Donald M. Borchert
David Stewart

OHIO UNIVERSITY

Exploring
Ethics

MACMILLAN PUBLISHING COMPANY
NEW YORK
COLLIER MACMILLAN PUBLISHERS
LONDON

Copyright © 1986, Macmillan Publishing Company, a division of Macmillan, Inc.

PRINTED IN THE UNITED STATES OF AMERICA

Macmillan Publishing Company
866 Third Avenue, New York, New York 10022

Collier Macmillan Canada, Inc.

LIBRARY OF CONGRESS CATALOGING-IN-PUBLICATION DATA

Main entry under title:

Exploring ethics.

  Bibliography: p.
  Includes index.
  1. Ethics.   2. Social ethics.   I. Borchert,
Donald M.,   II. Stewart, David,
BJ1012.E97   1986   170   85–13606
ISBN 0–02–312430–X

Printing: 1 2 3 4 5 6 7 8   Year: 6 7 8 9 0 1 2 3 4 5

ISBN 0-02-312430-X

Preface

At the outset, we wish to acknowledge the valuable suggestions of the following reviewers: Thomas Benson, University of Maryland; Owen Dukelow, Washington and Jefferson College; Jerry Kreyche, De Paul University; Leonard O'Brian, Elgin Community College; William Radke, Seton Hall University; and Michael Vengrin, Radford University. Their careful review of the text and helpful comments have contributed significantly to whatever virtues this book has. It is, of course, we and not they who bear the responsibility for any inadequacies the book still may have.

Why Another Ethics Text?

There are already so many ethics texts on the market, why did we undertake the writing of another one? Chief among the reasons is that our experience in teaching ethics revealed the need for the kind of text that currently does not exist. We have become convinced during our years of teaching ethics to beginning philosophy students that an introductory text should perform four basic functions:

1. Introduce beginning philosophy students to the nature of ethics with clarity and appeal.
2. Examine and assess carefully some of the key metaethical issues and major normative positions in ethics.
3. Lead students carefully through significant primary sources.
4. Elucidate how major normative positions can be applied in specific situations.

Currently available texts seem to be of one or two types. One type is the reader or anthology, which offers selections from writers in ethics, either classic or contemporary, or both. Our experience has been that, at the introductory level, students unaccustomed to reading philosophical writing find such collections formidable and discouraging. Not only is the level of difficulty of many selections beyond what could reasonably be expected of the beginning philosophy student, the materials are sometimes chosen on the basis of what the editors thought was important to other philosophers rather than on the basis of readability or accessibility to beginning students.

The other type of ethics text currently available is a purely secondary text with copious discussions of various ethical positions, often supported by intricate taxonomies of positions drawn from the history of ethics. We believe that such approaches leave the student without one of the major values of a philosophy course: direct contact with the writings of philosophical figures in the western tradition.

Books of both types also frequently embody another flaw that we want to avoid. They offer the student merely a "cafeteria approach" (i.e., a little of this, a little of that) and not much help in discriminating those positions that culminate in philosophical dead ends from those that open up additional possibilities for insight and analysis. One response that students make to such presentations is to dismiss the textbook as confusing, or worse, they conclude that philosophy in general, and ethics in particular, is simply a lot of pointless arguments, and that no progress in philosophical understanding has been made through the centuries.

The Approach of This Book

We agree with Kant that ethics is a rational activity embodying objective principles, not principles of self-interest, and that to be moral we must be free. In order to make these points early on, we discuss in the first section four positions that are rejections of the Kantian position described above. These four positions—egoism, determinism, ethical relativism, and emotivism—we believe, would jettison the moral experience of humankind and make the philosophical examination of ethics a restricted, if not impossible, business. The discussion of each of these positions provides an advocate and a critic of the position together with our own analysis of what is at stake for ethics.

The second section of the book offers a survey of four of the major theories in ethics: ethical views based on human nature, divine will theories, teleological ethics, and deontological ethics. Aristotle and Epicurus are offered as representatives of an ethical theory based on human nature. Aristotle's emphasis on ethics as a rational activity resulting in happiness, is an example of the Greek desire for the contemplative life. Epicurus represents a hedonistic ideal, but tempered with the Greek goal of moderation. Paley and Brunner are presented as representatives of the divine will theory. Bentham and John Stuart Mill are spokesmen for utilitarianism; Kant and W. D. Ross present the deontological perspective.

Finally, the third section connects normative issues to the metaethical concerns discussed in the first two sections. Among the many possible issues, we have included three topics: ethical issues in medicine, in business, and in public policy concerns.

We have argued that the role of ethical theory is not to provide a "cookbook" solution to an ethical concern, but rather to help us isolate the morally relevant aspects of the topics being analyzed.

Throughout the book, we have chosen significant primary sources for their readability for beginning philosophy students. Where aspects of the primary sources seem to be difficult to the beginner, we have provided explanatory notes either as insertions in the readings or as introductions to them. We have also prepared substantial introductions to the issues to acquaint students with the problems of ethics, and to elucidate the contributions made by the anthologized philosophers. To aid students further, we have included a glossary of terms and an annotated bibliography for suggested further readings.

To characterize this book generally, we would say that it has been designed as an introductory work to be used primarily by freshmen and sophomore students for whom a course in ethics might be their only encounter with philosophy.

A Note on the Text

Bibliographical information on the citations has been included for each reading. In some instances we have suppressed the scholarly apparatus in the readings, leaving in only those footnotes that referred to quoted material or that were, in our judgment, crucial to an understanding of the issue under discussion.

Our experience with the readings from Hobbes and Butler has been that students have more difficulty with the language used than with the philosophical issues discussed. We felt it would be appropriate to provide a revision of the language of these two philosophers of the late seventeenth and early eighteenth centuries so that the form would not obscure the substance of their views. Accordingly, we offer our own "translation" (or to use our friend P. Lal's salient phrase, "transcreation") of the selections from Hobbes and Butler. As a sample, here are Hobbes's original words followed by our translation.

And from this diffidence of one another, there is no way for any man to secure himself, so reasonable, as anticipation; that is, by force, or wiles, to master the persons of all men he can, so long, till he see no other power great enough to endanger him; and this is no more than his own conservation requireth, and is generally allowed.

And our translation:

From this lack of confidence in others there is no protection as reasonable as that of planning. That is, through force or cleverness one can control others until there is no power great enough to be a danger. This is no more than a person's own security requires and is generally allowed.

For those teachers who prefer to have students grapple with the original text from Hobbes and Butler, we considered including the text in this book as an appendix, but the ready availability of both writers in a variety of editions seemed to us to make this step unnecessary.

We wish to thank our Macmillan editors, Gene Panhorst and Helen McInnis, for their help and encouragement at every step of the way, and we also wish to thank our students at Ohio University who have worked through this material with us at various stages in its development. We also wish to acknowledge the many suggestions given to us by colleagues both at Ohio University and elsewhere, while also stating the obvious: any shortcomings or inadequacies in the book are our fault alone.

We urge users of the book to send their comments and suggestions for improving the book to us. We hope this book proves to be useful to you, and we solicit your help in making future editions of it better.

Donald Borchert
David Stewart

Athens, Ohio

Contents

Introduction

On the 17th of January 1912, Captain Robert Scott and his four companions reached the South Pole after a march of eighty-one days. They quickly discovered that Roald Amundsen had reached the pole a month earlier. Their disappointment was keen. The return journey added misfortune and disaster. Petty Officer Evans fell ill and became a burden to the party. Accordingly, Captain Scott had to make a decision. He could drag Evans along, slow the trek down, and risk being stranded in the approaching blizzards. Or he could abandon Evans to die alone in the wilderness in the hope that the remainder of his party could be saved.

What ought Scott to do? Take Evans or abandon him? Scott decided on the first alternative. The team dragged Evans along until he died. The delay proved fatal. The blizzards overtook them. Oates, in a weakened condition, tried to assist his companions by sacrificing himself. The three survivors struggled toward the safety of their depot, but they fell victim to the Antarctic snows. Had they sacrificed Evans originally, they might have been saved. Their frozen bodies were later discovered only eleven miles or one day's march from the depot they had been unable to reach.

Captain Scott was not in an enviable position as he faced the task of deciding the fate of Evans and his companions. Few of us would want to be in his situation. Yet, in a certain sense, we are. The question he no doubt pondered—What ought I to do?—is our question too. It is *the* ethical question. It lurks behind all our moral decisions and, as such, reveals a great deal about the primary beliefs that we hold concerning the human situation.

When you or I or Captain Scott ask the ethical question, What ought I to do? we presuppose at least five features about our human condition.

1. We assume that we have alternative futures open to us.
2. We assume that we are burdened with choice. We cannot avoid choosing a future. For Captain Scott to try to delay or escape choosing a future was to choose a future. Choosing to do nothing is still to choose.
3. We assume that one of those futures is more desirable than the others, but we do not know which one. That is why Captain Scott would, no doubt, have raised the question with such anxiety.
4. We assume that the more desirable future possesses certain objective characteristics that we can identify that make it the more desirable future. It is precisely those characteristics that Captain Scott would have been trying to identify in order to answer the ethical question.
5. We assume that we are obliged to pursue the more desirable future. Captain Scott's anxiety would also reveal this sense of obligation.

In short, when we raise the question, What ought I to do? in a moral context, we are assuming that we are free and that we can obtain moral knowledge. To be free means at least to have the capacity to identify and pursue alternative futures; and moral knowledge refers to a certain kind of information about the world. If we are mistaken in our assumptions—if freedom and moral knowledge are merely illusions—then we really cannot raise the ethical question in any significant way. And if this is the case, then the business of ethics—whose chief task is to help us formulate rational answers to the ethical question—becomes a futile exercise.

Challenges to Ethics

Some thinkers have developed positions that call into question the possibility of human freedom and moral knowledge, either by maintaining that freedom and moral knowledge are illusory, or by reshaping the concepts in such a way that what we ordinarily mean by "freedom" and "moral knowledge" appears to be mistaken.

For example, *psychological egoism* claims that all persons all of the time act selfishly. If true, this claim would narrow the boundaries of human freedom in such a way that the scope of the ethical question would be limited to a selfish perspective. Rather than ask, What ought I to do? Captain Scott should have asked, Which selfish deed shall I do? Such a modified question would certainly alter radically the whole business of ethics.

Another challenge to ethics is *determinism* which, in its extreme form, claims that human beings are not free at all. If true, this claim would render the ethical question meaningless and substitute for it the question, What in the light of my hereditary and environmental factors will I do?

In addition, there is *ethical relativism* which, in its most interesting form, attacks the ordinary meaning of "moral knowledge" by claiming that such knowledge is culturally conditioned and culturally specific. The relativist claims that there are no cross-cultural norms by which to evaluate the conduct of persons in all societies. If true, this claim would modify the ethical question to read, What do the standards that are fashioned by my particular cultural group at this specific time direct me to do? Captain Scott's way of putting the question would be both imprecise and mistaken.

Finally, we should note *emotivism* which, in effect, rules out moral knowledge. Emotivism claims that moral terms and the sentences that contain them simply express the emotions of the speaker and perhaps attempt to evoke similar responses from the hearers. Expressing emotions, however, is not at all the same thing as possessing and expressing moral knowledge. Thus, if emotivism is true, it would undermine the seriousness of our fundamental ethical question.

Clearly, these four positions constitute major challenges to the pursuit of ethics. Before we attempt to formulate responses to our ethical question, our first task is accordingly to examine these challenges. Such preparation for ethics is an important part of the inquiry philosophers usually call *metaethics*.

A Glimpse Ahead

Before beginning the readings in Chapter 1, it may be useful for the reader to get an overall view of how this book is organized.

Part I deals with metaethical issues, specifically with an examination of four major challenges to ethics: psychological egoism, determinism, ethical relativism, and emotivism.

Part II proceeds to consider ethics proper. It explores and assesses answers to the fundamental ethical question, What ought I to do? A ready response to the question is, I ought to do what is right. Yet this response inspires the further question, What makes an act right? Two major answers to this question are identified. Some ethicists—whose point of view is referred to as *teleological*—argue that the rightness or wrongness of acts depends upon their consequences. Other ethicists—whose perspective is called *deontological*—claim that considerations other than, or in addition to, consequences determine the rightness or wrongness of acts and place the primary emphasis on the recognition of a sense of duty.

In Part II we examine two teleological views: one that emphasizes the consequences of the action with primary emphasis on individual happiness and self-actualization (Aristotle and Epicurus), and a second that emphasizes the broader consequences of an action for society as a whole (Jeremy Bentham and John Stuart Mill). We also look at two deontological views: one that sees the rightness of an action as a duty to follow the dictates of divine authority (William Paley and Emil Brunner) and the other that sees the morality of an action as a duty to follow the commands of reason (Immanuel Kant and W. D. Ross).

Part III, the final section of the book, examines a series of specific ethical issues that range from personal and professional to issues of public policy. In thinking through responses to these issues, we examine the responses that teleologists and deontologists might provide.

Few of us will have to answer the question, What ought I to do? under the critical circumstances that confronted Captain Scott. Yet few of us can avoid a daily encounter with that recurring human question. The study of ethics can aid us in answering that question by sharpening our critical awareness of the nature of the question, by encouraging the formulation of a defensible perspective from which to respond to the question, and by enhancing our capacity for imaginative response to problems. We hope that your study of the materials assembled in *Exploring Ethics* will assist you in responding clearly, coherently, and courageously to the fundamental ethical question.

PART I

The Fundamental Ethical Question: Challenges to its Meaningfulness

CHAPTER 1

Psychological Egoism

Introduction

Have you ever encountered a person who said, All people act always to promote their own self-interest, or, Everyone is really always looking out for Number One? If you have, then you were faced with a psychological egoist. The egoist's doctrine can be expressed in a number of different ways, but it has four basic features.

1. It makes a *universal* claim that embraces all human beings.
2. It makes a totally *inclusive* claim about all the acts, or motives, of every person.
3. It makes a *factual* claim about every human act or motive. The doctrine does not approve or disapprove of human acts or motives. It simply makes a claim about the nature of those acts or motives.
4. It makes the claim that every human act is ultimately *selfish* or *egoistic*.

This is a far-reaching doctrine. It claims that every act that you have done or will do is ultimately selfish. However altruistic your act may appear to be on the surface, at bottom it is fundamentally selfish. The same is true for all humans who have lived in the past or will live in the future.

If this doctrine is true, the consequences for our ethical question are enormous. The domain of the possible responses to the ethical question would be strikingly narrowed. The possibility of altruism or benevolence—unselfishly acting for the sake of others—would be ruled out. That does not mean that you would be unable to do something kind and beneficial for another person. Rather it means that whenever you would do something kind for someone else, you would be inescapably involved in seeking some kind of payoff for yourself. Answering the question, What ought I to do? would become the business of selecting one of several possible egoistic futures.

If we ask psychological egoists to prove their doctrine, we might find ourselves in this kind of a dialogue.

EGOIST: Let's be honest! Look at the way people act. Don't people act selfishly most of the time? Consider your own actions. Aren't you interested most of the time in some kind of personal payoff? You have to admit that, don't you? Then doesn't such a widespread appearance of selfishness establish a presumption in favor of the truth of psychological egoism?

YOU: I certainly can't disagree with your claim that most people most of the time seem to act selfishly. But consider the case of a very intelligent medical student I met last night. She is in her last year of studies and has been accepted for a residency in eye surgery at the Wills Eye Hospital in Philadelphia. After her residency she plans to work for Operation Eyesight Universal, a charitable organization headquartered in Calgary, Alberta, Canada that seeks to restore the sight of the poor curable blind in the world's developing countries. When I asked her why she wanted to pursue this low-paying course of action rather than a much more lucrative practice in Philadelphia itself, she responded that she had a reverence for human life and wanted to help the blind poor to see again. She said she was acting out of love for people. Doesn't such a person falsify your doctrine?

EGOIST: I am glad you raised the example of this medical student, because you must come to recognize the deceptive appearance of allegedly unselfish acts. This woman is either deceiving herself or she is deceiving us when she tells us that she is doing this out of love for humankind. If she is deceiving herself, she is simply the victim of a weak ego. She has probably bought into the myth of the benevolent do-gooder that society has drummed into her ears. Or she's too weak to admit that she is selfish just like you and me. Maybe someday she will give up her self-deception and become refreshingly honest, admitting that she is selfish like the rest of us.

YOU: Listen! This student has been through psychoanalysis. She knows the score. You can't pin that assessment on her.

EGOIST: Fine. So she has been through analysis. Granted, then, that she is not deceiving herself. Then she must be deceiving us. She tells us she is going to dedicate her surgical skills to the service of the world's poor because the model of the unselfish person is getting something for her. We just have to identify her payoff. That should be simple enough. I'll bet she comes from a conservative religious family that believes in God and in life after death. I'll bet that she is trying to please God so that she can get a heavenly reward. You know the old slogan: no cross on earth, no crown in glory. That's what she's after, that's her selfish payoff.

YOU: Wrong again! She doesn't believe in God at all. She is an atheistic humanist. Your analysis fails again.

EGOIST: Oh, now I know the medical student you are talking about. Her family has political connections, and I bet she has her sights set on an important position in the state's new Department of Health and Human Services. What better qualifications could she have—excellent academic credentials, world-wide experience in hundreds of eye operations, the backing of a grand old political family, but also the aura of a sacrificial humanitarian.

YOU: You have just dreamed up a rather unrealistic prospect to account for her actions. No matter how much evidence I present that is contrary to the specific egoistic goals that you suggest motivate this medical student, you will always try to dream up another selfish payoff. We are limited only by your capacity to imagine possible payoffs, and I can see that your imagination seems to be limitless.

EGOIST: You flatter me; but my imagination has its limits. I am pleased, however, that you responded the way you did. You have given me the opportunity to make an important point. If we cannot identify the specific selfish payoff that she is seeking, then we are forced to the conclusion that she is being driven to pursue her apparently unselfish plans by unconscious forces. Deep within her unconscious are selfish desires that she is attempting to satisfy. Needless to say, she is not aware of these selfish origins of her actions.

YOU: What can I say to that? You really exercise your mind to show that every human act is selfish, don't you? You must be completely convinced that your doctrine is true.

EGOIST: I am. But, of course, I am willing to scrutinize any new data or arguments that you would care to suggest. Do you have any?

The psychological egoist leaves us with that challenge. Let us see if we can discover some additional relevant insights through an analysis of the positions of Thomas Hobbes and his critic, Joseph Butler.

Advocate of Egoism: Thomas Hobbes

It is not only important that you were born, it is also important when and where you were born. Thomas Hobbes (1588–1679), the classic advocate of psychological egoism, was born in England at a time when the modern era of science was dawning on Europe. Hobbes's philosophy must be understood within the context of the new science.

The Emergence of the New Science

Basic to the new view of the world that emerged in the sixteenth and seventeenth centuries was the idea that knowledge is derived from empirical data and reasoning based on such data. Especially important to such reasoning was the role of mathematics. The new scientist was one who quantified observed facts, expressed those quantities in formulae, synthesized those formulae into explanatory systems, used those systems to predict the behavior of the phenomena, and then subjected those systems to empirical verification.

It was especially in astronomy that the new mathematical method was developed. Copernicus (1473–1543) and Kepler (1571–1630) construed God as a cosmic mathematician who created the world in accordance with simple mathematical principles. The challenge was to discern those mathematical principles. In so doing, humans would be virtually thinking God's thoughts after him. Kepler used the mathematical data of Tycho Brahe (1546–1601) to generate hypotheses that could be checked against data expressed in mathematical form. He thereby produced his laws of planetary motion. Galileo (1564–1642) pushed mathematical reasoning beyond the mathematical expression of data and the formation of hypotheses to the formulation of a rationale or system that binds the separate truths together. Galileo achieved such a system on the twofold assumption that empirical facts can be quantified and measured, and that the behavior of bodies can be explained in geometric terms.

In the view of reality that emerged from the new science, physical reality was pictured as matter in motion. Matter objectively possessed position, shape, size, mass, and velocity. All these characteristics were measurable, quantifiable. Those characteristics that were not quantifiable, such as colors, smells, sounds, and tastes, were not objectively real. They were rather "appearances" that arise in us when our sense organs are stimulated by the objectively real bodies with their quantifiable characteristics. The objective world, then, was a mechanical world of quantifiable, measurable objects in motion. What place did this view leave for human freedom and God—subjects that exercised medieval minds? The answer was clear: there is no room for freedom and God in a completely mechanistic, quantifiable world.

The Challenge for Philosophy

Philosophers had at least two paths of thought open to them. They could postulate a second separate domain where human freedom and God operated beyond the constraints of the mechanistic, objective world and then be forced to wrestle with the perplexing difficulty of figuring out how the two domains are related. Or they could admit the exclusive truth of the picture of reality suggested by the new science and try to cope with the death of freedom and the absence of God that this view seemed to demand. Thomas Hobbes—a child of his time who was committed to the new science and the materialism it seemed to imply—embraced the second option, but retained a residual belief in God. God is the cause of the world, but the laws of God are the laws of nature. Some interpreters think that Hobbes included in his works this limited role for God to protect himself from charges of atheism.

Hobbes's student days at Oxford were devoted to the traditional program in scholastic logic, and he proved himself sufficiently competent to be hired as a tutor for the important aristocratic Cavendish family. Not until he was in his forties did the mathematical logic of Euclid and the explanations of planetary motion by Galileo create a significant impact on him. When the new science did grasp him, Hobbes set out to interpret all reality in terms of that new science. Like a Euclidean geometrician, he identified his basic axioms, set forth his definitions, and proceeded to generate truths about human beings and their world. As physicists did following Galileo's lead, he viewed reality as fundamentally reducible to moving particles that obey simple laws.

Kinds of Human Motions

What distinguishes human beings within the universe of moving particles is the kind of motion that takes place in them. Hobbes analyzed and categorized that motion for us. He discerned two sorts of animal motion within us: vital and voluntary. Note that voluntary motion has its roots in our fancy or imagination which is the residue of motion left within us from past sense experience.

* There are two sorts of motions belonging to animals: (1) *vital*, begun at birth and continued without interruption through their whole life (such as the circulation of blood, pulse, breathing, digestion, nutrition, excretion, and so forth), motion that is further characterized by having no need of help from the mind; and (2) *animal* or *voluntary* motion (going, speaking and moving limbs) in such manner as is first conceived in the mind. In the first and second chapters it was shown that the five senses are motions in the sense organs and interior parts of the human body caused by the action of things we see, hear, and so forth, and that a conception in the mind is nothing but the residue of the same motion remaining after sense experience. Because going, speaking, and similar voluntary motions always depend on a prior thought (Where to? Which way? What?), it is evident that the mind is the internal beginning of all voluntary motion. Although persons who have not studied such things think there is no motion there at all due either to the fact that it cannot be seen or is of short duration, this does not argue against the reality of such motion. Even that which is moved over a great distance must first be moved over a small distance. Small beginnings of motion within the human body are called *endeavor* before they appear in walking, speaking, striking and other visible actions.

Endeavor that is directed toward something that causes it is called *appetite* or *desire*. Desire is the general term; appetite usually refers to desire for food, i.e., hunger or thirst. Endeavor that is directed away from something is generally called *aversion*. Appetite and aversion are both Latin derivatives and signify motion, one the motion of approaching, the other the motion of withdrawing. . . .

People are said to love what they desire and hate those things for which they have aversion. Love and desire are the same, except desire always signifies the absence of the object and love most commonly its presence. Similarly, aversion signifies the absence and hate the presence of the object.

People are born with some appetites and aversions, such as the appetite for food. . . . Other appetites are for particular things and come from experience and trial and error, either by the individual or by other people. . . .

The things we neither desire nor hate we are said to hold in *contempt*. Contempt is nothing but an immobility or stubborness of the heart in resisting the action of certain things. This is due to the fact that the heart is already

* FROM Thomas Hobbes, *Leviathan*. Translated into modern idiom by the authors.

moving differently because of other more potent objects, or from lack of experience of them. Also, the heart may be unmoved by certain things because of a lack of experience of them. . . .

All persons consider their voluntary acts to have as their object something that is good for them.

Values Depend on Personal Preferences

Note how strongly this last statement expresses the egoism espoused by Hobbes. Things have no intrinsic value. If we judge that something is good, or valuable, it is because the object is good for us. That is to say, we project values onto things. Things in themselves have only quantity and motion. Accordingly, *things in themselves* are neither good, evil nor vile. Those values are properties that you and I bestow on objects. My values differ from yours even as my preferences in matters of taste differ from yours. Furthermore, because I am in constant motion, what I call "good" today I may call "evil" tomorrow, and "vile" the next day. Similarly, pleasure and displeasure are subjective states or "appearances" within each person and are associated with the presence of goods and evils.

> Because the constitution of the human body is continually changing, it is impossible that all the same things should always cause a person to have the same appetites and aversions. Still less should we expect that all people would agree in desiring any particular object.
>
> But whatever the object of any person's appetite or desire may be, that person calls the object desired *good* and the object hated *evil*. Whatever a person has contempt for is labeled *vile* or not worthy of consideration. The words *good, evil* and *contemptible* are always used relative to the person who uses them. There is nothing that is simply and absolutely good or evil or vile. . . .
>
> As I have said before, since that which is really within us is only motion caused by the action of external objects (but in appearance light and color to sight, sound to the ear, odor to the nostril, and so forth), then the action of the same object is continued from the eyes, ears and other organs to the heart, the real effect there is nothing but motion or endeavor. And endeavor consists of appetite or aversion, to or from the object moving. But the appearance or sense of that motion is what we either call *delight* or *trouble of mind*. . . .
>
> Pleasure or delight, therefore, is the appearance or sense of good; displeasure is the appearance or sense of evil. Consequently, all appetite, desire and love is accompanied by some degree of delight, and all hatred and aversion with some degree of displeasure.

The Origin of War and the State of Nature

Hobbes now explains for us the origin of war. He reminds us that happiness is a process of achieving our desires rather than a static state of enjoyment. Accordingly, human beings thirst for more and more power to assure that their future desires can be satisfied. Nature has, however, made humans virtually equal in ability or power. When such equal beings compete with each other for scarce resources, the result is war. Similarly, they distrust each other, and the solution they seize upon is to subdue or destroy the other person first. Again, they contend with each other for glory, one of the forms of power, which can only be gained at the expense of others. Selfish beings, then, endowed by nature with virtually equal capacities, struggle with each other in unceasing warfare. In such a state of nature, there is no significant cultural development. Nor is there any legitimate distinction between right and wrong, justice and injustice. Why? Hobbes's answer relates to the absence of an authoritative, coercive power.

> Happiness in life does not consist of the calm of a satisfied mind. There is no *finis ultimus* ("ultimate aim") or *summum bonum* ("greatest good") as is spoken of in the books of the old moral philosophers. Nor can a person live whose desires are at an end any more than can one whose senses and mind have ceased functioning. Happiness is a continual progress of desire from one object to another, the attaining of the former being merely a stage on the way to the latter. The reason for this is that the object of a person's desire is not simply to enjoy something only once but also to assure that the object can be possessed whenever it is desired again in the future. Therefore, the voluntary actions and inclinations of all persons tend not only to procuring but also to assuring a contented life. They differ only in the way which stems, in part, from the diversity of passions in different people and partly from the differences in the knowledge, or opinion, each one has of the causes that produce the desired effect.
>
> So in the first place I put as a general inclination of all mankind a perpetual and restless desire of power after power that ceases only in death. The cause for this is not always that a person hopes for a more intensive delight than has already been attained or that the person cannot be content with moderate power. Rather it is because the person cannot be assured of the present power and means to live well without acquiring more. This is why kings, whose power is greatest, turn their efforts to assuring it by laws at home or by wars abroad. When that is done, a new desire follows—of fame from new conquest in some, of ease and sensual pleasure in others, of admiration or being flattered for excellence in some art or other ability of mind in still others. . . .
>
> Nature has made people so equal in the faculties of body and mind that, although one person may be obviously stronger in body or quicker in mind than another, the difference is not so great as to allow one person to claim a benefit that another cannot also claim. As to strength of body, the weakest has enough strength to kill the strongest, either by secret machination or by confederacy with others who are in the same danger.
>
> As to the faculties of mind, setting aside verbal abilities or scientific skill which very few have, and then about only a few things (and which, incidentally, is not an in-born ability or attained along with something else like prudence is), I find an even greater equality among people than equality of strength. For prudence is but experience which time equally bestows on all persons in those things they equally apply themselves to. That which

may perhaps make such equality difficult to believe is the vain conceit regarding one's own wisdom, which everybody thinks they have in greater degree than "common people" (which means everybody but themselves, and perhaps a few others they happen to agree with). Human nature is such that no matter how many others a person acknowledges as more witty or more eloquent or more learned, no one will believe that there are many others as wise. People see their own wit at hand and that of others at a distance. But this proves that people are in that point equal rather than unequal. There is ordinarily no greater indication of the equal distribution of anything than that everybody is contented with their share.

From this equality of ability arises equality of hope in attaining our goals. Therefore, if any two people desire the same thing, which they nevertheless cannot both enjoy, they become enemies in their pursuit of their goal, which is mainly their own survival and sometimes only their enjoyment. From this it follows that when an invader has nothing to fear but the power of a single person, if one plants, sows, builds or possesses a suitable estate, others may be expected to come prepared with united forces to dispossess and deprive that person not only of the efforts of work but also of life or liberty. That invader, in turn, is in similar danger from another.

From this lack of confidence in others there is no protection as reasonable as that of planning. That is, through force or cleverness, one can control others until there is no power great enough to be a danger. This is no more than a person's own security requires and is generally allowed. Also, there are some who, taking pleasure in contemplating their own power in the acts of conquest, pursue it further than their own security requires. Those who are content with modest means and do not increase their power by invasion would not be able to hold out against such persons very long. Consequently, increasing domination over others that is necessary for self-protection ought to be allowed.

Again, people get no pleasure, but rather a great deal of grief, from human association where there is no power able to encompass them all. For all persons want to be valued in the same way they value themselves. When there is no common power to keep them quiet, people react to indications of contempt or undervaluing from others by attempting to destroy each other or by trying to force a greater expression of value from those who have not expressed it either by injury or by threat.

The upshot is that in human nature we find three principal causes of quarrels: first, competition; second, distrust; third, glory.

The first makes people invade for gain, the second for safety, and the third for reputation. The first uses violence to make themselves masters of other people's person or possessions; the second, to defend them; the third, for trifles—the wrong word, a smirk, a different viewpoint, and any other indication of undervalue directed toward themselves, their family, friends, nation, profession, or even their name.

Thus it is clear that during the time people live without a common power to keep them all in check, they are in that condition which is called war. This is war of every person against every other person. For war consists

not only in battle or fighting but in that period of time in which the will
to engage in battle is sufficiently known. Therefore, the notion of *time* is
to be considered in understanding the nature of war just as it is in
understanding the nature of weather. The nature of foul weather does not
consist in one or two rain showers but in a tendency to rain for many
days. So the nature of war consists not in actual fighting alone but in the
known disposition to do so during all the time there is no guarantee of
the opposite. All other time is peace.

Whatever holds true of war, when every person is enemy to every other
person, also holds true of the time in which people live without other security
than what their own strength and their own cleverness supplies. In such
condition there is no place for work, because the results of it are uncertain.
Consequently, there is no cultivation of the earth, no navigation or use of
the goods that may be imported from across the sea, no comfortable
buildings, no powerful machinery for transportation or building, no
knowledge of the face of the earth, no history, no arts, no letters, in short,
no society. What is worst of all, there is continual fear and danger of violent
death; and human life is solitary, poor, nasty, brutish, and short. . . .

Following from this war of every person against every other person is
that nothing can be unjust. The notions of right and wrong, justice and
injustice, have no place. Where there is no common power, there is no
law; where no law, no injustice. Force and fraud are the two cardinal virtues
in war. Justice and injustice are not innate faculties of the body or mind.
If they were, they might be found in a person alone in the world, as are
the person's senses and passions. Justice and injustice are qualities of people
in society, not in solitude. It would also follow that apart from human society
there would be no sense of social decorum, no common authority to enforce
individual ownership; there would only be a dog-eat-dog attitude on every
person's part.

The Articles of Peace and the Commonwealth

The "solitary, poor, nasty, brutish and short" life of human beings in this state
of warfare can only be overcome through the establishment of civil society. Although
we are considering Hobbes's views as representative of an egoistic attitude toward
ethics, his writings are also important in political philosophy, for he was the first
philosopher to suggest that the basis for civil government is a contract between
the governed and the ruler. Although Hobbes did not develop these views in great
detail, the social contract theory of government was given considerable attention
in the eighteenth century by such thinkers as John Locke and J. J. Rousseau. It
also had a significant influence on Thomas Jefferson. Social contract language, as
well as references to the laws of nature and nature's God, run throughout the
American Declaration of Independence. Hobbes wrote the following:

So much for the bad situation of people in the state of nature. But there
are possibilities grounded both in reason and in the emotions for getting
out of such a state.

The emotions that incline people to peace are fear of death, desire of things that are necessary to comfortable living, and a hope that by their work they can obtain them. Reason therefore supports articles of peace in terms of which people can be brought to agreement. These articles are sometimes called the *Laws of Nature.*

The *right of nature,* which writers commonly call the *jus naturale,* is the freedom all persons have to use their own power as they will to preserve their own nature, that is, their life, and consequently to do anything which will enhance it.

Properly understood, *freedom* means the absence of external constraints which prevent people from doing what they want to do. It also includes the ability to use whatever power people have as their judgment and reason dictate.

A law of nature, a *lex naturalis,* is a precept or general rule discovered by reason by which people are forbidden to do that which destroys or takes away the means of preserving life. . . .

And because the human condition, as was indicated above, is a condition of war of everyone against everyone else—at least when there is no governing power other than the individual to help preserve a person against enemies— it follows that in such a condition every person has a "right" to everything, even to another person's body. Therefore, as long as the natural right of every person to everything persists, there can be no security for anyone, no matter how strong or wise, during the natural course of life. Consequently, it is a precept or general rule of reason that all people ought, as far as possible, to desire peace; and only when peace is unobtainable may they seek and use the advantages of war. The first part of this rule contains the first and fundamental law of nature, namely, *seek peace and follow it.* The second sums up the right of nature: *defend ourselves by all means possible.*

From this fundamental law of nature, which commands people to strive for peace, is derived this second law: people should be willing, in order to achieve peace and self-defense, to lay down their natural rights to all things and be content with as much freedom against other people as they will allow other people to have against themselves. As long as people think they can do anything they like, they are in a state of war. But unless everybody gives up their rights, there is no reason for any individual to give up rights. A person who unilaterally gives up rights would be preyed upon, which one can expect nobody to do. This is also consistent with the Golden Rule: "whatever you would that others should do to you, do also to them."

Words alone, as I have already noted, being too weak to hold people to the performance of their promises, there are in human nature only two possible ways to strengthen it. Those are either a fear of the consequences of breaking their word, or a glory or pride in appearing not to need to break it. The latter is too rarely found to count on, especially when people are pursuing wealth, command, or sensual pleasure (this includes almost everybody). The emotion to be counted on is fear. There are two general objects of fear: (1) the power of invisible spirits, (2) the power of the people we offend. Of these two, though the former be greater, the fear of the latter is commonly greater. . . .

From the law of nature in terms of which we are obligated to transfer to others those rights that hinder the peace of human beings, there follows a third law: men ought to keep their covenants. Without this, covenants are vain and are but empty words. And since the right of all persons to all things remains, we are still in the condition of war.

Justice is based in this third law of nature. For where there is no covenant, there is no transfer of rights, and every person has right to everything. Consequently, no action can be unjust. But when a covenant is made, then to break it is unjust. The definition of injustice is therefore the failure to keep a covenant. Whatever is not unjust is just.

Because covenants demand mutual trust, where there is fear of nonperformance on either side, as was noted earlier, covenants are invalid. Though the origins of justice reside in the making of covenants, there can be no real justice until the cause of such fear is removed. While people are in the natural condition of war, this cannot be done. Therefore, before the terms "just" and "unjust" have meaning, there must be some coercive power to force people equally to keep their covenants out of fear of punishment greater than the benefit they expect by violating their covenants. A second function of this coercive power is to protect the property people acquire through their own effort in return for the rights they give up. Apart from the establishment of a commonwealth, there is no such power.

Hobbes goes on to discuss additional laws of nature which we need not examine at this time because the train of his thought has already become evident. According to Hobbes, humans are basically matter in motion, particles seeking their own interests. These selfish humans battle each other to achieve happiness. The same selfish drive for happiness, however, leads them to seek peace and security as the conditions essential to happiness. Reason suggests certain articles of peace, but most human beings are not sufficiently enlightened to see that obedience to these laws would ultimately promote their selfish interests. Accordingly, a sovereign authority is needed who will compel human beings to conform to these laws. Such is the situation within the commonwealth: selfish humans must be compelled by absolute authority to do those things that will promote most effectively their own self interests.

Is this an adequate portrayal of the human condition? Are all human beings fundamentally selfish? Do the value terms—*good, evil* and *vile*—have no objective meaning? Is their meaning basically subjective, varying from person to person in accordance with personal selfish interests? Is psychological egoism true? Joseph Butler says, "No!" Let us look at his critique.

Critic of Egoism: Joseph Butler

Shortly after the death of Hobbes, Joseph Butler (1692–1752) was born at Wantage, Berkshire. Like Hobbes he attended Oxford and soon came under the influence of the new science. The central message he derived from the new science, however, was quite different from the one received by Hobbes. Whereas Hobbes took from the new science a view that reduced reality to a continuum of quantifiable particles in motion, Butler embraced the new science's emphasis on the inductive method and the interpretation of data within relationships and systems. Hobbes's world of particles moving according to set laws allowed no room for God and human freedom. Butler's position did not exclude these features from the outset. Instead, Butler set out to account for all the data of human experience and to interpret the human being as a functioning system. Because contemporary science has not only abandoned the reductionistic, mechanistic world-view that undergirded Hobbes's discussion, and has also followed the method of interpreting data in terms of relationships within a system, Butler's point of view bears a much closer kinship to current science than does Hobbes's.

It may seem rather unusual that the bulk of the material cited in this chapter comes from sermons preached by Butler. We are not accustomed to think of sermons as philosophical treatises. Butler, however, used the pulpit for some heavy philosophizing. He found no basic incompatibility between the truths of nature and the truths of revelation, between the new science and traditional Christianity. Nature and revelation, for him, were complementary. Accordingly, the vocations of churchman and philosopher could be readily blended, and sermons could be occasions for philosophizing. Butler served the Church of England first as a priest and later as a bishop. At the same time, he contributed to philosophy the classic refutation of psychological egoism. One commentator observes that Butler "killed the theory so thoroughly that he sometimes seems to the modern reader to be flogging dead horses."* Indeed, few contemporary philosophers would care to defend psychological egoism in the wake of Butler's attack. Yet, the doctrine that human beings are fundamentally selfish enjoys considerable popularity in contemporary society. Let us consider how convincing Butler's attack really is.

Questioning Hobbes on Benevolence

First of all, let us assume for the sake of argument that Hobbes's psychological egoism is true. To what implications would such an assumption commit us? Butler suggests several of these implications that he finds objectionable.

> ** Suppose a learned person were writing a serious book about human nature designed to show that the author had an insight into the subject. Among other things that would need to be explained is the phenomenon of benevolence or good will among people both toward their relatives and toward others. Wanting to avoid being misled by outward appearances, the author appeals to introspection to see exactly what it is in the human mind that is the source of this appearance of good will. If, upon deep reflection, the author asserts that the principle of good will in the mind is due only to the love of power and delight in its exercise, would not everybody

---

* C. D. Broad, *Five Types of Ethical Theory* (Patterson, N.J.: Littlefield, Adams & Co., 1959), p. 55.
** FROM Joseph Butler, *Sermons.* Translated into modern idiom by the authors.

think this was a confusion of terms, that the philosopher was thinking about and explaining some *other* human action and behavior than good will? Could anyone really believe that what we commonly call benevolence or good will was the feeling meant? Or would it be more plausible to believe that the author had a general hypothesis to which the fact of good will could not otherwise be reconciled?

To be sure, what appears to be good will is often nothing but ambition. And benevolence is often (perhaps even always) mixed in with the enjoyment of superiority. But this makes it all the more specious to call good will ambition (one might as well call it hunger), for ambition no more accounts for the phenomenon of good will than hunger does. Is there not often the phenomenon of people desiring good things for others even though they know they are unable to procure them? Further, don't they rejoice when a third person delivers them? And can love of power possibly account for this desire or delight? Is there not also often the phenomenon of people distinguishing between two or more persons, preferring to do good to one over another, in cases where love of power cannot possibly account for this distinction? Love of power cannot distinguish between objects; all one could say is that it is a greater example and effort of power to do good to one rather than to another.

Again, suppose that good will in the human mind is nothing but delight in the exercise of power. People might indeed be restrained by distant and incidental considerations. But since these restraints are far away, people would have a tendency to enjoy creating mischief as an exercise in and proof of power. This disposition and delight in it would arise from—or even be the same principle in the mind—as a disposition to and delight in charity. Thus cruelty, as distinct from envy and resentment, would be exactly the same in the human mind as good will. That one person tends to the happiness of our fellow creatures while another person tends to their misery would be merely an accidental circumstance which the mind is unconcerned about. These are the absurdities which even intelligent people face when they misrepresent their nature and perversely deny the image of God which was originally stamped upon that nature. The traces of the image of God, no matter how faint, are plainly discernible upon the human mind.

Butler argues that Hobbes's view would commit us to saying that benevolence or good will is really delight in the use of power. That is to say, benevolent persons selfishly seek and derive personal satisfaction from deploying their power in behalf of someone else. Benevolence or good will is reduced to an ego-trip or a power-trip. Do we really want to accept that as an adequate meaning of the term *benevolence*? Suppose, for example, that your parents are comfortably situated but not rich enough to assist you and your spouse to meet the economic challenges of life. Suppose, however, that your spouse's parents are billionaires and that they not only gave you and your spouse a luxury yacht with arrangements for an around-the-world cruise as a wedding gift but they also turned over to you one of the lucrative family businesses. Suppose, further, that your parents rejoiced and wished you well in the lifestyle that they themselves could not provide for you. Does it make sense, Butler would ask, to call your parents' good will toward you the "delight in the use of power"? What power have *they* used?

In addition, is not cruelty a clear example of persons taking delight in using their power against weaker persons? Does not Hobbes's position, therefore, commit us to saying that benevolence and cruelty are fundamentally the same thing?

An Alternative to Hobbes's View

Given the problems in Hobbes's view, Butler invites us to look beyond it. Hobbes, Butler says, is a "learned person" who, having embraced a "general hypothesis" about reality, is able to reconcile benevolence with that hypothesis only by reducing benevolence to something it is not, namely, to cruelty. In effect, Hobbes's interpretation defines benevolence out of existence. But, says Butler, the existence of benevolence or good will is an established fact. The testimony of humankind that benevolence exists must be taken seriously. Butler argues that this means that we must abandon the simplistic procedure of reducing all voluntary behavior to the one motivating principle of selfishness. Human beings are complex systems with several motivating principles. We must identify those principles and then try to discern their interrelationships.

> If anybody seriously doubts whether there is such a thing as one person's having good will toward another, it should be noted that, no matter what an individual's personal disposition toward this subject is, we are dealing here with a question of fact not immediately provable by reason. The question is not about the degree or extensiveness of good will but the existence of the phenomenon itself. We should therefore deal with this issue the same way we would other factual matters, that is by appealing to the senses or introspection, depending on the matter under consideration, or by arguing from acknowledged facts and actions. A great number of actions of the same kind in different circumstances, and directed toward different objects, will prove with certainty what principles these actions do not proceed from and will prove with a high degree of probability what principles they do proceed from. Finally, there is also the testimony of mankind. That there is some degree of benevolence among people can be as strongly and clearly proved by all these ways as anything can be proved. . . .
>
> Whoever thinks it is worthwhile to consider this matter thoroughly should begin by noting exactly what the idea of an organized system entails. Obviously it involves a whole made up of parts; but even the parts collectively do not equal the whole unless one includes the relations those parts have to each other. Every organized system, whether natural or artificial, has some use or purpose beyond itself. So to the characteristics of an organized system must be added its conduciveness to one or more ends.
>
> Consider a watch, for instance. Suppose it is disassembled and its parts laid out separately. No matter how clear an understanding a person might have of these individual parts, without knowing the relations they have to one another that person will not have understood the watch. Suppose these different parts are assembled somehow. Even if the parts are connected

together, a person would not gain from this the idea of a watch and its function. But let that person see these pieces put together as a watch, and assuming that person also understands the relations these different pieces have to each other when they form the watch whose function is to tell time, then that observer has the idea of a watch.

The same principle applies to the inner workings of human beings. Appetites, passions, affections, and the principle of reflection, considered merely as individual parts of our inward nature, do not at all give us an idea of the system or constitution of our nature. This is due to the fact that our inner nature results from something not taken into consideration, namely the relations these various parts have to each other, the chief of which is the authority of reflection or conscience. It is from considering the relations which the different appetites and passions in the inner structure of human beings have to each other—and above all the supremacy of reflection or conscience, that we get the idea of the system or constitution of human nature.

Further examination will reveal that, when we understand the idea of virtue, we will see that our nature is adapted to virtue as much as it is clear from the idea of a watch that its nature is adapted to measure time. The usual course of events does not disprove this. Every artificial system can be put out of order. But this is so inconsistent with its nature as a system that a great enough increase in disorder will totally destroy it. This is merely a further explanation of what an ordered system is. Thus far the cases are perfectly parallel. But if we go further there is one major difference which, though too important to be omitted, does not really bear on the present topic. A machine is inanimate and passive, but we are moral agents. Our constitution is under our own power. We are responsible for it and are therefore accountable for any disorder or violation of it.

The Human System of Decision Making

Like animals and machines, the human being is a system of interrelated parts. The human, however, can decide for or against the smooth operation and interfacing of those parts, that is to say, for or against the proper functioning of human nature. A decision in favor of proper function is the core of virtue. A decision in favor of malfunction is the heart of vice. In the following passages Butler identifies the key parts of human decision making and indicates their proper functions. Try to detect how this analysis strikes at the heart of psychological egoism.

There is a natural principle of benevolence in human beings which, to some extent, has the same relation to society that self-love has to the individual. If there is any such thing as compassion (i.e., momentary love), if there is any such thing as paternal or filial affections, if there is any affection in human nature which has as its aim the good of another, this is benevolence itself, or the love of another. No matter how short, lowly, or unfortunately restricted, it proves the claim and points out what we were designed for as surely as it would were it in a higher degree and more extensive.

I should remind you, however, that though benevolence and self-love are different—the former concerning itself most directly with the public good, the latter with private—they are yet so perfectly overlapping that our greatest satisfactions depend upon our having benevolence to the proper extent. Further, self-love is the single chief guarantee of our right behavior toward society. One might also add that the mutual overlapping of benevolence and self-love being such that one can scarcely encourage the one without the other is equally a proof that we were made for both.

This point is underscored by the observation that the various passions and affections which are distinct from both benevolence and self-love generally contribute and lead us to public as readily as to private good. It would require a too detailed and lengthy analysis here to compare and contrast the several passions or appetites distinct from benevolence whose primary use and aim is the security and good of society as well as the passions distinct from self-love whose primary aim is the security and good of the individual. It suffices for the present argument to point to the following public affections or passions having an immediate reference to others that will naturally lead us to regulate our behavior in such a way as to be of service to our fellow creatures: desire for esteem from others, contempt and esteem of them, love of society as distinct from affections for its good, and indignation against vice that succeeds. If any or all of these may also be considered as private affections that support private good, this does not prevent them from being public affections too or destroy the good influence they have upon society and their support of public good.

Similarly, just as people who have no rational conviction to continue their life will nonetheless preserve their life merely because of the appetite of hunger, so by acting merely out of concern for their reputation and without any thought for the good of others, people often contribute to public good. In both these cases people are plainly instruments in the hands of another—Providence—in support of the aim of preserving the individual and the good of society, which is not the intention or aim they have for themselves. The bottom line is that people have various appetites, passions, and particular affections quite different from self-love and from benevolence, and all of these have a tendency to promote both public and private good and may be considered equally supportive of the common good for ourselves and others. But some of these passions seem primarily to concern others or to support the public good; others seem primarily to concern self, or support the private good. Just as the former are not benevolence, so the latter are not self-love. Neither of these types of passions are instances of our love for ourselves or others but are rather examples of our Maker's care and love both for the individual and the species and proofs that he intended that we should be instruments of good to each other as well as to ourselves. . . .

Everybody makes a distinction between self-love and the various particular passions, appetites, and affections. Yet it is easy to confuse them. That they are totally different will be seen by anyone who will distinguish between the passions and appetites themselves and the attempts to gratify them.

Consider the appetite of hunger and the desire of esteem. Since either can be the occasion both of pleasure or pain, the coolest self-love, as well as the appetites and passions themselves, may direct us toward methods for obtaining that pleasure and avoiding that pain. But the *feelings themselves,* the pain of hunger and shame, the delight from esteem, are no more self-love than they are anything else in the world. Even when people hate themselves, they will feel the pain of hunger as they would that of the gout. And it is clearly possible that there may be individuals with such a high self-love that they are insensible and indifferent (as people in some cases are) to the contempt and esteem of those upon whom their happiness does not in some respects depend.

That self-love and the various particular passions and appetites are in themselves totally different, and that some actions proceed from one and some from the other, will be clear to anyone who will consider the following two very believable cases. One person is heading toward certain ruin in order to gratify a present desire. Nobody will call the principle of this action self-love. Suppose another person goes through some difficult work upon the promise of a great reward but without any clear knowledge of what the reward will be. This course of action cannot be ascribed to any particular passion.

The former of these actions is plainly to be attributed to some particular passion or affection, the latter to the general affection or principle of self-love. That there are some particular pursuits or actions concerning which we cannot determine how much they owe to one passion or another stems from the fact that the two principles are frequently mixed together and confused. . . .

There is a principle of reflection in people by which they distinguish between and approve and disapprove their own actions. We are plainly constituted to be the sort of creatures that reflect upon their own nature. The mind can take a view of what passes within itself, its inclinations, aversions, passions, affections as they are directed toward various objects and to various degrees and toward the various resulting actions. In this survey the mind approves of one, disapproves of another, and toward a third is affected in neither of these ways but is quite indifferent.

This principle in human beings, by which they approve or disapprove their heart, temper, and actions is conscience. This is the strict sense of the word, though sometimes it is used to include more. That this faculty tends to restrain people from doing mischief to each other and leads them to do good is too manifest to need being insisted upon.

Butler further clarifies the operation of conscience in another sermon.

But there is a superior principle of reflection or conscience in every person which distinguishes between the internal principles of their hearts as well as their external actions. The conscience passes judgment upon the person and the person's actions, pronounces some actions to be in themselves just, right, good, others to be in themselves evil, wrong, unjust. . . .

It is by this faculty, natural to human beings, that they are moral agents, laws unto themselves. By this faculty I do not mean merely a principle in the person's heart which is to have some influence on the person as well as others but rather the faculty supreme in kind and nature over all the other faculties and which bears its own authority of being so.

This natural supremacy of the faculty which surveys, approves or disapproves the various affections of our mind and actions of our lives is that by which people are a law unto themselves, and their conformity or disobedience to this law of our nature makes their actions, in the highest and most proper sense, natural or unnatural. . . .

A person may act according to conscience or according to inclination, whichever happens at the moment to be strongest, and act in a way that violates the proper nature of a human being. Suppose a brute creature is allured by bait into a trap which destroys it. It plainly followed the bent of its nature, which led the creature to gratify its appetite. There is a full correspondence between the brute's nature and its actions; such action is therefore natural. But suppose a human being, forseeing the same danger of certain ruin, should rush into it for the sake of a present gratification. That person in this instance followed the strongest desire, just as the brute creature did. But there is a major difference between the nature of a human being and such an action as there is between the crudest work of art and the skill of the greatest master of that art.

This disproportion arises not from considering the action by itself or even from its consequences but from comparing it with the nature of the agent. Since such an action is utterly disproportionate to the nature of a human being, it is in the strictest and most proper sense unnatural, the very term itself expressing disproportion. Therefore, instead of the term "disproportionate to human nature," the word "unnatural" should be used, this being more familiar to us. But let it be noted that the meaning is exactly the same.

But what is it that renders such a rash action unnatural? Is it that the person went against the principle of reasonable and cool self-love considered *merely* as a part of that person's nature? No, for if that person had acted the contrary way, that would equally have gone against a principle or aspect of that person's nature—namely, passion or appetite. But to deny a present appetite from advance knowledge that gratifying it would end in immediate ruin or extreme misery is by no means an unnatural action, whereas to contradict or go against cool self-love for the sake of such gratification would be. Such an action, then, being unnatural, and its unnaturalness arising not from a person's going against a principle or desire, it necessarily follows that there must be some other difference between these two principles, passion and cool self-love, than what I have already referred to.

This difference, not being a difference in strength or degree, I call a difference in *nature* and in *kind*. And since, in the example just given, if passion prevails over self-love, the resulting action is unnatural. But if self-love prevails over passion, the action is natural. It is therefore clear that self-love is in human nature a superior principle to passion. The latter may be contradicted without violating that nature, whereas the former cannot. So, if we act consistently according to the organization of human nature, reasonable self-love must govern. Without specifically considering conscience, we may have a clear understanding of the superior nature of one inward principle to another and see that there really is this natural superiority quite distinct from degrees of strength and prevalency.

Let us now look at human nature as consisting partly of various appetites, passions, affections, and partly of the principle of reflection or conscience. We will leave out of consideration the various degrees of strength required for either of them to prevail; and it will still appear that there is a natural superiority of one inward principle to another and that it is even part of the idea of reflection or conscience.

Passion or appetite implies a direct tendency toward particular objects with no concern for the means by which they are to be obtained. Consequently, it is often the case that there is a desire of particular objects in those cases where they cannot be obtained without clear injury to others. Reflection or conscience enters the picture and disapproves the pursuit of them in these circumstances; but the desire remains. Which is to be obeyed, appetite or reflection? Cannot this question be answered from the regulation and constitution of human nature merely without saying which is the strongest?

Would not the question be intelligibly and fully answered by saying that the principle of reflection of conscience, when compared with the various appetites, passions, and affections in human beings, shows itself to be superior and highest in authority without regard to strength? And whenever the passions and appetites and affections happen to prevail, it is mere usurpation. Conscience remains in nature and in kind superior, and every instance of the prevalence of passions is an instance of breaking in upon and violation of the constitution of the human being.

All this is no more than the distinction which everyone is acquainted with between *mere power* and *authority*. But instead of using these terms to express the difference between what is possible and what is lawful in civil government, here it applies to the various principles in the human mind. Thus that principle by which we survey and either approve or disapprove our own heart, temper and actions is not only to be considered as having only some influence (which may be said of every passion, even of the lowest appetites) but as rather being superior. In its very nature conscience clearly claims superiority over all the other principles, inasmuch as you cannot form a notion of conscience without including judgment, direction, oversight. This is an integral part of the idea of the faculty itself. To preside and govern over the regulation and constitution of the human being belongs to it. Had it strength as it has right, had it power as it has manifest authority, it would absolutely govern the world.

All this gives us a further view of human nature. It shows us what course of life we were made for and that not only does our real nature lead us to be influenced to some degree by reflection and conscience but to what degree we should be influenced by it if we act in accordance with the constitution of our nature. This faculty was placed within to be our proper governor, to direct and regulate all the principles and motives of action. This is its right and position, a sacred trust. No matter how often people violate and rebelliously refuse to submit to it, either for supposed gain which they cannot otherwise obtain or for the sake of passion which they cannot otherwise gratify, this makes no difference as to the natural right and position of conscience. . . .

The natural supremacy of reflection or conscience having been established, we may from it form a distinct notion of what is meant by human nature when virtue is said to consist in following it and vice in deviating from it.

The idea of a civil constitution implies united strength, various subordinations under one direction of the supreme authority; the different strength of each particular member of the society does not come into this idea. But if you leave out the subordination, the union, and the one direction, you destroy and lose it. In the same way, reason, various appetites, passions and affections prevailing in different degrees of strength do not constitute the idea of human nature. Rather, human nature consists in these several principles having relations to each other such that the various passions are naturally subordinate to the one superior principle of reflection or conscience. Every bias, instinct, internal inclination, is a real part of our nature but not the whole of it. Add to these the superior faculty whose position it is to adjust, manage, and preside over them, and add to this its natural superiority and you complete the idea of human nature. And just as in civil government the constitution is broken in upon and violated by power and strength prevailing over authority, so the human constitution is broken in upon and violated by the lower faculties or principles within prevailing over that which is in its nature supreme over them all. . . .

The Weakness of Egoism

According to Butler, then, we have a whole cluster of particular passions, that is, drives toward and away from specific things. Some of these passions can make us happy, some of them can make us miserable. And some of them can make others happy; some of them can make others sad. Fortunately we also have two rational regulating principles that assess our passions to determine their tendencies. On the one hand, we have cool self-love which operates when we sort out those passions which are likely to make us happy from those which are likely to make us sad. On the other hand, we have benevolence which performs the same sorting operation relative to the happiness of humankind. Do we always obey the counsel of cool self-love that urges us to yield to those passions which will promote our happiness and to refrain from those passions which will generate our misery? Unfortunately, we do not. Too often we yield to a passion of the moment which we know will occasion much misery for us. In addition, sometimes we find ourselves so intent on listening to the advice of cool self-love that we neglect the counsel of benevolence. This neglect will sooner or later bring us to grief. Also, sometimes we are so intent upon obeying the dictates of benevolence that we forget to love ourselves adequately and consequently stumble again into misery.

It is this very human experience of the frustrated desire to achieve happiness that Butler uses to expose the weakness of psychological egoism. Hobbes would proclaim that all our actions are motivated by self-love. Butler would retort that he wished it were so. How can people be said to love themselves when they frustrate their deep desires for happiness? Indeed, how can we be said to love ourselves when we yield to a particular passion for LSD? How can we be said to love ourselves when we are so self-centered that we cut ourselves off from bonds with others whose support is essential for our happiness? How can we be said to love ourselves when we so concentrate on benevolence that we make ourselves a doormat for the heels of humanity?

According to Butler, the problem is that there is not enough self-love in the world. But bear in mind that, for Butler, cool self-love and benevolence are two sides of the same coin. When these regulating principles are functioning properly, they are not in conflict. It is the task of conscience, a third rational regulating principle, to arbitrate the conflicts between cool self-love and benevolence, and thereby to bring harmonious functioning and happiness to human nature.

Assessment of Psychological Egoism

In assessing the debate between Butler and Hobbes over the issue of psychological egoism, it is important to understand what they mean by self-love. Hobbes, you will recall, says that "desire and love are the same, except desire always signifies the absence of the object and love most commonly its presence." Love, then, is a passion or motion toward an object. Hobbes goes on to say that all voluntary actions are motivated by the desire to achieve some good for the self, which is presumably self-love. Thus in possessing the objects of one's desires a person is both loving the objects and loving his or her self.

Butler finds this account of love inadequate. He distinguishes clearly between loving objects and loving self. He argues that the objects toward which our drives or passions are directed are always specific, particular things. That is why he calls them the *particular* passions. The object of self-love, however, is not a specific object but is rather a life-long experience of happiness. Self-love, then, evaluates and calculates which of the particular passions will generate happiness. Because of its calculating, regulative role, Butler calls it *cool* self-love. By carefully distinguishing the particular passions from cool self-love, Butler has cleared the way for showing that not all particular passions lead to happiness and therefore that not all voluntary acts are motivated by self-love.

Has Butler refuted the doctrine of psychological egoism? There are a number of ways of refuting a philosophical position. One method involves showing how the position under attack leads to absurdities. Another method seeks to generate counterexamples that the philosophical position is supposed to explain but in fact cannot. Does Butler's contention that psychological egoism commits one to equating benevolence with cruelty demonstrate that psychological egoism leads to absurdity?

Does Butler's analysis of the frustrated desire to achieve happiness demonstrate that not all acts are motivated by self-love, and does that analysis thereby constitute a refutation of psychological egoism by counterexample?

Butler certainly has mounted a formidable attack against psychological egoism. Perhaps, if we took the time and spent the energy, we could enrich and refine Hobbes's theory to make it less vulnerable to Butler's criticism. Yet we do not need an unassailable refutation in order to reject a philosophical doctrine. We can also reject a doctrine if it is confused or fails to provide adequate guidance for our actions. Remember that Hobbes's view suggests that human beings are fundamentally selfish and that good and bad are values relative to the particular person at a particular time. Nothing is good absolutely. A thing is good if it is the object of someone's desire or love.

Suppose that a power company proposes to build a hydroelectric dam that will flood a wilderness area. An environmentalist group has mounted strong opposition to the dam. On the basis of Hobbes's psychological egoism, how can the dispute be settled? The supporters of the power company desire the dam, and *for them* building the dam is good. The supporters of the environmentalists have a strong aversion to the dam, and *for them* building the dam is evil. Is the action good or evil? Psychological egoism cannot really decide the question on rational grounds. From the perspective of psychological egoism, whether the dam will be built depends not on whether it is good or evil but on which group has the greatest power to enforce its perspective. Psychological egoism, therefore, leads to the conclusion that "might makes right." There seems to be no court of appeal beyond conflicting self-interests for the psychological egoist other than power or force. And this was precisely what Hobbes proposed: a sovereign with the power to enforce a resolution of such disagreements not necessarily on rational grounds but by might.

Given Butler's refutation of psychological egoism, as well as the objectionable practical consequences to which the position leads, why do so many people still accept the doctrine? Perhaps its appeal rests on confused thinking about the particular passions. Suppose that I am hungry and go to the local pizza parlor to stuff myself with an extra large sausage-mushroom-anchovy pizza. I would have had a particular passion for food, which was satisfied by the pizza. The passion was *mine,* and the satisfaction was *mine.* Because this passion and satisfaction were mine, some people may conclude that I was concerned about myself—indeed, that I was loving myself in the pizza parlor. But possession of a passion and its satisfaction is not equivalent to self-love. In fact, in my case, fulfilling the passion to eat pizza would probably hasten my death by aggravating my metabolism problem. In any case, self-love would be violated if I ate the pizza even though the passion and the satisfaction were mine. That the particular passions and their satisfactions are mine may be the rather faulty basis on which some people uncritically conclude that I am basically selfish.

Do you find this criticism of psychological egoism convincing? If you do, then presumably you will agree that when we try to respond to our ethical question, What ought I to do? we are not inevitably committed to selfish answers and selfish actions. Presumably you will agree that psychological egoism is unacceptable and that genuinely unselfish actions are possible. Having reached those judgments, you are ready to move on to consider our next challenge—determinism.

Review Questions

1. Describe how the new science influenced the ethical perspectives of Thomas Hobbes and Joseph Butler.
2. Consider Hobbes's "State of Nature." Do right and wrong exist there? How does war originate? How is peace brought into being?
3. According to Butler, what are the four major facets of the human system of decision making? How does that system generate "virtue"? "vice"?
4. Contrast the interpretations of self-love given by Hobbes and Butler. How does Butler's interpretation contribute to his critique of psychological egoism?
5. Briefly describe how Hobbes's view can be criticized using the stagies of reducing to absurdity, generating counterexamples, and rejection on pragmatic grounds.

Chapter 2

Determinism

Introduction

Psychological egoism presents a challenge to the significance of the ethical question, What ought I to do? by transforming it into quite a different question. The fundamental ethical question presupposes that we are free and have the capacity to identify and pursue alternative futures. Psychological egoism would confine those alternative futures to selfish or egoistic ones. The range of our freedom would be considerably narrowed, and the fundamental ethical question would be transformed into a different question: Which egoistic future shall I pursue? In the previous chapter we explored some of the theoretical and practical objections to psychological egoism and suggested that those objections were strong enough to make us question that doctrine as a basis for ethics. We now turn to another philosophical position that would also erode the meaningfulness of ethics: determinism.

If psychological egoism reduces the range of our possible alternative futures to only egoistic ones, determinism eliminates the very possibility of having alternative futures at all. Determinism replaces the question, What ought I to do? with the question, What *will* I do? With the fundamental ethical question discarded, the business of ethics would become something quite different. Here is how a determinist might describe it.

DETERMINIST: We determinists believe that every event is caused by some other event. For example, the ripples moving across a placid pond are caused by something such as a pebble thrown into the water by a playful child or a fish leaping into the air to catch a low-flying insect. Ripples on ponds don't just suddenly appear by chance. They have causes. Every event has a cause. There are no uncaused events. Nothing happens by chance.

YOU: Does your doctrine apply also to human beings?

DETERMINIST: Of course. When you have a toothache, headache, or stomachache, something has caused that ache. When you hear pleasant sounds, smell fragrant odors, taste delicious foods, and see beautiful sights, something has caused those sensations. When you think, choose, and act, once again something has caused you to do what you do. Indeed, all the events that take place in, through, and around you are caused by something.

YOU: When you say that all events associated with me are caused by something, are you saying that something causes or forces me to think what I think, choose what I choose, and act how I act? Are you saying that I am not free to think, to choose and to act?

DETERMINIST: Well, yes. We determinists maintain that human beings are not free. Would you say that a cucumber is free? Of course not. A cucumber is the product of forces beyond its control. It doesn't freely decide to be a cucumber rather than a grape, any more than a grape freely decides to be a grape rather than a carrot. Would you say that a caterpillar is free? Of course you wouldn't. A caterpillar doesn't freely decide to become a moth rather than an eagle. Nature mandates what the caterpillar will be. What makes you think human beings are any different from cucumbers, grapes, and caterpillars?

YOU: I have always thought that human beings are different, that we are free. You are familiar, no doubt, with the expedition of Captain Scott to the Antarctic. You know that he was faced with the dilemma of taking Evans with him or abandoning him in that frozen wilderness. Surely the fact that in such a situation, having to wrestle with the question, What ought I to do? points to the existence of human freedom. How can we meaningfully raise that question unless we are free? We do raise that question. You must admit that.

DETERMINIST: Yes, I admit that people raise that question, but really they are using language rather loosely, and they are unfortunately mistaken when they assume that human beings are free. Let's look more closely at Captain Scott's alleged freedom. You would maintain, wouldn't you, that Captain Scott was free to act in accordance with his choice?

YOU: Yes, I would accept that. Surely Captain Scott was free to take Evans along if he chose to do so, and free to abandon Evans if he chose to do that. Presumably no one held a gun to his head and demanded that he act in one way or another.

DETERMINIST: Why did Scott choose to drag Evans along?

YOU: I suppose because he wanted to. That was his desire.

DETERMINIST: Fine. Then tell me, do you think that Scott was free to choose in accordance with his desires?

YOU: I don't imagine he was completely free to choose in accordance with his desires. He probably wished that he could take Evans to a hospital, but that was an empty desire. He could not choose that alternative and act on it. He might have wished that he had never brought his team on this futile campaign to be the first people to reach the South Pole, but that wish also would have been empty. To be sure, Scott could desire many alternative futures that presented no real choice to him. His freedom to choose in accordance with his desires was hedged in by a number of practical limitations. But surely within those boundaries he was free to choose in accordance with his desires. If he desired to take Evans, he was free to choose that alternative. If he desired to abandon him, he was also free to choose that course of action.

DETERMINIST: You have answered with considerable precision, but allow me to press the analysis a bit further. You would say that Scott freely took Evans along because he chose to do so, and that he freely chose to do that because he desired to do it. But why did he desire to drag Evans along? Was he free to desire that?

YOU: Continue. No doubt you have more to say.

DETERMINIST: Thank you. I am about to urge my most important point. Were not Scott's desires caused by his character? And was not his character the product of his heredity and environment? Nature and nurture, genes and society—that's what made him the kind of person he was. Do you see the implications of this truth for the freedom you believe that Scott possessed? Scott was not free to desire. His desires were the direct consequence of his character which, in turn, was shaped by forces beyond his control—his heredity and environment. The cause of Scott's action was his choice to take Evans along. The cause of his choice was his desire. The cause of his desire was his character. The cause of his character was his heredity and environment. In the final analysis, Scott did not act freely. He acted the way he did because of his unique hereditary and environmental factors. Given those factors, he could not have acted otherwise. The same applies to you and me. We are the products of heredity and environment, forces beyond our control.

YOU: I can see now why you think the ethical question, What ought I to do? is a misuse of language. You think the real question is, Given the hereditary and environmental forces working on me, what *will* I do?

DETERMINIST: Precisely. I can see that you understand my position perfectly.

Such, then, is the challenge of determinism: human beings really do not have alternative futures open to them; the futures that they pursue are the only ones they could follow. They are not free, and ethics—understood as the attempt to find principles that should guide our actions—is a futile human enterprise.

We will follow further the debate between the advocates and critics of determinism by looking at writings from each. From the advocates we will examine a selection by the contemporary American philosopher Brand Blanshard. From determinism's critics, we will look at the counterattack by another contemporary philosopher, C. A. Campbell.

Advocate of Determinism: Brand Blanshard

An Ancient Doctrine

The doctrine of determinism, in various forms, has been around for centuries. In ancient Greece, the disciples of Democritus (circa 460–360 B.C.) held that everything consists of indivisible and imperceptible small particles called atoms. All events, including human actions, can be explained in terms of the motions and combinations of these atoms. Atoms for these thinkers were small bits that could not be further analyzed (in fact, the term "atom" means "indivisible"), not the complex configuration of neutrons, protons, and electrons spoken of by contemporary physicists.

The followers of another atomist, Epicurus (341–270 B.C.), adopted this atomic theory but modified it to make a place—albeit a small place—for human freedom. The chief concern of the Epicureans was to discover and practice the means for achieving a happiness that was safe from the changing fortunes of everyday life. It made little sense for them to pursue happiness actively if human beings were not free and if human action was explainable in terms of atoms in motion hitting each other like so many billiard balls. Epicureans thought that the way out of this difficulty was to say that although the motions of atoms were generally altered by the impact of other atoms, atoms have the capacity to swerve spontaneously from their paths. By inserting into the atomic theory this notion of a spontaneous swerve, the Epicureans were able to affirm an element of uncertainty and unpredictability in nature and thereby to allow a place for human freedom in an otherwise determined world.

From a somewhat different perspective, medieval theologians such as Saint Augustine (354–430) struggled with the problem of how to reconcile the personal experience of free will with the belief in an omniscient God who knows all events before they happen. If God knows that an event will happen, how can it *not* happen? Does God's foreknowledge of all events imply a form of determinism in which all events are inevitable from the beginning of time? Augustine's answers to these and related questions shaped the thinking of Christian theologians on the subject of human freedom for centuries to come.

Support from Modern Science

With the emergence of modern science, determinism found a new and stalwart ally. As is indicated in Chapter 1, the new science emphasized the mathematical model of thinking, which reduced the complex variety of phenomena to simple, abstract quantities of matter in motion and which enabled scientists to predict the behavior of phenomena. The new science brought with it the view that the objective world was a mechanical interplay of quantifiable, measurable objects. This was a world operating according to fixed laws, a world without spontaneity, a world devoid of freedom. One of the classic advocates of the determinism implied in the new science was Baron d'Holbach (1723–1789) whose book *The System of Nature* became known as "The Bible of Materialism." As an uncompromising materialist, d'Holbach claimed that nature or matter is all that there is. The human soul or mind or spirit, which was traditionally considered to be the source of free acts, was discarded by d'Holbach as an illusion. For him, a "man's life is a line that nature commands him to describe upon the surface of the earth, without his ever being able to swerve from it, even for an instant." Many other modern thinkers added their voices to that of d'Holbach in affirming determinism and denying free will. One of these thinkers on the contemporary scene is B. F. Skinner, whose book *Beyond Freedom and Dignity,* published in 1971, called upon us to discard the notion of an "autonomous inner man" or "soul" that allegedly is the source of our so-called free acts. He asks us to begin to think of ourselves as complex organisms without freedom and as parts of nature without special dignity.

Not every advocate of determinism, however, wishes to do away entirely with free will. Some determinists believe that it is possible to reconcile free will with determinism either by redefining free will, by reinterpreting causality, or by both of these tactics. Such determinists have come to be called "soft" determinists, using the term suggested by William James (the critic of determinism we will encounter later in this chapter). Those determinists who maintain that determinism and free will are completely irreconcilable are called "hard" or sometimes "extreme" determinists.

Blanshard's Case

The thinker we have selected as the advocate of determinism is Brand Blanshard, a representative of the soft determinist position. Born in Fredericksburg, Ohio in 1892, Blanshard became a philosopher and educator, holding appointments at the University of Michigan, Swarthmore College, and Yale University. Blanshard presents his case for determinism with admirable clarity in three phases. First, he defines several of the key terms that enter into his discussion. Second, he introduces and criticizes three of the major reasons thoughtful people often use to support their belief in indeterminism. Third, he proposes an interpretation of causality which, he suggests, allows one not only to affirm determinism but also to talk meaningfully about the human experience of freedom while avoiding repulsive mechanistic metaphors for human volition.

Key Definitions

At the outset, leaving no doubt as to where he stands in the debate, Blanshard offers definitions of *determinism, indeterminism, event* and *cause.*

> * I am a determinist. None of the arguments offered on the other side seem of much weight except one form of the moral argument, and that itself is far from decisive. Perhaps the most useful thing I can do . . . is explain why the commoner arguments for indeterminism do not, to my mind, carry conviction. In the course of this explanation the brand of determinism to which I am inclined should become gradually apparent.
>
> But first a definition or two. Determinism is easier to define than indeterminism, and at first glance there seems to be no difficulty in saying what one means by it. It is the view that all events are caused. But unless one also says what one means by "event" and "caused," there is likely to be trouble later. Do I include among events not only changes but the lack of change, not only the fall of the water over the cataract's edge, but the persistence of ice in the frozen river? The answer is "Yes." By an event

* FROM Brand Blanshard, "The Case for Determinism" in *Determinism and Freedom in the Age of Modern Science,* edited by Sidney Hook (New York: Collier Books, 1961), pp. 19–30. Used by permission of New York University Press.

I mean any change or persistence of state or position. And what is meant
by saying that an event is caused? The natural answer is that the event is
so connected with some preceding event that unless the latter had occurred
the former would not have occurred. Indeterminism means the denial of
this. And the denial of this is the statement that there is at least one event
to which no preceding event is necessary. But that gets us into trouble at
once, for it is doubtful if any indeterminist would want to make such an
assertion. What he wants to say is that his decision to tell the truth is
undetermined, not that there is no preceding event necessary to it. He
would not contend, for example, that he could tell the truth if he had
never been born. No, the causal statement to which the indeterminist takes
exception is a different one. He is not saying that there is any event to
which some namable antecedents are not necessary; he is saying that there
are some events whose antecedents do not make them necessary. He is
not denying that all consequents have necessary antecedents; he is denying
that all antecedents have necessary consequents. He is saying that the state
of things just before he decided to tell the truth might have been exactly
what it was and yet he might have decided to tell a lie.

By determinism, then, I mean the view that every event A is so connected
with a later event B that, given A, B must occur. By indeterminism I mean
the view that there is some event B that is not so connected with any
previous event A that, given A, it must occur. Now, what is meant here
by "must"? We cannot in the end evade that question, but I hope you
will not take it as an evasion if at this point I am content to let you fill in
the blank in any way you wish. Make it a logical "must," if you care to,
or a physical or metaphysical "must," or even the watered-down "must"
that means "A is always in fact followed by B." We can discuss the issue
usefully though we leave ourselves some latitude on this point.

Feelings and Freedom

Blanshard now summarizes the three reasons used by reflective people to support
indeterminism. He proceeds to critique the *first* of those reasons.

With these definitions in mind, let us ask what are the most important
grounds for indeterminism. This is not the same as asking what commonly
moves people to be indeterminists; the answer to that seems to me all
too easy. Everyone vaguely knows that to be undetermined is to be free,
and everyone wants to be free. My question is rather, When reflective
people accept the indeterminist view nowadays, what considerations seem
most cogent to them? It seems to me that there are three: first, the stubborn
feeling of freedom, which seems to resist all dialectical solvents; second,
the conviction that natural science itself has now gone over to the
indeterminist side; and, third, that determinism would make nonsense of
moral responsibility. The third of these seems to me the most important,
but I must try to explain why none of them seem to me conclusive.

One of the clearest heads that ever devoted itself to this old issue was

Henry Sidgwick. Sidgwick noted that, if at any given moment we stop to think about it, we always feel as if more than one course were open to us, that we could speak or be silent, lift our hand or not lift it. If the determinist is right, this must be an illusion, of course, for whatever we might have done, there must have been a cause, given which we had to do what we did. Now, a mere intuitive assurance about ourselves may be a very weak ground for belief; Freud has shown us that we may be profoundly deceived about how we really feel or why we act as we do. But the curious point is that, though a man who hates his father without knowing it can usually be shown that he does and can often be cured of his feeling, no amount of dialectic seems to shake our feeling of being free to perform either of two proposed acts. By this feeling of being free I do not mean merely the freedom to do what we choose. No one on either side questions that we have that sort of freedom, but it is obviously not the sort of freedom that the indeterminist wants, since it is consistent with determinism of the most rigid sort. The real issue, so far as the will is concerned, is not whether we can do what we choose to do, but whether we can choose our own choice, whether the choice itself issues in accordance with law from some antecedent. And the feeling of freedom that is relevant as evidence is the feeling of an open future as regards the choice itself. After the noise of argument has died down, a sort of intuition stubbornly remains that we can not only lift our hand if we choose, but that the choice itself is open to us. Is this not an impressive fact?

No, I do not think it is. The first reason is that when we are making a choice our faces are always turned toward the future, toward the consequences that one act or the other will bring us, never toward the past with its possible sources of constraint. Hence these sources are not noticed. Hence we remain unaware that we are under constraint at all. Hence we feel free from such constraint. The case is almost as simple as that. When you consider buying a new typewriter your thought is fixed on the pleasure and advantage you would gain from it, or the drain it would make on your budget. You are not delving into the causes that led to your taking pleasure in the prospect of owning a typewriter or to your having a complex about expenditure. You are too much preoccupied with the ends to which the choice would be a means to give any attention to the causes of which your choice may be an effect. But that is no reason for thinking that if you did preoccupy yourself with these causes you would not find them at work. You may remember that Sir Francis Galton was so much impressed with this possibility that for some time he kept account in a notebook of the occasions on which he made important choices with a full measure of this feeling of freedom; then shortly after each choice he turned his eye backward in search of constraints that might have been acting on him stealthily. He found it so easy to bring such constraining factors to light that he surrendered to the determinist view.

But this, you may say, is not enough. Our preoccupation with the future may show why we are not aware of the constraints acting on us, and hence why we do not feel bound by them; it does not explain why our sense of freedom persists after the constraints are disclosed to us. By disclosing the causes of some fear, for example, psychoanalytic therapy can remove the fear, and when these causes are brought to light, the fear commonly does go. How is it, then, that when the causes of our volition are brought to light volition continues to feel as free as before? Does this not show that it is really independent of those causes?

No again. The two cases are not parallel. The man with the panic fear of dogs is investing all dogs with the qualities—remembered, though in disguised form—of the monster that frightened him as a child. When this monster and his relation to it are brought to light, so that they can be dissociated from the Fidos and Towsers around him, the fear goes, because its appropriate object has gone. It is quite different with our feeling of freedom. We feel free, it was suggested, because we are not aware of the forces acting on us. Now, in spite of the determinist's conviction that when a choice is made there are always causal influences at work, he does not pretend to reveal the influences at work in our present choice. The chooser's face is always turned forward; his present choice is always unique; and no matter how much he knows about the will and the laws, his present choice always emerges out of deep shadow. The determinist who buys a typewriter is as little interested at the moment in the strings that may be pulling at him from his physiological or subconscious cellars as his indeterminist colleague, and hence feels just as free. Thus, whereas the new knowledge gained through psychoanalysis does remove the grounds of fear, the knowledge gained by the determinist is not at all of the sort that would remove the grounds for the feeling of freedom. To make the persistence of this feeling in the determinist an argument against his case is therefore a confusion.

Blanshard's response to those who cite their stubborn feelings of freedom as a reason for believing they are free is that when they choose, their attention is always turned toward future consequences rather than toward past causes for the choice. The resulting ignorance of past determining events of one's choice supports the feeling of freedom and the false belief that one is truly free to choose. Inattention to, and ignorance of, past constraints accounts for the stubborn feeling of freedom.

Physics and Freedom

The *second* reason often used to support indeterminism is the claim that modern physics has affirmed indeterminism in the physical world; accordingly, one is justified in maintaining indeterminism in the realm of the human will. Blanshard's criticism of this follows.

The second reason, I suggested, why so many thoughtful persons remain indeterminists is that they are convinced that science has gone indeterminist. Well, has it? If you follow Heisenberg, Eddington, and Born, it has. If you follow Russell, Planck, and Einstein, it has not. When such experts disagree it is no doubt folly for the layman to rush in. But since I am discussing the main reasons why people stick to indeterminism, and have admitted that the new physics is one of them, I cannot afford to be quite prudent. Let me say, then, with much hesitation that, as far as I can follow the argument, it provides no good evidence for indeterminism even in the physical world, and that, if it did, it would provide no good evidence for indeterminism in the realm of will.

First as to physical indeterminism. Physicists now tell us that descriptive statements about the behavior of bodies are really statistical statements. It was known long ago that the pressure that makes a football hard is not the simple quality one feels in pushing something: it is the beating on the inner surface of the football of millions of molecular bullets. We now know that each of these bullets is a swarm of atoms, themselves normally swarms of still minuter somethings, of which the proton and the electron are typical. The physicist admits that the behavior of an enormous mass of these particles, such as a billiard ball, is so stable that we may safely consider it as governed by causal law. But that is no reason, he adds, for assigning a like stability to the ultimate particles themselves. Indeed, there is good reason, namely the principle of indeterminacy, for saying that they sometimes act by mere chance. That principle tells us that whereas, when we are talking about a billiard ball, we can say that it has a certain momentum and direction at point *B* as a result of having a certain momentum and direction at point *A,* we can never say that sort of thing about an electron. Why? Because the conditions of observation are such that, when they allow us to fix the position exactly, they make it impossible to fix the momentum exactly. Suppose that we can determine the position of a moving particle with more accuracy the shorter the wave length of light we use. But suppose that the shorter the wave length, the more it interferes with the momentum of the particle, ma' g it leap unpredictably about. And suppose there is no way of determining the position without in this way leaving the momentum vague, or of determining the momentum without leaving the position vague. It will then be impossible to state any precise law that governs the particle's movement. We can never say that such-and-such a momentum at point *A* was necessarily followed by such-and-such a momentum at point *B,* because these statements can have no precise meaning, and can be given none, for either antecedent or consequent. Hence to speak any longer of nature as governed ultimately by causal laws—i.e., statements of precise connection between antecedent and consequent—is simply out of the question.

This argument, as Sir David Ross has pointed out, may be interpreted in different ways. It may be taken to say that, though the particle does have a certain position and momentum, we can never tell, definitely and for both at the same time, what they are. Many interpreters thus understand the theory. But so taken, there is of course nothing in it to throw the slightest doubt on the reign of causality. It is merely a statement that in a certain region our knowledge of causal law has limits. Secondly, the theory might be taken to mean that electrons are not the sort of things that have position and momentum at all in the ordinary sense, but are fields, perhaps, or widespreading waves. This, too, has no suggestion of indeterminism. It would not mean that general statements about the nature and behavior of electrons could not be made, but only that such statements would not contain references to position and momentum, the theory might mean that, though these particles do have a position and a momentum, the position or momentum is not definitely this rather that that. Even laymen must rise at this point and protest, with all respect, that this is meaningless. Vagueness in our thought of a position makes sense; vagueness of actual position makes none. Or, finally, the argument may mean that, though the particle does have a definite position and momentum, these cannot even in theory be correlated with anything that went before. But how could we possibly know this? The only ground for accepting it is that we do not know of any such correlates. And that is no reason for denying that any exist. Indeed, to deny this is to abandon the established assumption and practice of science. Science has advanced in the past precisely because, when things happened whose causes were unknown, it was assumed that they had causes nevertheless. To assume that a frustration of present knowledge, even one that looks permanent, is a sign of chance in nature is both practically uncourageous and theoretically a *non sequitur*.

But let us suppose that the Eddingtonians are right and that what has been called "free will among the electrons" is the fact. Would that imply indeterminism in the realm that most nearly concerns us, the realm of choice? I cannot see that it would. The argument supposed to show that it would is as follows: Psychical processes depend on physical processes. But physical processes are themselves at bottom unpredictable. Hence the psychical processes dependent on them must share this unpredictability. Stated in the abstract, the argument sounds impressive. But what does it actually come to? We are told that, even if there is inconstancy in the behavior of single particles, there is no observable inconstancy in the behavior of masses of them; the particles of a billiard ball are never able to get together and go on a spree simultaneously. Eddington admitted that they might, just as he admitted that an army of monkeys with a million typewriters might produce all the books in the British Museum, but he admitted also that the chance of a billiard ball's behaving in this way were so astronomically remote that he would not believe it if he saw it.

The question of importance for us, then, is whether, if acts of choice are dependent on physical processes at all, they depend on the behavior of particles singly or on that of masses of particles. To this there can be but one answer. They depend on mass behavior. An act of choice is an extremely complex process. It involves the idea of one or more ends, the association of that idea with more or less numerous other ideas, the presence of desires and repulsions, and the operation of habits and impulses; indeed, in those choices for which freedom is most demanded, the whole personality seems to be at work. The cortical basis for so complex a process must be extremely broad. But if it is, the great mass of cells involved must, by the physicist's admission, act with a high stability, and the correlated psychical processes must show a similar stability. But that is what we mean by action in accordance with causal law. So, even if the physicists are right about the unstable behavior of single particles, there is no reason whatever for translating this theory into a doctrine of indeterminism for human choice.

Blanshard is not convinced by those who advance the physical principle of indeterminacy as proof of free will. It is not clear, he maintains, that modern physics has in fact committed itself to indeterminism. The principle of indeterminacy may simply be an expression of the current ignorance of physics of the causal connectedness of things rather than a proof of their lack of connectedness. Yet, says Blanshard, even if one grants that modern physics has demonstrated indeterminism at the microlevel, that does not lead to the conclusion that indeterminism prevails at the macrolevel. There may be instability at the level of subatomic particles without a corresponding instability at the level of human will.

Morality and Freedom

The *third* reason often cited to uphold indeterminism is the assertion that determinism lays waste to morality. For example, surely one would not wish to blame or praise cucumbers, or butterflies, or stones for being what they are. Are they not, after all, what they are because of environmental or genetic factors over which they have no control? In a similar way, would it not be inappropriate to blame or praise human beings for being what they are and for doing what they do if, in fact, human actions are also the result of environmental or genetic factors over which we have no control? If determinism is true, then human beings have no real choices, no control over their actions, no alternative futures. And if blaming and praising are rendered inappropriate, has not morality been radically undercut? How could we say that a person is morally wrong for doing something if that person could not have done otherwise? Notice how Blanshard handles this reason for rejecting determinism.

We now come to the third of the reasons commonly advanced in support of indeterminism. This is that determinism makes a mess of morality. The charge has taken many forms. We are told that determinism makes praise and blame meaningless, punishment brutal, remorse pointless, amendment hopeless, duty a deceit. All these allegations have been effectively answered except the one about duty, where I admit I am not quite satisfied. But none of them are in the form in which determinism most troubles the plain man. What most affronts him, I think, is the suggestion that he is only a machine, a big foolish clock that seems to itself to be acting freely, but whose movements are controlled completely by the wheels and weights inside, a Punch-and-Judy show whose appearance of doing things because they are right or reasonable is a sham because everything is mechanically regulated by wires from below. He has no objections to determinism as applied by physicists to atoms, by himself to machines, or by his doctor to his body. He has an emphatic objection to determinism as applied by anyone to his reflection and his will, for this seems to make him a gigantic mechanical toy, or worse, a sort of Frankenstein monster.

In this objection I think we must agree with the plain man. If anyone were to show me that determinism involved either materialism or mechanism, I would renounce it at once, for that would be equivalent, in my opinion, to reducing it to absurdity. The "physicalism" once proposed by Neurath and Carnap as a basis for the scientific study of behavior I could not accept for a moment, because it is so dogmatically antiempirical. To use empirical methods means, for me, not to approach nature with a preconceived notion as to what facts must be like, but to be ready to consider all kinds of alleged facts on their merits. Among these the introspectively observable fact or reflective choice, and the inference to its existence in others, are particularly plain, however different from anything that occurs in the realm of the material or the publicly observable or the mechanically controlled.

In response to the objection that "determinism makes a mess of morality," Blanshard dismisses the charge simply by saying that this claim has already been effectively answered by philosophers. Then he proceeds to indicate that the real concern behind this objection is the suggestion that if one accepts determinism, then one is committed to saying that human beings are simply mechanical toys. Blanshard joins the "plain man" in being offended by such a metaphor for human beings. But how can one avoid such a metaphor if one accepts determinism? That question brings Blanshard to the third and final phase of his case for determinism.

Causality Interpreted

To avoid repulsive mechanistic metaphors for human volition, while affirming determinism, Blanshard proposes the following interpretation of causality.

Now, what can be meant by saying that such choice, though not determined mechanically, is still determined? Are you suggesting, it will be asked, that in the realm of reflection and choice there operates a different kind of causality from any we know in the realm of bodies? My answer is: Yes, just that. To put it more particularly, I am suggesting (1) that even within the psychical realm there are different causal levels, (2) that a causality of higher level may supervene on one of lower level, and (3) that when causality of the highest level is at work, we have precisely what the indeterminists, without knowing it, want.

1. First, then, as to causal levels. I am assuming that even the indeterminist would admit that most mental events are causally governed. No one would want to deny that his stepping on a tack had something to do with his feeling pain, or that his touching a flame had something to do with his getting burned, or that his later thought of the flame had something to do with his experience of its hotness. A law of association is a causal law of mental events. In one respect it is like a law of physical events: in neither case have we any light as to *why* the consequent follows on the antecedent. Hume was right about the billiard balls. He was right about the flame and the heat; we do not see why something bright and yellow should also be

hot. He was right about association; we do not understand how one idea calls up another; we only know that it does. Causality in all such cases means to us little if anything more than a routine of regular sequence.

Is all mental causation like that? Surely not. Consider a musician composing a piece or a logician making a deduction. Let us make our musician a philosopher also, who after adding a bar pauses to ask himself, "Why did I add just that?" Can we believe he would answer, "Because whenever in the past I have had the preceding bars in mind, they have always been followed by this bar?" What makes this suggestion so inept is partly that he may never have thought of the preceding bars before, partly that, if he had, the repetition of an old sequence would be precisely what he would avoid. No, his answer, I think, would be something like this: "I wrote what I did because it seemed the right thing to do. I developed my theme in the manner demanded to carry it through in an aesthetically satisfactory way." In other words, the constraint that was really at work in him was not that of association; it was something that worked distinctly against association; it was the constraint of an aesthetic ideal. And, if so, there is a causality of a different level. It is idle to say that the musician is wholly in the dark about it. He can see not only *that* B succeeded A; as he looks back, he can see in large measure *why* it did.

It is the same with logical inference, only more clearly so. The thinker starts, let us say, with the idea of a regular solid whose faces are squares, and proceeds to develop in thought the further characteristics that such a solid must possess. He constructs it in imagination and then sees that it must have six faces, eight vertices, and twelve edges. Is this association merely? It may be. It is, for example, if he merely does in imagination what a child does when it counts the edges on a lump of sugar. This is not inference and does not feel like it. When a person, starting with the thought of a solid with square faces, deduces that it must have eight vertices, and then asks why he should have thought of that, the natural answer is, Because the first property entails the second. Of course this is not the only condition, but it seems to me contrary to introspectively plain fact to say that it had nothing to do with the movement of thought. It is easy to put this in such a way as to invite attack. If we say that the condition of our thinking of B is the observed necessity between A and B, we are assuming that B is already thought of as a means of explaining how it comes to be thought of. But that is not what I am saying. I am saying that in thinking at its best thought comes under the constraint of necessities in its object, so that the objective fact that A necessitates B partially determines our passing in thought from A to B. Even when the explanation is put in this form, the objection has been raised that necessity is a timeless link between concepts, while causality is a temporal bond between events, and that the two must be kept sharply apart. To which the answer is: Distinct, yes; but always apart, no. A timeless relation may serve perfectly well as the condition of a temporal passage. I hold that in the course of our thinking we can easily verify this fact, and because I do, I am not put off by pronouncements about what we should and should not be able to see.

2. My second point about the causal levels is that our mental processes seldom move on one level alone. The higher is always supervening on the lower and taking over partial control. Though brokenly and imperfectly rational, rational creatures we still are. It must be admitted that most of our so-called thinking moves by association, and is hardly thinking at all. But even in the dullest of us, "bright shoots of everlastingness," strands of necessity, aesthetic or logical, from time to time appear. "The quarto and folio editions of mankind" can follow the argument with fewer lapses than most of us; in the texts of the greatest of all dramas, we are told, there was seldom a blot or erasure; but Ben Johnson added, and no doubt rightly, that there ought to have been a thousand. The effort of both thought and art is to escape the arbitrary, the merely personal, everything that, causal and capricious, is irrelevant, and to keep to lines appointed by the whole that one is constructing. I do not suggest that logical and aesthetic necessity are the same. I do say that they are both to be distinguished from association or habit as representing a different level of control. That control is never complete; all creation in thought or art is successful in degree only. It is successful in the degree to which it ceases to be an expression of merely personal impulses and becomes the instrument of a necessity lying in its own subject matter.

3. This brings us to our last point. Since moral choice, like thought and art, moves on different causal levels, it achieves freedom, just as they do, only when it is determined by its own appropriate necessity. Most of our so-called choices are so clearly brought about by association, impulse, and feeling that the judicious indeterminist will raise no issue about them. When we decide to get a drink of water, to take another nibble of chocolate, to go to bed at the usual hour, the forces at work are too plain to be denied. It is not acts like these on which the indeterminist takes his stand. It is rather on those where, with habit, impulse, and association prompting us powerfully to do *X,* we see that we ought to do *Y* and therefore do it. To suppose that in such cases we are still the puppets of habit and impulse seems to the indeterminist palpably false.

So it does to us. Surely about this the indeterminist is right. Action impelled by the sense of duty, as Kant perceived, is action on a different level from anything mechanical or associative. But Kant was mistaken in supposing that when we were determined by reason we were not determined at all. This supposition seems to me wholly unwarranted. The determination is still there, but since it is a determination by the moral necessities of the case, it is just what the moral man wants and thus is the equivalent of freedom. For the moral man, like the logician and the artist, is really seeking self-surrender. Through him as through the others an impersonal ideal is working, and to the extent that this ideal takes possession of him and molds him according to its pattern, he feels free and is free.

The logician is most fully himself when the wind gets into his sails and carries him effortlessly along the line of his calculations. Many an artist and musician have left it on record that their best work was done when the whole they were creating took the brush or pen away from them and completed the work itself. It determined them, but they were free, because to be determined by this whole was at once the secret of their craft and the end of their desire. This is the condition of the moral man also. He has caught a vision, dimmer perhaps than that of the logician or the artist, but equally objective and compelling. It is a vision of the good. This good necessitates certain things, not as means to ends merely, for that is not usually a necessary link, but as integral parts of itself. It requires that he should put love above hate, that he should regard his neighbor's good as of like value with his own, that he should repair injuries, and express gratitude, and respect promises, and revere truth. Of course it does not guide him infallibly. On the values of a particular case he may easily be mistaken. But that no more shows that there are no values present to be estimated, and no ideal demanding a special mode of action, than the fact that we make a mistake in adding figures shows that there are no figures to be added, or a right way of adding them. In both instances what we want is control by the objective requirements of the case. The saint, like the thinker and the artist, has often said this in so many words. I feel most free, said St. Paul, precisely when I am most a slave.

According to Blanshard, the mental life of human beings is subject to different kinds of causality. When one feels pain after stepping on a tack, one normally associates the pain with the tack and assumes that the contact with the tack caused the mental event of pain. Another type of causality operating in one's mental life is the necessity imposed upon one when a person is caught up by an aesthetic, logical or moral ideal. When a person surrenders to such an ideal, that ideal shapes the person according to its own pattern. When a person so surrenders and is thus shaped, causality of a higher order than either that of the association of a bodily event with a mental event or that of the functioning of a mechanistic toy is operative. When the artist, the logician, and the saint are seized by their respective ideals, causality is still present, and determinism still prevails. Being determined by such ideals is, Blanshard argues, the human experience of freedom.

Summary and Questions

Blanshard sums up his case for determinism as follows:

> We have now dealt, as best we can in a restricted space, with the three commonest objections to determinism. They all seem to admit of answers. To the objection that we always feel free, we answer that it is natural to feel so, even if we are determined, since our faces are set toward results and not toward causes, and the causes of present action always elude us. To the objection that science has gone indeterminist, we answer that this is only one interpretation of recent discoveries, and not the most plausible one, and that, even if it were true, it would not carry with it indeterminism for human choice. To the objection that determinism would reduce us to the level of mechanical puppets, we answer that though we are puppets in part we live, as Aristotle said, on various levels. And so far as causality

in reflection, art, and moral choice involves control by immanent ideal, mechanism has passed over into that rational determinism that is the best kind of freedom.

Has Blanshard presented a conclusive case for determinism? In responding to the claim that modern physics supports indeterminism, Blanshard correctly indicates that the significance of indeterminacy at the microlevel is still being debated. Yet if Blanshard and others allow for such indeterminacy at the microlevel and limit determinism to the macrolevel, has not determinism, which claims that all events (not just those on the macrolevel) are caused, been seriously compromised? Then, too, has Blanshard provided sufficient assurance that determinism does not lead to a devastation of morality? In addition, is Blanshard's notion of constraint by an ideal appropriately termed an example of the causality that is at the heart of determinism? Does not determinism claim that "every event A is so connected with a later event B that, given A, B must occur"? Can ideals appropriately be construed as *current events* which cause later events? Or are ideals more appropriately construed to be *future possibilities* rather than current events? And if they are seen as future possibilities, does not the ideal then function as a beckoning call rather than as a driving force? And if an ideal is a future possibility, are we not free to choose it or reject it?

It is precisely the beckoning call of an ideal in the situation of moral temptation upon which our next author, C. A. Campbell, focuses in order to make his case for indeterminism.

Critic of Determinism: C. A. Campbell

Determinism Contrasted with Indeterminism

Before we look at the views of a critic of determinism, let us delineate the issues that separate determinists from indeterminists. The determinist claims that all events are caused. The indeterminist denies this claim. The indeterminist, however, does not deny that many events are caused. What the indeterminist denies is that *all* events are caused. If *all* events are caused, as the determinist claims, then there would be no real alternative futures facing us. The future would be determined by past and present events; only *one* future would be compatible with the present state of the world. Does the future present us with real alternatives, or does it present us with only one mandated course of action? This is the issue that separates determinists and indeterminists.

William James (1842–1910), a distinguished American psychologist, philosopher, and physician, presents a case for indeterminism in his famous essay "The Dilemma of Determinism." He sets in sharp relief the issue dividing determinists and indeterminists.

> * It [determinism] professes that those parts of the universe already laid

* The passages in this chapter are from William James, "The Dilemma of Determinism" found in William James, *The Will to Believe and Other Essays in Popular Philosophy* (New York: Longmans, Green and Co., 1897), pp. 145–83. First published in *Unitarian Review* 22 (1884); 193–224.

down absolutely appoint and decree what the other parts shall be. The future has no ambiguous possibilities hidden in its womb: the part we call the present is compatible with only one totality. Any other future complement than the one fixed from eternity is impossible. The whole is in each and every part, and welds it with the rest into an absolute unity, an iron block, in which there can be no equivocation or shadow of turning.

> "With earth's first clay they did the last man knead,
> And there of the last harvest sowed the seed.
> And the first morning of creation wrote
> What the last dawn of reckoning shall read."

Indeterminism, on the contrary, says that the parts have a certain amount of loose play on one another, so that the laying down of one of them does not necessarily determine what the others shall be. It admits that possibilities may be in excess of actualities, and that things not yet revealed to our knowledge may really in themselves be ambiguous. Of two alternative futures which we conceive, both may now be really possible; and the one becomes impossible only at the very moment when the other excludes it by becoming real itself. Indeterminism thus denies the world to be one unbending unit of fact. It says there is a certain ultimate pluralism in it; and, so saying, it corroborates our ordinary unsophisticated view of things. To that view, actualities seem to float in a wider sea of possibilities from out of which they are chosen; and, *somewhere,* indeterminism says, such possibilities exist, and form a part of truth.

Determinism, on the contrary, says they exist *nowhere,* and that necessity on the one hand and impossibility on the other are the sole categories of the real. Possibilities that fail to get realized are, for determinism, pure illusions: they never were possibilities at all. There is nothing inchoate, it says, about this universe of ours, all that was or is or shall be actual in it having been from eternity virtually there. The cloud of alternatives our minds escort this mass of actuality withal is a cloud of sheer deceptions, to which 'impossibilities' is the only name that rightfully belongs.

The issue, it will be seen, is a perfectly sharp one, which no eulogistic terminology can smear over or wipe out. The truth *must* lie with one or the other, and its lying with one side makes the other false.

Advocates of Freedom

To maintain that we have real alternative possibilities is to say that we are free in the most important sense. Numerous thinkers have addressed and defended just such a sense of freedom. Immanuel Kant (1724–1804) argued that the real and undeniable experience of moral oughtness requires that we postulate the existence of human freedom. In the twentieth century, human freedom has been at the core of continental philosophy and was espoused by thinkers who disagreed about many things but were united on the central importance of free will: exponents have included Martin Heidegger, Nicholas Berdyaev, Gabriel Marcel, and Martin Buber, just to name a few.

Perhaps the most intense and famous of the twentieth-century critics of determinism and defenders of human freedom was Jean-Paul Sartre (1905–1980). Important in the development of the series of views that came to be called existentialism, Sartre through his novels, plays, essays, and treatises insisted on keeping distinct the difference between *persons* and *things.* In Sartre's analysis, a human being is not a thing, an object, but is rather a subject who knows, wills, and judges. To treat a person as a thing, which determinism does, is to fail to understand the uniqueness of human reality. What, in fact, makes persons different from things is that a person does not have a predetermined essence, as do such things as trees, stones, or manufactured objects. Human persons create themselves through their actions and choices. What a person will become is not caused by anything. You and you alone choose what you will be. Out of the myriad possibilities that lie before you, the choice of what you will be is yours and yours alone. With freedom goes a tremendous responsibility, a responsibility so overwhelming that we try to escape it by various forms of self-deception. We blame our choices on our heredity, our environment, on others (the anonymous "they," as when we say, They made me do it). In short, we find almost any explanation acceptable to the one that is truest to our own experience of freedom. All such forms of self-deception Sartre calls "bad faith."

Sartre's point of view helps us understand both the origin and attractiveness of determinism. Its origin is in the assumption that human beings are no different from things. Its attractiveness is in the lifting of a burden from our shoulders— the burden of freedom. In viewing human beings as things, determinism shifts the responsibility for what a person is to one's heredity or environment, thereby removing it from us.

Campbell's Case for Freedom

We have chosen to explore the works of C. A. Campbell as a critic of determinism and advocate of indeterminism. Although he is not so famous as the other critics we have mentioned, his writings on determinism repay careful study with beneficial insight. Charles Arthur Campbell (1897–1974), a Scotsman, was educated at Glasgow University and Oxford. After serving as a professor of philosophy at University College of North Wales, he became professor of logic and rhetoric at Glasgow University in 1938 and remained there until his retirement in 1961. The following essay by Campbell was originally presented by him in 1938 as his inaugural lecture when he assumed the Chair of Logic and Rhetoric at Glasgow.

In 1938 advocates of determinism were numerous. Modern science with its mechanistic models for interpreting the universe seemed to endorse the theory. Many people still assumed with the nineteenth-century physicist the Marquis de Laplace that, given the position and velocity of all the particles in the universe, one could theoretically calculate the future positions and velocities of these particles. The universe seemed to be one whose future was mandated by the ancient motions of objects. Yet just a decade before Campbell made his presentation, a German physicist, Werner Heisenberg, wrote a paper explaining quantum mechanics in which he articulated his famous uncertainty principle. According to that principle, it is impossible to know simultaneously the exact velocity and position of even a single particle, much less of all the particles in the universe. Laplace's dream seemed to be even more remote.

Heisenberg's principle, however, did not overturn determinism. Indeed, the influence of determinism was becoming more solidly entrenched, particularly in the social sciences with the development of the behavioristic psychology of J. B. Watson and B. F. Skinner and with the adoption of Marxian economic analyses by increasing numbers of sociologists, economists and historians.

Campbell begins his attack on determinism by seeking to identify at least one human action that is undeniably a free act. Because determinists claim that *all* acts are necessitated by prior causes, the indeterminist need find only a single free action to falsify the determinist's claim. If Campbell is successful in his task, he thus generates a refutation of determinism by counterexample. Let us watch his moves carefully.

> * In casting about for a suitable topic upon which to address you to-day, I have naturally borne in mind that an inaugural lecture of this sort should be devoted to some theme of much more than merely esoteric import: to some theme, for preference, sufficiently central in character to have challenged the attention of all who possess a speculative interest in the nature of the universe and man's place within it. That is a principal reason why I have chosen to-day to speak on free will. Mighty issues turn, and turn directly, on the solution of the free will problem. It is in no way surprising that for centuries past it has exercised a fascination for thinkers both within and without the ranks of the professional philosophers that is probably not paralleled in the case of any of the other great problems of metaphysics.
>
> There are, however, other considerations also which have governed my choice of subject. More particularly, I have been influenced by a conviction that the present state of philosophical opinion on free will is, for certain definitely assignable reasons, profoundly unsatisfactory. In my judgment, a thoroughly perverse attitude to the whole problem has been created by the almost universal acquiescence in the view that free will in what is often called the "vulgar" sense is too obviously nonsensical a notion to deserve serious discussion. Free will in a more "refined" sense—which is apt to mean free will purged of all elements that may cause embarrassment to a Deterministic psychology or a Deterministic metaphysics—is, it is understood, a conception which may be defended by the philosopher without loss of caste. But in its "vulgar" sense, as maintained, for example, by the plain man, who clings to a belief in genuinely open possibilities, it is (we are told) a wild and even obnoxious delusion, long ago discredited for sober thinkers.

* FROM C. A. Campbell's Inaugural Lecture "In Defense of Free Will" delivered on assuming the Glasgow University Chair of Logic and Rhetoric, 1938. Reprinted with permission of Macmillan Publishing Company from *An Introduction to Ethics* by Robert E. Dewey and Robert H. Hurlbutt III. Copyright © 1977 by Macmillan Publishing Company.

Now, as it happens, I myself firmly believe that free will, in something extremely like the "vulgar" sense, is a fact. And I am anxious to-day to do what I can, within the limits of a single lecture, to justify that belief. I propose therefore to develop a statement of the Libertarian's position which will try to make clear why he finds himself obliged to hold what he does hold, and to follow this up with a critical examination of the grounds most in vogue among philosophers for impugning this position. Considerations of time will, I fear, compel a somewhat close economy in my treatment of objections. But I shall hope to say enough to instigate a doubt in some minds concerning the validity of certain very fashionable objections whose authority is often taken to be virtually final. And if no other good purpose is served, it will at least be of advantage if I can offer, in my positive statement, a target for the missiles of the critics more truly representative of Libertarianism than the targets at which they sometimes direct their fire— targets, I may add, upon which even the clumsiest of marksmen could hardly fail to register bull's-eyes.

Moral Responsibility and Freedom

His preliminary remarks over, Campbell proceeds with his analysis. To begin, he indicates that if we hold a person morally responsible for an act (that is, if we deem the person worthy of praise or blame), then that person's act must have been a free act. Then he identifies two conditions which must obtain in a free act if that act is to incorporate moral responsibility.

Let us begin by noting that the problem of free will gets its urgency for the ordinary educated man by reason of its close connection with the conception of moral responsibility. When we regard a man as morally responsible for an act, we regard him as a legitimate object of moral praise or blame in respect of it. But it seems plain that a man cannot be a legitimate object of moral praise or blame for an act unless in willing the act he is in some important sense a "free" agent. Evidently free will in some sense, therefore, is a pre-condition of moral responsibility. Without doubt it is the realization that any threat to freedom is thus a threat to moral responsibility—with all that that implies—combined with the knowledge that there are a variety of considerations, philosophic, scientific, and theological, tending to place freedom in jeopardy, that gives to the problem of free will its perennial and universal appeal. And it is therefore in close connection with the question of the conditions of moral responsibility that any discussion of the problem must proceed, if it is not to be academic in the worse sense of the term.

We raise the question at once, therefore, what are the conditions, in respect of freedom, which must attach to an act in order to make it a morally responsible act? It seems to me that the fundamental conditions are two. I shall state them with all possible brevity, for we have a long road to travel.

The first condition is the universally recognized one that the act must be *self*-caused, *self*-determined. But it is important to accept this condition in its full rigour. The agent must be not merely *a* cause but the *sole* cause of that for which he is deemed morally responsible. If entities other than the self have also a causal influence upon an act, then that act is not one for which we can say without qualification that the *self* is morally responsible. If in respect of it we hold the self responsible at all, it can only be for some feature of the act—assuming the possibility of disengaging such a feature—of which the self *is* the sole cause. I do not see how this conclusion can be evaded. But it has awkward implications which have led not a few people to abandon the notion of individual moral responsibility altogether.

This first condition, however, is quite clearly not sufficient. It is possible to conceive an act of which the agent is the sole cause, but which is at the same time an act *necessitated* by the agent's nature. Some philosophers have contended, for example, that the act of Divine creation is an act which issues necessarily from the Divine nature. In the case of such an act, where the agent could not do otherwise than he did, we must all agree, I think, that it would be inept to say that he *ought* to have done otherwise and is thus morally blameworthy, or *ought not* to have done otherwise and is thus morally praiseworthy. It is perfectly true that we do sometimes hold a person morally responsible for an act, even when we believe that he, being what he now is, virtually could not do otherwise. But underlying that judgment is always the assumption that the person has *come* to be what he now is in virtue of past acts of will in which he *was* confronted by real alternatives, by genuinely open possibilities: and, strictly speaking, it is in respect of these *past* acts of his that we praise or blame the agent *now*. For ultimate analysis, the agent's power of alternative action would seem to be an inexpugnable condition of his liability to moral praise or blame, i.e. of his moral responsibility.

We may lay down, therefore, that an act is a "free" act in the sense required for moral responsibility only if the agent (a) is the sole cause of the act; and (b) could exert his causality in alternative ways. And it may be pointed out in passing that the acceptance of condition (b) implies the recognition of the inadequacy for moral freedom of mere "self-determination". . . .

Moral Temptation and Freedom

Having defined in general terms the conditions of free will, Campbell singles out and proceeds to analyze the situation of moral temptation as the locus where a free act can occur.

There seems to me to be one, and only one, function of the self with respect to which the agent can even pretend to have an assurance of that absolute self-origination which is here at issue. But to render precise the nature of that function is obviously of quite paramount importance; and we can do so, I think, only by way of a somewhat thorough analysis—

which I now propose to attempt—of the experiential situation in which it occurs, viz., the situation of "moral temptation."

It is characteristic of that situation that in it I am aware of an end A which I believe to be morally right, and also of an end B, incompatible with A, towards which, in virtue of that system of conative dispositions which constitutes my "character" as so far formed, I entertain a strong desire. There may be, and perhaps must be, desiring elements in my nature which are directed to A also. But what gives to the situation its specific character as one of moral temptation is that the urge of our desiring nature towards the right end, A, is felt to be *relatively* weak. We are sure that if our desiring nature is permitted to issue directly in action, it is end B that we shall choose. That is what is meant by saying, as William James does, that end B is "in the line of least resistance" relatively to our conative dispositions. The expression is, of course, a metaphorical one, but it serves to describe, graphically enough, a situation of which we all have frequent experience, viz., where we recognize a specific end as that towards which the "set" of our desiring nature most strongly inclines us, and which we shall indubitably choose if no inhibiting factor intervenes.

But inhibiting factors, we should most of us say, *may* intervene: and that in two totally different ways which it is vital to distinguish clearly. The inhibiting factor may be of the nature of another desire (or aversion), which operates by changing the balance of the desiring situation. Though at one stage I desire B, which I believe to be wrong, more strongly than I desire A, which I believe to be right, it may happen that before action is taken I become aware of certain hitherto undiscerned consequences of A which I strongly desire, and the result may be that now not *B* but *A* presents itself to me as the end in the line of least resistance. Moral temptation is here overcome by the simple process of ceasing to be a moral temptation.

That is one way, and probably by far the commoner way, in which an inhibiting factor intervenes. But it is certainly not regarded by the self who is confronted by moral temptation as the *only* way. In such situations we all believe, rightly or wrongly, that even although B *continues* to be in the line of least resistance, even although, in other words, the situation remains one with the characteristic marks of moral temptation, we *can* nevertheless align ourselves with A. We can do so, we believe, because we have the power to introduce a new energy, to make what we call an "effort of will," whereby we are able to act contrary to the felt balance of mere desire, and to achieve the higher end despite the fact that it continues to be in the line of greater resistance relatively to our desiring nature. The self in practice believes that it has this power; and believes, moreover, that the decision rests solely with its self, here and now, whether this power be exerted or not.

Now the objective validity or otherwise of this belief is not at the moment in question. I am here merely pointing to its existence as a psychological fact. No amount of introspective analysis, so far as I can see, even tends to disprove that we do as a matter of fact believe, in situations of moral temptation, that it rests with our self absolutely to decide whether we exert the effort of will which will enable us to rise to duty, or whether we shall allow our desiring nature to take its course.

Campbell's point is that in the situation of moral temptation we are confronted by two goals: *A*, which we perceive to be morally right, and *B*, which we perceive to be incompatible with *A* and morally wrong. Our desires, arising out of our characters formed through heredity and interaction with our environment, urge us in the direction of *B*. We might, however, pursue *A* under two circumstances. First, we might become aware of certain previously unnoticed consequences of *A* that lead us to desire *A* more strongly than *B*. Second, we might, through an effort of will, pursue *A* even though our desires continue to urge us in the direction of *B*. In the first instance, moral temptation is overcome simply by being eliminated through a shift in our desires. In the second instance, moral temptation is overcome by an effort of will whereby we respond to the beckoning call of duty which is much less attractive than the pursuit of *B*. When we do this through an effort of will, in our heart of hearts we firmly believe that the decision rests solely with us. That such an act fulfills the two conditions of a free act previously stated, Campbell now seeks to demonstrate.

I have now to point out, further, how this act of moral decision, at least in the significance which it has for the agent himself, fulfils in full the two conditions which we found it necessary to lay down at the beginning for the kind of "free" act which moral responsibility presupposes.

For obviously it is, in the first place, an act which the agent believes he could perform in alternative ways. He believes that it is genuinely open to him to put forth effort—in varying degrees, if the situation admits of that— or withhold it altogether. And when he *has* decided—in whatever way— he remains convinced that these alternative courses were really open to him.

It is perhaps a little less obvious, but I think, equally certain, that the agent believes the second condition to be fulfilled likewise, i.e., that the act of decision is determined *solely* by his self. It appears less obvious, because we all realize that formed character has a great deal to do with the choices that we make; and formed character is, without a doubt, partly dependent on the external factors of heredity and environment. But it is crucial here that we should not misunderstand the precise nature of the influence which formed character brings to bear upon the choices that constitute conduct. No one denies that it determines, at least largely, what things we desire, and again how greatly we desire them. It may thus fairly be said to determine the felt balance of desires in the situation of moral temptation. But all that that amounts to is that formed character describes the nature of the situation *within* which the act of moral decision takes place. It does not in the least follow that it has any influence whatsoever in determining the act of decision itself—the decision as to whether we shall exert effort or take the easy course of following the bent of our desiring nature: take, that is, the course which, in virtue of the determining influence of our character as so far formed, we feel to be in the line of least resistance.

When one appreciates this, one is perhaps better prepared to recognize the fact that the agent himself in the situation of moral temptation does not, and indeed could not, regard his formed character as having any influence whatever upon his act of decision as such. For the very nature of that decision, as it presents itself to him, is as to whether he will or will not permit his formed character to dictate his action. In other words, the agent distinguishes sharply between the self which makes the decision, and the self which, as formed character, determines not the decision but the situation within which the decision takes place. Rightly or wrongly, the agent believes that through his act of decision he can oppose and transcend his own formed character in the interest of duty. We are therefore obliged to say, I think, that the agent *cannot* regard his formed character as in any sense a determinant of the act of decision as such. The act is felt to be a genuinely creative act, originated by the self *ad hoc,* and by the self alone.

Here then, if my analysis is correct, in the function of moral decision in situations of moral temptation, we have an act of the self which at least *appears to the agent* to satisfy both of the conditions of freedom which we laid down at the beginning. The vital question now is, is this "appearance" true or false? Is the act of decision really what it appears to the agent to be, determined solely by the self, and capable of alternative forms of expression? If it is, then we have here a free act which serves as an adequate basis for moral responsibility. We shall be entitled to regard the agent as morally praiseworthy or morally blameworthy according as he decides to put forth effort or to let his desiring nature have its way. We shall be entitled, in short, to judge the agent as he most certainly judges himself in the situation of moral temptation. If, on the other hand, there is good reason to believe that the agent is the victim of illusion in supposing his act of decision to bear this character, then in my opinion the whole conception of moral responsibility must be jettisoned altogether. For it seems to me certain that there is no other function of the self that even looks as though it satisfied the required conditions of the free act.

Now in considering the claim to truth of this belief of our practical consciousness, we should begin by noting that the onus of proof rests upon the critic who rejects this belief. Until cogent evidence to the contrary is adduced, we are entitled to put our trust in a belief which is so deeply embedded in our experience as practical beings as to be, I venture to say, ineradicable from it. Anyone who doubts whether it is ineradicable may be invited to think himself imaginatively into a situation of moral temptation as we have above described it, and then to ask himself whether in that situation he finds it possible to *disbelieve* that his act of decision has the characteristics in question. I have no misgivings about the answer. It is possible to disbelieve only when we are thinking abstractly about the situation; not when we are living through it, either actually or in imagination. This fact certainly establishes a strong prima facie presumption in favour of the Libertarian position. . . .

Campbell has argued that the agent who through an effort of will pursues *A* instead of *B*, genuinely believes not only that B could have been chosen (that is, that two alternative futures were really present) but also that the decision to pursue *A* was an act solely determined by the self. Is the agent correct in this belief? It could be objected, as did the determinist in the opening dialogue of this chapter, that the decision was really caused by the agent's character which, in turn, was formed by the interplay of hereditary and environmental factors over which the person had no control. Campbell's response is that formed character merely sets the stage for moral temptation. Formed character only determines that the agent's desires for *B* are stronger than the agent's desires for *A*. Formed character does not force the agent to pursue *A*. In pursuing *A* the self somehow negates the pressure of formed character (which is in the direction of *B*) and instead obeys the beckoning call of duty. Indeed, in moral temptation, the agent experiences two selves in conflict: the self that determines the relative attractiveness of *A* and *B;* and the self that is able, on occasion, to pursue the less attractive *A*. Introspection leads the agent to believe that a decision to overcome moral temptation (the pursuit of *A* rather than *B*) does in fact fulfill the two conditions of a free act. If the determinist continues to claim that this belief is wrong, the burden of proof, says Campbell, rests with the determinist to show why this belief is mistaken.

Criticisms of Indeterminism Answered

Campbell now responds to two major criticisms that have been lodged against libertarianism. First, it is claimed that the libertarian position is incompatible with the predictability of human behavior and that, because such prediction is in fact possible, libertarianism must be false. Second, it is claimed that libertarianism is an unintelligible, self-contradictory doctrine in that it says that the act of overcoming moral temptation is an act of the self but that the act is not influenced by the hereditary and environmental factors which have made the self what it is. Here is Campbell's response to the first criticism.

> The charge made is that the Libertarian view is incompatible with the *predictability* of human conduct. For we do make rough predictions of people's conduct, on the basis of what we know of their character, every day of our lives, and there can be no doubt that the practice, within certain limits, is amply justified by results. Indeed if it were not so, social life would be reduced to sheer chaos. The close relationship between character and conduct which prediction postulates really seems to be about as certain as anything can be. But the Libertarian view, it is urged, by ascribing to the self a mysterious power of decision uncontrolled by character, and capable of issuing in acts inconsistent with character, denies that continuity between character and conduct upon which prediction depends. If Libertarianism is true, prediction is impossible. But prediction *is* possible, therefore Libertarianism is untrue.
>
> My answer is that the Libertarian view is perfectly compatible with prediction within certain limits, and that there is no empirical evidence at

all that prediction is in fact possible beyond these limits. The following considerations will, I think, make the point abundantly clear.

(1) There is no question, on our view, of a free will that can will just anything at all. The range of possible choices is limited by the agent's character in every case; for nothing can be an object of possible choice which is not suggested by either the agent's desires or his moral ideals, and these depend on "character" for us just as much as for our opponents. We have, indeed explicitly recognized at an earlier stage that character determines the situation within which the act of moral decision takes place, although not the act of moral decision itself. This consideration obviously furnishes a broad basis for at least approximate predictions.

(2) There is *one* experiential situation and *one only,* on our view, in which there is any possibility of the act of will not being in accordance with character: viz. the situation in which the course which formed character prescribes is a course in conflict with the agent's moral ideal: in other words, the situation of moral temptation. Now this is a situation of comparative rarity. Yet with respect to all other situations in life we are in full agreement with those who hold that conduct is the response of the agent's formed character to the given situation. Why should it not be so? There could be no reason, in our view any more than on another, for the agent even to consider deviating from the course which his formed character prescribes and he most strongly desires, *unless* that course is believed by him to be incompatible with what is right.

(3) Even within that one situation which is relevant to free will, our view can still recognize a certain basis for prediction. In that situation our character as so far formed prescribes a course opposed to duty, and an effort of will is required if we are to deviate from that course. But of course we are all aware that a greater effort of will is required in proportion to the degree in which we have to transcend our formed character in order to will the right. Such action is, as we say, "harder." But if action is "harder" in proportion as it involves deviation from formed character, it seems reasonable to suppose that, on the whole, action will be of rarer occurrence in that same proportion: though perhaps we may not say that at any level of deviation it becomes flatly impossible. It follows that even with respect to situations of moral temptation we may usefully employ our knowledge of the agent's character as a clue to prediction. It will be a clue of limited, but of by no means negligible, value. It will warrant us in predicting, e.g., of a person who has become enslaved to alcohol, that he is unlikely, even if fully aware of the moral evil of such slavery, to be successful immediately and completely in throwing off its shackles. Predictions of this kind we all make often enough in practice. And there seems no reason at all why a Libertarian doctrine should wish to question their validity.

Now when these three considerations are borne in mind, it becomes quite clear that the doctrine we are defending is compatible with a very substantial measure of predictability indeed. And I submit that there is not a jot of empirical evidence that any larger measure than this obtains in fact.

Campbell's response to the second charge brings us to the end of his discussion.

Let us pass on then to consider a much more interesting and, I think, more plausible criticism. It is constantly objected against the Libertarian doctrine that it is fundamentally *unintelligible.* Libertarianism holds that the act of moral decision is the *self's* act, and yet insists at the same time that it is not influenced by any of those determinate features in the self's nature which go to constitute its "character." But, it is asked, do not these two propositions contradict one another? Surely a *self*-determination which is determination by something other than the self's *character* is a contradiction in terms? What meaning is there in the conception of a "self" in abstraction from its "character"? If you really wish to maintain, it is urged, that the act of decision is not determined by the self's character, you ought to admit frankly that it is not determined by the *self* at all. But in that case, of course, you will not be advocating a freedom which lends any kind of support to moral responsibility; indeed very much the reverse.

Now this criticism, and all of its kind, seem to me to be the product of a simple, but extraordinarily pervasive, error: the error of confining one's self to the categories of the external observer in dealing with the actions of human agents. Let me explain.

It is perfectly true that the standpoint of the external observer, which we are obliged to adopt in dealing with physical processes, does not furnish us with even a glimmering of a notion of what can be meant by an entity which acts causally and yet not through any of the determinate features of its character. So far as we confine ourselves to external observation, I agree that this notion must seem to us pure nonsense. But then we are *not* obliged to confine ourselves to external observation in dealing with the human agent. Here, though here alone, we have the inestimable advantage of being able to apprehend operations from the *inside,* from the standpoint of *living experience.* But if we do adopt this internal standpoint—surely a proper standpoint, and one which we should be only too glad to adopt if we could in the case of other entities—the situation is entirely changed. We find that we not merely can, but constantly do, attach meaning to a causation which is the self's causation but is yet not exercised by the self's character. We have seen as much already in our analysis of the situation of moral temptation. When confronted by such a situation, we saw, we are certain that it lies with our *self* to decide whether we shall let our character as so far formed dictate our action or whether we shall by effort oppose its dictates and rise to duty. We are certain, in other words, that the act is *not* determined by our *character,* while we remain equally certain that the act *is* determined by our *self.*

Or look, for a further illustration (since the point we have to make here is of the very first importance for the whole free will controversy), to the experience of effortful willing itself, where the act of decision has found expression in the will to rise to duty. In such an experience we are certain that it is our self which makes the effort. But we are equally certain that the effort does not flow from that system of conative dispositions which we call our formed character; for the very function that the effort has for us is to enable us to act against the "line of least resistance," i.e. to act in a way *contrary* to that to which our formed character inclines us.

I conclude, therefore, that those who find the Libertarian doctrine of the self's causality in moral decision inherently unintelligible find it so simply because they restrict themselves, quite arbitrarily, to an inadequate standpoint: a standpoint from which, indeed, a genuinely creative activity, if it existed, never *could* be apprehended.

It will be understood, of course, that it is no part of my purpose to deny that the act of moral decision is in *one* sense "unintelligible." If by the "intelligibility" of an act we mean that it is capable, at least in principle, of being inferred as a consequence of a given ground, then naturally my view is that the act in question is "*un*intelligible." But that, presumably, is not the meaning of "intelligibility" in the critic's mind when he says that the Libertarian holds an "unintelligible" doctrine. If it were all he means, he would merely be pointing out that Libertarianism is not compatible with Determinism! And that tautologous pronouncement would hardly deserve the title of "criticism." Yet, strangely enough, not all of the critics seem to be quite clear on this matter. The Libertarian often has the experience of being challenged by the critic to tell him *why,* in his view, the agent now decides to put forth moral effort and now decides not to, with the obviously intended implications that if the Libertarian cannot say "why" he should give up his theory. Such critics apparently fail to see that if the Libertarian *could* say why he would already have given up his theory! Obviously to demand "intelligibility" in this sense is simply to prejudge the whole issue in favour of Determinism. The sense in which the critic is entitled to demand intelligibility of our doctrine is simply this; he may demand that the kind of action which our doctrine imputes to human selves should not be, for ultimate analysis, meaningless. And in that sense, as I have already argued, our doctrine is perfectly intelligible.

Has Campbell been successful in his criticism of determinism? Does the overcoming of moral temptation really constitute a free act such that determinism is falsified by counterexample? Can the overcoming of moral temptation be given a coherent and plausible deterministic interpretation? Has Campbell defended indeterminism (or libertarianism) adequately against the two charges he cites? Are there other significant charges against indeterminism that he has not addressed?

We will look at these and related questions as we turn to an assessment of the debate between Blanshard and Campbell.

Assessment of Determinism

Determinism presents a challenge to ethics because it denies the kind of freedom (genuinely possible alternative futures) apart from which our ethical question, What ought I to do? is meaningless. If we are to take that question seriously and attempt to answer it reasonably, we must reject determinism, and we must do so with good reasons.

An Inconclusive Debate

Has Campbell provided us with good enough reasons for rejecting determinism? Has he refuted it by counterexample? Campbell focused upon the call of duty in the situation of moral temptation. As he analyzed that situation he discovered that the causal chain of past events had made the call of duty less attractive than the call of immorality. The causal chain pushes the self in the direction of immorality. Yet on some occasions the self does countermand the deterministic demand of past events and does pursue the weaker voice of duty. Campbell concluded that this interruption of the direction of the causal chain is the activity of the self as a free agent.

Although this interpretation of the call of duty may seem to be more in agreement with our experience than does Blanshard's redefinition of causality to include logical, moral, and aesthetic ideals as necessitating elements in human experience, Campbell's argument is not conclusive. Could not the determinist respond that in the situation of moral temptation in which one vacillates between the call of duty and the call of immorality, the self is really the battleground of conflicting causally determined factors? On the one hand, a certain set of hereditary and environmental factors drives the self in the direction of duty. On the other hand, another set of hereditary and environmental factors drives the self in the direction of immorality. In moral temptation, the second set always *appears* to be the stronger. Yet, the stronger set is not *really* revealed until the agent acts. Prior to that time, the two sets of forces struggle with each other. The really stronger set always prevails, and the so-called decision is always causally determined.

Are we left with a stalemate in which both determinists and indeterminists almost endlessly refine their positions? And are we, who witness the debate, left unable to decide which side has the best evidence for its position? Fortunately, we need not fall into such a stalemate if we follow the lead of William James, with whom we began this chapter.

William James on Freedom

First as a student in science, then as a professor of physiology, psychology, and philosophy at Harvard, James was constantly exposed to the deterministic model of the world, and he found that model depressingly appealing. It was appealing because it seemed to correspond to the observed data that all human behavior is in accordance with physical laws. It was depressing to him because it seemed to cast a shroud of futility over his efforts to pursue a moral life. James wanted to take morality seriously, but how could he justifiably do so in a deterministic world? This problem was not just an intellectual game for James to be played now and then. It was instead a problem that struck at the very heart of his sense of meaning and being. James's biographer, Ralph Barton Perry, emphasizes the gravity of this question by characterizing it as a matter of "personal salvation" for James.

James received philosophical aid from the French philosopher Charles Renouvier (1815–1903), from whom he learned to think that freedom means "the sustaining of a thought *because I choose to,* when I might have other thoughts."* In addition, he owed to Renouvier a justification for this view of freedom. That justification is contained for the most part in his famous essay "The Dilemma of Determinism," selections from which are included at the beginning of this chapter and in the paragraphs below.

At the outset, James renounces any attempt to *prove* the truth of the claim that human beings have free will. Indeed, he suggests that it would be inconsistent for us to be coerced by an irrefutable argument to believe that we are free. More consistent is the perspective which declares that your first act of freedom should be to affirm that freedom.

A common opinion prevails that the juice has ages ago been pressed out of the free-will controversy, and that no new champion can do more than warm up stale arguments which every one has heard. This is a radical mistake. I know of no subject less worn out, or in which inventive genius has a better chance of breaking open new ground,—not, perhaps, of forcing a conclusion or of coercing assent, but of deepening our sense of what the issue between the two parties really is, of what the ideas of fate and of free-will imply. . . . My ambition limits itself to just one little point. If I can make two of the necessarily implied corollaries of determinism clearer to you than they have been made before, I shall have made it possible for you to decide for or against that doctrine with a better understanding of what you are about. And if you prefer not to decide at all, but to remain doubters, you will at least see more plainly what the subject of your hesitation is. I thus disclaim openly on the threshold all pretension to prove to you that the freedom of the will is true. The most I hope is to induce some of you to follow my own example in assuming it true, and acting as if it were true. If it be true, it seems to me that this is involved in the strict logic of the case. Its truth ought not to be forced willy-nilly down our indifferent throats. It ought to be freely espoused by men who can equally well turn their backs upon it. In other words, our first act of freedom if we are free, ought in all inward propriety to be to affirm that we are free. This should exclude, it seems to me, from the free-will side of the question all hope of a coercive demonstration,—a demonstration which I, for one, am perfectly contented to go without.

Two Presuppositions

James proceeds to indicate two fundamental presuppositions of his argument. First, philosophical theories about the world are generated to produce personal satisfaction. Second, given two competing theories of the world, the one that is "more rational" is probably truer. It is important to note that for James "rationality"

* *The Letters of William James,* I, 147.

relates to many facets of human experience, ranging from the domain of logic to the realm of morality. Accordingly, one theory may be "more rational" than another theory in the sense that it fits in with our moral experience, whereas the other theory violates that part of human experience. From these two presuppositions we can see already the tendency of James's argument: he is especially concerned with the practical consequences of determinism. Is it a philosophy that is capable of sustaining human life with inner peace? Is it a philosophy that coheres with our moral experience?

> The arguments I am about to urge all proceed on two suppositions: First, when we make theories about the world and discuss them with one another, we do so in order to attain a conception of things which shall give us subjective satisfaction; and, second, if there be two conceptions, and the one seems to us, on the whole, more rational than the other, we are entitled to suppose that the more rational one is the truer of the two. I hope that you are all willing to make these suppositions with me; for I am afraid that if there be any of you here who are not, they will find little edification in the rest of what I have to say. I cannot stop to argue the point; but I myself believe that all the magnificent achievements of mathematical and physical science—our doctrines of evolution, of uniformity of law, and the rest—proceed from our indomitable desire to cast the world into a more rational shape in our minds than the shape into which it is thrown there by the crude order of our experience. The world has shown itself, to a great extent, plastic to this demand of ours for rationality. How much farther it will show itself plastic no one can say. Our only means of finding out is to try; and I, for one, feel as free to try conceptions of moral as of mechanical or of logical rationality. If a certain formula for expressing the nature of the world violates my moral demand, I shall feel as free to throw it overboard, or at least to doubt it, as if it disappointed my demand for uniformity of sequence, for example; the one demand being, so far as I can see, quite a subjective and emotional as the other is. The principle of causality, for example,—what is it but a postulate, an empty name covering simply a demand that the sequence of events shall some day manifest a deeper kind of belonging of one thing with another than the mere arbitrary juxtaposition which now phenomenally appears? It is as much an altar to an unknown god as the one that Saint Paul found at Athens. All our scientific and philosophic ideals are altars to unknown gods. Uniformity is as much so as is free-will. If this be admitted, we can debate on even terms. But if any one pretends that while freedom and variety are, in the first instance, subjective demands, necessity and uniformity are something altogether different, I do not see how we can debate at all.

The Pragmatic Approach

According to James, an appeal to the facts will not decide the debate between determinism and indeterminism. Indeterminism holds that the world as it now is could have been different. Determinism denies this. Could the world have been different? Were there really other possibilities that could have been realized? All we have is the facts of *this* world, and those facts cannot be used to demonstrate that other facts could or could not have been in their place. Neither position in the debate rests securely upon facts. Both positions are rooted in faith: one faith holds that freedom is real, that possibilities really do exceed actualities; the other faith holds that there is no freedom, that the world could not have been different from what it is. Accordingly, James moves the debate away from the facts, away from refutation by counterexample, to an assessment of the viability of those faiths. What are the practical consequences of accepting one faith over the other? With which of these faiths can I live most comfortably? James proceeds to show that determinism leads to an uncomfortable dilemma.

> I wish first of all to show you just what the notion that this is a deterministic world implies. The implications I call your attention to are all bound up with the fact that it is a world in which we constantly have to make what I shall, with your permission, call judgments of regret. Hardly an hour passes in which we do not wish that something might be otherwise. . . . Some regrets are pretty obstinate and hard to stifle,—regrets for acts of wanton cruelty or treachery, for example, whether performed by others or by ourselves. Hardly any one can remain *entirely* optimistic after reading the confession of the murderer at Brockton the other day: how, to get rid of the wife whose continued existence bored him, he inveigled her into a desert spot, shot her four times, and then, as she lay on the ground and said to him, "You didn't do it on purpose, did you, dear?" replied, "No, I didn't do it on purpose," as he raised a rock and smashed her skull. Such an occurrence, with the mild sentence and self-satisfaction of the prisoner, is a field for a crop of regrets, which one need not take up in detail. We feel that, although a perfect mechanical fit to the rest of the universe, it is a bad moral fit, and that something else would really have been better in its place.
>
> But for the deterministic philosophy the murder, the sentence, and the prisoner's optimism were all necessary from eternity; and nothing else for a moment had a ghost of a chance of being put into their place. To admit such a chance, the determinists would tell us, would be to make a suicide of reason; so we must steel our hearts against the thought. And here our plot thickens, for we see the first of those difficult implications of determinism and monism which it is my purpose to make you feel. If this Brockton murder was called for by the rest of the universe, if it had to come at its preappointed hour, and if nothing else would have been consistent with the sense of the whole, what are we to think of the universe? Are we stubbornly to stick to our judgment of regret, and say, though it *couldn't* be, yet it *would* have been a better universe with something different from this Brockton murder in it? That, of course, seems the natural and spontaneous thing for us to do; and yet it is nothing short of deliberately espousing a kind of pessimism. The judgment of regret calls the murder bad. Calling a thing bad means, if it means anything at all, that the thing ought not to be, that something else ought to be in its stead. Determinism,

in denying that anything else can be in its stead, virtually defines the universe as a place in which what ought to be is impossible,—in other words, as an organism whose constitution is afflicted with an incurable taint, an irremediable flaw. The pessimism of a Schopenhauer says no more than this,—that the murder is a symptom; and that it is a vicious symptom because it belongs to a vicious whole, which can express its nature no otherwise than by bringing forth just such a symptom as that at this particular spot. Regret for the murder must transform itself, if we are determinists and wise, into a larger regret. It is absurd to regret the murder alone. Other things being what they are, *it* could not be different. What we should regret is that whole frame of things of which the murder is one member. I see no escape whatever from this pessimistic conclusion, if, being determinists, our judgment of regret is to be allowed to stand at all.

The only deterministic escape from pessimism is everywhere to abandon the judgment of regret. That this can be done, history shows to be not impossible. The devil, *quoad existentiam,* may be good. That is, although he be a *principle* of evil, yet the universe, with such a principle in it, may practically be a better universe than it could have been without. On every hand, in a small way, we find that a certain amount of evil is a condition by which a higher form of good is brought. There is nothing to prevent anybody from generalizing this view, and trusting that if we could but see things in the largest of all ways, even such matters as this Brockton murder would appear to be paid for by the uses that follow in their train. An optimism *quand meme,* a systematic and infatuated optimism like that ridiculed by Voltaire in his *Candide,* is one of the possible ideal ways in which a man may train himself to look on life. Bereft of dogmatic hardness and lit up with the expression of a tender and pathetic hope, such an optimism has been the grace of some of the most religious characters that ever lived.

> "Throb thine with Nature's throbbing breast,
> And all is clear from east to west."

Even cruelty and treachery may be among the absolutely blessed fruits of time, and to quarrel with any of their details may be blasphemy. The only real blasphemy, in short, may be that pessimistic temper of the soul which lets it give way to such things as regrets, remorse, and grief.

Thus, our deterministic pessimism may become a deterministic optimism at the price of extinguishing our judgments of regret.

But does not this immediately bring us into a curious logical predicament? Our determinism leads us to call our judgments of regret wrong, because they are pessimistic in implying that what is impossible yet ought to be. But how then about the judgments of regret themselves? If they are wrong, other judgments, judgments of approval presumably, ought to be in their place; and the universe is just what it was before,—namely, a place in which what ought to be appears impossible. We have got one foot out of the pessimistic bog, but the other one sinks all the deeper. We have rescued our actions from the bonds of evil, but our judgments are now held fast. When murders and treacheries cease to be sins, regrets are theoretic absurdities and errors. The theoretic and the active life thus play a kind of seesaw with each other on the ground of evil. The rise of either sends the other down. Murder and treachery cannot be good without regret being bad: regret cannot be good without treachery and murder being bad. Both, however, are supposed to have been foredoomed; so something must be fatally unreasonable, absurd, and wrong in the world. It must be a place of which either sin or error forms a necessary part. From this dilemma there seems at first sight no escape. Are we then so soon to fall back into the pessimism from which we thought we had emerged? And is there no possible way by which we may, with good intellectual consciences, call the cruelties and the treacheries, the reluctances and the regrets, *all* good together?

Certainly there is such a way, and you are probably most of you ready to formulate it yourselves. But, before doing so, remark how inevitably the question of determinism and indeterminism slides us into the question of optimism and pessimism, or, as our fathers called it, 'the question of evil.' The theological form of all these disputes is the simplest and the deepest, the form from which there is the least escape,—not because, as some have sarcastically said, remorse and regret are clung to with a morbid fondness by the theologians as spiritual luxuries, but because they are existing facts of the world, and as such must be taken into account in the deterministic interpretation of all that is fated to be. If they are fated to be error, does not the bat's wing of irrationality still cast its shadow over the world?

The refuge from the quandary lies, as I said, not far off. The necessary acts we erroneously regret may be good, and yet our error in so regretting them may be also good, on one simple condition; and that condition is this: The world must not be regarded as a machine whose final purpose is the making real of any outward good, but rather as a contrivance for deepening the theoretic consciousness of what goodness and evil in their intrinsic natures are. Not the doing either of good or of evil is what nature cares for, but the knowing of them. Life is one long eating of the fruit of the tree of *knowledge*. I am in the habit, in thinking to myself, of calling this point of view the *gnostical* point of view. According to it, the world is neither an optimism nor a pessimism, but a *gnosticism*. But as this term may perhaps lead to some misunderstandings, I will use it as little as possible here, and speak rather of *subjectivism,* and the *subjectivistic* point of view.

Subjectivism has three great branches,—we may call them scientificism, sentimentalism, and sensualism, respectively. They all agree essentially about the universe, in deeming that what happens there is subsidiary to what we think or feel about it. Crime justifies its criminality by awakening our intelligence of that criminality, and eventually our remorses and regrets; and the error included in remorses and regrets, the error of supposing that the past could have been different, justifies itself by its use. Its use is to quicken our sense of *what* the irretrievably lost is. When we think of it as that which might have been ('the saddest words of tongue or pen'), the quality of its worth speaks to us with a wilder sweetness; and, conversely, the dissatisfaction wherewith we think of what seems to have driven it from its natural place gives us the severer pang. Admirable artifice of nature! we might be tempted to exclaim,—deceiving us in order the better to enlighten us, and leaving nothing undone to accentuate to our consciousness the yawning distance of those opposite poles of good and evil between which creation swings.

We have thus clearly revealed to our view what may be called the dilemma of determinism, so far as determinism pretends to think things out at all. A merely mechanical determinism, it is true, rather rejoices in not thinking them out. It is very sure that the universe must satisfy its postulate of a physical continuity and coherence, but it smiles at any one who comes forward with a postulate of moral coherence as well. I may suppose, however, that the number of purely mechanical or hard determinists among you this evening is small. The determinism to whose seductions you are most exposed is what I have called soft determinism,—the determinism which allows considerations of good and bad to mingle with those of cause and effect in deciding what sort of a universe this may rationally be held to be. The dilemma of this determinism is one whose left horn is pessimism and whose right horn is subjectivism. In other words, if determinism is to escape pessimism, it must leave off looking at the goods and ills of life in a simple objective way, and regard them as materials, indifferent in themselves, for the production of consciousness, scientific and ethical in us. . . .

For my own part, . . . whatever difficulties may beset the philosophy of objective right and wrong, and the indeterminism it seems to imply, determinism, with its alternative of pessimism or romanticism, contains difficulties that are greater still. But you will remember that I expressly repudiated awhile ago the pretension to offer any arguments which could be coercive in a so-called scientific fashion in this matter. And I consequently find myself, at the end of this long talk, obliged to state my conclusions in an altogether personal way. This personal method of appeal seems to be among the very conditions of the problem; and the most any one can do is to confess as candidly as he can the grounds for the faith that is in him, and leave his example to work on others as it may.

Let me, then, without circumlocution say just this. The world is enigmatical enough in all conscience, whatever theory we may take up toward it. The indeterminism I defend, the free-will theory of popular sense based on the judgment of regret, represents the world as vulnerable, and liable to be injured by certain of its parts if they act wrong. And it represents their acting wrong as a matter of possibility or accident neither inevitable nor yet to be infallibly warded off. In all this, it is a theory devoid either of transparency or of stability. It gives us a pluralistic, restless universe, in which no single point of view can ever take in the whole scene; and to a mind possessed of the love of unity at any cost, it will, no doubt, remain forever inacceptable.

The Determinist's Dilemma

In summary, James has argued that if a determinist regrets the actions of the Brockton murderer, then that is equivalent to wishing that something else would have taken place. But, according to determinism, nothing else could have happened at that time and place. Accordingly, to continue to regret the murder is to regret the whole universe whose conditioning forces required the murder to take place. However, to regret the entire universe is to live by the doctrine of pessimism—not an entirely satisfying philosophy by which to live.

In order to avoid pessimism, one could maintain that some evil is necessary in the universe along with some good in order to produce a balanced whole. Then the murder becomes something to celebrate because it contributes to a beautiful balance of contrasts. One can then abandon the original deterministic pessimism in favor of a deterministic optimism. The implication, however, would be that the original pessimism was wrongheaded and something to be regretted. But to regret pessimism is to wish for other thoughts. Yet, according to determinism, those were the only thoughts possible at that time. Therefore, to continue to regard the original pessimism as wrongheaded and regrettable is to be committed to regretting the whole universe that mandated those thoughts at that time. Once again, determinism seems to lead to a doctrine of pessimism.

One could attempt to escape from this pessimism by maintaining that the universe is a giant mechanism whose goal is the production of theoretical consciousness (or mind) that is capable of making increasingly refined and subtle distinctions between good and evil. Then one could celebrate both the evil murder and also the original regrets as significant contributions to developing a theoretical capacity to distinguish between good and evil.

This new-found optimism, however, would be secured by a commitment to subjectivism. What matters is the development of theoretical consciousness. Each of us is at different stages of theoretical development because the forces acting upon us are different. My ideas are consonant with the forces acting on me: they are the only ideas I could have. The ideas others have are consonant with the forces acting on them: they are the only ideas these people could have. I cannot legitimately say that they should have my ideas, and they cannot legitimately claim that I should have their ideas. After all, our conditioning forces are different. The values I embrace are appropriate for me. The values they affirm are appropriate for them. This position is the doctrine of subjectivism.

The determinist who entertains regrets is committed either to pessimism or to subjectivism. That is the determinist's dilemma. Of the two, James would choose subjectivism, but he finds that this alternative is repugnant because it leads to standardlessness and moral anarchy. Although indeterminism is not without problems, James concludes that it is in practice a more satisfying and morally coherent philosophy by which to live.

James's advice to us in responding to the debate between determinism and indeterminism is to table the attempts to prove that determinism is false. Instead, he recommends that when we are faced with two competing doctrines, both of which cannot be true and neither of which we can disprove beyond doubt, then we should affirm the one that possesses the greatest "sentiment of rationality" (that is, the one that coheres most completely with our lived experience). By focusing on the sentiment of rationality, James directs our attention to the practical consequences that accrue to the person who accepts a particular doctrine.

Let us be as clear as possible about the practical consequences to which the determinist would be committed. The major consequence that provides a ground for rejecting determinism is that it violates our sense of moral rationality. From the standpoint of morality, we normally regret certain things. We regret vicious murders like the Brockton case, and we regret organized persecutions like the Jewish Holocaust by the Third Reich. We wish that these things had not happened. We call them evil, and we hold the people who did them blameworthy, and we punish them if we can capture them, because we believe that they ought to have done something different. At the heart of moral rationality are the notions that events can be regretted because they could have been different and that people are to be held responsible or accountable for their actions because they could have acted differently.

When faced with a moral outrage as overwhelming as is the Holocaust, a determinist who chooses to regret that systematic murder of millions of Jews would have only two paths open. On the one hand, the determinist could regret the Holocaust as a pessimist; that means accepting this incredible sacrifice as something *required* by the universe and saying, "It could not have been otherwise." Does not that seem like an empty, almost meaningless regret? On the other hand, the determinist could regret the Holocaust as an optimistic subjectivist. But does not that position commit the determinist to celebrating the Holocaust as *beneficial* to our developing capacity to make moral distinctions? Furthermore, does not that position lead to moral anarchy; namely, the doctrine that one person's moral distinctions are just as correct as another person's, that Hitler's moral ideas were just as right as Martin Luther King's?

Such, then, is the cost of determinism: the moral domain is emptied of its traditional significance, and one is committed either to pessimism or subjectivism. What would we lose if we chose indeterminism, if we affirmed free will? We would surrender the satisfaction produced from having a tidy, causal explanation of the universe. In comparing the costs, James concludes that determinism has priced itself out of the marketplace of ideas. Determinism is simply too costly; too much of traditional human experience would have to be surrendered.

Do you share James's conclusion? If you reject determinism, then you will affirm human freedom and consider the basic moral question, What ought I to do? to be a serious and meaningful one. And if that be the case, it is time to move on to consider our next challenge—ethical relativism.

Review Questions

1. Distinguish determinism from indeterminism and indicate which position you think is supported by modern science.
2. What criticisms does Blanshard level against the three reasons people often present to support indeterminism?

3. What does Blanshard mean by "causality of the highest level"?
4. How, according to Campbell, does the situation of moral temptation provide the occasion for a free act?
5. How does Campbell respond to two of the major criticisms registered against indeterminism?
6. What, according to James, is the determinist's dilemma, and how does that dilemma constitute an argument against determinism?

CHAPTER 3

Ethical Relativism

Introduction

The moral question, What ought I to do? presupposes that we are free in the sense that we have the capacity to identify and pursue genuine alternative futures. Without such freedom the significance of this question would be eroded. Psychological egoism would modify the question to, Which selfish act should I do? Determinism would transform the question into, What will I be compelled to do by the forces acting on me? Ethical relativism, the viewpoint to be examined in this chapter, would change the question to, Within the context of my social group, what ought I to do?

For the ethical relativist, the fundamental ethical question cannot legitimately be raised in general; ethical issues must always be considered relative to a specific social group. The reason the ethical relativist insists on this revision of the fundamental ethical question is that the relativist believes there are no universal cross-cultural ethical norms. Instead, the relativist holds that there are only the norms that a particular society sets up, and these norms vary greatly from one society to another.

The relativist thinks there is little sense to the general question, What ought I to do? because that question, by not being limited to a specific social group, is addressed to all persons and, therefore, assumes universal cross-cultural moral norms that are applicable to everyone. Asking the question, What ought I to do? as we have done commits us to belief in universal cross-cultural norms. That is the position of *ethical objectivism,* sometimes called *ethical absolutism.* The objectivist in ethics defends the view that when different cultures, or different individuals, hold opposing moral values, both of them cannot be right. The ethical relativist would say, in contrast, that right and wrong are defined by each culture *for that culture,* and that what a given culture defines as right really is right for that culture even though it may be the only culture in the world with such a view. It is easy to see how relativism is the opposite of objectivism in ethics, with its view that there are objective moral principles that are true regardless of how many people agree, or disagree, with them. Although the terms *objectivism* and *absolutism* are interchangeable, we will throughout this chapter use the term *absolutism,* as it is the term used consistently by one of the readings in this chapter.

The Case for Relativism: Anthropological Facts

The case for ethical relativism rests chiefly on two sets of considerations: a set of anthropological facts and a set of methodological assumptions. We will look at both in examining the case for relativism.

The central anthropological fact is *the existence of cultural diversity.* For decades, anthropologists have been amassing a vast array of data on different cultures. Even a quick review of that data reveals how widely human societies diverge from each other in their beliefs and moral practices. How can we account for such diversity? The ethical relativist claims that such differences exist because there are no universal ethical norms to which all societies can look for guidance in evaluating their acts. If there were universal norms, then surely we could expect some fundamental ethical uniformity among various human societies. But no such uniformity seems to exist. Accordingly, an attractive conclusion is that there simply are no such universal norms.

A second anthropological fact to which ethical relativists appeal is the *cultural origin of values.* It is almost universally acknowledged that human beings develop their beliefs and values within a social context. That is to say, one is not born with a whole set of moral values already formed. Those beliefs are acquired slowly through a sustained encounter with the values of the people who make up society. Where did those people get their values? No doubt they acquired theirs also in an encounter with their social environment. That is to say, values are the product of society's customs. How can we account for those customs? Ethical relativists like to suggest that those customs are based ultimately on the emotions of pain and pleasure that a society in its collective wisdom associates with various actions. By trial and error, and guided by pain and pleasure, our ancestors discovered those actions that satisfied their needs and promoted their pleasure. Similarly they discovered those actions that failed to satisfy their needs and generated pain. The former came to be regarded as "right" or "good," and the latter came to be seen as "wrong" or "evil." The results of these learning experiences were enshrined in society's customs for the benefit of succeeding generations.

If moral values are derived from society's customs, and if those customs are derived from the pains and pleasures of that society's ancestors, then it becomes clear why one society's moral beliefs differ from those of another society. What caused pain and pleasure for one society's ancestors did not necessarily generate pain or pleasure for the ancestors of a different society. Given different ancestral emotional responses in the struggle of different societies for survival, it is understandable that societies would develop different values and practices. Differing ancestral emotional responses, says the relativist, account much better for different current moral beliefs than do assumed universal moral norms.

A third anthropological fact cited by ethical relativists to bolster the case for relativism is *the pervasiveness of ethnocentrism*. Many people at different times and places have believed that their culture in general and their moral values in particular were superior to those of others. Such beliefs of moral superiority, says the relativist, are not based on the knowledge that a culture's morality is perfectly compatible with certain absolute moral norms. Those beliefs spring instead from the respect for one's culture that society has instilled in its people from early childhood. When that respect escalates into feelings of superiority, the phenomenon of ethnocentrism is present. Ethnocentrism can explain why ethical absolutists are willing to go around evaluating human behavior in other cultures as inferior to their own culture's values.

The Case for Relativism: Methodology

In addition to these anthropological considerations, some relativists also appeal to methodological issues. One issue involves the claim that because the meanings of moral concepts vary from culture to culture, those concepts cannot be understood outside the moral system of a specific culture. For example, *good* in one society may mean "that which is approved by the gods," whereas *good* in another society may mean "that which promotes the happiness of the majority." In yet another society *good* may mean "that which hastens the coming of the communist revolution." How can any person, standing within one society's moral system, really understand the meanings of the key concepts of a different society's morality? Some ethical relativists declare that such understanding is impossible. If that is the case, then cross-cultural evaluations become doubly impossible. The ethical relativist would not only deny any universal moral norms by which all cultures can be judged, but would also argue that no one really has the intimate knowledge of another society's moral concepts that is essential for passing judgment on that society's morality.

A second methodological issue that is sometimes urged by ethical relativists involves the claim that the basis for justifying moral obligation varies from culture to culture. Suppose, for example, I said, It is wrong to murder. And suppose, further, that someone asked me on what grounds I based that claim. What convincing basis could I specify? Would it be convincing if I appealed to a divine revelation from God that declared murder to be wrong? Would it be convincing if I said that murder was contrary to my feelings? Or, what if I appealed to the majority of the world's scientists who denounced murder? Or, how would it be if I said that murder violated universal human nature? We could probably find persons who would endorse one or more of these reasons for justifying moral claims; but it is unlikely that we would find all people agreeing on any one of them. Without such agreement, so the relativist argues, it is foolish to expect that we can have an answer to the question What ought I to do? that will be acceptable to all people. In other words, we do not have a universally agreed upon way of demonstrating what one ought to do. Some people appeal to one basis, others appeal to another. The basis you select is derived from the culture in which you live.

A third methodological basis for ethical relativism comes from the practice of anthropology itself. As a social science, anthropology offers a *description* of cultures and human behavior. The philosophical study of ethics, in contrast, is not so concerned about how people in fact behave but with how they ought to behave; it is *prescriptive* rather than descriptive. Anthropologists who started making value judgments about the behavior of the peoples they were studying would not only cease being anthropologists in so doing, but they would also probably find the people they were studying unwilling to talk with them. There is also the ever-present danger of ethnocentrism, of simply assuming that one's own cultural values are the best. Such an assumption would not only blind one to the values of the culture under study, but it also might simply be wrong. For these and many other reasons, anthropologists have adopted a value-free method of inquiry. As an anthropologist, the investigator does not make value judgments about a society or culture under study but instead seeks as clear an understanding as possible of what values, beliefs, and norms underlie a given society. Some anthropologists, though not all by any means, make the jump from this value-free method of research to the conclusion that no cross-cultural value judgments are ever warranted. Such an assumption apparently has been made by the advocate of ethical relativism presented in this chapter. As you read through the selection from M. J. Herskovits, you should ask yourself whether his relativistic position is supported by the findings of anthropology or if the anthropological data he advances is being interpreted by him in the light of relativistic assumptions for which he does not argue.

The Attractiveness of Relativism

Part of the attractiveness of relativism lies in the attitude of tolerance it seems to promote. There seems to be a humility attached to the relativist position ("I can't say *my* views are right for everybody, although they are right for me") and an arrogance associated with the absolutist view ("There are absolute moral principles, and I know what they are"). Undoubtedly this is one reason many people find ethical objectivism so unattractive. We have seen too many examples of people trying to remake the world in terms of their own religious or ideological views for which they claim absolute certainty. A live-and-let-live attitude, which seems to follow from the relativist position, strikes most of us as an attractive alternative to the dogmatism of the absolutist.

To characterize the two viewpoints in this way is not quite accurate. The degree of intolerance a person has toward others may not be directly related to the philosophical basis for that person's views. A relativist could be just as dogmatic as an absolutist. Ethical absolutists could also realize that tolerance of other views is called for, as their own views may in the future prove to have been wrong. A better characterization of the absolutist's point of would be: "There are absolute moral principles, but I may not have a full grasp of them; I act on the basis of the best knowledge I have." Throughout the history of philosophy one will find these two views, though perhaps under different labels. One view assumes that there are no fixed moral norms, and that right or wrong is solely determined by society. The other view is that we should keep on searching for a clearer understanding of morality and looking for better ways to relate to other people. We may not know the ultimate truth about things, but we should keep pursuing a better understanding of the true, the good, and the beautiful.

Given the central role played by anthropology in the case for ethical relativism, it is appropriate that the advocate position in this debate be represented by an American anthropologist, M. J. Herskovits. It is to his writings that we now turn.

Advocate of Relativism: M. J. Herskovits

A prominent American anthropologist, Melville Jean Herskovits was born in 1895 in Bellefontaine, Ohio. His studies at the Hebrew Union College and the University of Cincinnati were interrupted by his service in the First World War. Following the Armistice he studied briefly in France at the University of Poitiers before returning to the United States to study at the University of Chicago. He pursued graduate work in anthropology under the celebrated Franz Boas at Columbia University and received a Ph.D. degree in 1923. While at Columbia, Herskovits met Frances Shapiro, a student of anthropology at the New School for Social Research, whom he married in 1924 and who collaborated with him in many of his research and writing projects. Aided by numerous research grants, Herskovits became an expert on American black culture, including its transatlantic roots. He joined the anthropology department at Northwestern University in Evanston, Illinois in 1927, where he remained for almost four decades. In 1938 he was selected as one of the twenty American collaborators to work with Gunnar Myrdal of the University of Stockholm on a project funded by the Carnegie Corporation to study blacks in the United States. Herskovits's contribution, *The Myth of the Negro Past,* appeared in 1941 and helped correct many false views about black history. Herskovits served on many national advisory committees and established the first university program on African studies in the United States. He died in 1963 at the age of 68.

Among Herskovits's many writings, his large single volume *Man and His Works,* published in 1948, sets forth his interpretation of the entire field of cultural anthropology. It is from this work that the following statement in defense of cultural relativism is taken.

Evaluations Vary with Different Definitions

Herskovits begins with the observation that the definition of what is desirable varies from society to society. Conflicting moral evaluations, based on these differing definitions of the desirable, are to be expected. Herskovits illustrates his point by analyzing the institution of the polygamous family. Those reared in a culture where monogamy is the norm would find a polygamous family arrangement abnormal, but for those for whom polygamy is the norm, the custom has many desirable features. This example is used by Herskovits to underscore his conclusion that "evaluations are relative to the cultural background out of which they arise."

* All peoples form judgments about ways of life that are different from their own. Where systematic study is undertaken, comparison gives rise to classification, and scholars have drawn many schemes for classifying ways of life. Moral judgments have been drawn regarding the ethical principles that guide the behavior and mold the value-systems of different peoples. Their economic and political structures, and their religious beliefs have been ranked in order of complexity, efficiency, desirability. Their art, music, and literary forms have been weighed.

It has become increasingly evident, however, that evaluations of this kind stand or fall with the acceptance of the premises from which they derive. But this is not the only reason. Many of the criteria on which judgment is based are in conflict, so that conclusions drawn from one definition of what is desirable will not agree with those based on another formulation.

A simple example will illustrate this. There are not many ways in which the primary family can be constituted. One man may live with one woman, one man may have a number of wives, one woman may have a number of husbands. But if we evaluate these forms on the basis of how they fulfil their function of perpetuating the group by assuring that the children are reared to adulthood, it is clear that they meet the pragmatic test. By the very fact of their existence, they prove that they perform their essential tasks. Otherwise, the societies wherein they function would not survive.

Such an answer will, however, by no means satisfy all those who have undertaken to study the problem of cultural evaluation. What of the status of the plural spouse, the moral questions inherent in the practice of monogamy as against polygamy, the adjustment of children raised in households where, for example, the mothers must compete in behalf of their offspring for the favors of a common husband? If monogamy is held to be the desired form of marriage, the responses to these questions are not conjectural. But when we consider these questions from the point of view of those who live in societies other than our own, the possibility of alternative answers, based on different conceptions of what is desirable, becomes clear.

Let us consider, for example, the life of a plural family in such a West African culture as that of Dahomey. Here, within a compound, live a man and his wives. The man has his own house, as has each of the women, in consonance with the basic principle of African procedure that two wives cannot successfully inhabit the same quarters. The children of each wife live with their mother. Each wife in turn spends a native week of four days with the common husband, cooking his food, washing his clothes, sleeping in his house during this interval, and then making way for the next wife. Her children, however, remain in their mother's hut. With

* FROM Man and His Works: The Science of Cultural Anthropology, by Melville J. Herskovits. Copyright 1947, 1948 by Melville J. Herskovits. Reprinted by permission of Alfred A. Knopf, Inc.

pregnancy, she drops out of this routine, and ideally, in the interest of her child's health and her own, does not resume her visits to her husband until the child has been born and weaned. This means a period of from three to four years, since infants are nursed two years and longer.

The compound, made up of these households, is a cooperative unit. The women who sell goods in the market or make pottery or have their gardens contribute to its support. This aspect, though of great economic importance, is secondary to the prestige that attaches to the larger unit, a prestige in which all its members share. This is why one often finds a wife not only urging her husband to acquire a second spouse but even aiding him by loans or gifts to make this possible. Since a woman's earnings are hers to dispose of and women as traders in the market enjoy high economic position in this polygamous society, there is an appreciable number who command substantial means in terms of the general economy, and can thus help a husband, if it is desired, to sustain the expenses incident upon each marriage.

That tensions arise between the women who inhabit a large compound goes without saying. Thirteen different ways of getting married have been recorded in this society, and in a large household those wives who are married in the same category tend to unite as against all others. Competition for the regard of the husband is also a factor, though this is as often in the interest of the children as for personal advantage. Rivalries are especially sharp when several wives try to influence the choice of an heir in favor of their own sons. Yet all the children of the compound play together, and the strength of the emotional ties between the children of the same mother more than compensates for whatever stresses may arise between brothers and sisters who share the same father but are of different mothers. Cooperation, moreover, is by no means absent among the wives. Many common tasks are performed in friendly unison, and there is solidarity in the interest of women's prerogatives, or where the status of the common husband, the father of their children, is threatened.

We may now return to the criteria to be applied in drawing judgments concerning polygamous as against monogamous families in the light of this portrayal of the Dahomean plural family. The family structure of Dahomey is obviously a complex institution. If we but consider one aspect of it, the many possible lines of personal relationships between the many individuals concerned, we see clearly how numerous are the ramifications of the reciprocal rights and obligations and, consequently, of areas of both security and conflict. Its effectiveness is, however, patent. It has, for untold generations, performed its function of rearing the young; more than this, the very size of the group gives it economic resources and a resulting stability that might well be envied by those who live under different systems of family organization. Moral values are always difficult to establish, but at least in this society marriage is clearly distinguished from casual sex relationships and from prostitution, which is also known to the Dahomeans. It is differentiated from them in its supernatural sanctions and in the prestige it confers, to say nothing of the economic obligations toward spouse and prospective offspring explicitly accepted by one who enters on a marriage.

Numerous problems of adjustment do present themselves in an aggregate of this sort. The clash of personalities is not to be underestimated where persons of different individual backgrounds are brought into such close and continuous contact. It does not call for much speculation to understand the plaint of the head of one large compound when he said, "One must be something of a diplomat if one has many wives." Yet the sly digs in proverb and song, and the open quarreling, are of no greater stress than that of any small rural community where people are also thrown closely together for long periods of time. Quarrels between co-wives are not greatly different from disputes over the back fence between neighbors. And Dahomeans who know European culture, when they argue for their system, stress the fact that it permits for the individual wife a spacing of her children that is in accord with the best precepts of modern gynecology.

Thus polygamy, when looked at from the point of view of those who practise it, is seen to hold values that are not apparent from the outside. A similar case can be made for monogamy, however, when it is attacked by those who are enculturated to a different kind of family structure. And what is true of a particular phase of culture such as this, is also true of others. Evaluations are *relative* to the cultural background out of which they arise.

Attitudes Result from Enculturation

Herskovits has provided an example of a way of establishing a family unit that differs markedly from the norm in Western societies. He concludes that how one evaluates such an arrangement—or a monogamous family or a polyandrous family—depends on attitudes instilled by one's own culture. *Enculturation,* he calls it. But not only are our ethical attitudes the product of our enculturation. Enculturation determines our attitudes toward a host of other things as well.

The principle of *cultural relativism* derives from a vast array of factual data gained from the application of techniques in field study that have permitted us to penetrate the underlying value-systems of societies having diverse customs. This principle, briefly stated, is as follows: *Judgments are based on experience, and experience is interpreted by each individual in terms of his own enculturation. . . .* When we reflect that such intangibles as right and wrong, normal and abnormal, beautiful and plain are absorbed from infancy, as a person learns the ways of the group into which he is born, we see that we are dealing here with a process of first importance. Even the facts of the physical world are discerned through the enculturative screen, so that the perception of time, distance, weight, size, and other "realities" is mediated by the conventions of any given group.

No culture, however, is a closed system, a series of rigid molds to which the behavior of all members of a society must conform. In stressing the psychological reality of culture, it was made plain that a culture, as such, can *do* nothing. It is, in its very nature, but the summation of the behavior and habitual modes of thought of the persons who, at a given time and in a given place, make up a particular society. These persons, as individuals, though by learning and habit they conform to the ways of the group into which they have been born, nonetheless vary in their reactions to the situations of living they commonly meet. They vary, too, in the degree to which they desire change, as whole cultures vary. It is difficult for us, living in a culture where change is prized, to see the values in attitudes that stress stability as a desired end. This is but another way in which we see that the summation of behavior we call culture is flexible, not rigid, and holds many possibilities of choice within its larger framework. To recognize the values held to by a given people in no wise implies that they are a constant factor in the lives of succeeding generations of the same group. As Dewey has phrased it, "Whatever are the native constituents of human nature, the culture *of a period and group* is the determining influence in their arrangement.". . .

Norms and Normality Vary

Herskovits has claimed that anthropological research has provided ample evidence of *cultural relativism,* which he understands as the view that a person's concepts, judgments, and attitudes are based on experience which, in turn, is interpreted in the light of that person's cultural conditioning, or enculturation. These concepts, judgments, and attitudes include the norms and values that an individual is taught from infancy; notice even how easily we assume that our *norms* are *normal* for everyone. Yet anthropological research has shown that what counts as a norm in one culture may be very different from the norms of other cultures. In other words, the *normal* varies considerably from one culture to another.

Numerous instances of how these norms vary are to be found in the anthropological literature. . . . Many peoples have conventions of relationship that, while recognizing the role of both father and mother in procreation, count descent on but one side of the family. In such societies, it is common for incest lines to be so arbitrarily defined that "first cousins" as we would say, on the mother's side, call each other brother and sister and regard marriage with one another with horror. Yet marriage within the same degree of biological relationship on the father's side may be held not only desirable, but sometimes mandatory. This is because two persons related in this way are by definition not considered blood relatives.

The very definition of what is normal or abnormal is relative to the cultural frame of reference. As an example of this, we may take the phenomenon of possession as found among African and New World Negroes. The supreme expression of their religious experience, possession, is a psychological state wherein a displacement of personality occurs when the god "comes to the head" of the worshiper. The individual thereupon is held to be the deity himself. He often exhibits a complete transformation in his personality; facial expression, motor behavior, voice, physical strength, and the character of his utterances are startlingly different from what they are when he is "himself."

This phenomenon has been described in pathological terms by many students whose approach is non-anthropological, because of its surface resemblance to cases in the records of medical practitioners, psychological clinicians, psychiatrists, and others. The hysteria-like trances, where persons, their eyes tightly closed, move about excitedly and presumably without purpose or design, or roll on the ground, muttering meaningless syllables, or go into a state where their bodies achieve complete rigidity, are not difficult to equate with the neurotic and even psychotic manifestations of abnormality found in Euroamerican society.

Yet when we look beneath behavior to meaning, and place such apparently random acts in their cultural frame of reference, such conclusions become untenable. For *relative to the setting in which these possession experiences occur, they are not to be regarded as abnormal at all,* much less psychopathological. They are *culturally* patterned, and often induced by learning and discipline. The dancing or other act of the possessed persons is so stylized that one who knows this religion can identify the god possessing a devotee by the behavior of the individual possessed. Furthermore, the possession experience does not seem to be confined to emotionally unstable persons. Those who "get the god" run the gamut of personality types found in the group. Observation of persons in New World Negro groups who are interested in this religion and frequent the cults, yet who, in the idiom of worship "have nothing in the head" and thus never experience possession, seems to show that they are far less adjusted than those who do get possessed. . . .

The terminology of psychopathology has been readily applied to these states of possession. Such designations as hysteria, autohypnosis, compulsion, have come to rest easily on the tongue. Employed solely as descriptive terms, their use in technical analysis of the possession phenomenon may be of some utility. But the connotation they carry of psychic instability, emotional imbalance, departure from normality recommends the use of other words that do not invite such a distortion of cultural reality. For in these Negro societies the interpretation given behavior under possession—the meaning this experience holds for the people—falls entirely in the realm of understandable, predictable, *normal* behavior. This behavior is known and recognized by all members as something which may come to any one of them and is to be welcomed not only for the psychological security that derives from assurances of oneness with the power of the universe it affords, but also for the status, economic gain, aesthetic expression, and emotional release it vouchsafes the devotee.

A Defense of Relativism

If, as the relativist maintains, moral evaluation depends upon norms that are generated within a particular group at a specific time, and if those norms vary considerably from group to group, is not moral valuing reduced to such an arbitrary business that it can hardly be taken seriously? Herskovits is aware of this criticism and responds to it.

> Before we terminate our discussion of cultural relativism, it is important that we consider certain questions that are raised when the cultural relativistic position is advanced. "It may be true," it is argued, "that human beings live in accordance with the ways they have learned. These ways may be regarded by them as best. A people may be so devoted to these ways that they are ready to fight and die for them. In terms of survival value, their effectiveness may be admitted, since the group that lives in accordance with them continues to exist. But does this not mean that all systems of moral values, all concepts of right and wrong, are founded on such shifting sands that there is no need for morality, for proper behavior, for ethical codes? Does not a relativistic philosophy, indeed, imply a negation of these?"
>
> To hold that values do not exist because they are relative to time and place, or to deny the psychological validity of differing concepts of reality, is to fall prey to a fallacy that results from a failure to take into account the positive contribution of the relativistic position. For cultural relativism is a philosophy which, in recognizing the values set up by every society to guide its own life, lays stress on the dignity inherent in every body of custom, and on the need for tolerance of conventions though they may differ from one's own. Instead of underscoring differences from absolute norms that, however objectively arrived at, are nonetheless the product of a given time or place, the relativistic point of view brings into relief the validity of every set of norms for the people whose lives are guided by them, and the values these represent.
>
> It is essential, in considering cultural relativism, that we differentiate absolutes from universals. *Absolutes* are fixed, and, in so far as convention is concerned, are not admitted to have variation, to differ from culture to culture, from epoch to epoch. *Universals,* on the other hand, are those least common denominators to be extracted, inductively, from comprehension of the range of variation which all phenomena of the natural or cultural world manifest. If we apply the distinction between these two concepts in drawing an answer to the points raised in our question, these criticisms are found to lose their force. To say that there is no absolute criterion of value or morals, or even, psychologically, of time or space, does not mean that such criteria, in differing *forms,* do not comprise universals in human culture. We shall see, in a later section, how certain values in human life are everywhere accorded recognition, even though the institutions of no two cultures are identical in form. Morality is a universal, and so is enjoyment of beauty, and some standard for truth. The many forms these concepts take are but products of the particular historical experience of the societies that manifest them. In each, criteria are subject to continuous questioning, continuous change. But the basic conceptions remain, to channel thought and direct conduct, to give purpose to living.
>
> It will later become apparent how dynamic culture can be. Whether by invention from within or borrowing from without, cultures continuously

change, not only in their totality, but in each of their aspects. Change may be resisted, or changes may be welcomed. In this process, the individual changes his attitude toward the intangibles in culture no less than toward the material objects of his world. The morals, the world-view of one age are not identical with those of the next, as only a cursory study of our own history demonstrates. Yet the validity of each, for its time, is such as too often to make change difficult to envisage for the man who lives at that time.

In a similar manner, we can dispose of the contention that cultural relativism negates the force of the codes that prevail at a given time in a given culture. Everywhere, man seemingly always sets up goals for himself, and ideals toward which he strives. Because these are subject to change, or differ from people to people, does not make them any the less effective within a particular society during the period they prevail. Each people, having standards, not only inculcate them in the young so that each generation is enculturated to the value-systems of its predecessors, but they see to it that transgressions of accepted codes are punished. Law, no less than education, is one of the universals of culture, in each society stabilizing sanctioned modes of behavior, and stressing their values. Yet every culture knows the rebel, which means that man's experience encompasses cultural change as well as cultural stability.

The point may be put in a somewhat different way. *Cultural* relativism must be sharply distinguished from concepts of the relativity of individual behavior, which would negate all social controls over conduct. The existence of integrative moral forces has been remarked in every human society. Conformity to the code of the group is a requirement for any regularity in life. Yet to say that we have a right to expect conformity to the code of our day for ourselves does not imply that we need expect, much less impose conformity to our code on persons who live by other codes. The very core of cultural relativism is the social discipline that comes of respect for differences—of mutual respect. Emphasis on the worth of many ways of life, not one, is an affirmation of the values in each culture. Such emphasis seeks to understand, and to harmonize goals, not to judge and destroy those that do not dovetail with our own. Cultural history teaches that, important as it is to discern and study the parallelisms in human civilizations, it is no less important to discern and study the different ways man has devised to fulfil his needs.

That it has been necessary to consider questions such as have been raised, in discussing cultural relativism, itself reflects an enculturative experience wherein absolutes are stressed. These questions could only be asked by those who were trained in a culture such as our own, where the prevalent system of morals is not only consciously inculcated, but its exclusive claim to excellence emphasized. There are not many cultures, for example, where a rigid dichotomy between good and evil, such as we have set up, is insisted upon. Rather it is recognized that good and evil are but the extremes of a continuously varied scale between these poles that produces only different degrees of greyness. We thus return to the principle enunciated earlier, that "judgments are based on experience, and experience is interpreted by each individual in terms of his enculturation." In a culture where absolute values are stressed, the relativism of a world that encompasses many ways of living will be difficult to comprehend. Rather, it will offer a field-day for value-judgments based on the degree to which a given body of customs resembles or differs from those of Euroamerican culture.

It is not chance that a philosophy of cultural relativism, of which only the barest sketch has been given here, has had to await the development of adequate ethnographic knowledge. As long as the customs of peoples could not be studied in terms of their context of values, they of necessity had to be evaluated in terms of the ethnocentrism of the appraiser. But with effective techniques and a broad range of data, the humility reflected in the tolerance of the cultural relativistic position and its breadth of approach, becomes possible. Employing the field methods of the scientific student of man, and with an awareness of the satisfactions the most varied bodies of custom yield, this position gives us a leverage to lift us out of the ethnocentric morass in which our thinking about ultimate values has for so long bogged down. With a means of probing deeply into all manner of differing cultural orientations, of reaching into the significance of the ways of living of different peoples, we can, however, turn again to our own culture with fresh perspective, and an objectivity that can be achieved in no other manner.

Questions to Ponder

Note the following considerations which Herskovits has urged in defense of relativism. First, he points out that the relativist tries to understand the validity of every morality within its appropriate social group. Such an understanding, he says, breeds tolerance for perspectives other than one's own. But how far would he press this tolerance? Would he go so far as to respect and tolerate a culture that engages in human sacrifice? That pursues racial genocide? That uses terrorism as a routine means to achieve desired goals? Is it really the case that respect for every culture's morality means endorsing equally every culture's morality?

Second, Herskovits distinguishes between cultural "absolutes" and cultural "universals." Applying his distinction to ethics we could say that *ethical* universals are values that seem to be recognized by all cultures even though the ways in which those values are expressed, served, and enforced vary from culture to culture. Does Herskovits allow for the existence of ethical universals? Certainly, he says that *cultural* universals exist, such as, morality, the enjoyment of beauty, and a standard for truth. That is to say, all peoples have some sort of morality. But is there universal agreement about some values within morality? Do all peoples value some similar thing as good? Would not such an ethical universal be similar to a universal ethical norm? Would not the affirmation of ethical universals be inconsistent with ethical relativism? Is not Herskovits, therefore, committed to denying the existence of both ethical absolutes and also ethical universals? Why does he then raise the distinction between absolutes and universals? Is it simply to inform us that human beings universally practice morality of some sort? If so, how does that strengthen his contention that relativism affirms the seriousness of moral valuing.

Third, Herskovits wishes to distinguish clearly between *cultural* relativism and *individual,* personal relativism. The former would affirm that individuals within a culture are legitimately assessed in terms of the standards of that culture. The latter would make each individual the determiner of morality, and that form of relativism Herskovits rejects. On what basis, however, does Herskovits accept cultural relativism and reject individual relativism? Does he not maintain that the one leads to social stability and should be affirmed, whereas the other leads to social chaos and should be rejected? If so, what would be his attitude toward a social reformer (Gandhi, Martin Luther King) who opposes society's customs and laws for the sake of a higher morality than that which society currently acknowledges? To be consistent, would Herskovits not have to say that, because the social reformer generates social instability, such behavior would have to be condemned on the basis of the criterion by which Herskovits accepts cultural but rejects individual relativism?

These are the kinds of questions that lead us to the criticism of ethical relativism presented by Walter T. Stace.

Critic of Relativism: Walter Stace

A person who lived in several different cultures for extended periods of time would have unusually rich opportunities to reflect on ethical relativism. Such a person was Walter T. Stace (1886–1967). He was born in London, England in 1886 into a family deeply embedded in governmental service. His great grandfather was a general in the Battle of Waterloo, his father was a lieutenant colonel in the British Army, and his brother became a lieutenant colonel in the Royal Engineers. Such a family background probably influenced Stace to enter the British Civil Service in Ceylon in 1910, two years after he had received his B.A. in philosophy from Trinity College at Dublin University. For the next twenty-two years he lived in Ceylon, serving in positions ranging from district judge to mayor of Colombo. In 1932, governmental changes in Ceylon induced him to leave the country, and he accepted a position at Princeton University, where he taught until his retirement in 1955.

Stace was a member of that vanishing breed of philosophers who became distinguished teachers and scholars without having had any formal graduate education. He did, however, receive a Litt.D. in 1929 from Dublin University in recognition of the contribution he made to the scholarly world with his book *The Philosophy of Hegel.* In the preface to that work Stace indicates that his goal is to reduce the notoriously complex thought of Hegel to an easily understood discussion. Stace succeeds remarkably well, and that same quest for clarity for the sake of communicating to others seems to inform most of his writings.

One of Stace's major philosophical concerns was the wave of ethical relativism that seemed to be flooding the minds of many persons prior to the Second World War. Relativists, though often of a disposition to do so, were unable to defend democracy as morally better than the totalitarian state of fascism. In *The Concept of Morals,* published in 1937 and from which the selection below is taken, Stace mounted a tough-minded attack on ethical relativism. Then in *The Destiny of Western Man,* published in 1942, he made a case for the moral superiority of democracy, and his discussion was so impressive that it won him the Reynal and Hitchcock Prize. Stace went on to publish altogether ten books and many articles, for which in 1959 he was selected as one of ten scholars to receive a prize from the American Council of Learned Societies for distinguished scholarship in the humanities.

Relativism Distinguished from Absolutism

At the beginning of his analysis of relativism, Stace describes clearly the disagreement that separates the ethical relativist from the ethical absolutist. That disagreement can be described in a number of ways: it can be discussed in terms of the differing beliefs about universal cross-cultural norms; the absolutist affirms such "absolutes" or norms, and the relativist denies them. Here is his definition of relativism.

> * Any ethical position which denies that there is a single moral standard which is equally applicable to all men at all times may fairly be called a species of ethical relativity. There is not, the relativist asserts, merely one moral law, one code, one standard. There are many moral laws, codes, standards. What morality ordains in one place or age may be quite different from what morality ordains in another place or age. The moral code of Chinamen is quite different from that of Europeans, that of African savages quite different from both. Any morality, therefore, is relative to the age, the place, and the circumstances in which it is found. It is in no sense absolute.

Another way the disagreement between the relativist and absolutist can be represented is in terms of distinctions that the absolutist affirms and the relativist denies. The absolutist, for example, distinguishes between what people *think* is right, and what *is actually* right. The relativist denies this distinction by affirming that what people *think* is right *is* in fact right. Notice how Stace, without mincing words, characterizes the relativist's creed as declaring, "Cannibalism is right for people who believe in it." We could add, Terrorism is right for people who believe in it. After defining relativism, Stace next makes clear the important distinction between *cultural* relativism and *ethical* relativism. The tendency to confuse them rests, in part, on using the term *standard* in two different senses.

> This does not mean merely—as one might at first sight be inclined to suppose—that the very same kind of action which is *thought* right in one country and period may be *thought* wrong in another. This would be a mere platitude, the truth of which everyone would have to admit. Even

the absolutist would admit this—would even wish to emphasize it—since he is well aware that different peoples have different sets of moral ideas, and his whole point is that some of these sets of ideas are false. What the relativist means to assert is, not this platitude, but that the very same kind of action which *is* right in one country and period may *be* wrong in another. And this, far from being a platitude, is a very startling assertion.

It is very important to grasp thoroughly the difference between the two ideas. For there is reason to think that many minds tend to find ethical relativity attractive because they fail to keep them clearly apart. It is so very obvious that moral ideas differ from country to country and from age to age. And it is so very easy, if you are mentally lazy, to suppose that to say this means the same as to say that no universal moral standard exists,— or in other words that it implies ethical relativity. We fail to see that the word "standard" is used in two different senses. It is perfectly true that, in one sense, there are many variable moral standards. We speak of judging a man by the standard of his time. And this implies that different times have different standards. And this, of course, is quite true. But when the word "standard" is used in this sense it means simply the set of moral ideas current during the period in question. It means what people *think* right, whether as a matter of fact it *is* right or not. On the other hand when the absolutist asserts that there exists a single universal moral "standard," he is not using the word in this sense at all. He means by "standard" what *is* right as distinct from what people merely think right. His point is that although what people think right varies in different countries and periods, yet what actually is right is everywhere and always the same. And it follows that when the ethical relativist disputes the position of the absolutist and denies that any universal moral standard exists he too means by "standard" what actually is right. But it is exceedingly easy, if we are not careful, to slip loosely from using the word in the first sense to using it in the second sense; and to suppose that the variability of moral beliefs is the same thing as the variability of what really is moral. And unless we keep the two senses of the word "standard" distinct, we are likely to think the creed of ethical relativity much more plausible than it actually is.

The genuine relativist, then, does not merely mean that Chinamen may think right what Frenchmen think wrong. He means that what *is* wrong for the Frenchman may *be* right for the Chinaman. And if one enquires how, in those circumstances, one is to know what actually is right in China or in France, the answer comes quite glibly. What is right in China is the same as what people think right in China; and what is right in France is the same as what people think right in France. So that, if you want to know what is moral in any particular country or age all you have to do is to ascertain what are the moral ideas current in that age or country. Those ideas are, *for that age or country,* right. Thus what is morally right is identified with what is thought to be morally right, and the distinction which we made above between these two is simply denied. To put the same thing in another way, it is denied that there can be or ought to be any distinction between the two senses of the word "standard." There is only one kind of standard of right and wrong, namely, the moral ideas current in any particular age or country.

Moral right *means* what people think morally right. It has no other meaning. What Frenchmen think right is, therefore, right for *Frenchmen.* And evidently one must conclude—though I am not aware that relativists are anxious to draw one's attention to such unsavoury but yet absolutely necessary conclusions from their creed—that cannibalism is right for people who believe in it, that human sacrifice is right for those races which practice it, and that burning widows alive was right for Hindus until the British stepped in and compelled the Hindus to behave immorally by allowing their widows to remain alive.

When it is said that, according to the ethical relativist, what is thought right in any social group is right for that group, one must be careful not to misinterpret this. The relativist does not, of course, mean that there actually is an objective moral standard in France and a different objective standard in England, and that French and British opinions respectively give us correct information about these different standards. His point is rather that there are no objectively true moral standards at all. There is no single universal objective standard. Nor are there a variety of local objective standards. All standards are subjective. People's subjective feelings about morality are the only standards which exist.

To sum up. The ethical relativist consistently denies, it would seem, whatever the ethical absolutist asserts. For the absolutist there is a single universal moral standard. For the relativist there is no such standard. There are only local, ephemeral, and variable standards. For the absolutist there are two senses of the word "standard." Standards in the sense of sets of current moral ideas are relative and changeable. But the standard in the sense of what is actually morally right is absolute and unchanging. For the relativist no such distinction can be made. There is only one meaning of the word standard, namely, that which refers to local and variable sets of moral ideas. Or if it is insisted that the word must be allowed two meanings, then the relativist will say that there is at any rate no actual example of a standard in the absolute sense, and that the word as thus used is an empty name to which nothing in reality corresponds; so that the distinction between the two meanings becomes empty and useless. Finally—though this is merely saying the same thing in another way—the absolutist makes a distinction between what actually is right and what is thought right. The relativist rejects this distinction and identifies what is moral with what is thought moral by certain human beings or groups of human beings. . . .

The Case for Relativism Examined

Stace now examines several of the major arguments usually made to support ethical relativism. The first argument, which we have already encountered in this chapter, suggests that the diversity of moral beliefs and practices is conclusive evidence for ethical relativism. Stace's attack on this argument is clear and strong. He does not deny that there are varieties of moral beliefs and practices among the world's peoples; there is ample data to support this claim. What he denies is that this data by itself leads to ethical relativism. Stace argues that the diversity of moral beliefs and practices is compatible with either ethical relativism or ethical absolutism. That is, the facts can be accounted for by either position and cannot be used to argue for the truth of only one of them. Stace begins by characterizing the argument as it would be put by an ethical relativist using anthropological data to undergird the argument.

There are [several] . . . main arguments in favour of ethical relativity. The first is that which relies upon the actual varieties of moral "standards" found in the world. It was easy enough to believe in a single absolute morality in older times when there was no anthropology, when all humanity was divided clearly into two groups, Christian peoples and the "heathen." Christian peoples knew and possessed the one true morality. The rest were savages whose moral ideas could be ignored. But all this is changed. Greater knowledge has brought greater tolerance. We can no longer exalt our own moralities as alone true, while dismissing all other moralities as false or inferior. The investigations of anthropologists have shown that there exist side by side in the world a bewildering variety of moral codes. On this topic endless volumes have been written, masses of evidence piled up. Anthropologists have ransacked the Melanesian Islands, the jungles of New Guinea, the steppes of Siberia, the deserts of Australia, the forests of central Africa, and have brought back with them countless examples of weird, extravagant, and fantastic "moral" customs with which to confound us. We learn that all kinds of horrible practices are, in this, that, or the other place, regarded as essential to virtue. We find that there is nothing, or next to nothing, which has always and everywhere been regarded as morally good by all men. Where then is our universal morality? Can we, in face of all this evidence, deny that it is nothing but an empty dream?

This argument, taken by itself, is a very weak one. It relies upon a single set of facts—the variable moral customs of the world. But this variability of moral ideas is admitted by both parties to the dispute, and is capable of ready explanation upon the hypothesis of either party. The relativist says that the facts are to be explained by the non-existence of any absolute moral standard. The absolutist says that they are to be explained by human ignorance of what the absolute moral standard is. And he can truly point out that men have differed widely in their opinions about all manner of topics including the subject-matters of the physical sciences—just as much as they differ about morals. And if the various different opinions which men have held about the shape of the earth do not prove that it has no one real shape, neither do the various opinions which they have held about morality prove that there is no one true morality.

Thus the facts can be explained equally plausibly on either hypothesis. There is nothing in the facts themselves which compels us to prefer the relativistic hypothesis to that of the absolutist. And therefore the argument fails to prove the relativist conclusion. If that conclusion is to be established, it must be by means of other considerations.

Because it is the anthropologists who have expanded so vastly our knowledge of cultural diversity, and because anthropologists are characterized as scientists in their work, and because science is accorded such great respect in our society, it is understandable why so many people accept as true the doctrine of ethical relativism when it is declared to be the truth by anthropologists. But, says Stace, it is an error to think that no one knew about ethical diversity before anthropologists appeared on the scene. Long before modern anthropological methods were brought to bear on the issue, it was known—even in antiquity—that various peoples of the world differed in their moral attitudes and practices. Although Stace does not mention it, one could also note that anthropology is a fairly recent academic discipline, and its great contribution to learning has not been in informing a previously ignorant world of cultural diversity.

The work of the anthropologists, upon which ethical relativists seem to rely so heavily, has as a matter of fact added absolutely nothing *in principle* to what has always been known about the variability of moral ideas. Educated people have known all along that the Greeks tolerated sodomy, which in modern times has been regarded in some countries as an abominable crime; that the Hindus thought it a sacred duty to burn their widows; that trickery, now thought despicable, was once believed to be a virtue; that terrible torture was thought by our own ancestors only a few centuries ago to be a justifiable weapon of justice; that it was only yesterday that western peoples came to believe that slavery is immoral. Even the ancients knew very well that moral customs and ideas vary—witness the writings of Herodotus. Thus the principle of the variability of moral ideas was well understood long before modern anthropology was ever heard of. Anthropology has added nothing to the knowledge of this principle except a mass of new and extreme examples of it drawn from very remote sources. But to multiply examples of a principle already well known and universally admitted adds nothing to the argument which is built upon that principle. The discoveries of the anthropologists have no doubt been of the highest importance in their own sphere. But in my considered opinion they have thrown no new light upon the special problems of the moral philosopher.

Although the multiplication of examples has no logical bearing on the argument, it does have an immense *psychological* effect upon people's minds. These masses of anthropological learning are impressive. They are propounded in the sacred name of "science." If they are quoted in support of ethical relativity—as they often are—people *think* that they must prove something important. They bewilder and over-awe the simple-minded, batter down their resistance, make them ready to receive humbly the doctrine of ethical relativity from those who have acquired a reputation by their immense learning and their claims to be "scientific." Perhaps this is why so much ado is made by ethical relativists regarding the anthropological evidence. But we must refuse to be impressed. We must discount all this mass of evidence about the extraordinary moral customs of remote peoples. Once we have admitted—as everyone who is instructed must have admitted these last two thousand years without any anthropology at all—the principle that moral ideas vary, all this new evidence adds nothing to the argument. And the argument itself proves nothing for the reasons already given.

Problematic Consequences of Relativism

Stace acknowledges that one of the difficulties the ethical absolutist faces is that of providing a foundation for morality to which everyone would agree. Stace acknowledges this difficulty in sections of his paper that are not included here. The various approaches to an objective basis for ethics will be explored in the second section of this book; to go into them here would require too much detail at the present time. But the difficulty that the absolutist faces, though considerable, is not so serious a challenge to the absolutist view as are the difficulties faced by relativists in defending their position. In an approach reminiscent of William James's evaluation of determinism, Stace argues that the practical consequences of relativism would be devastating.

It is time that we turned our attention from the case in favour of ethical relativity to the case against it. Now the case against it consists, to a very large extent, in urging that, if taken seriously and pressed to its logical conclusion, ethical relativity can only end in destroying the conception of morality altogether, in undermining its practical efficacy, in rendering meaningless many almost universally accepted truths about human affairs, in robbing human beings of any incentive to strive for a better world, in taking the life-blood out of every ideal and every aspiration which has ever ennobled the life of man. In short, the charge against it is that it revolts and outrages man's moral *feelings.*

To all such arguments it is always possible to reply that they are merely pragmatic, mere appeals to feeling which have no logical cogency and no scientific value. . . . Perhaps we shall find that the purely logical and scientific procedure, which would rule out all feeling as irrelevant, is not wholly applicable to the subject matter of morals; that it rests upon a too rigorous dichotomy between feeling and cognition. But however that may be, let us hear what the anti-relativist has to say. It cannot be wrong, it cannot be irrelevant for us, and for the relativist himself, to see what his doctrine actually implies in the way of practical consequences; to see how it tallies with the demands of the "moral consciousness."

The *first* effect of ethical relativism would be to render meaningless any cross-cultural moral comparisons. No matter how depraved a society's attitudes might be—the Nazi's attitude toward Jews, South Africa's official policy of apartheid, a society's official endorsement of terrorism as a political weapon, the list could go on and on—the ethical relativist in our society would not have any grounds on which to condemn such attitudes. Why? Because, in the relativist view, there are no cross-cultural standards to which one could appeal.

First of all, then, ethical relativity, in asserting that the moral standards of particular social groups are the only standards which exist, renders meaningless all propositions which attempt to compare these standards with one another in respect of their moral worth. And this is a very serious matter indeed. We are accustomed to think that the moral ideas of one nation or social group may be "higher" or "lower" than those of another. We believe, for example, that Christian ethical ideas are nobler than those of the savage races of central Africa. Probably most of us would think that the Chinese moral standards are higher than those of the inhabitants of New Guinea. In short we habitually compare one civilization with another and judge the sets of ethical ideas to be found in them to be some better, some worse. The fact that such judgments are very difficult to make with any justice, and that they are frequently made on very superficial and prejudiced grounds, has no bearing on the question now at issue. The question is whether such judgments have any *meaning*. We habitually assume that they have.

But on the basis of ethical relativity they can have none whatever. For the relativist must hold that there is no *common* standard which can be applied to the various civilizations judged. Any such comparison of moral standards implies the existence of some superior standard which is applicable to both. And the existence of any such standard is precisely what the relativist denies. According to him the Christian standard is applicable only to Christians, the Chinese standard only to Chinese, the New Guinea standard only to the inhabitants of New Guinea.

Stace's *second* objection to relativism is that it makes impossible even the comparison of different epochs within the same culture.

What is true of comparisons between the moral standards of different races will also be true of comparisons between those of different ages. It is not unusual to ask such questions as whether the standard of our own day is superior to that which existed among our ancestors five hundred years ago. And when we remember that our ancestors employed slaves, practiced barbaric physical tortures, and burnt people alive, we may be inclined to think that it is. At any rate we assume that the question is one which has meaning and is capable of rational discussion. But if the ethical relativist is right, whatever we assert on this subject must be totally meaningless. For here again there is no common standard which could form the basis of any such judgments.

The *third* objection to relativism is that it makes the whole idea of moral progress meaningless.

This in its turn implies that the whole notion of moral *progress* is a sheer delusion. Progress means an advance from lower to higher, from worse to better. But on the basis of ethical relativity it has no meaning to say that the standards of this age are better (or worse) than those of a previous age. For there is no common standard by which both can be measured. Thus it is nonsense to say that the morality of the New Testament is higher than that of the Old. And Jesus Christ, if he imagined that he was introducing into the world a higher ethical standard than existed before his time, was merely deluded.

The ethical relativist, however, can salvage some meaning from cross-cultural comparisons, intracultural comparisons, and notions of moral progress. But the salvaged meaning ends up being simply the affirmation that another culture is more like one's own (if one assesses that culture positively) or less like one's own (if one assesses the culture negatively).

There is indeed one way in which the ethical relativist can give some sort of meaning to judgments of higher or lower as applied to the moral ideas of different races or ages. What he will have to say is that we assume *our* standards to be the best simply because they are ours. And we judge other standards by our own. If we say that Chinese moral codes are better than those of African cannibals, what we *mean* by this is that they are better *according to our standards.* We mean, that is to say, that Chinese standards are *more like our own* than African standards are. "Better" accordingly *means* "more like us." "Worse" means "less like us." It thus becomes clear that judgments of better and worse in such cases do not express anything that is really true at all. They merely give expression to our perfectly groundless satisfaction with our own ideas. In short, they give expression to nothing but our egotism and self-conceit. Our moral ideals are not really better than those of the savage. We are simply deluded by our egotism into thinking they are. The African savage has just as good a right to think his morality the best as we have to think ours the best. His opinion is just as well grounded as ours, or rather both opinions are equally groundless. And on this view Jesus Christ can only have been led to the quite absurd belief that his ethical precepts were better than those of Moses by his personal vanity. If only he had read Westermarck and Dewey he would have understood that, so long as people continued to believe in the doctrine of an eye for an eye and a tooth for a tooth, that doctrine was morally *right;* and that there could not be any point whatever in trying to make them believe in his new-fangled theory of loving one's enemies. True, the new morality would *become* right as soon as people came to believe in it, for it would then be the accepted standard. And what people think right is right. But then, if only Jesus Christ and persons with similar ideas had kept these ideas to themselves, people might have gone on believing that the old morality was right. And in that case it would have *been* right, and would have remained so till this day. And that would have saved a lot of useless trouble. For the change which Jesus Christ actually brought about was merely a change from one set of moral ideas to another. And as the new set of ideas was in no way better than the set it displaced— to say that it was better would be meaningless for the reasons already given— the change was really a sheer waste of time. And of course it likewise follows that anyone who in the future tries to improve the moral ideas of humanity will also be wasting his time.

Stace's *fourth* objection to relativism is similar to the third one. He charges that ethical relativism undercuts the seriousness of moral striving for higher ideals. If, as ethical relativism maintains, one cannot say that one moral ideal is superior to another, what is the point in striving for so-called higher ideals? Why should anyone bother to change a comfortable pattern of life?

> Thus the ethical relativist must treat all judgments comparing different moralities as either entirely meaningless; or, if this course appears too drastic, he has the alternative of declaring that they have for their meaning-content nothing except the vanity and egotism of those who pass them. We are asked to believe that the highest moral ideals of humanity are not really any better than those of an Australian bushman. But if this is so, why strive for higher ideals? Thus the heart is taken out of all effort, and the meaning out of all human ideals and aspirations.
>
> The ethical relativist may perhaps say that he is being misjudged. It is not true that, on the basis of his doctrine, all effort for moral improvement is vain. For if we take such a civilization as our own, and if we assume that the standard of morals theoretically accepted by it is that of Christian ethics, then there is surely plenty of room for improvement and "progress" in the way of making our practice accord with our theory. Effort may legitimately be directed towards getting people to live up to whatever standards they profess to honour. Such effort will be, on the relativistic basis, perfectly meaningful; for it does not imply a comparison of standards by reference to a common standard, but only a comparison of actual achievements with an admitted and accepted standard within a social group.
>
> Now I do not believe that even this plea can be accepted. For as soon as it comes to be effectively realized that our moral standard is no better than that of barbarians, why should anyone trouble to live up to it? It would be much easier to adopt some lower standard, to preach it assiduously until everyone believes it, when it would automatically become right. But even if we waive this point, and admit that the exhortation to practice what we preach may be meaningful, this does not touch the issue which was raised above. It will still be true that efforts to improve moral *beliefs,* as distinguished from moral *practice,* would be futile. It will still be true that Jesus Christ would have done better had he tried only to persuade humanity to live up to the old barbaric standards than he did in trying to propagate among them a new and more enlightened moral code. It will still be true that any reformer in the future who attempts to make men see even more noble ideals than those which we have inherited from the reformers of the past will be wasting his time.

The *fifth* objection made to relativism is that it tends to produce moral anarchy, the view that one moral view is just as legitimate as any other, that anything goes. This consequence results from the serious difficulty of defining what one means by "social group." According to the relativist, the ethical question, What ought I to do? must be restated into the form, Within the context of my social group, what ought I to do? But what is one's social group? All the people in the nation? Does everyone who lives in a nation subscribe to the same moral standards? Hardly. Is one's social group all the people in the province, state, or territory? Or is it the people in one's city, district, neighborhood, or home? When pressed to identify the meaning of the term *social group,* the relativist encounters these kinds of difficulties. Perhaps the only group that affirms exactly the same moral standards I do is a group of one person—myself. If so, I alone determine what is right and wrong; and so does everyone else. If that is the logical consequence of relativism, then we have a situation of moral anarchy where conflicts of interest are settled not by an appeal to an acknowledged cross-group standard but by force. In the situation of moral neutrality, might makes right.

Up to the present I have allowed it to be taken tacitly for granted that, though judgments comparing different races and ages in respect of their moral codes are impossible for the ethical relativist, yet judgments of comparison between individuals living with the same social group would be quite possible. For individuals living within the same social group would presumably be subject to the same moral code, that of their group, and this would therefore constitute, as between these individuals, a common standard by which they could both be measured. We have not here, as we had in the other case, the difficulty of the absence of any common standard of comparison. It should therefore be possible for the ethical relativist to say quite meaningfully that President Lincoln was a better man than some criminal or moral imbecile of his own time and country, or that Jesus was a better man than Judas Iscariot.

But is even this minimum of moral judgment really possible on relativist grounds? It seems to me that it is not. For when once the whole of humanity is abandoned as the area covered by a single moral standard, what smaller areas are to be adopted as the *loci* of different standards? Where are we to draw the lines of demarcation? We can split up humanity, perhaps,— though the procedure will be very arbitrary—into races, races into nations, nations into tribes, tribes into families, families into individuals. Where are we going to draw the *moral* boundaries? Does the *locus* of a particular moral standard reside in a race, a nation, a tribe, a family, or an individual? Perhaps the blessed phrase "social group" will be dragged in to save the situation. Each such group, we shall be told, has its own moral code which is, for it, right. But what *is* a "group"? Can anyone define it or give its boundaries? . . .

The difficulty is not, as might be thought, merely an academic difficulty of logical definition. If that were all, I should not press the point. But the ambiguity has practical consequences which are disastrous for morality. No one is likely to say that moral codes are confined within the arbitrary limits of the geographical divisions of countries. Nor are the notions of race, nation, or political state likely to help us. To bring out the essential practical character of the difficulty let us put it in the form of concrete questions. Does the American nation constitute a "group" having a single moral standard? Or does the standard of what I ought to do change continuously as I cross the continent in a railway train? Do different States of the Union have different moral codes? Perhaps every town and village has its own peculiar standard. This may at first sight seem reasonable enough. "In Rome do as Rome does" may seem as good a rule in morals as it is in etiquette. But can we stop there? Within the village are numerous cliques each having its own set of ideas. Why should not each of these claim to be bound only by its own special and peculiar moral standards? And if it comes to that, why should not the gangsters of Chicago claim to constitute a group having its own morality, so that its murders and debaucheries must be viewed as "right" by the only standard which can legitimately be applied to it? And if it be answered that the nation will not tolerate this, that may be so. But this is to put the foundation of right simply in the superior force of the majority. In that case whoever is stronger will be right, however monstrous his ideas and actions. And if we cannot deny to any set of people the right to have its own morality, is it not clear that, in the end, we cannot even deny this right to the individual? Every individual man and woman can put up, on this view, an irrefutable claim to be judged by no standard except his or her own.

   If these arguments are valid, the ethical relativist cannot really maintain that there is anywhere to be found a moral standard binding upon anybody against his will. And he cannot maintain that, even within the social group, there is a common standard as between individuals. And if that is so, then even judgments to the effect that one man is morally better than another become meaningless. All moral valuation thus vanishes. There is nothing to prevent each man from being a rule unto himself. The result will be moral chaos and the collapse of all effective standards. . . .

Even if it were possible to identify a morally relevant social group, the relativist's problem is not solved. Within a social group, however defined, complete agreement on moral attitudes is most unlikely to be present. When complete agreement is lacking, how does one decide what really is the standard of the group? Either one takes the majority opinion, or goes with the minority. If one takes the majority view, then one must judge all social reformers to be misfits. If one goes with the minority view, then one seems to be led into individualism and moral anarchy. Such is the dilemma of the relativist.

But even if we assume that the difficulty about defining moral groups has been surmounted, a further difficulty presents itself. Suppose that we have now definitely decided what are the exact boundaries of the social group within which each moral standard is to be operative. And we will assume—as is invariably done by relativists themselves—that this group is to be some actually existing social community such as a tribe or nation. How are we to know, even then, what actually *is* the moral standard within that group? How is anyone to know? How is even a member of the group to know? For there are certain to be within the group—at least this will be true among advanced peoples—wide differences of opinion as to what is right, what wrong. Whose opinion, then, is to be taken as representing *the* moral standard of the group? Either we must take the opinion of the majority within the group or the opinion of some minority. If we rely upon the ideas of the majority, the results will be disastrous. Wherever there is found among a people a small band of select spirits, or perhaps one man, working for the establishment of higher and nobler ideals than those commonly accepted by the group, we shall be compelled to hold that, for that people at that time, the majority are right, and that the reformers are wrong and are preaching what is immoral. We shall have to maintain, for example, that Jesus was preaching immoral doctrines to the Jews. Moral goodness will have to be equated always with the mediocre and sometimes with the definitely base and ignoble. If on the other hand we say that the moral standard of the group is to be identified with the moral opinions of some minority, then what minority is this to be? We cannot answer that it is to be the minority composed of the best and most enlightened individuals of the group. This would involve us in a palpably vicious circle. For by what standard are these individuals to be judged the best and the most enlightened? There is no principle by which we could select the right minority. And therefore we should have to consider every minority as good as every other. And this means that we should have no logical right whatever to resist the claim of the gangsters of Chicago—if such a claim were made— that their practices represent the highest standards of American morality. It means in the end that every individual is to be bound by no standard save his own.

The ethical relativists are great empiricists. *What* is the actual moral standard of any group can only be discovered, they tell us, by an examination on the ground of the moral opinions and customs of that group. But will they tell us how they propose to decide, when they get to the ground, which of the many moral opinions they are sure to find there is *the* right one in that group? To some extent they will be able to do this for the Melanesian Islanders—from whom apparently all lessons in the nature of morality are in future to be taken. But it is certain that they cannot do it for advanced peoples whose members have learnt to think for themselves and to entertain among themselves a wide variety of opinions. They cannot do it unless they accept the calamitous view that the ethical opinion of the majority is always right. We are left therefore once more with the conclusion that, even within a particular social group, anybody's moral opinion is as good as anybody else's, and that every man is entitled to be judged by his own standards.

Stace's *sixth* and final criticism of relativism is that it has a disastrous effect on human conduct. Relativism breeds the kind of indifference toward the actions of others that allows those other groups to do terrible things to people without the relativist raising an objection or striking a defensive blow.

Finally, not only is ethical relativity disastrous in its consequences for moral theory. It cannot be doubted that it must tend to be equally disastrous in its impact upon practical conduct. If men come really to believe that one moral standard is as good as another, they will conclude that their own moral standard has nothing special to recommend it. They might as well then slip down to some lower and easier standard. It is true that, for a time, it may be possible to hold one view in theory and to act practically upon another. But ideas, even philosophical ideas, are not so ineffectual that they can remain for ever idle in the upper chambers of the intellect. In the end they seep down to the level of practice. They get themselves acted on.

Speaking of the supposedly dangerous character of ethical relativity Westermarck says "Ethical subjectivism instead of being a danger is more likely to be an advantage to morality. Could it be brought home to people that there is no absolute standard in morality, they would perhaps be on the one hand more tolerant, and on the other hand more critical in their judgments." Certainly, if we believe that any one moral standard is as good as any other, we *are* likely to be more tolerant. We shall tolerate widow-burning, human sacrifice, cannibalism, slavery, the infliction of physical torture, or any other of the thousand and one abominations which are, or have been, from time to time approved by one moral code or another. But this is not the kind of toleration that we want, and I do not think its cultivation will prove "an advantage to morality."

Stace sums up his analysis of the weaknesses of relativism by placing his criticism in the frame of reference of our contemporary society.

These, then, are the main arguments which the anti-relativist will urge against ethical relativity. And perhaps finally he will attempt a diagnosis of the social, intellectual, and psychological conditions of our time to which the emergence of ethical relativism is to be attributed. His diagnosis will be somewhat as follows.

We have abandoned, perhaps with good reason, the oracles of the past. Every age, of course, does this. But in our case it seems that none of us knows any more whither to turn. We do not know what to put in the place of that which has gone. What ought we, supposedly civilized peoples, to aim at? What are to be our ideals? What is right? What is wrong? What is beautiful? What is ugly? No man knows. We drift helplessly in this direction and that. We know not where we stand nor whither we are going. . . .

And the philosophers of our age, where have they stood? They too, as is notorious, speak with many voices. But those who preach the various relativisms have taken upon themselves a heavy load of responsibility. By formulating abstractly the defeatism of the age they have made themselves the aiders and abettors of death. They are injecting poison into the veins of civilization. Their influence upon practical affairs may indeed be small. But it counts for something. And they cannot avoid their share of the general responsibility. They have failed to do what little they could to stem the tide. They have failed to do what Plato did for the men of his own age— find a way out of at least the intellectual confusions of the time.

Assessment of Relativism

The fundamental ethical question, What ought I to do? is addressed to each and every human being. The answer we are seeking is a statement of moral obligation, You ought to do such and such, that likewise holds for each and every human being. Ethical relativism is radically opposed to this whole approach. For the relativist, there are no universal moral obligations because, according to the relativist, there is no universal moral basis of obligation (such as a god whose uniform moral commands are made known to all persons). For the relativist, the only moral obligations are those that have been commanded by a specific social group. Herskovits has defended ethical relativism. Stace has attacked it. Now we must decide which position has the best support.

We cannot appeal to the range of empirical facts to decide the issue. Stace correctly points out that the vast array of differing moral attitudes and practices can be integrated into either perspective without difficulty. The ethical relativist can argue that the great diversity of moral beliefs and practices indicates that there are no universal norms to guide the human moral enterprise. The ethical absolutist can argue that the diversity simply indicates human ignorance of the objective moral norms under which all persons are held accountable. To be sure, absolutism would be in a stronger position if it would point to a series of norms that legitimately would apply to all persons. But absolutists so far have not been successful in doing that. The relativist could falsify absolutism by demonstrating that there are no universal norms; but this, too, has proved to be an unsuccessful venture.

The upshot is that we have two opposing theories—ethical relativism and ethical absolutism—both vying for our assent and both compatible with the facts. Herskovits has argued that relativism leads to a greater sense of tolerance of the views of others. Stace finds this tolerance to be precisely one of the objectionable features in relativism, for it leads to tolerance of actions that are injurious to other human beings. Stace also points us to other undesirable consequences of relativism, not the least of which is that it requires that we give up all striving for higher moral ideals, all attempts at moral improvement, and any goal of moral progress.

Given these consequences that are offensive to our moral sensibilities, why are there any advocates of ethical relativism at all? The attractiveness of ethical relativism is not only in the aura of science within which it clothes itself but also in the tolerance it seems to encourage, in contrast to the bigotry that is often associated with moral absolutism. When people believe that they have possession of *the* universal morality, that belief has often been justification for imperialistic, dehumanizing moves against other people who espouse a different morality. No doubt such a justification contributed to the wars of religion, the heresy hunts of the Inquisition, the brutalization of primitive peoples by colonial empires, and the destruction of whole races and groups in the name of some monstrous ideology.

But note the irony of this attack on ethical absolutism: such immoralities as mentioned above can be recognized *as immoralities* only if there is some objective standard by which to judge these actions. Relativism denies that there is any such standard; therefore, if consistent, the relativist would have to say that the actions of the Inquisition were right for that social group at that time. It is only from the viewpoint of ethical absolutism that the barbarities of the past, and present, can be condemned as morally wrong. How one justifies such a claim requires a moral foundation within which such judgments are made. It is precisely to the pursuit of such a foundation that the second section of this book is dedicated.

Before we go on to the task of examining the foundations of morality, we must analyze one final view. This is the view that denies that moral statements have any cognitive meaning at all; it claims that they are merely expressions of a person's feelings. This view, known as emotivism, will be the topic of the next chapter.

Review Questions

1. What are the anthropological facts and methodological considerations often used to support ethical relativism?
2. Outline the case Herskovits makes for ethical relativism.
3. Comment on the statement, Herskovits's discussion of cultural "universals" seems to be inconsistent with the claims of ethical relativism.
4. "Neither ethical relativists nor ethical absolutists can appeal to facts to support their claims." Explain that statement.
5. What are the pragmatic (that is, practical) difficulties encountered by the absolutist and by the relativist? Which difficulties do you consider to be the most serious? Is the seriousness of pragmatic difficulties adequate reason for rejecting an ethical point of view?

CHAPTER 4

Ethical Emotivism

Introduction

Psychological egoists, determinists, and ethical relativists would all object in one way or another to the fundamental ethical question, What ought I to do? On the basis of their point of view we would have to reformulate that question in various ways. There is still another attitude toward ethics that many people—not just professional philosophers—share. That is the view that ethics is fundamentally about feelings or emotions. This view is sometimes called emotivism. According to emotivists, when people respond to the ethical question by making moral pronouncements, what they are doing is simply expressing their feelings about something and probably also trying to evoke similar feelings in others.

Historical Roots of Emotivism

Although certain features of ethical emotivism are as old as the ancient Greeks, the widespread interest in this view of ethics during the twentieth century arose largely from influences created by a philosophical movement called *logical positivism* or *logical empiricism*. Logical positivism as a distinct philosophical point of view began in Vienna during the early decades of the twentieth century. At first the mathematician Hans Hahn, the economist Otto Neurath, and the physicist Philipp Frank met to discuss the philosophy of science. Later they were joined by other prominent intellectuals including Friedrich Waismann, Felix Kaufmann, Herbert Fiegl and especially Moritz Schlick, trained as a scientist under Max Planck, and Rudolf Carnap, a physicist and mathematician. This gathering of impressive scientists and scholars soon came to be called the "Vienna Circle," and their outspoken goal was to propagate the scientific outlook in all fields of human knowledge.

This scientific outlook, however, held some rather startling consequences for traditional philosophy. In its search for more powerful modes of investigation, science broke away from the syllogistic method of reasoning that characterized medieval science. In its place, modern science developed a mathematical method of reasoning that quantified data, formulated explanatory systems, predicted the behavior of phenomena, and tested those predictions against experience. So successful was this modern scientific method at penetrating and interpreting reality that what counted as "real" came to be defined in terms of that method. The method dealt with quantifiable reality—that which could be observed, measured, counted, and reduced to a mathematical formula. If something could not be so quantified, then the suspicion was that it was not objectively real. The traditional concerns of philosophy—religion, aesthetic experience, metaphysics, ethics—did not fit this new scheme. The conclusion? All these areas dealt not with knowledge, least of all with scientific understanding, but with human feelings. If philosophy was to become truly scientific, it would have to purge itself of all emotive factors and reshape itself to consider the supporting role it could serve for science by placing its logical and analytical skills at the service of physics and mathematics. During the Middle Ages philosophy was often considered the handmaiden of theology; during the twentieth century it was to become the mistress of science.

Logical Positivism Illustrated

How this purging and reshaping of traditional philosophical concerns took place can be illustrated by a positivist-like analysis of the following cluster of sentences.

1. There is a tall stepladder in that closet.
2. There are subterranean life forms on Mars.
3. The square root of four is two.
4. Oh, to be in England now that April's there!
5. Don't shoot until you see the whites of their eyes!
6. Is Paris burning?

If we tried to group these sentences into similar sets, we might be inclined first of all to group 4, 5 and 6 together as rather famous quotations and to put the rest of the sentences together as rather common utterances. Such a grouping is certainly justifiable, but its basis is philosophically uninteresting. If, however, we look at these sentences more closely, we would discover that the first three give us some sort of information: 1 and 2 inform us about states of affairs in the world, and 3 expresses a relation that holds between certain symbols. The last three sentences do not convey information. Sentence 4 is an expression of a feeling; sentence 5 is a command; and the last sentence is a question. Another way of making this distinction is to say that the first three sentences have a truth value: they are either true or false. The last three sentences do not have truth value. We can assess them in terms of sincerity, appropriateness, intelligibility, and so forth, but not in terms of truth or falsity. Accordingly, the sentences that people use can be categorized as either cognitive (that is, informational) or noncognitive (that is, noninformational).

We can go on to subdivide cognitive sentences according to the way we check up on them. To find out if sentence 1 is true or false, we locate the closet and look inside to see if, in fact, there is a tall stepladder in it. We put together, or synthesize, various elements from our experience to check up on statements of the type represented by sentence 1. Such sentences are therefore known as *synthetic* statements. Although we cannot go to Mars at the present time and penetrate its surface to discover if, in fact, there are life forms there, nevertheless the way we would check up on sentence 2 is similar in principle to the way we would check up on sentence 1. Thus sentence 2 is also a synthetic statement. Sentence 3, however, presents a different situation. To check up on it we do not have to go somewhere and gather data; we simply examine or *analyze* the sentence itself to see if the terms in the sentence (e.g., square root, four, two) are being used according to the accepted rules. Sentences like 3 are called *analytic*, and if the terms in the sentence are used correctly we say that the sentence is tautological, but if they are used incorrectly we say that the sentence is contradictory.

Here is how these distinctions look when put into a tree diagram.

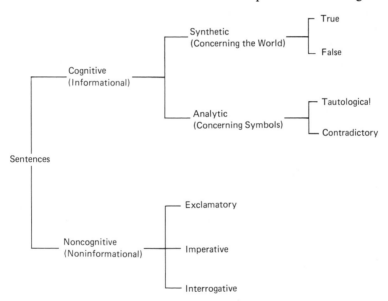

Consider now the following additional sentences.

7. There is a shy purple unicorn under my lectern that disappears whenever someone tries to check up on him.
8. The Absolute is beyond space and time.
9. God loves us.
10. The President of the United States is good.

What happens when we try to place these sentences in the categories listed above? At first glance, sentence 7 seems to be a cognitive, synthetic sentence: it purports to give information about a unicorn. Yet as we look at what this sentence tells us, we discover that this unicorn presumably always resists detection. How then can we check up on the information purportedly being conveyed in the sentence? Although sentence 7 seems to convey information, we cannot verify it or check up on it as we can a cognitive sentence of the synthetic kind. What, then, is sentence 7? We would probably all agree that it is *nonsense,* and rightly so, because we would consider claims about unicorns hiding behind doors and so forth to be obvious nonsense. From considerations such as these, the positivists generalized the principle that sentences claiming to be cognitive, but which are unverifiable in principle, are really nonsense.

How shall we classify sentences 8 and 9? Both of them seem to be conveying information; they seem to be cognitive and synthetic. Yet if we press on to ask what procedures we should use to check up on them, we encounter grave difficulties. Consider sentence 8. How is it possible for space-time creatures like us to check up on a presumed state of affairs beyond space and time? Is not the only verification that we can do in space and time? Must we not, therefore, conclude that sentence 8, like sentence 7, falls into the category of nonsense? Similarly, sentence 9 also poses serious problems when we try to verify it. The "God" of sentence 9 is like the "Absolute" of sentence 8—beyond the space-time domain and thus beyond human verification. Sentence 9 must, according to positivist principles, also be considered nonsense. By disposing of sentences 8 and 9 in this fashion we have adopted the logical positivist technique for dismissing much of traditional philosophy and theology.

Sentence 10 appears to be a moral pronouncement. How shall we categorize it? At first glance, sentence 10 seems to be cognitive and synthetic; it seems to be informing us that the President is morally good, that he possesses the property of moral goodness. Now if sentence 10 is to function in this way, it must be verifiable. What would verifying it involve? Presumably we would have to be able to identify the property of moral goodness and then be able to examine the President to determine if, in fact, he possessed that property. But identifying this property of moral goodness is no easy matter. The difficulty of defining moral goodness has contributed greatly to the formulation of ethical emotivism.

The Problem of Defining Goodness

The problem of identifying and defining goodness was central to the ethical thought of G. E. Moore (1873–1958), whose work inspired a movement in ethics called *intuitionism*—a movement that captured the attention of many philosophers before it was forced to yield center stage to emotivism. According to Moore, most philosophers have blundered seriously in their efforts to define goodness because they have invariably identified goodness with a certain property that some—but not all—good things have. Regardless of the property we select to define goodness (for example, "benevolence"), and even though we would all agree that a certain person has this property of benevolence (for example, the President of the United States), it is still an *open question* whether that person is really good. After all, some benevolent people are downright vicious. The case is the same for any property we might select to define goodness; and this situation is referred to as Moore's "Open Question Argument." The judgment that Moore reached was that goodness is a unique, simple, indefinable property. In addition, he argued that goodness is not an empirical or natural property that can be discerned by our usual methods of observation, and that no amount of factual data will lead to moral obligation. We cannot derive what *ought* to be from what *is* the case. That is to say, we cannot taste, touch, see, hear, or smell goodness. Goodness is not a naturalistic property: it is detected not by our organs of sense but by intuition. Anyone who attempts to interpret goodness as a natural property commits what Moore called "The Naturalistic Fallacy."

In brief, then, Moore considered goodness to be an indefinable, nonnaturalistic property present in some things and detectable only by intuition. Because "goodness" is the central category of ethics, all of ethics rests ultimately on intuition. And as intuition is a rather personal and idiosyncratic functioning of the mind, ethics ends up being founded on intensely subjective judgments.

Now if goodness is this indefinable, nonnaturalistic property, how does one check up on a sentence like sentence 10? The observable data of human experience are of no help because that data deals with empirical, naturalistic properties— properties that can be seen, or heard, or smelled, or tasted, or touched. Presumably, one is to use intuition to verify sentence 10. Presumably, we are to compare the contents of our intuitions. But what if you intuit the President to be good, and I intuit him to be evil, and others say they have no clear intuition one way or the other? Who is correct? Seemingly, intuitions are so private, so subjective, so idiosyncratic that they are beyond the realm of verifiability, which is in the public, objective, and nonidiosyncratic domain. Must we not, therefore, relegate a sentence like, "The President of the United States is Good"—and all of ethics with it—to the category of nonsense?

Although many logical positivists were content to allow much of traditional philosophy and theology to fall on the scrapheap of discarded nonsense, they were unwilling to permit the same fate to overtake ethics. Many of the positivists proposed that ethical sentences are really noncognitive sentences masquerading as cognitive ones. This proposal allowed ethical sentences to be meaningful if they were removed from the problematic domain of verifiability. Carnap suggested that such sentences were really imperatives. Schlick said they functioned as rules. A. J. Ayer, the "father" of ethical emotivism, considered them to be exclamations of emotions. It is to his interpretation of ethics that we will now turn.

Advocate of Emotivism: A. J. Ayer

Variously described as "the most representative and influential philosopher in England" and as "the one who stands at the pinnacle of the British philosophic Establishment," A. J. Ayer was born in London on October 29, 1910. A brilliant student, he was awarded a King's Scholarship in 1923 to attend Eton, one of England's best known public schools. Upon graduating from Eton in 1929, he received another scholarship to study at Oxford University. In that same year he spent several months in Vienna, attending meetings of the Vienna Circle. Stimulated by the views of the logical positivists, Ayer returned to Oxford to lecture in philosophy, to pursue graduate studies leading to his Master of Arts degree in 1936, and to write his first book, which is regarded by some as one of the most influential philosophical books of the twentieth century.

That book, *Language, Truth and Logic,* published in 1936, blended insights from his contemporaries (Bertrand Russell and Ludwig Wittgenstein), from earlier empiricists (George Berkeley and David Hume) and from the positivism of the Vienna Circle. Ayer's book attacked with clarity and force much of the prevailing philosophy. Imagine the situation: a twenty-six-year-old fellow who had barely started his teaching career at Oxford University publishes a book that attacks without stint the traditional philosophy being offered at his own university. The fact that his book was not simply dismissed by the traditionalists as an immature radical outburst, but was strongly debated, testifies to the cogency of Ayer's argument. Indeed, the book became a philosophical manifesto for many young intellectuals.

Ayer's academic life was interrupted by the Second World War. In 1945, he was appointed dean of Wadham College, Oxford. The next year he was appointed Grote Professor of the Philosophy of Mind and Logic at London University, and in 1959 he was named Sykeham Professor of Logic at Oxford. Within twenty-five years, the radical young critic of the established philosophy had himself become the key figure in the Establishment.

Although the logical positivism of the Vienna Circle which influenced Ayer enormously is now dead as a philosophical movement, and although Ayer has shown signs of moderating the radical posture he assumed in *Language, Truth and Logic,* and although ethical emotivism's most carefully articulated case is to be found probably in the writings of C. L. Stevenson (especially in his *Ethics and Language,* published in 1944), there are nevertheless good reasons for using the following material from *Language, Truth and Logic* as the representative expression of emotivism. Ayer's discussion is the classic piece on emotivism that every student of ethics should know. In addition, his discussion is exceptionally clear and provides easy access to the emotive theory.

Ayer's Agenda

Ayer begins his discussion of ethics by indicating how traditional views of ethics present a problem for his philosophical perspective. He claims that "all synthetic propositions are empirical hypotheses." That is to say, he maintains that all statements that purportedly convey information are statements about the empirical world which we experience with our sense organs; these statements are verifiable by the standard procedures of investigation. Traditional views of ethics, however, maintain that "statements of value"—moral judgments—are "synthetic"; they presumably convey information about "moral facts" that are objectively real and that may or may not be detectable by the sense organs. The case is similar concerning traditional views of aesthetic values. Ayer must, therefore, give an account of moral and aesthetic judgments that both explains them as human speech acts and that also explains away their possibility of conveying information about objective facts.

> * There is still one objection to be met before we can claim to have justified our view that all synthetic propositions are empirical hypotheses. This objection is based on the common supposition that our speculative knowledge is of two distinct kinds—that which relates to questions of empirical fact, and that which relates to questions of value. It will be said that "statements of value" are genuine synthetic propositions, but that they cannot with any show of justice be represented as hypotheses, which are used to predict the course of our sensations; and, accordingly, that the existence of ethics and aesthetics as branches of speculative knowledge presents an insuperable objection to our radical empiricist thesis.
>
> In face of this objection, it is our business to give an account of "judgements of value" which is both satisfactory in itself and consistent with our general empiricist principles.

Ayer's account of value judgments (both moral and aesthetic ones) involves showing (1) that insofar as these judgments are "significant," that is, informational or about matters of fact, they are really "scientific" statements, that is, statements about *empirical* matters of fact that are verifiable by standard investigative procedures; (2) and insofar as they are not "significant," they merely express emotion, that is, the speaker's feelings with perhaps the desire to evoke a similar emotional response in someone else.

> We shall set ourselves to show that in so far as statements of value are significant, they are ordinary "scientific" statements; and that in so far as they are not scientific, they are not in the literal sense significant, but are simply expressions of emotion which can be neither true nor false. In maintaining this view, we may confine ourselves for the present to the case of ethical statements. What is said about them will be found to apply *mutatis mutandis,* to the case of aesthetic statements also.

Four Kinds of Sentences

Ayer begins this account by sorting out the four major kinds of sentences containing ethical language that philosophers often scramble together: (1) definitions, (2) descriptions, (3) exhortations, and (4) moral judgments.

> The ordinary system of ethics, as elaborated in the works of ethical philosophers, is very far from being a homogeneous whole. Not only is it apt to contain pieces of metaphysics, and analyses of non-ethical concepts: its actual ethical contents are themselves of very different kinds. We may

* FROM A. J. Ayer, *Language, Truth and Logic* (New York: Dover Publications, 1952), pp. 102–13. Copyright 1952 by Dover Publications. Used by permission of Dover Publications.

divide them, indeed, into four main classes. There are, first of all, propositions which express definitions of ethical terms, or judgements about the legitimacy or possibility of certain definitions. Secondly, there are propositions describing the phenomena of moral experience, and their causes. Thirdly, there are exhortations to moral virtue. And, lastly, there are actual ethical judgements. It is unfortunately the case that the distinction between these four classes, plain as it is, is commonly ignored by ethical philosophers; with the result that it is often very difficult to tell from their works what it is that they are seeking to discover or prove.

The sentence, "The term 'promise' means keeping one's word," is a sentence of the first type in that it defines a term used in ethical discourse. According to Ayer, this type of statement is acceptable because it states a definition of a term and can be checked with reference to common usage if it is looked up in a dictionary. Propositions of the second type are statements such as, "People feel obligated to tell the truth because of fear of punishment rooted in childhood experiences." Statements like this attempt to explain the origins and nature of moral experience and are also acceptable in Ayer's system. Exhortations to moral virtue, the third class of statements, are sentences that give commands: "Tell the truth!" or, "Don't lie!" Although not verifiable, because they are commands, exhortations are straight-forward enough as an attempt by one person to get another person to adopt a certain kind of behavior.

The fourth kind of sentence is one that makes a moral judgment: "It is wrong to tell a lie," "One ought to keep one's promises," or, "We have a duty to tell the truth." Each of these sentences makes a claim about the moral acceptability of an action. Ayer will argue later on that sentences of the fourth type can be understood as really being sentences of one of the first three types. The addition of a moral term such as "wrong," "ought," or "duty" does not add anything significant to the statement.

Many philosophers would object to the assumptions underlying Ayer's next move. He assumes that the task of ethics is to analyze ethical terms and that there is no room in ethical philosophy for moral judgments or pronouncements. Traditionally, philosophers have tried not only to analyze and clarify ethical terms but also to offer carefully reasoned responses to the question, What ought I to do? In so doing, they make moral judgments: they make normative claims. Ayer rejects this more expansive view of the role of moral philosophy. In discussing further the four classes of statements containing ethical terms, he regards sentences of the first type as the domain of moral philosophy, sentences of the second type as the province of social science, type-three statements as emotive, and type-four assertions as puzzling. He sets about to resolve the puzzle of sentences of the fourth type.

In fact, it is easy to see that only the first of our four classes, namely that which comprises the propositions relating to the definitions of ethical terms, can be said to constitute ethical philosophy. The propositions which describe the phenomena of moral experience, and their causes, must be assigned to the science of psychology, or sociology. The exhortations to moral virtue are not propositions at all, but ejaculations or commands which are designed to provoke the reader to action of a certain sort. Accordingly, they do not belong to any branch of philosophy or science. As for the expressions of ethical judgements, we have not yet determined how they should be classified. But inasmuch as they are certainly neither definitions nor comments upon definitions, nor quotations, we may say decisively that they do not belong to ethical philosophy. A strictly philosophical treatise on ethics should therefore make no ethical pronouncements. But it should, by giving an analysis of ethical terms, show what is the category to which all such pronouncements belong. And this is what we are now about to do.

Moral Judgments Rejected as Synthetic

In analyzing the fourth type of ethical sentence—moral judgments—Ayer explores the possibility that these sentences might be synthetic, that is, statements about facts. He discerns two ways in which they could be factually significant.

First, moral judgments could be factually significant if they could be translated into statements about empirical facts. For example, perhaps the sentence, "The President of the United States is good," could be translated into the sentence, "The President of the United States is approved by our group." That is the approach of *subjectivism*, according to which moral judgments are reduced to the likes and dislikes of a particular group. Or, perhaps the sentence in question could be translated into, "The President of the United States promotes the pleasure of humankind." This is the approach of *utilitarianism*, which interprets moral values in terms of pleasure and pain. Although it would be hard to verify the sentence, "The President of the United States is good," because it is particularly difficult to define "good," it would not be nearly so difficult to check up on whether the President is in fact approved by a certain group, or whether he in fact promotes the pleasure of humankind.

These translations would reduce ethical sentences of type-four to sentences of type-two. Ayer's concern to limit synthetic statements to empirical statements would thereby be achieved. Ayer, however, considers these translations to be inadequate accounts of moral judgments. In the following selection he refers to "ethical symbols." By this he means the words we use in ethical discourse. *Descriptive* ethical symbols are terms that describe how ethical language functions or what a group or society believes about certain kinds of behavior (i.e., "Most Americans believe we ought to keep our promises"). A sentence containing the term "ought" used as a *normative* ethical symbol would be, "One ought to keep one's promises."

A question which is often discussed by ethical philosophers is whether it is possible to find definitions which would reduce all ethical terms to one or two fundamental terms. But this question, though it undeniably belongs to ethical philosophy, is not relevant to our present enquiry. We are not now concerned to discover which term, within the sphere of ethical terms, is to be taken as fundamental; whether, for example, "good" can be defined in terms of "right" or "right" in terms of "good," or both in terms of "value." What we are interested in is the possibility of reducing the whole sphere of ethical terms to non-ethical terms. We are enquiring whether statements of ethical value can be translated into statements of empirical fact.

That they can be so translated is the contention of those ethical philosophers who are commonly called subjectivists, and of those who are known as utilitarians. For the utilitarian defines the rightness of actions, and the goodness of ends, in terms of the pleasure, or happiness, or satisfaction, to which they give rise; the subjectivist, in terms of the feelings of approval which a certain person, or group of people, has towards them. Each of these types of definition makes moral judgements into a sub-class of psychological or sociological judgements; and for this reason they are very attractive to us. For, if either was correct, it would follow that ethical assertions were not generically different from the factual assertions which are ordinarily contrasted with them; and the account which we have already given of empirical hypotheses would apply to them also.

Nevertheless we shall not adopt either a subjectivist or a utilitarian analysis of ethical terms. We reject the subjectivist view that to call an action right, or a thing good, is to say that it is generally approved of, because it is not self-contradictory to assert that some actions which are generally approved of are not right, or that some things which are generally approved of are not good. And we reject the alternative subjectivist view that a man who asserts that a certain action is right, or that a certain thing is good, is saying that he himself approves of it, on the ground that a man who confessed that he sometimes approved of what was bad or wrong would not be contradicting himself. And a similar argument is fatal to utilitarianism. We cannot agree that to call an action right is to say that of all the actions possible in the circumstances it would cause, or be likely to cause, the greatest happiness, or the greatest balance of pleasure over pain, or the greatest balance of satisfied over unsatisfied desire, because we find that it is not self-contradictory to say that it is sometimes wrong to perform the action which would actually or probably cause the greatest happiness, or the greatest balance of pleasure over pain, or of satisfied over unsatisfied desire. And since it is not self-contradictory to say that some pleasant things are not good, or that some bad things are desired, it cannot be the case that the sentence "x is good" is equivalent to "x is pleasant," or to "x is desired." And to every other variant of utilitarianism with which I am acquainted the same objection can be made. And therefore we should, I think, conclude that the validity of ethical judgements is not determined by the felicific tendencies of actions, any more than by the nature of people's feelings; but that it must be regarded as "absolute" or "intrinsic," and not empirically calculable.

If we say this, we are not, of course, denying that it is possible to invent a language in which all ethical symbols are definable in non-ethical terms, or even that it is desirable to invent such a language and adopt it in place of our own; what we are denying is that the suggested reduction of ethical to non-ethical statements is consistent with the conventions of our actual language. That is, we reject utilitarianism and subjectivism, not as proposals to replace our existing ethical notions by new ones, but as analyses of our existing ethical notions. Our contention is simply that, in our language, sentences which contain normative ethical symbols are not equivalent to sentences which express psychological propositions, or indeed empirical propositions of any kind.

It is advisable here to make it plain that it is only normative ethical symbols, and not descriptive ethical symbols, that are held by us to be indefinable in factual terms. There is a danger of confusing these two types of symbols, because they are commonly constituted by signs of the same sensible form. Thus a complex sign of the form "x is wrong" may constitute a sentence which expresses a moral judgement concerning a certain type of conduct, or it may constitute a sentence which states that a certain type of conduct is repugnant to the moral sense of a particular society. In the latter case, the symbol "wrong" is a descriptive ethical symbol, and the sentence in which it occurs expresses an ordinary sociological proposition; in the former case, the symbol "wrong" is a normative ethical symbol, and the sentence in which it occurs does not, we maintain, express an empirical proposition at all. It is only with normative ethics that we are at present concerned; so that whenever ethical symbols are used in the course of this argument without qualification, they are always to be interpreted as symbols of the normative type.

In addition to being factually significant if they could be translated into statements about empirical facts, a *second* way moral judgments could be factually significant is if they referred to nonempirical moral facts, facts that are not detectable by standard empirical investigative procedures. This is the claim of G. E. Moore's intuitionism, and Ayer firmly rejects it also.

In admitting that normative ethical concepts are irreducible to empirical concepts, we seem to be leaving the way clear for the "absolutist" view of ethics—that is, the view that statements of value are not controlled by observation, as ordinary empirical propositions are, but only by a mysterious "intellectual intuition." A feature of this theory, which is seldom recognized by its advocates, is that it makes statements of value unverifiable. For it is notorious that what seems intuitively certain to one person may seem doubtful, or even false, to another. So that unless it is possible to provide some criterion by which one may decide between conflicting intuitions, a mere appeal to intuition is worthless as a test of a proposition's validity. But in the case of moral judgements, no such criterion can be given. Some moralists claim to settle the matter by saying that they "know" that their own moral judgements are correct. But such an assertion is of purely psychological interest, and has not the slightest tendency to prove the validity of any moral judgement. For dissentient moralists may equally well "know" that their ethical views are correct. And, as far as subjective certainty goes, there will be nothing to choose between them. When such differences of opinion arise in connection with an ordinary empirical proposition, one may attempt to resolve them by referring to, or actually carrying out, some relevant empirical test. But with regard to ethical statements, there is, on the "absolutist" or "intuitionist" theory, no relevant empirical test. We are therefore justified in saying that on this theory ethical statements are held to be unverifiable. They are, of course, also held to be genuine synthetic propositions.

Moral Judgments Regarded as Emotive

Of course, unverifiable synthetic propositions are, as any philosopher sympathetic to logical positivism knows, "not factually significant" (if one wants to put it diplomatically) or simply "nonsense" (if one wants to be completely candid).

After rejecting two attempts to interpret moral judgments as factually significant, Ayer presents his own interpretation. According to him, moral judgments are not informative or factually significant at all. They are purely *emotive*.

> Considering the use which we have made of the principle that a synthetic proposition is significant only if it is empirically verifiable, it is clear that the acceptance of an "absolutist" theory of ethics would undermine the whole of our main argument. And as we have already rejected the "naturalistic" theories which are commonly supposed to provide the only alternative to "absolutism" in ethics, we seem to have reached a difficult position. We shall meet the difficulty by showing that the correct treatment of ethical statements is afforded by a third theory, which is wholly compatible with our radical empiricism.
>
> We begin by admitting that the fundamental ethical concepts are unanalysable, inasmuch as there is no criterion by which one can test the validity of the judgements in which they occur. So far we are in agreement with the absolutists. But, unlike the absolutists, we are able to give an explanation of this fact about ethical concepts. We say that the reason why they are unanalysable is that they are mere pseudo-concepts. The presence of an ethical symbol in a proposition adds nothing to its factual content. Thus if I say to someone, "You acted wrongly in stealing that money," I am not stating anything more than if I had simply said, "You stole that money." In adding that this action is wrong I am not making any further statement about it. I am simply evincing my moral disapproval of it. It is as if I had said, "You stole that money," in a peculiar tone of horror, or written it with the addition of some special exclamation marks. The tone, or the exclamation marks, adds nothing to the literal meaning of the sentence. It merely serves to show that the expression of it is attended by certain feelings in the speaker.

Here Ayer introduces the distinction between genuine and pseudo-propositions. Logicians use the term "proposition" to refer to a statement that has truth value, that is, a proposition which is either true or false. Another characteristic of a proposition is that it has factual content. A statement of the type, "Don't lie!" is not a proposition; it merely gives a command and is no different in principle from the command, "Close the door!" A statement of the form, "It is warm today," is a proposition. It has factual content and can be shown to be either true or false, depending on the state of affairs to which it refers. The statement, "It is wrong to lie," looks like a proposition, but, according to Ayer, it is a pseudo-proposition and has no factual content.

> If now I generalise my previous statement and say, "Stealing money is wrong," I produce a sentence which has no factual meaning—that is, expresses no proposition which can be either true or false. It is as if I had written "Stealing money!!"—where the shape and thickness of the exclamation marks show, by a suitable convention, that a special sort of moral disapproval is the feeling which is being expressed. It is clear that there is nothing said here which can be true or false. Another man may disagree with me about the wrongness of stealing, in the sense that he may not have the same feelings about stealing as I have, and he may quarrel with me on account of my moral sentiments. But he cannot, strictly speaking, contradict me. For in saying that a certain type of action is right or wrong, I am not making any factual statement, not even a statement about my own state of mind. I am merely expressing certain moral sentiments. And the man who is ostensibly contradicting me is merely expressing his moral sentiments. So that there is plainly no sense in asking which of us is in the right. For neither of us is asserting a genuine proposition.
>
> What we have just been saying about the symbol "wrong" applies to all normative ethical symbols. Sometimes they occur in sentences which record ordinary empirical facts besides expressing ethical feeling about those facts: sometimes they occur in sentences which simply express ethical feeling about a certain type of action, or situation, without making any statement of fact. But in every case in which one would commonly be said to be making an ethical judgement, the function of the relevant ethical word is purely "emotive." It is used to express feeling about certain objects, but not to make any assertion about them.
>
> It is worth mentioning that ethical terms do not serve only to express feeling. They are calculated also to arouse feeling, and so to stimulate action. Indeed some of them are used in such a way as to give the sentences in which they occur the effect of commands. Thus the sentence "It is your duty to tell the truth" may be regarded both as the expression of a certain sort of ethical feeling about truthfulness and as the expression of the command "Tell the truth." The sentence "You ought to tell the truth" also involves the command "Tell the truth," but here the tone of the command is less emphatic. In the sentence "It is good to tell the truth" the command has become little more than a suggestion. And thus the "meaning" of the word "good," in its ethical usage, is differentiated from that of the word "duty" or the word "ought." In fact we may define the meaning of the various ethical words in terms both of the different feelings they are ordinarily taken to express, and also the different responses which they are calculated to provoke.
>
> We can now see why it is impossible to find a criterion for determining

the validity of ethical judgements. It is not because they have an "absolute" validity which is mysteriously independent of ordinary sense-experience, but because they have no objective validity whatsoever. If a sentence makes no statement at all, there is obviously no sense in asking whether what it says is true or false. And we have seen that sentences which simply express moral judgements do not say anything. They are pure expressions of feeling and as such do not come under the category of truth and falsehood. They are unverifiable for the same reason as a cry of pain or a word of command is unverifiable—because they do not express genuine propositions.

A New Kind of Subjectivism

Ayer admits that his emotive theory can be viewed as subjectivistic, but he is careful to distinguish his form of subjectivism from the traditional form. To do this he distinguishes between *evincing* or *expressing* a feeling and *asserting* that one has the feeling. A clever actor, for example, can evince or express anger by clenching his fists, flushing red in his face, gritting his teeth, and stomping across the stage without really being angry himself. He is just playing a role: evincing feelings without possessing them. If I uttered the moral judgment, "The President of the United States is good," the traditional subjectivist would say that I was asserting my approval of the President. As we have already noted, such a translation of my moral judgment would be verifiable. Ayer, however, is so determined to remove ethical judgments from the realm of the verifiable that he would interpret my moral judgment to be simply my evincing the feeling of approval without any indication necessarily being present that I in fact possessed such a feeling.

Thus, although our theory of ethics might fairly be said to be radically subjectivist, it differs in a very important respect from the orthodox subjectivist theory. For the orthodox subjectivist does not deny, as we do, that the sentences of a moralizer express genuine propositions. All he denies is that they express propositions of a unique non-empirical character. His own view is that they express propositions about the speaker's feelings. If this were so, ethical judgements clearly would be capable of being true or false. They would be true if the speaker had the relevant feelings, and false if he had not. And this is a matter which is, in principle, empirically verifiable. Furthermore, they could be significantly contradicted. For if I say, "Tolerance is a virtue," and someone answers, "You don't approve of it," he would, on the ordinary subjectivist theory, be contradicting me. On our theory, he would not be contradicting me, because, in saying that tolerance was a virtue, I should not be making any statement about my own feelings or about anything else. I should simply be evincing my feelings, which is not at all the same thing as saying that I have them.

The distinction between the expression of feeling and the assertion of feeling is complicated by the fact that the assertion that one has a certain feeling often accompanies the expression of that feeling, and is then, indeed, a factor in the expression of that feeling. Thus I may simultaneously express boredom and say that I am bored, and in that case my utterance of the words, "I am bored," is one of the circumstances which make it true to say that I am expressing or evincing boredom. But I can express boredom without actually saying that I am bored. I can express it by my tone and gestures, while making a statement about something wholly unconnected with it, or by an ejaculation, or without uttering any words at all. So that even if the assertion that one has a certain feeling always involves the expression of that feeling, the expression of a feeling assuredly does not always involve the assertion that one has it. And this is the important point to grasp in considering the distinction between our theory and the ordinary subjectivist theory. For whereas the subjectivist holds that ethical statements actually assert the existence of certain feelings, we hold that ethical statements are expressions and excitants of feeling which do not necessarily involve any assertions.

Criticisms of Subjectivism Answered

There are, according to Ayer, two major criticisms that can be levelled against subjectivist ethics. The first criticism urges that "the validity of ethical judgments is not determined by the nature of their author's feelings." For example, according to the subjectivist, to determine the validity of the judgment, "The President of the United States is good," you must check to see if the person who made the judgment did, in fact, have a feeling of approval toward the President, because to say that he is "good" means to approve of him. Suppose, however, that a person said, "I approve of the President, but I consider him to be morally bad." In checking the validity of this judgment, according to subjectivism, we would discover that the sentence held a self-contradictory claim, namely, "I approve of the President, but I do not approve of him." From the subjectivist perspective, such a sentence would be self-contradictory nonsense. Clearly, however, ordinary language usage does not take such a sentence to be self-contradictory nonsense. It does make sense to approve of someone and yet to consider him morally bad. Accordingly, in checking up on the validity of a moral judgment, it is inadequate simply to determine whether or not the speaker has the appropriate feelings of approval or disapproval. Subjectivism's account of moral judgments, therefore, seems fundamentally inadequate. While admitting this criticism as telling against standard forms of subjectivism, Ayer believes that his brand of subjectivism escapes the criticism.

> We have already remarked that the main objection to the ordinary subjectivist theory is that the validity of ethical judgements is not determined by the nature of their author's feelings. And this is an objection which our theory escapes. For it does not imply that the existence of any feelings is a necessary and sufficient condition of the validity of an ethical judgement. It implies, on the contrary, that ethical judgements have no validity.

The second criticism of subjectivist theories of ethics is that "if ethical statements were simply statements about the speaker's feelings, it would be impossible to argue about questions of value." Ayer considers this criticism to be irrelevant because it is fundamentally mistaken about the nature of moral disputes.

There is, however, a celebrated argument against subjectivist theories which our theory does not escape. It has been pointed out by Moore that if ethical statements were simply statements about the speaker's feelings, it would be impossible to argue about questions of value. To take a typical example: if a man said that thrift was a virtue, and another replied that it was a vice, they would not, on this theory, be disputing with one another. One would be saying that he approved of thrift, and the other that *he* didn't; and there is no reason why both these statements should not be true. Now Moore held it to be obvious that we do dispute about questions of value, and accordingly concluded that the particular form of subjectivism which he was discussing was false.

It is plain that the conclusion that it is impossible to dispute about questions of value follows from our theory also. For as we hold that such sentences as "Thrift is a virtue" and "Thrift is a vice" do not express propositions at all, we clearly cannot hold that they express incompatible propositions. We must therefore admit that if Moore's argument really refutes the ordinary subjectivist theory, it also refutes ours. But, in fact, we deny that it does refute even the ordinary subjectivist theory. For we hold that one really never does dispute about questions of value.

This may seem, at first sight, to be a very paradoxical assertion. For we certainly do engage in disputes which are ordinarily regarded as disputes about questions of value. But, in all such cases, we find, if we consider the matter closely, that the dispute is not really about a question of value, but about a question of fact. When someone disagrees with us about the moral value of a certain action or type of action, we do admittedly resort to argument in order to win him over to our way of thinking. But we do not attempt to show by our arguments that he has the "wrong" ethical feeling toward a situation whose nature he has correctly apprehended. What we attempt to show is that he is mistaken about the facts of the case. We argue that he has misconceived the agent's motive: or that he has misjudged the effects of the action, or its probable effects in view of the agent's knowledge; or that he has failed to take into account the special circumstances in which the agent was placed. Or else we employ more general arguments about the effects which actions of a certain type tend to produce, or the qualities which are usually manifested in their performance. We do this in the hope that we have only to get our opponent to agree with us about the nature of the empirical facts for him to adopt the same moral attitude towards them as we do. And as the people with whom we argue have generally received the same moral education as ourselves, and live in the same social order, our expectation is usually justified. But if our opponent happens to have undergone a different process of moral "conditioning" from ourselves, so that, even when he acknowledges all the facts, he still disagrees with us about the moral value of the actions under discussion, then we abandon the attempt to convince him by argument. We say that it is impossible to argue with him because he has a distorted or underdeveloped moral sense; which signifies merely that he employs a different set of values from our own. We feel that our own system of values is superior, and therefore speak in such derogatory terms of his. But we cannot bring forward any arguments to show that our system is superior. For our judgement that it is so is itself a judgement of value, and accordingly outside the scope of argument. It is because argument fails us when we come to deal with pure questions of value, as distinct from questions of fact, that we finally resort to mere abuse.

In short, we find that argument is possible on moral questions only if some system of values is presupposed. If our opponent concurs with us in expressing moral disapproval of all actions of a given type t, then we may get him to condemn a particular action A, by bringing forward arguments to show that A is of type t. For the question whether A does or does not belong to that type is a plain question of fact. Given that a man has certain moral principles, we argue that he must, in order to be consistent, react morally to certain things in a certain way. What we do not and cannot argue about is the validity of these moral principles. We merely praise or condemn them in the light of our own feelings.

If anyone doubts the accuracy of this account of moral disputes, let him try to construct even an imaginary argument on a question of value which does not reduce itself to an argument about a question of logic or about an empirical matter of fact. I am confident that he will not succeed in producing a single example. And if that is the case, he must allow that its involving the impossibility of purely ethical arguments is not, as Moore thought, a ground of objection to our theory, but rather a point in favour of it.

A Redefined Task for Ethical Inquiry

Ayer now sums up the implications of his emotive theory for all ethical inquiries. Ethical philosophy is reduced to the task of presenting the emotivist theory of ethics. Ethical philosophy cannot legitimately seek to discover moral truth because there is no such thing. And insofar as ethical inquiry is related to facts, it is to the facts of psychology and sociology.

Having upheld our theory against the only criticism which appeared to threaten it, we may now use it to define the nature of all ethical enquiries. We find that ethical philosophy consists simply in saying that ethical concepts are pseudo-concepts and therefore unanalysable. The further task of describing the different feelings that the different ethical terms are used to express, and the different reactions that they customarily provoke, is a task for the psychologist. There cannot be such a thing as ethical science, if by ethical science one means the elaboration of a "true" system of morals. For we have seen that, as ethical judgements are mere expressions of feeling, there can be no way of determining the validity of any ethical system, and, indeed, no sense in asking whether any such system is true. All that one may legitimately enquire in this connection is, What are the moral habits of a given person or group of people, and what causes them to have precisely those habits and feelings? And this enquiry falls wholly within the scope of the existing social sciences.

It appears, then, that ethics, as a branch of knowledge, is nothing more than a department of psychology and sociology. And in case anyone thinks that we are overlooking the existence of casuistry, we may remark that casuistry is not a science, but is a purely analytical investigation of the structure of a given moral system. In other words, it is an exercise in formal logic.

When one comes to pursue the psychological enquiries which constitute ethical science, one is immediately enabled to account for the Kantian and hedonistic theories of morals. For one finds that one of the chief causes of moral behavior is fear, both conscious and unconscious, of a god's displeasure, and fear of the enmity of society. And this, indeed, is the reason why moral precepts present themselves to some people as "categorical" commands. And one finds, also, that the moral code of a society is partly determined by the beliefs of that society concerning the conditions of its own happiness—or, in other words, that a society tends to encourage or discourage a given type of conduct by the use of moral sanctions according as it appears to promote or detract from the contentment of the society as a whole. And this is the reason why altruism is recommended in most moral codes and egotism condemned. It is from the observation of this connection between morality and happiness that hedonistic or eudaemonistic theories of morals ultimately spring, just as the moral theory of Kant is based on the fact, previously explained, that moral precepts have for some people the force of inexorable commands. As each of these theories ignores the fact which lies at the root of the other, both may be criticized as being one-sided; but this is not the main objection to either of them. Their essential defect is that they treat propositions which refer to the causes and attributes of our ethical feelings as if they were definitions of ethical concepts. And thus they fail to recognise that ethical concepts are pseudo-concepts and consequently indefinable.

With a single sweep, Ayer disposes of all ethical theories: Kant's (the "categorical imperative"), Aristotle's (the eudaemonistic), as well as any morality based on the notion of divine commands. We will look at these theories in Part Two of this book, although if we agreed with Ayer there would be no Part Two of this book.

Such, then, is Ayer's resolution of the puzzling nature of moral judgments. At the heart of the puzzle is the view that moral judgments somehow convey information about objective facts, but there seems to be no agreed-upon procedure for checking up on the truth of those information-bearing judgments. Ayer resolves the problem not by finding a procedure for checking up on moral judgments, but by saying the problem is not a real problem at all because moral judgments are not information-bearing and are, in principle, unverifiable. Thus, when you say, "The President of the United States is good," you are not informing us that the President has certain moral qualities, you are not necessarily informing us that you approve of the President, you are not conveying any information about the President or yourself. You are simply evincing or expressing feelings that you may or may not have; you may, after all, be a very good actor who can display the signs of a feeling without having the feeling yourself.

Has Ayer really resolved the puzzle of the nature of moral judgments? Has he really given an adequate account of them? Brand Blanshard, our next author, says "No!" Let us turn now to his response to Ayer.

Critic of Emotivism: Brand Blanshard

In Chapter 2 we encountered Brand Blanshard (1892–), the advocate of soft determinism who presented his arguments with clarity and conviction. With a similar style, Blanshard writes as the able critic of emotivism. Like his opponent Ayer, Blanshard is the recipient of many honors, including appointments as a Rhodes scholar, a Guggenheim fellow, a corresponding fellow of the British Academy, and a member of the American Academy of Arts and Sciences. He held professorships at the University of Michigan, Swarthmore College, and Yale University, from which he retired in 1961.

Historical Roots of the New Subjectivism

Blanshard calls emotivism "the new subjectivism in ethics" and reviews its position and its roots in the logical positivists' theory of knowledge. That theory, as we have already noted, recognizes only two types of sentences that can convey knowledge: *synthetic* (Blanshard calls these "empirical") and *analytic*. Because emotivists regard moral judgments as neither empirical nor analytic, the judgments are not cognitive; that is, they do not convey knowledge.

> * By the new subjectivism in ethics I mean the view that when anyone says "this is right" or "this is good," he is only expressing his own feeling; he is not asserting anything true or false, because he is not asserting or judging at all; he is really making an exclamation that expresses a favorable feeling.
>
> This view has recently come into much favor. With variations of detail, it is being advocated by Russell, Wittgenstein and Ayer in England, and by Carnap, Stevenson, Feigl, and others, in this country. Why is it that the theory has come into so rapid a popularity? Is it because moralists of insight have been making a fresh and searching examination of moral experience and its expression? No, I think not. A consideration of the names just mentioned suggests a truer reason. All these names belong, roughly speaking, to a single school of thought in the theory of knowledge. If the new view has become popular in ethics, it is because certain persons who were at work in the theory of knowledge arrived at a new view *there,* and found, on thinking it out, that it required the new view in ethics; the view comes less from ethical analysis than from logical positivism.
>
> As positivists, these writers held that every judgment belongs to one or

* FROM Brand Blanshard, "The New Subjectivism in Ethics," *Philosophy and Phenomenological Research* 9(1948–1949):504–11. Copyright 1948 by *Philosophy and Phenomenological Research.* Used by permission of *Philosophy and Phenomenological Research.*

other of two types. On the one hand, it may be *a priori* or necessary. But then it is always analytic, i.e., it unpacks in its predicate part or all of its subject. Can we safely say that 7 + 5 make 12? Yes, because 12 is what we mean by "7 + 5." On the other hand, the judgment may be empirical, and then, if we are to verify it, we can no longer look to our meanings only; it refers to sense experience and there we must look for its warrant. Having arrived at this division of judgments, the positivists raised the question where value judgments fall. The judgment that knowledge is good, for example, did not seem to be analytic; the value that knowledge might have did not seem to be part of our concept of knowledge. But neither was the statement empirical, for goodness was not a quality like red or squeaky that could be seen or heard. What were they to do, then, with these awkward judgments of value? To find a place for them in their theory of knowledge would require them to revise the theory radically, and yet that theory was what they regarded as their most important discovery. It appeared that the theory could be saved in one way only. If it could be shown that judgments of good and bad were not judgments at all, that they asserted nothing true or false, but merely expressed emotions like "Hurrah" or "Fiddlesticks," then these wayward judgments would cease from troubling and weary heads could be at rest. This is the course the positivists took. They explained value judgments by explaining them away.

Now I do not think their view will do. But before discussing it, I should like to record one vote of thanks to them for the clarity with which they have stated their case. It has been said of John Stuart Mill that he wrote so clearly that he could be found out. This theory has been put so clearly and precisely that it deserves criticism of the same kind, and that I will do my best to supply. The theory claims to show by analysis that when we say, "That is good," we do not mean to assert a character of the subject of which we are thinking. I shall argue that we do mean to do just that.

To distinguish his position clearly from the subjectivist's, Blanshard contrasts the ways in which he and a subjectivist would interpret a statement about the painful death of a rabbit caught in a steel trap: "It was a bad thing that the little animal should suffer so." The subjectivist views this as an expression of present emotion. Blanshard views it as a statement about an animal's pain. For Blanshard, the speaker is making a claim about a state of affairs in the world. For the subjectivist, the speaker is simply expressing emotion. (Ayer would refine this representation of subjectivism to say that the speaker is simply evincing the emotion without claiming to have that emotion.) Blanshard explains his position.

Let us work through an example, and the simpler and commoner the better. There is perhaps no value statement on which people would more universally agree than the statement that intense pain is bad. Let us take a set of circumstances in which I happen to be interested on the legislative side and in which I think every one of us might naturally make such a statement. We come upon a rabbit that has been caught in one of the brutal traps in common use. There are signs that it has struggled for days to escape and that in a frenzy of hunger, pain, and fear, it has all but eaten off its own leg. The attempt failed: the animal is now dead. As we think of the long and excruciating pain it must have suffered, we are very likely to say: "It was a bad thing that the little animal should suffer so." The positivist tells us that when we say this we are only expressing our present emotion. I hold, on the contrary, that we mean to assert something of the pain itself, namely, that it was bad—bad when and as it occurred.

Five Objections to Emotivism

Blanshard proceeds to give five objections to emotivism, or the "new subjectivism." *First*, emotivism would commit us to saying that there was no badness in the rabbit's pain until someone came along and expressed a disapproving emotion. Such a view, Blanshard implies, violates common usage: when we judge the rabbit's pain to be bad, we normally imply that it was bad when it happened even before an observer was on the scene. That is to say, we are normally making a claim about the pain itself, about an actual state of affairs.

> Consider what follows from the positivist view. On that view, nothing good or bad happened in the case until I came on the scene and made my remark. For what I express in my remark is something going on in me at that time, and that of course did not exist until I did come on the scene. The pain of the rabbit was not itself bad; nothing evil was happening when that pain was being endured; badness, in the only sense in which it is involved at all, waited for its appearance till I came and looked and felt. Now that this is at odds with our meaning may be shown as follows. Let us put to ourselves the hypothesis that we had not come on the scene and that the rabbit never was discovered. Are we prepared to say that in that case nothing bad occurred in the sense in which we said it did? Clearly not. Indeed we should say, on the contrary, that the accident of our later discovery made no difference whatever to the badness of the animal's pain, that it would have been every whit as bad whether a chance passer-by happened later to discover the body and feel repugnance or not. If so, then it is clear that in saying the suffering was bad we are not expressing our feelings only. We are saying that the pain was bad when and as it occurred and before anyone took an attitude toward it.
>
> The first argument is thus an ideal experience in which we use the method of difference. It removes our present expression and shows that the badness we meant would not be affected by this, whereas on positivist grounds it should be.

Blanshard's *second* objection is that emotivism would not allow us to retract our original judgment as false if we later discovered that the rabbit did not in fact suffer at all. Such a view, however, seems to violate common usage because we would normally wish to retract our original judgment under these circumstances. Our desire to retract that judgment shows that we intended to make a claim about an actual state of affairs, and that being mistaken about such a state of affairs is justification for disavowing our original claim.

The second argument applies the method in the reverse way. It ideally removes the past event, and shows that this would render false what we mean to say, whereas on positivist grounds it should not. Let us suppose that the animal did not in fact fall into the trap and did not suffer at all, but that we mistakenly believe it did, and say as before that its suffering was an evil thing. On the positivist theory, everything I sought to express by calling it evil in the first case is still present in the second. In the only sense in which badness is involved at all, whatever was bad in the first case is still present in its entirety, since all that is expressed in either case is a state of feeling, and that feeling is still there. And our question is, is such an implication consistent with what we meant? Clearly it is not. If anyone asked us, after we made the remark that the suffering was a bad thing, whether we should think it relevant to what we said to learn that the incident had never occurred and no pain had been suffered at all, we should say that it made all the difference in the world, that what we were asserting to be bad was precisely the suffering we thought had occurred back there, that if this had not occurred, there was nothing left to be bad, and that our assertion was in that case mistaken. The suggestion that in saying something evil has occurred we were after all making no mistake, because we had never meant anyhow to say anything about the past suffering, seems to me merely frivolous. If we did not mean to say this, why should we be so relieved on finding that the suffering had not occurred? On the theory before us, such relief would be groundless, for in that suffering itself there was nothing bad at all, and hence in its non-occurrence there would be nothing to be relieved about. The positivist theory would here distort our meaning beyond recognition.

So far as I can see, there is only one way out for the positivist. He holds that goodness and badness lie in feelings of approval or disapproval. And there is a way in which he might hold that badness did in this case precede our own feeling of disapproval without belonging to the pain itself. The pain in itself was neutral; but unfortunately the rabbit, on no grounds at all, took up toward this neutral object an attitude of disapproval, and that made it for the first time, and in the only intelligible sense, bad. This way of escape is theoretically possible, but since it has grave difficulties of its own and has not, so far as I know, been urged by positivists, it is perhaps best not to spend time over it.

The *third* objection to emotivism is that it would make our original judgment empty of meaning if we restated it when our original feelings had cooled and were no longer present. Once again, emotivism seems to violate common usage because, even though our original emotions at seeing the rabbit might have faded away when we repeated the original judgment, nevertheless we would normally maintain that we were still conveying the original meaning. We are able to maintain this position because we assume that our original moral judgment was about a state of affairs (the rabbit's pain) and not simply an expression of passing emotions.

I come now to a third argument, which again is very simple. When we come upon the rabbit and make our remark about its suffering being a bad thing, we presumably make it with some feeling; the positivists are plainly right in saying that such remarks do usually express feeling. But suppose that a week later we revert to the incident in thought and make our statement again. And suppose that the circumstances have now so changed that the feeling with which we made the remark in the first place has faded. The pathetic evidence is no longer before us; and we are now so fatigued in body and mind that feeling is, as we say, quite dead. In these circumstances, since what was expressed by the remark when first made is, on the theory before us, simply absent, the remark now expresses nothing. It is as empty as the word "Hurrah" would be when there was no enthusiasm behind it. And this seems to me untrue. When we repeat the remark that such suffering was a bad thing, the feeling with which we made it last week may be at or near the vanishing point, but if we were asked whether we meant to say what we did before, we should certainly answer Yes. We should say that we made our point with feeling the first time and little or no feeling the second time, but that it was the same point we were making. And if we can see that what we meant to say remains the same, while the feeling varies from intensity to near zero, it is not the feeling that we primarily meant to express.

Fourth, subjectivism would preclude the assessment of attitudes as fitting or unfitting with respect to certain acts or effects. To say that a person's attitude of disapproval regarding a certain act is "fitting," assumes that there is a quality within the act that makes it worthy of disapproval. Subjectivism, however, considers all acts and effects to be morally neutral. That is, acts and effects have no qualities within them that are inherently worthy of approval or disapproval. "Fittingness" and "unfittingness" are, accordingly, ruled out. Here again, subjectivism seems to violate common usage because in making moral judgments we normally assume the possibility and legitimacy of assessing attitudes as fitting or unfitting.

I come now to a fourth consideration. We all believe that toward acts or effects of a certain kind one attitude is fitting and another not; but on the theory before us such a belief would not make sense. Broad and Ross have lately contended that this fitness is one of the main facts of ethics, and I suspect they are right. But that is not exactly my point. My point is this: whether there is such fitness or not, we all assume that there is, and if we do, we express in moral judgments more than the subjectivists say we do. Let me illustrate.

In his novel *The House of the Dead,* Dostoevsky tells of his experiences in a Siberian prison camp. Whatever the unhappy inmates of such camps are like today, Dostoevsky's companions were about as grim a lot as can be imagined. "I have heard stories," he writes, "of the most terrible, the most unnatural actions, of the most monstrous murders, told with the most spontaneous childishly merry laughter." Most of us would say that in this delight at the killing of others or the causing of suffering there is something very unfitting. If we were asked why we thought so, we should say that these things involve great evil and are wrong, and that to take delight in what is evil or wrong is plainly unfitting. Now in the subjectivist view, this answer is ruled out. For before someone takes up an attitude toward death, suffering, or their infliction, they have no moral quality at all. There is therefore nothing about them to which an attitude of approval or condemnation could be fitting. They are in themselves neutral, and, so far as they get a moral quality, they get it only through being invested with it by the attitude of the onlooker. But if that is true, why is any attitude more fitting than any other? Would applause, for example, be fitting if, apart from the applause, there were nothing good to applaud? Would condemnation be fitting if, independently of the condemnation, there were nothing bad to condemn? In such a case, any attitude would be as fitting or unfitting as any other, which means that the notion of fitness has lost all point.

Indeed, we are forced to go much farther. If goodness and badness lie in attitudes only and hence are brought into being by them, those men who greeted death and misery with childishly merry laughter are taking the only sensible line. If there is nothing evil in these things, if they get their moral complexion only from our feeling about them, why shouldn't they be greeted with a cheer? To greet them with repulsion would turn what before was neutral into something bad; it would needlessly bring badness into the world; and even on subjectivist assumptions that does not seem very bright. On the other hand, to greet them with delight would convert what before was neutral into something good; it would bring goodness into the world. If I have murdered a man and wish to remove the stain, the way is clear. It is to cry, "Hurrah for murder."

What is the subjectivist to reply? I can only guess. He may point out that the inflicting of death is *not* really neutral before the onlooker takes his attitude, for the man who inflicted the death no doubt himself took an attitude, and thus the act had a moral quality derived from this. But that makes the case more incredible still, for the man who did the act presumably approved it, and if so it was good in the only sense in which anything is good, and then our conviction that the laughter is unfit is more unaccountable still. It may be replied that the victim, too, had his attitude and that since this was unfavorable, the act was not unqualifiedly good. But the answer is plain. Let the killer be expert at his job; let him despatch his victim instantly before he has time to take an attitude, and then gloat about his perfect crime without ever telling anyone. Then, so far as I can see, his act will be good without any qualification. It would become bad only if someone found out about it and disliked it. And that would be a curiously irrational procedure, since the man's approving of his own killing is in itself just as neutral as the killing that it approves. Why then should anyone dislike it?

It may be replied that we can defend our dislike on this ground that, if the approval of killing were to go unchecked and spread, most men would have to live in insecurity and fear, and these things are undesirable. But surely this reply is not open; these things are not, on the theory, undesirable, for nothing is; in themselves they are neutral. Why then should I disapprove men's living in this state? The answer may come that if other men live in insecurity and fear, I shall in time be infected myself. But even in my own insecurity and fear there is, on the theory before us, nothing bad whatever, and therefore, if I disapprove them, it is without a shadow of ground and with no more fitness in my attitude than if I cordially cheered them. The theory thus conflicts with our judgments of fitness all along the line.

Fifth, for emotivism there are no mistakes about values. But everyday moral experience normally assumes that such mistakes are possible. Moralists, for example, have traditionally distinguished between what a person thinks is the right act in a certain situation (the subjectively right thing) and what in fact is the right act in the situation (the objectively right). Suppose that my preschool son was uncooperative and somewhat rude to his violin teacher during a lesson. Suppose that I, embarrassed and annoyed by his deplorable behavior, gave him a solid paddling after the lesson. No doubt I would be doing what I considered to be the right act. I would have done the subjectively right thing. But that is no guarantee that I did what was objectively right. An observer more skilled in interpreting children's behavior than I, might have suggested that my son's response to his teacher was his way of saying that the Bach minuet he was learning was extremely difficult for his little fingers. He needed comfort and encouragement from his father rather than punishment. Although I did what was subjectively right when I spanked the little fellow, I missed by a mile what was objectively right. In short, I was mistaken about what was the right act in the situation. Blanshard maintains that the possibility of being mistaken in this way is at the heart of the notion of duty, the basis for self-criticism, and the motive for self-improvement. By precluding this possibility, emotivism seems once again to contradict certain fundamental aspects of human moral experience.

I come now to a fifth and final difficulty with the theory. It makes mistakes about values impossible. There is a whole nest of inter-connected criticisms here, some of which have been made so often that I shall not develop them again, such as that I can never agree or disagree in opinion with anyone else about an ethical matter, and that in these matters I can never be inconsistent with others or with myself. I am not at all content with the sort of analysis which says that the only contradictions in such cases have regard to facts and that contradictions about value are only differences of feeling. I think that if anyone tells me that having a bicuspid out without an anaesthetic is not a bad experience and I say it is a very nasty experience indeed, I am differing with him in opinion, and differing about the degree of badness of the experience. But without pressing this further, let me apply the argument in what is perhaps a fresh direction.

There is an old and merciful distinction that moralists have made for many centuries about conduct—the distinction between what is subjectively and what is objectively right. They have said that in any given situation there is some act which, in view of all the circumstances, would be the best act to do; and this is what would be objectively right. The notion of an objectively right act is the ground of our notion of duty: our duty is always to find and do this act if we can. But of course we often don't find it. We often hit upon and do acts that we think are the right ones, but we are mistaken; and then our act is only subjectively right. Between these two acts the disparity may be continual; Professor Prichard suggested that probably few of us in the course of our lives ever succeed in doing *the* right act.

Now so far as I can see, the new subjectivism would abolish this difference at a stroke. Let us take a case. A boy abuses his small brother. We should commonly say, "That is wrong, but perhaps he doesn't know any better. By reason of bad teaching and a feeble imagination, he may see nothing wrong in what he is doing, and may even be proud of it. If so, his act may be subjectively right, though it is miles away from what is objectively right." What concerns me about the new subjectivism is that it prohibits this distinction. If the boy feels this way about his act, then it is right in the only sense in which anything is right. The notion of an objective right lying beyond what he has discovered, and which he ought to seek and do is meaningless. There might, to be sure, be an act that would more generally arouse favorable feelings in others, but that would not make it right for him unless he thought of it and approved it, which he doesn't. Even if he did think of it, it would not be obligatory for him to feel about it in any particular way, since there is nothing in any act, as we have seen, which would make any feeling more suitable than any other.

Now if there is no such thing as an objectively right act, what becomes of the idea of duty? I have suggested that the idea of duty rests on the idea of such an act, since it is always our duty to find that act and do it if we can. But if whatever we feel approval for at the time is right, what is the point of doubting and searching further? Like the little girl in Boston who was asked if she would like to travel, we can answer, "Why should I travel when I'm already there?" If I am reconciled in feeling to my present act, no act I could discover by reflection could be better, and therefore why reflect or seek at all? Such a view seems to me to break the mainspring of duty, to destroy the motive for self-improvement, and to remove the ground for self-criticism. It may be replied that by further reflection I can find an act that would satisfy my feelings more widely than the present one, and that this is the act I should seek. But this reply means either that such general satisfaction is objectively better, which would contradict the theory, or else that, if at the time I don't feel it better, it isn't better, in which case I have no motive for seeking it. When certain self-righteous persons took an inflexible line with Oliver Cromwell, his very Cromwellian reply was, "Bethink ye, gentlemen, by the bowels of Christ, that ye may be mistaken." It was good advice. I hope nobody will take from me that privilege of finding myself mistaken. I should be sorry to think that the self of thirty years ago was as far along the path as the self of today, merely because he was a smug, young jackanapes, or even that the paragon of today has a little room for improvement as would be allowed by his myopic complacency.

Emotivism and Moral Anarchy

In a final rhetorical flourish, Blanshard raises the specter of moral anarchy that would haunt a world committed to emotivism, or the new subjectivism, in ethics.

> One final remark. The great problems of the day are international problems. Has the new subjectivism any bearing upon these problems? I think it has, and a somewhat sinister bearing . . . For its general acceptance would, so far as one can see, be an international disaster. The assumption behind the old League and the new United Nations was that there is such a thing as right and wrong in the conduct of a nation, a right and wrong that do not depend on how it happens to feel at the time. It is implied, for example, that when Japan invaded Manchuria in 1931 she might be wrong, and that by discussion and argument she might be shown to be wrong. It was implied that when the Nazis invaded Poland they might be wrong, even though German public sentiment overwhelmingly approved it. On the theory before us, it would be meaningless to call these nations mistaken; if they felt approval for what they did, then it was right with as complete a justification as could be supplied for the disapproval felt by the rest of the world. In the present dispute between Russia and our own country over southeast Europe, it is nonsense to speak of the right or rational course for either of us to take; if with all the facts before the two parties, each feels approval for its own course, both attitudes are equally justified or unjustified; neither is mistaken; there is no common reason to which they can take an appeal; there are no principles by which an international court could pronounce on the matter; nor would there be any obligation to obey the pronouncement if it were made. This cuts the ground from under any attempt to establish one's case as right or anyone else's case as wrong. So if our friends the subjectivists still hold their theory after I have applied my little ruler to their knuckles, which of course they will, I have but one request to make of them: Do keep it from Mr. Molotov and Mr. Vishinsky.

Assessment of Emotivism

Are moral judgments cognitive or non-cognitive? That question is at the center of emotivism. Ayer says that they are noncognitive, whereas Blanshard considers them to be cognitive. Before we assess the debate, let us be as clear as possible about the substance of the two positions.

Suppose I made the moral judgment, "Martin Luther King was a good man." Ayer would say that I was not making a claim that Dr. King had a certain quality or characteristic that we call "goodness." Nor would I be claiming that I approved of King but would simply be evincing or exhibiting feelings of approval for him without claiming that I possessed such feelings. Even if I did in fact possess such feelings of approval for Dr. King, my moral judgment would not necessarily entail the claim that I possessed those feelings.

In contrast, Blanshard would maintain that in my moral judgment I was making a claim about Dr. King. I would be saying that he possessed a certain property called "goodness." To be sure, my judgment would probably have some emotive content, but it would not be limited to that. I would be making a claim about an objective state of affairs. I would allegedly be conveying certain information about Dr. King.

Which of these interpretations should we accept? If we use the criterion of ordinary usage—that is, what people generally construe themselves to be doing when they make moral judgments—we would prefer Blanshard's view. Blanshard argues that people assume that their moral judgments involve factually significant claims about the world, rather than just emotive outbursts.

If, as it surely seems to be the case, Blanshard's interpretation of moral judgments is a more comprehensive and accurate representation of what people think they are doing when they make such judgments, would that fact be troublesome for Ayer? Perhaps not. Philosophers as far back as Socrates have often rejected, at great cost to themselves, the opinions of the masses because those opinions seemed to be false. Yet Ayer, and philosophers in his tradition, often construe one of the major tasks of philosophy to be the analysis of the language people use. Failure of a philosopher to give an adequate account of what people are intending to do with their language would be a serious shortcoming, according to Ayer and his followers. Is perhaps Ayer guilty of such a shortcoming when he empties moral judgments of all cognitive significance? That Ayer's interpretation violates ordinary usage must be admitted. Whether that fact represents a telling criticism of Ayer's position is certainly debatable.

If we turn, however, to a consideration of the practical consequences that would result from a commitment to Ayer's position, the case against Ayer takes on added weight. Suppose, for example, that Mr. K. considered the terroristic random killing of political opponents to be morally good, and Mr. C. regarded such activity to be morally bad. How, according to emotivism, could we settle this disagreement? Ayer suggests that, first of all, we must be perfectly clear about the facts relating to the disagreement, because many moral disagreements can be resolved if human beings can get the facts of the case straightened out. We might discover, for instance, that K. considered the killing of political opponents to be an execution, whereas C. regarded it as murder. Perhaps all that divided them was a factual dispute, namely, whether the killing should be classified as execution or murder. Yet, as we probe the disagreement further, we might learn that K. considered the killing to be an execution because he believed that all people who disagreed with his political philosophy were criminals worthy of execution, whereas C. refused to brand political opponents as morally reprehensible criminals. Accordingly, we might conclude that the disagreement was not simply about the facts in the case, but that it embraced also opposing values: K. considered political opponents to be morally bad, but C. did not.

At this point, when we have attempted to straighten out the facts relating to a moral disagreement and we have reached the judgment that persons give different values to the same fact, what could emotivism advise? First, it is apparent that emotivism could provide no basis for preferring one position over the other. According to emotivism, the opposing moral judgments of K. and C. are simply different *evinced* feelings and perhaps different *possessed* feelings about killing political opponents. Because you cannot argue about the validity of feelings, K.'s feelings are just as legitimate as C.'s, and vice versa. Does not this position then lead to moral anarchy? Does not emotivism imply that a person's feelings of approval and disapproval are beyond dispute and stand with equal legitimacy beside all other people's feelings of approval and disapproval? Do we not then have to say that the moral judgments of Hitler, who approved the slaughter of over a million Jewish children in the Holocaust, have equal legitimacy with the moral judgments of Jesus, who blessed little children as living illustrations of the nature of God's kingdom?

Second, because emotivism provides no basis for assessing opposing moral judgments, does it not run aground on the same problem upon which psychological egoism faltered? Emotivism seems to lead to the judgment that where divergent subjective evaluations are competing with each other in the absence of objective norms, the competition can be resolved only by an appeal to force. Does not emotivism, accordingly, lead to the conclusion that "might makes right"?

In brief, adopting ethical emotivism would seem to involve (1) a radical reinterpretation of what people think they are doing when they make moral judgments, (2) a facilitation of moral anarchy, and (3) a commitment to force as the only arbiter of value conflicts. Do not these implications of emotivism make it an ethical theory too costly to adopt?

If we reject Ayer's position and adopt Blanshard's view that moral judgments are cognitive, then we face the perplexing puzzle of figuring out in what sense those judgments are cognitive. Many philosophers prefer living with that puzzle to existing in a world where every moral judgment has equal legitimacy and where force is the only court of appeal to settle value conflicts. Part Two of this book examines several answers to the question of what criteria we should use in judging an action to be right or wrong.

Review Questions

1. How did logical positivism and ethical intuitionism contribute to the development of modern ethical emotivism?
2. Describe G. E. Moore's "Open Question Argument" and "The Naturalistic Fallacy."
3. Ayer discerns two ways in which moral judgments could be synthetic. What are they, and why does Ayer reject them?
4. How does Ayer distinguish his "new" subjectivism from traditional subjectivism in ethics?
5. What objections to emotivism does Blanshard present, and do you consider those criticisms to be compelling?

Retrospective to Part I

The fundamental ethical question, we have suggested, is, What ought I to do? When people ask that question, they usually make several assumptions. They assume that human beings are free, in the sense that alternative futures really are open to them. They also assume that we can assess these alternative futures in terms of objective standards that allow us to evaluate some of those futures as better than others.

The four positions we have examined in Part One of this book are challenges to these basic assumptions. Psychological egoism constricts freedom by narrowing the range of human futures to egoistic ones. Determinism eliminates freedom by making human beings completely subject to hereditary and environmental forces beyond their control. Ethical relativism abolishes objective criteria for evaluating actions. Ethical emotivism eliminates the possibility of objective criteria for evaluating actions by interpreting moral language as having no cognitive content. Clearly, these four positions, if adopted, would commit us to a radical reshaping of the meaning ordinarily associated with the fundamental ethical question.

Where does the survey of these challenges leave us? For each of the issues, we have presented an advocate and a critic. Several standard refutation strategies were adopted by the critics. Refutation by counterexample was used by Butler against psychological egoism in his analysis of the frustrated desire to achieve happiness. Campbell used the same methods to argue against determinism in his discussion of the situation of overcoming moral temptation. Refutation by reduction of the position under attack to absurdity was used by Butler against psychological egoism; he showed that Hobbes's view implied the equating of cruelty and benevolence. Although these strategies are formidable, there is still another reason to reject the four positions covered in this section.

The authors of this book believe that William James's pragmatic approach provides a worthy alternative to a formal refutation of the four positions surveyed in this section. James argued that if one confronts two mutually incompatible doctrines, and it is impossible to know definitely which of the doctrines is true, and one must decide for one or the other, then the truth probably resides in the doctrine that most adequately coheres with lived experience. The pragmatic approach asks, What are the practical consequences for me if I accept this doctrine as true? Then the pragmatic approach declares, If those consequences are radically incompatible with my lived experience, then I am justified in rejecting the doctrine as probably false.

Now, in examining psychological egoism, determinism, ethical relativism, and ethical emotivism, we have seen that each of these doctrines seems to slip into a state of standardlessness. Suppose, for example, that we asked each of these positions to assess the morality of horrendous actions such as the behavior of Nazis toward the Jews or Stalin's purges of the 1930s. What would proponents of each of the positions covered in this section be able to say about these abominable events?

The psychological egoist would no doubt be appalled by the holocaust, but on what grounds could the egoist legitimately condemn the holocaust? For Thomas Hobbes, the classic psychological egoist, nothing is good or evil in itself. A thing becomes good when it is the object of someone's desires, and evil when it is the object of someone's aversions. There is no standard beyond one's personal preference to judge good or evil. Accordingly, while a psychological egoist could shout condemnation at the Nazis, the Nazis could reply that it was in *their* egoistic interests to exterminate the Jews; in fact, Stalin's purges were justified on more or less this exact basis. The point is that the egoist could not point to an objective standard independent of egoistic impulses to condemn the death camps. To be sure, Hobbes indicates that within the commonwealth there are objective standards—the laws fashioned by selfish people in order to promote their own interests. Yet those laws are laws of convenience that can be jettisoned if they no longer serve the interests of the self. The self's own interests define what is good and evil. This implies standardlessness and points toward moral anarchy.

Similarly, determinists might be repulsed by the horrors of Hitler's death camps, but on what grounds can determinists legitimately condemn Buchenwald and Auschwitz? Is not the determinist ultimately committed to saying that the thoughts and values a person has are so causally interconnected with the other events in the universe that those thoughts and values are the only ones that that person could have possessed at that time and place? If so, how can the determinist legitimately condemn Nazi behavior? If nature and the person's environment caused the value assumptions operative in the behavior of the Nazis, how could a determinist be consistent with deterministic assumptions and still condemn Nazi behavior? If one person is determined by nature to develop hatred for Jews and another to have the values of a caring social worker, must not the determinist accept both as merely variations within nature?

To be sure, determinists could say that they would not have done what the exterminators did. Yet can determinists *justifiably* go beyond that declaration to reject and condemn such behavior as inappropriate and unacceptable on moral grounds? How can determinists avoid accepting as equally legitimate all the moral views held by earth's teeming millions, however idiosyncratic, deviant and repulsive they may be—inasmuch as each person's moral vales are the result of a unique ensemble of conditioning forces? Does not determinism, then, preclude the generation of a standard by which some behaviors can be legitimately rejected and condemned on moral grounds?

Ethical relativists would also face something of the same problem. The cultural group that developed the death camps was acting on its principles; what could a relativist say about this behavior except that our cultural group abhors such behavior? Cross-cultural moral judgments are not acknowledged by relativism because, according to relativist presuppositions, there are no cross-cultural standards. Furthermore, as Walter Stace pointed out, the relativist has serious difficulty defining and defending what is to be considered the relevant social group in terms of which a person's behavior can be legitimately evaluated. Stace suggested that this difficulty leads the relativist to admit that the relevant social group, in the final analysis, is the self. Once again, the outcome is standardlessness and the threat of moral anarchy in which each person defines good and evil.

Emotivists would certainly have grounds for a strong reaction against Nazi behavior. But the moral judgments offered by emotivists would, in terms of the theory, be noncognitive. That is, for the emotivist, when people make moral judgments they are either evincing or asserting feelings, and possibly trying to evoke similar feelings in others. Moral values, accordingly, do not have an objective status independent of a person's emotions or attitudes. Without an objective standard, it is not even possible to say that some emotions are more *fitting* than others when a person is confronted by the activities of the death camps. When moral judgments are reduced in this fashion to a matter of subjective feelings, have we not, once again, encountered standardlessness and the threat of moral anarchy?

In sum, psychological egoism, determinism, ethical relativism, and ethical emotivism all seem to entail standardlessness as the logical outcome of an acceptance of their viewpoints. Without objective standards—that is, without standards that are independent of subjective feelings and reactions—we would be unable to raise our voices in a legitimate moral protest against the holocaust, a protest that condemns as evil and monstrous the actions of those who brutalized and butchered so many human beings.

If such moral evaluation is rendered unsupportable because we have concluded that we live in a world without objective moral standards, then surely the entire moral experience of humankind would be called into question. That is, the overall consequences of adopting any of these four doctrines would be to abandon the search for objective criteria by which to judge the moral issues that face us. Because such abandonment would mean a gutting of the moral experience of humankind, we have sided with the critics in rejecting these four positions. The great challenge for us who reject the subjectivism and standardlessness inherent in these doctrines is to specify and defend the objective standards which we believe are the basis for legitimately pronouncing the holocaust and similar events to be morally abhorrent. That challenge is engaged in the next section of this book.

PART II

What Makes an Action Right?

CHAPTER 5

Actualizing Human Nature

Introduction

One of the oldest and most attractive responses to the question, What ought I to do? is that, I ought to actualize my potentialities as a human being. That response immediately raises the question of which potentialities I ought to actualize, inasmuch as many potentialities that are often incompatible, are presented to me. After all, few of us, if any, can become an artist, attorney, athlete, banker, butcher, baker, poet, philosopher, physician, soldier, sailor, and statesman in one lifetime. We must be selective and somewhat idiosyncratic in these matters. Yet in spite of the different careers we select, is there perhaps something all of us can share as we pursue those careers? Is there perhaps a distinctively human way of pursuing our diverse personal goals? Is there perhaps a distinctive humanness that we all can share and that can be nourished as well as starved? Is there a human nature that can be the common goal of all of us amidst the diversity of our individual pursuits?

Of the many philosophers who answer "Yes" to these questions, we have selected one of Western civilization's monumental thinkers, Aristotle. Aristotle affirmed that we ought to strive to actualize our humanness, and he defined our humanness in terms of that which is distinctive in our nature. As we proceed to an examination of his writings, consider whether or not you agree with Aristotle on the nature of this humanness we ought to actualize, and whether or not you think he presents convincing cases on behalf of his views.

Aristotle: Strive for Happiness

Aristotle was born in 384 B.C. in the city of Stagira in Thrace, where his father, Nicomachus, was physician to Amyntas II, the king of Macedon. At the age of seventeen, Aristotle went to Athens to pursue his education and entered Plato's Academy. For the next twenty years he engaged in continual philosophical dialogue with Plato, who was the most illustrious disciple of Socrates. When Plato died in 347 B.C., leadership of the Academy passed into the hands of Plato's nephew, Speusippus, with whom Aristotle did not see eye to eye. Accordingly, Aristotle departed from the Academy. After several years of travel with extended stays in Assos and Mitylene, he accepted the invitation of Philip II of Macedon to supervise the education of Philip's thirteen-year-old son.

Thus, in 342, Aristotle took up residence at the royal Macedonian court in Pella to instruct a young man who would become known to posterity as Alexander the Great. When Alexander ascended the throne in 335 B.C., Aristotle left Macedon, presumably because his work as a princely tutor had ended. Legend has it, however, that Alexander never forgot his old teacher, because wherever his armies went they were instructed, so we are told, to send back to Aristotle any unusual biological specimens they encountered so that Aristotle's ever-inquisitive mind would have fresh data to analyze and classify.

Aristotle returned to Athens, where he established his own school that took on two different names: the Lyceum, because it was located in the precincts of Apollo Lyceus, and the Peripatos. Its members were known as the Peripatetics, because they often carried on their philosophical discussions while walking back and forth in the school's portico. The Lyceum was somewhat similar to a university in that instruction was given and research was pursued. When Alexander died in 323 B.C., reaction against the Macedonian hegemony in Greece spread through Athens. Aristotle consequently left Athens and took refuge at Chalcis in Euboea, where he enjoyed the protection of a Macedonian garrison. Later, in reflecting upon his departure from Athens, he is reputed to have said that he did not want "the Athenians to sin twice against philosophy." After all, they had been responsible for the death of Socrates, and could conceivably conspire against another philosopher. He died of poor health in 322 B.C. at Chalcis, leaving behind a wealth of philosophical treatises.

Accounting for Change

In seeking to discover Aristotle's answer to the question, What ought I to do? we discover that he based his answer on his analysis of the nature of humanness. A survey of his works reveals that he used many expressions to describe human uniqueness. He defined the human as an animal capable of acquiring knowledge, and as an animal that walks on two feet. He also described the human as the only animal that can learn to use both hands equally, that can contract white leprosy, that can suffer from gallstones, that has speech, that laughs, and that deliberates. These descriptions reveal to us the breadth of Aristotle's learning, but they do not indicate the depth of his insight into the nature of humanness. To encounter that insight we must turn to one of his extended discussions of human nature, such as is found in *Nicomachean Ethics*. This treatise, from which the following passages have been taken, was probably given its present title by Aristotle's disciples to honor either Aristotle's father (Nicomachus) or Aristotle's son (also named Nicomachus), who edited the work after the death of Aristotle.

To gain an adequate perspective on Aristotle's view of humanness, we must comment briefly on one of the important philosophical questions that Aristotle inherited from his predecessors, namely, the problem of explaining change. Some commentators on Aristotle prefer to talk about the problem of accounting for motion, but it will perhaps be easier to understand Aristotle's position if we think in terms of change rather than motion alone. In responding to this challenge, Aristotle suggested that change involves the actualization of potentialities. All things, except God, he claimed, are a combination of actuality (or "isness") and potentiality (or "maybeness"). All things, except God, are subject to change, that is, are striving to actualize their potentialities. God, however, is pure actuality. He has no potentialities to actualize. He is perfectly at rest. He is the loftiest of beings—pure thought, contemplating the loftiest of thoughts—himself. This God, engaged in perpetual contemplation of himself, causes change not by doing something but by being what he is. He is perfect actuality, and all things desire to be like him—fully actualized. He is the object of desire of all beings. He is, so to speak, an irresistible attractive force that draws all beings toward himself, toward actuality: he attracts them into change. This God, however, is not aware of these beings he is influencing. To be aware of them would open up the possibility of change in God (that is, God moving from one thought to another). If this were to happen, God would no longer be that ultimate force that is the source of all change. If God changed, there would have to be a force beyond God that was the source of his change. Aristotle rejected the notion of an infinite regress of changing changers as providing no satisfactory explanation of change. He adopted instead the concept of an "Unmoved Mover"—a God who does not move or change but moves all things.

One of the beings that God produces change in is the human. We are all changing, actualizing potentialities. Over some of these changes we have virtually no control, such as the sudden pain from a bee sting or the excretion of certain glands. Over other changes we exercise control, and we call these changes or motions voluntary. The task of ethics is to analyze and assess the nature of and conditions associated with these voluntary motions. In other words, ethics analyzes and assesses the potentialities that are open to human beings, and seeks to provide guidance for humans when they are confronted by competing, alternative potentialities.

Identifying Humankind's Chief Good

Aristotle begins *Nicomachean Ethics* by indicating that his discussion will seek to identify and clarify the chief good (that is, the chief, desirable potentiality) for human beings. Aristotle believes that this good must embrace all the persons of the state, because a corporate good is more complete, and hence more godlike than an individual good. Indeed, Aristotle construes the human being to be inherently social. Because it is the role of politics to identify and legislate the chief good for humankind, Aristotle calls his inquiry "political science" and occasionally addresses his readers as "students of political science." At the heart of a political science that is doing its job, then, is sound ethical inquiry.

In attempting to identify the chief good for human beings, the chief desirable potentiality, Aristotle draws an important distinction between goods or ends that are desired for the sake of something else, and goods or ends that are desirable in themselves. Philosophers today commonly refer to the former as instrumental goods and to the latter as intrinsic goods.

> * Since there are evidently more than one end, and we choose some of these (e.g. wealth, flutes, and in general instruments) for the sake of something else, clearly not all ends are final ends; but the chief good is evidently something final. Therefore, if there is only one final end, this will be what we are seeking, and if there are more than one, the most final of these will be what we are seeking. Now we call that which is in itself worthy of pursuit more final than that which is worthy of pursuit for the sake of something else, and that which is never desirable for the sake of something else more final than the things that are desirable both in themselves and for the sake of that other thing, and therefore we call final without qualification that which is always desirable in itself and never for the sake of something else.
>
> Now such a thing happiness, above all else, is held to be; for this we choose always for itself and never for the sake of something else, but honour, pleasure, reason, and every virtue we choose indeed for themselves (for if nothing resulted from them we should still choose each of them), but we choose them also for the sake of happiness, judging that by means of them we shall be happy. Happiness, on the other hand, no one chooses for the sake of these, nor, in general, for anything other than itself.
>
> From the point of view of self-sufficiency the same result seems to follow; for the final good is thought to be self-sufficient. Now by self-sufficient we do not mean that which is sufficient for a man by himself, for one who lives a solitary life, but also for parents, children, wife, and in general for his friends and fellow citizens, since man is born for citizenship. But some limit must be set to this; for if we extend our requirement to ancestors and descendants and friends' friends we are in for an infinite series. Let us examine this question, however, on another occasion; the self-sufficient we now define as that which when isolated makes life desirable and lacking in nothing; and such we think happiness to be; and further we think it most desirable of all things, without being counted as one good thing among others—if it were so counted it would clearly be made more desirable by the addition of even the least of goods; for that which is added becomes

* FROM Aristotle, *Nichomachean Ethics,* translated by W.D. Ross in *The Oxford Translation of Aristotle,* edited by W.D. Ross (Oxford: Oxford University Press, 1925) Vol. 9. Used by permission of Oxford University Press.

an excess of goods, and of goods the greater is always more desirable. Happiness, then, is something final and self-sufficient, and is the end of action.

Clarifying Human Happiness

The chief good, then, is happiness. But human beings differ considerably about the meaning of happiness. Some identify happiness with sensual pleasure. Others say that to be happy is to be wealthy, or to be happy is to be honored by other people, or to be happy is to be contemplating truth. To sort out what human happiness really is, we must identify that over-all human function which is uniquely human because the performing of that function harbors the possibility of distinctively human happiness. Notice how godlike the distinctively human function is, according to Aristotle. Also, notice that this function must be performed with the appropriate "excellence" or "virtue" in order to generate happiness.

Presumably, however, to say that happiness is the chief good seems a platitude, and a clearer account of what it is is still desired. This might perhaps be given, if we could first ascertain the function of man. For just as for a flute-player, a sculptor, or any artist, and, in general, for all things that have a function or activity, the good and the 'well' is thought to reside in the function, so would it seem to be for man, if he has a function. Have the carpenter, then, and the tanner certain functions or activities, and has man none? Is he born without a function? Or as eye, hand, foot, and in general each of the parts evidently has a function, may one lay it down that man similarly has a function apart from all these? What then can this be? Life seems to be common even to plants, but we are seeking what is peculiar to man. Let us exclude, therefore, the life of nutrition and growth. Next there would be a life of perception, but *it* also seems to be common even to the horse, the ox, and every animal. There remains, then, an active life of the elements that has a rational principle; of this, one part has such a principle in the sense of being obedient to one, the other in the sense of possessing one and exercising thought. And, as 'life of the rational element' also has two meanings, we must state that life in the sense of activity is what we mean; for this seems to be the more proper sense of the term. Now if the function of man is an activity of soul which follows or implies a rational principle, and if we say 'a so-and-so' and 'a good so-and-so' have a function which is the same in kind. e.g. a lyre-player and a good lyre-player, and so without qualification in all cases, eminence in respect of goodness being added to the name of the function (for the function of a lyre-player is to play the lyre, and that of a good lyre-player to do so well): if this is the case, [and we state the function of man to be a certain kind of life, and this to be an activity or actions of the soul implying a rational principle, and the function of a good man to be the good and noble performance of these, and if any action is well performed when it is performed in accordance with the appropriate excellence: if this is the case,] human good turns out to be activity of soul in accordance with virtue, and if there are more than one virtue, in accordance with the best and most complete.

But we must add 'in a complete life'. For one swallow does not make a summer, nor does one day; and so too one day, or a short time, does not make a man blessed and happy. . . .

Understanding Virtue and the Soul

A human being's chief good is happiness. And happiness is to be realized through that function which is distinctively human. That function is action in accordance with a rational principle. Such action generates happiness when it is performed with the appropriate excellence or virtue. To clarify happiness further we need to explore the nature of virtue and the nature of the soul (which is the seat of this distinctively human activity).

Since happiness is an activity of soul in accordance with perfect virtue, we must consider the nature of virtue; for perhaps we shall thus see better the nature of happiness. The true student of politics, too, is thought to have studied virtue above all things; for he wishes to make his fellow citizens good and obedient to the laws. . . .

But clearly the virtue we must study is human virtue; for the good we were seeking was human good and the happiness human happiness. By human virtue we mean not that of the body but that of the soul; and happiness also we call an activity of soul. But if this is so, clearly the student of politics must know somehow the facts about soul, as the man who is to heal the eyes or the body as a whole must know about the eyes or the body; and all the more since politics is more prized and better than medicine; but even among doctors the best educated spend much labour on acquiring knowledge of the body. The student of politics, then, must study the soul, and must study it with these objects in view, and do so just to the extent which is sufficient for the questions we are discussing; for further precision is perhaps something more laborious than our purposes require.

Some things are said about it, adequately enough, even in the discussions outside our school, and we must use these; e.g. that one element in the soul is irrational and one has a rational principle. Whether these are separated as the parts of the body or of anything divisible are or are distinct by definition but by nature inseparable, like convex and concave in the circumference of a circle, does not affect the present question.

Of the irrational element one division seems to be widely distributed, and vegetative in its nature, I mean that which causes nutrition and growth; for it is this kind of power of the soul that one must assign to all nurslings and to embryos, and this same power to full-grown creatures; this is more reasonable than to assign some different power to them. Now the excellence of this seems to be common to all species and not specifically human; for this part or faculty seems to function most in sleep, while goodness and badness are least manifest in sleep (whence comes the saying that the happy are no better off than the wretched for half their lives; and this happens naturally enough, since sleep is an inactivity of the soul in that respect in which it is called good or bad), unless perhaps to a small extent some of the movements actually penetrate to the soul, and in this respect the dreams of good men are better than those of ordinary people. Enough of this subject, however; let us leave the nutritive faculty alone, since it has by its nature no share in human excellence.

There seems to be also another irrational element in the soul—one which in a sense, however, shares in a rational principle. For we praise the rational principle of the continent man and of the incontinent, and the part of their soul that has such a principle, since it urges them aright and towards the best objects; but there is found in them also another element naturally opposed to the rational principle, which fights against and resists that principle. For exactly as paralysed limbs when we intend to move them to the right turn on the contrary to the left, so is it with the soul; the impulses of incontinent people move in contrary directions. But while in the body we see that which moves astray, in the soul we do not. No doubt, however, we must none the less suppose that in the soul too there is something contrary to the rational principle, resisting and opposing it. In what sense it is distinct from the other elements does not concern us. Now even this seems to have a share in a rational principle, as we said; at any rate in the continent man it obeys the rational principle—and presumably in the temperate and brave man it is still more obedient; for in him it speaks, on all matters, with the same voice as the rational principle.

Therefore the irrational element also appears to be twofold. For the vegetative element in no way shares in a rational principle, but the appetitive, and in general the desiring element in a sense shares in it, in so far as it listens to and obeys it; this is the sense in which we speak of 'taking account' of one's father or one's friends, not that in which we speak of 'accounting' for a mathematical property. That the irrational element is in some sense persuaded by a rational principle is indicated also by the giving of advice and by all reproof and exhortation. And if this element also must be said to have a rational principle, that which has a rational principle (as well as that which has not) will be twofold, one subdivision having it in the strict sense and in itself, and the other having a tendency to obey as one does one's father.

Virtue too is distinguished into kinds in accordance with this difference; for we say that some of the virtues are intellectual and others moral, philosophic wisdom and understanding and practical wisdom being intellectual, liberality and temperance moral. For in speaking about a man's character we do not say that he is wise or has understanding but that he is good-tempered or temperate; yet we praise the wise man also with respect to his state of mind; and of states of mind we call those which merit praise virtues.

The human soul, accordingly, has two major divisions: the irrational part (subdivided into the vegetative and appetitive elements) and the rational part (subdivided into the scientific and calculative elements, which Aristotle discusses in a later selection). The rational part, of course, possesses rational principles and evidences the distinctive human function of reasoning. When that part is functioning properly, intellectual virtue or excellence is present. The irrational part does not possess a rational principle, but the appetitive element can be obedient to a rational principle. When that appetitive element is obeying properly a rational principle, moral virtue of excellence is present. Intellectual virtue is acquired through teaching, whereas moral virtue is developed through habit.

Acquiring Moral Virtue

Aristotle now focuses his attention on moral virtue, exploring the meaning of acquiring moral virtue by habit. That is, he asks what it means to say that we become just by doing just acts, brave by doing brave acts, and so forth.

> The question might be asked, what do we mean by saying that we must become just by doing just acts, and temperate by doing temperate acts; for if men do just and temperate acts, they are already just and temperate, exactly as, if they do what is in accordance with the laws of grammar and of music, they are grammarians and musicians.
>
> Or is this not true even of the arts? It is possible to do something that is in accordance with the laws of grammar, either by chance or at the suggestion of another. A man will be a grammarian, then, only when he has both done something grammatical and done it grammatically; and this means doing it in accordance with the grammatical knowledge in himself.
>
> Again, the case of the arts and that of the virtues are not similar; for the products of the arts have their goodness in themselves, so that it is enough that they should have a certain character, but if the acts that are in accordance with the virtues have themselves a certain character it does not follow that they are done justly or temperately. The agent also must be in a certain condition when he does them; in the first place he must have knowledge, secondly he must choose the acts, and choose them for their own sakes, and thirdly his action must proceed from a firm and unchangeable character. These are not reckoned in as conditions of the possession of the arts, except the bare knowledge; but as a condition of the possession of the virtues knowledge has little or no weight, while the other conditions count not for a little but for everything, i.e. the very conditions which result from often doing just and temperate acts.
>
> Actions, then, are called just and temperate when they are such as the just or the temperate man would do; but it is not the man who does these that is just and temperate, but the man who also does them *as* just and temperate men do them. It is well said, then, that it is by doing just acts that the just man is produced, and by doing temperate acts the temperate man; without doing these no one would have a prospect of becoming good.
>
> But most people do not do these, but take refuge in theory and think they are being philosophers and will become good in this way, behaving somewhat like patients who listen attentively to their doctors, but do none of the things they are ordered to do. As the latter will not be made well

in body by such a course of treatment, the former will not be made well in soul by such a course of philosophy.

So one acquires moral virtues by doing deeds *as* a morally virtuous person would do them. The nature of moral virtue, however, needs further clarification. Already Aristotle has noted that moral virtue involves the disciplining of the appetites by a rational principle. Now he proceeds to call this disciplining a "state of character." He articulates the rational principle to which the appetites should be subject. That principle is his famous dictum that virtue is the mean between extremes.

> We must, however, not only describe virtue as a state of character, but also say what sort of state it is. We may remark, then, that every virtue or excellence both brings into good condition the thing of which it is the excellence and makes the work of that thing be done well; e.g. the excellence of the eye makes both the eye and its work good; for it is by the excellence of the eye that we see well. Similarly the excellence of the horse makes a horse both good in itself and good at running and at carrying its rider and at awaiting the attack of the enemy. Therefore, if this is true in every case, the virtue of man also will be the state of character which makes a man good and which makes him do his own work well. . . .
>
> If it is . . . that every art does its work well—by looking to the intermediate and judging its works by this standard (so that we often say of good works of art that it is not possible either to take away or to add anything, implying that excess and defect destroy the goodness of works of art, while the mean preserves it; and good artists, as we say, look to this in their work), and if, further, virtue is more exact and better than any art, as nature also is, then virtue must have the quality of aiming at the intermediate. I mean moral virtue; for it is this that is concerned with passions and actions, and in these there is excess, defect, and the intermediate. For instance, both fear and confidence and appetite and anger and pity and in general pleasure and pain may be felt both too much and too little, and in both cases not well; but to feel them at the right times, with reference to the right objects, towards the right people, with the right motive, and in the right way, is what is both intermediate and best, and this is characteristic of virtue. Similarly with regard to actions also there is excess, defect, and the intermediate. Now virtue is concerned with passions and actions, in which excess is a form of failure, and so is defect, while the intermediate is praised and is a form of success; and being praised and being successful are both characteristics of virtue. Therefore virtue is a kind of mean, since, as we have seen, it aims at what is intermediate.
>
> Again, it is possible to fail in many ways (for evil belongs to the class of the unlimited, as the Pythagoreans conjectured, and good to that of the limited), while to succeed is possible only in one way (for which reason also one is easy and the other difficult—to miss the mark easy, to hit it difficult); for these reasons also, then, excess and defect are characteristic of vice, and the mean of virtue;

For men are good in but one way, but bad in many.

Virtue, then, is a state of character concerned with choice, lying in a mean, i.e. the mean relative to us, this being determined by a rational principle, and by that principle by which the man of practical wisdom would determine it. Now it is a mean between two vices, that which depends on excess and that which depends on defect; and again it is a mean because the vices respectively fall short of or exceed what is right in both passions and actions, while virtue both finds and chooses that which is intermediate. Hence in respect of its substance and the definition which states its essence virtue is a mean, with regard to what is best and right an extreme.

But not every action nor every passion admits of a mean; for some have names that already imply badness, e.g. spite, shamelessness, envy, and in the case of actions adultery, theft, murder; for all of these and suchlike things imply by their names that they are themselves bad, and not the excesses or deficiencies of them. It is not possible, then, ever to be right with regard to them; one must always be wrong. Nor does goodness or badness with regard to such things depend on committing adultery with the right woman, at the right time, and in the right way, but simply to do any of them is to go wrong. It would be equally absurd, then, to expect that in unjust, cowardly, and voluptuous action there should be a mean, an excess, and a deficiency; for at that rate there would be a mean of excess and of deficiency, an excess of excess, and a deficiency of deficiency. But as there is no excess and deficiency of temperance and courage because what is intermediate is in a sense an extreme, so too of the actions we have mentioned there is no mean nor any excess and deficiency, but however they are done they are wrong; for in general there is neither a mean of excess and deficiency, nor excess and deficiency of a mean.

We must, however, not only make this general statement, but also apply it to the individual facts. For among statements about conduct those which are general apply more widely, but those which are particular are more genuine, since conduct has to do with individual cases, and our statements must harmonize with the facts in these cases. . . . With regard to feelings of fear and confidence courage is the mean; of the people who exceed he who exceeds in fearlessness has no name (many of the states have no name), while the man who exceeds in confidence is rash, and he who exceeds in fear and falls short in confidence is a coward. With regard to pleasures and pains—not all of them, and not so much with regard to the pains—the mean is temperance, the excess self-indulgence. Persons deficient with regard to the pleasures are not often found; hence such persons also have received no name. But let us call them insensible.

With regard to giving and taking of money the mean is liberality, the excess and the defect prodigality and meanness. In these actions people exceed and fall short in contrary ways; the prodigal exceeds in spending and falls short in taking, while the mean man exceeds in taking and falls short in spending. . . .

With regard to honour and dishonour the mean is proper pride, the excess is known as a sort of 'empty vanity', and the deficiency is undue humility. . . .

With regard to anger also there is an excess, a deficiency, and a mean. Although they can scarcely be said to have names, yet since we call the intermediate person good-tempered let us call the mean good temper; of the persons at the extremes let the one who exceeds be called irascible, and his vice irascibility, and the man who falls short an inirascible sort of person, and the deficiency inirascibility. . . .

That moral virtue is a mean, then, and in what sense it is so, and that it is a mean between two vices, the one involving excess, the other deficiency, and that it is such because its character is to aim at what is intermediate in passions and in actions, has been sufficiently stated. Hence also it is no easy task to be good. For in everything it is no easy task to find the middle, e.g. to find the middle of a circle is not for every one but him who knows; so, too, any one can get angry—that is easy—or give or spend money; but to do this to the right person, to the right extent, at the right time, with the right motive, and in the right way, *that* is not for every one, nor is it easy; wherefore goodness is both rare and laudable and noble. . . .

Pursuing the Golden Mean

This last passage explains what has come to be called the "golden mean" (although Aristotle did not call it that any more than Jesus called his own famous statement the "golden rule"). Aristotle has argued that moral virtue is midway, a mean, between an excess and a deficiency of activity. Perhaps his point will be clearer when seen in the following tabular form.

ACTIVITY	DEFECT	MEAN	EXCESS
Confidence	Cowardice	Courage	Rashness
Pleasures/Pains	No Name	Temperance	Self-Indulgence
Giving/Taking of Money	Meanness	Liberality	Prodigality
Honor/Dishonor	Undue Humility	Proper Pride	Empty Vanity
Anger	Inirascibility	Good Temper	Irascibility

Aristotle says that some actions have no mean because they are excessive in themselves, murder and theft being good examples. It is also important to note that the mean is not the same for everybody. A large person may need twice as much food as a small person, so the mean for each differs. The obese person may need twice as much food to be "moderate," in Aristotle's sense of the term, as a thin person needs to be moderate. How do we determine, then, what the mean is? Aristotle answers that we must seek the interpretation of a rational person. Recall Aristotle's definition of virtue: "Virtue . . . is a state of character concerned with choice, lying in a mean . . . relative to us, this being determined by a rational principle, and by that principle by which the man of practical wisdom would determine it."

Developing Intellectual Virtue

Turning now to Aristotle's analysis of the rational part of the soul, we are afforded not only a discussion of intellectual virtue but also additional insight concerning the nature of moral virtue. Like the irrational part, the rational part is divided into two elements: the scientific part that contemplates invariable or unchanging things, and the calculative part that contemplates variable things.

> We divided the virtues of the soul and said that some are virtues of character and others of intellect. Now we have discussed in detail the moral virtues; with regard to the others let us express our view as follows, beginning with some remarks about the soul. We said before that there are two parts of the soul—that which grasps a rule or rational principle, and the irrational; let us now draw a similar distinction within the part which grasps a rational principle. And let it be assumed that there are two parts which grasp a rational principle—one by which we contemplate the kind of things whose originative causes are invariable, and one by which we contemplate variable things; for where objects differ in kind the part of the soul answering to each of the two is different in kind, since it is in virtue of a certain likeness and kinship with their objects that they have the knowledge they have. Let one of these parts be called the scientific and the other the calculative; for to deliberate and to calculate are the same thing, but no one deliberates about the invariable. Therefore the calculative is one part of the faculty which grasps a rational principle. We must, then, learn what is the best state of each of these two parts; for this is the virtue of each.

The proper work of both intellectual parts of the soul is truth, and the states of mind by which truth is possessed are the intellectual virtues. Aristotle identifies five such virtues. First, there is scientific knowledge (not to be confused with modern scientific knowledge), whose object is things that are invariable, that are necessarily so, that are eternal, that are the conclusions demonstrated by logic and observation. Second, there is art, which is concerned with making things, with contriving and considering how something can be brought into being. An object of art could just as readily not have been made. Art, accordingly, deals with the variable, with things that could have been made other than they were. Third, there is practical wisdom, which also deals with the variable. Practical wisdom involves commendable deliberation about the means to achieve a good end (to achieve a worthy goal other than making an object of art). Practical wisdom entails assessing the appropriate actions for achieving the good life. Practical wisdom relates to things done or to actions. Art encompasses things made. Fourth, there is intuitive reason, which involves grasping the first principles upon which scientific knowledge is founded. Fifth, there is philosophic wisdom, which is based upon intuitive reason combined with scientific knowledge. The aim of philosophic wisdom is to generate a knowledge of the highest and best objects (and, of course, the highest and best object is not man but the Unmoved Mover). Of these intellectual virtues, it is practical wisdom that relates to moral virtue.

Practical wisdom is not simply the capacity to determine the most effective way of acting in order to achieve a goal. The desired goal itself must be worthy. Morally virtuous action, then, originates in choice, which in turn is based upon reasoning about the appropriate means to achieve a worthy end.

> The virtue of a thing is relative to its proper work. Now there are three things in the soul which control action and truth—sensation, reason, desire.
>
> Of these sensation originates no action; this is plain from the fact that the lower animals have sensation but no share in action.
>
> What affirmation and negation are in thinking, pursuit and avoidance are in desire; so that since moral virtue is a state of character concerned with choice, and choice is deliberate desire, therefore both the reasoning must be true and the desire right, if the choice is to be good, and the latter must pursue just what the former asserts. Now this kind of intellect and of truth is practical; of the intellect which is contemplative, not practical nor productive, the good and the bad state are truth and falsity respectively (for this is the work of everything intellectual); while of the part which is practical and intellectual the good state is truth in agreement with right desire.
>
> The origin of action—its efficient, not its final cause—is choice, and that of choice is desire and reasoning with a view to an end. This is why choice cannot exist either without reason and intellect or without a moral state; for good action and its opposite cannot exist without a combination of intellect and character. Intellect itself, however, moves nothing, but only the intellect which aims at an end and is practical; for this rules the productive intellect as well, since every one who makes makes for an end, and that which is made is not an end in the unqualified sense (but only an end in a particular relation, and the end of a particular operation)—only that which is *done* is that; for good action is an end, and desire aims at this. Hence choice is either desiderative reason or ratiocinative desire, and such an origin of action is a man.

Achieving Human Happiness

Toward the end of his treatise Aristotle returns to the issue of the nature of human happiness—the chief good. Having identified reasoning as the distinctive human function, and having discussed how moral virtue arises within the irrational part of the soul when the appetites are disciplined by a rational principle, and having explored the states of the rational soul which exhibit intellectual virtues, Aristotle is prepared to declare which virtues are superior to the rest and to argue that those who practice those superior virtues are the happiest, the most godlike, and the dearest to the gods. Why? That which is the distincively human trait is reason. When we act rationally—in the sense with which Aristotle has analyzed this term—we are using that aspect of our nature that is uniquely human. By developing this uniquely human capacity to the fullest, we will achieve happiness.

If happiness is activity in accordance with virtue, it is reasonable that it should be in accordance with the highest virtue; and this will be that of the best thing in us. Whether it be reason or something else that is this element which is thought to be our natural ruler and guide and to take thought of things noble and divine, whether it be itself also divine or only the most divine element in us, the activity of this in accordance with its proper virtue will be perfect happiness. That this activity is contemplative we have already said.

Now this would seem to be in agreement both with what we said before and with the truth. For, firstly, this activity is the best (since not only is reason the best thing in us, but the objects of reason are the best of knowable objects); and, secondly, it is the most continuous, since we can contemplate truth more continuously than we can *do* anything. And we think happiness has pleasure mingled with it, but the activity of philosophic wisdom is admittedly the pleasantest of virtuous activities; at all events the pursuit of it is thought to offer pleasures marvellous for their purity and their enduringness, and it is to be expected that those who know will pass their time more pleasantly than those who inquire. And the self-sufficiency that is spoken of must belong most to the contemplative activity. For while a philosopher, as well as a just man or one possessing any other virtue, needs the necessaries of life, when they are sufficiently equipped with things of that sort the just man needs people towards whom and with whom he shall act justly, and the temperate man, the brave man, and each of the others is in the same case, but the philosopher, even when by himself, can contemplate truth, and the better the wiser he is; he can perhaps do so better if he has fellow-workers, but still he is the most self-sufficient. And this activity alone would seem to be loved for its own sake; for nothing arises from it apart from the contemplating, while from practical activities we gain more or less apart from the action. And happiness is thought to depend on leisure; for we are busy that we may have leisure, and make war that we may live in peace. Now the activity of the practical virtues is exhibited in political or military affairs, but the actions concerned with these seem to be unleisurely. Warlike actions are completely so (for no one chooses to be at war, or provokes war, for the sake of being at war; any one would seem absolutely murderous if he were to make enemies of his friends in order to bring about battle and slaughter); but the action of the statesman is also unleisurely, and—apart from the political action itself—aims at despotic power and honours, or at all events happiness, for him and his fellow citizens—a happiness different from political action, and evidently sought as being different. So if among virtuous actions political and military actions are distinguished by nobility and greatness, and these are unleisurely and aim at an end and are not desirable for their own sake, but the activity of reason, which is contemplative, seems both to be superior in serious worth and to aim at no end beyond itself, and to have its pleasure proper to itself (and this augments the activity), and the self-sufficiency, leisureliness, unweariedness (so far as this is possible for man), and all the other attributes ascribed to the supremely happy man are evidently those connected with this activity, it follows that this will be the complete happiness of man, if it be allowed a complete term of life (for none of the attributes of happiness is *in*complete).

But such a life would be too high for man; for it is not in so far as he is man that he will live so, but in so far as something divine is present in him; and by so much as this is superior to our composite nature is its activity superior to that which is the exercise of the other kind of virtue. If reason is divine, then, in comparison with man, the life according to it is divine in comparison with human life. But we must not follow those who advise us, being men, to think of human things, and, being mortal, of mortal things, but must, so far as we can make ourselves immortal, and strain every nerve to live in accordance with the best thing in us; for even if it be small in bulk, much more does it in power and worth surpass everything. This would seem, too, to be each man himself, since it is the authoritative and better part of him. It would be strange, then, if he were to choose not the life of his self but that of something else. And what we said before will apply now; that which is proper to each thing is by nature best and most pleasant for each thing; for man, therefore, the life according to reason is best and pleasantest, since reason more than anything else *is* man. This life therefore is also the happiest.

But in a secondary degree the life in accordance with the other kind of virtue is happy; for the activities in accordance with this befit our human estate. Just and brave acts, and other virtuous acts, we do in relation to each other, observing our respective duties with regard to contracts and services and all manner of actions and with regard to passions; and all of these seem to be typically human. Some of them seem even to arise from the body, and virtue of character to be in many ways bound up with the passions. Practical wisdom, too, is linked to virtue of character, and this to practical wisdom, since the principles of practical wisdom are in accordance with the moral virtues and rightness in morals is in accordance with practical wisdom. Being connected with the passions also, the moral virtues must belong to our composite nature; and the virtues of our composite nature are human; so, therefore, are the life and the happiness which correspond to these. The excellence of the reason is a thing apart; we must be content to say this much about it, for to describe it precisely is a task greater than our purpose requires. It would seem, however, also to need external equipment but little, or less than moral virtue does. Grant that both need the necessaries, and do so equally, even if the statesman's work is the more concerned with the body and things of that sort; for there will be little difference there; but in what they need for the exercise of their activities there will be much difference. The liberal man will need money for the doing of his liberal deeds, and the just man too will need it for the returning of services (for wishes are hard to discern, and even people who are not just pretend to wish to act justly); and the brave man will need power if he is to accomplish any of the acts that correspond to his virtue, and the temperate man will need opportunity; for how else is either he or any of the others to be recognized? It is debated, too, whether the will or the deed is more essential to virtue, which is assumed to involve both; it is surely clear that its perfection involves both; but for deeds many things are needed, and more, the greater and nobler the deeds are. But the man who is contemplating the truth needs no such thing, at least with a view to the exercise of his activity; indeed they are, one may say, even hindrances, at all events to his contemplation; but in so far as he is a man and lives with a number of people, he chooses to do virtuous acts; he will therefore need such aids to living a human life.

But that perfect happiness is a contemplative activity will appear from the following consideration as well. We assume the gods to be above all other beings blessed and happy; but what sort of actions must we assign to them? Acts of justice? Will not the gods seem absurd if they make contracts and return deposits, and so on? Acts of a brave man, then, confronting dangers and running risks because it is noble to do so? Or liberal acts? To whom will they give? It will be strange if they are really to have money or anything of the kind. And what would their temperate acts be? Is not such praise tasteless, since they have no bad appetites? If we were to run through them all, the circumstances of action would be found trivial and unworthy of gods. Still, every one supposes that they *live* and therefore that they are active; we cannot suppose them to sleep like Endymion. Now if you take away from a living being action, and still more production, what is left but contemplation? Therefore the activity of God, which surpasses all others in blessedness, must be contemplative; and of human activities, therefore, that which is most akin to this must be most of the nature of happiness.

This is indicated, too, by the fact that the other animals have no share in happiness, being completely deprived of such activity. For while the whole life of the gods is blessed, and that of men too in so far as some likeness of such activity belongs to them, none of the other animals is happy, since they in no way share in contemplation. Happiness, therefore, must be some form of contemplation.

But, being a man, one will also need external prosperity; for our nature is not self-sufficient for the purpose of contemplation, but our body also must be healthy and must have food and other attention. Still, we must not think that the man who is to be happy will need many things or great things, merely because he cannot be supremely happy without external goods; for self-sufficiency and action do not involve excess, and we can do noble acts without ruling earth and sea; for even with moderate advantages one can act virtuously (this is manifest enough; for private persons are thought to do worthy acts no less than despots—indeed even more); and it is enough that we should have so much as that; for the life of the man who is active in accordance with virtue will be happy. Solon, too, was perhaps sketching well the happy man when he described him as moderately furnished with externals but as having done (as Solon thought) the noblest acts, and lived temperately; for one can with but moderate possessions do what one ought. Anaxagoras also seems to have supposed the happy man not to be rich nor a despot, when he said that he would not be surprised if the happy man were to seem to most people a strange person; for they judge by externals, since these are all they perceive. The opinions of the wise seem, then, to harmonize with our arguments. But while even such things carry some conviction, the truth in practical matters is discerned from the facts of life; for these are the decisive factor. We must therefore survey what we have already said, bringing it to the test of the facts of life, and if it harmonizes with the facts we must accept it, but if it clashes with them we must suppose it to be mere theory. Now he who exercises his reason and cultivates it seems to be both in the best state of mind and the most dear to the gods. For if the gods have any care for human affairs, as they are thought to have, it would be reasonable both that they should delight in that which was best and most akin to them (i.e. reason) and that they should reward those who love and honour this most, as caring for the things that are dear to them and acting both rightly and nobly. And that all these attributes belong most of all to the philosopher is manifest. He, therefore, is the dearest to the gods. And he who is that will presumably be also the happiest; so that in this way too the philosopher will more than any other be happy.

In summary, if we posed our ethical question, What ought I to do? to Aristotle, his response would be that we should develop our human uniqueness with the appropriate excellence or virtue. That is to say, we should practice the moral virtues as a good person would, and we should develop the intellectual virtues as a wise person would. Especially, we should give our attention to the pursuit of philosophic wisdom and thereby actualize our highest potentialities, and thereby become most truly happy. No doubt Aristotle would be quick to add that our happiness must never be construed individualistically, as if it were possible apart from society. For Aristotle, "He who is unable to live in society, or who has no need because he is sufficient for himself, must be either a beast or a god . . ."* The human is by nature inescapably social.

It is important to note that Aristotle's discussion of ethics depends upon a model of the good and wise person that Aristotle simply assumes and does not defend. Over and over again he declares that a particular human excellence is defined and delineated by the performance of the good and wise man. No doubt Aristotle's contemporaries understood, and perhaps many endorsed, the model of the good and wise man that informed his ethic. Yet Aristotle's model was much more than a reflection of public opinion concerning goodness and wisdom. For him, his model was probably the product of intuitive reason grasping the first principles of human virtue. His ethic, then, is to be seen more as an explanation than as a defense of his model of humanness. In short, Aristotle assumes what he is trying to prove. If we accept the premise that to be human is to be rational, then we could conclude that the life of reason is the highest to which we can aspire. If we reject the premise, then Aristotle's conclusion does not follow.

* *Politics,* 1253ᵃ, 25–30.

Epicurus: Seek Tranquility

As the second representative of the perspective that counsels us to actualize our potentialities as human beings, we have chosen Epicurus (341–270 B.C.), a younger contemporary of Aristotle. Although we know of no direct contact between Aristotle and Epicurus, we can see some similarity in their points of view. Partly this is due to the general milieu in ancient Greece. The view that moderation, contemplation, and happiness were important to self-fulfillment was in the air, and what we see in Epicurus is another variation on these themes. Epicurus is usually classified as an egoistic hedonist, inasmuch as he emphasized the pursuit of pleasure for each individual (*hedonism* comes from the Greek word for pleasure; it refers to any ethical view whose primary emphasis is on pleasure).

Another reason for including Epicurus in this textbook is to illustrate the limitations that a person of reason will place on the pursuit of pleasure. The term *epicurean* has entered our language to refer to someone profligate in their lifestyle, someone who goes to excess in pursuit of the ultimate in pleasurable experiences. As we look further into Epicurus's writings, we will see that the association of his name with excesses in the pursuit of pleasure is a great injustice.

Epicurus was born in 341 B.C. on the Athenian island colony of Samos across the Aegean Sea. Although his parents were apparently rather poor, Epicurus was able at the age of fourteen to study at a famous school on the neighboring island of Teos, where he learned the atomic philosophy of Democritus. According to Democritus, all reality can be explained ultimately in terms of physical matter, small bits of "stuff" (atoms) moving about in the void. He denied that there was a God or any transcendent reality.

When Epicurus was eighteen, his studies were interrupted by a year of compulsory military service in Athens. At this time, the death of Alexander the Great (356–323 B.C.) contributed to the unrest and social instability brewing in the vast Greek empire. While Alexander's generals were carving up their departed leader's empire, Perdiccas of Thrace attacked Samos and drove out the Athenian colonists who took refuge on the mainland of Asia Minor at Colophon. Epicurus soon joined his refugee family at Colophon, where human suffering was intense. There he puzzled out his secret for a happy life.

The refugees at Colophon suffered from economic deprivation, as is the case with most refugees of war. Apparently they believed that they had sinned egregiously against the gods; they viewed the invasion by Perdiccas as divine retribution. Yet they seem to have been unable to identify the specific sins that occasioned their punishment, and accordingly were unable to perform the proper penance. What was even more disquieting was the thought of dying and confronting the displeased gods and being ignorant of the reasons for their displeasure. In short, the refugees were wretched in their living and afraid of dying. They thirsted for peace and joy, for knowledge and forgiveness, for happiness beyond pain.

Epicurus thirsted with them and found a pathway to happiness that he began to teach at the age of thirty-two, first at Mytilene and then at Lampsacus. So impressed with his teaching were his disciples that they purchased a villa in Athens which they gave to their master so that his voice could be heard at the very center of Greek philosophizing. To that villa Epicurus repaired in 306 B.C. and resided there for the rest of his life. The villa became a quasi-religious community where Epicurus taught his secret of happiness and lived a tranquil and simple life among his friends.

Epicurus was a prolific writer, according to Diogenes Laertius, an early biographer of the ancient philosophers, who credits Epicurus with having written about three hundred works. Unfortunately, most of these documents have been lost. What has survived provides us with an appealing but tantalizingly incomplete view of his moral theory. From the available sources we are not able to reconstruct a taxonomy of human nature analogous to Aristotle's in which reason is clearly identified as the truly distinctive feature of human nature, which when pursued leads to human self-realization and distinctively human happiness. Yet we do have some correspondence in which he offers advice on how to achieve truly human happiness—a happiness that, like Aristotle's, is attained by the use of reason and that involves the actualization of a human's highest potentialities.

We have included these excerpts from Epicurus because, within the context of the Greek ideal of actualizing human nature in the pursuit of happiness, his advice for obtaining that happiness is so clear, so direct, and so compelling. In his Letter to Menoeceus he offers several recommendations to his friend. Notice how the recommendations are founded upon confidence in reason as the agent that dissolves the fears and anxieties which rob us of tranquility.

Thinking Correctly About the Gods

First, if we wish to achieve happiness, we must learn to think correctly about the gods.

> * Let no one when young delay to study philosophy, nor when he is old grow weary of his study. For no one can come too early or too late to secure the health of his soul. And the man who says that the age for philosophy has either not yet come or has gone by is like the man who says that the age for happiness is not yet come to him, or has passed away. Wherefore both when young and old a man must study philosophy, that as he grows old he may be young in blessings through the grateful recollection of what has been, and that in youth he may be old as well, since he will know no fear of what is to come. We must then meditate on the things that make our happiness, seeing that when that is with us we have all, but when it is absent we do all to win it.
>
> The things which I used unceasingly to commend to you, these do and practise, considering them to be the first principle of the good life. First of all believe that god is a being; immortal and blessed, even as the common idea of a god is engraved on men's minds, and do not assign to him anything

* FROM *Epicurus: The Extant Remains,* translated by Cyril Bailey (Oxford: Oxford University Press, 1926), pp. 83–95. Copyright 1926 by Oxford University Press. Used by permission of Oxford University Press.

alien to his immortality or ill-suited to his blessedness: but believe about him everything that can uphold his blessedness and immortality. For gods there are, since the knowledge of them is by clear vision. But they are not such as the many believe them to be: for indeed they do not consistently represent them as they believe them to be. And the impious man is not he who denies the gods of the many, but he who attaches to the gods the beliefs of the many. For the statements of the many about the gods are not conceptions derived from sensations, but false suppositions, according to which the greatest misfortunes befall the wicked and the greatest blessings the good by the gift of the gods. For men being accustomed always to their own virtues, welcome those like themselves, but regard all that is not of their nature as alien.

In another of his writings, Epicurus adds this terse comment: "The blessed and immortal nature knows no trouble itself nor causes trouble to any other, so that it is never constrained by anger or favour. For all such things exist only in the weak." In effect, Epicurus removes the suffering associated with fear of the gods, not by denying the existence of the gods, but by denying the nature ascribed to the gods by the masses. Contrary to popular beliefs, Epicurus taught that the gods do not interfere in human affairs: they neither punish nor reward humankind. Therefore, penance, propitiation, repentance, fear, and worry about one's standing with the gods are just so many superstitions. The gods live in tranquility, uninvolved in and undisturbed by the heat and turmoil of human existence.

Thinking Correctly About Death

Second, we must learn to think correctly about death.

> Become accustomed to the belief that death is nothing to us. For all good and evil consists in sensation, but death is deprivation of sensation. And therefore a right understanding that death is nothing to us makes the mortality of life enjoyable, not because it adds to it an infinite span of time, but because it takes away the craving for immortality. For there is nothing terrible in life for the man who has truly comprehended that there is nothing terrible in not living. So that the man speaks but idly who says that he fears death not because it will be painful when it comes, but because it is painful in anticipation. For that which gives no trouble when it comes, is but an empty pain in anticipation. So death, the most terrifying of ills, is nothing to us, since so long as we exist death is not with us; but when death comes, then we do not exist. It does not then concern either the living or the dead, since for the former it is not, and the latter are no more.
>
> But the many at one moment shun death as the greatest of evils, at another yearn for it as a respite from the evils in life. But the wise man neither seeks to escape life nor fears the cessation of life, for neither does life offend him nor does the absence of life seem to be any evil. And just as

with food he does not seek simply the larger share and nothing else, but rather the most pleasant, so he seeks to enjoy not the longest period of time, but the most pleasant.

And he who counsels the young man to live well, but the old man to make a good end, is foolish, not merely because of the desirability of life, but also because it is the same training which teaches to live well and to die well. Yet much worse still is the man who says it is good not to be born but

> once born make haste to pass the gates of death.
>
> (*Theognis,* 427)

For if he says this from conviction why does he not pass away out of life? For it is open to him to do so, if he had firmly made up his mind to this. But if he speaks in jest, his words are idle among men who cannot receive them.

We must then bear in mind that the future is neither ours, nor yet wholly not ours, so that we may not altogether expect it as sure to come, nor abandon hope of it, as if it will certainly not come.

Thus, to remove the fear of death, Epicurus taught that death means that one ceases to exist. Because you will not survive death, there is nothing painful beyond the grave—such as divine judgment—that you must fear. Furthermore, in accepting death for what it is you will cease to fear its coming: death means the end of living, not the beginning of anything to be feared. Only the person who accepts death for what it is, is freed to live life devoid of fear.

Scrutinizing Our Desires

Third, we must learn to think correctly about our desires and the nature of pleasure.

We must consider that of desires some are natural, others vain, and of the natural some are necessary and others merely natural; and of the necessary some are necessary for happiness, others for the repose of the body, and others for very life. The right understanding of these facts enables us to refer all choice and avoidance to the health of the body and the soul's freedom from disturbance, since this is the aim of the life of blessedness. For it is to obtain this end that we always act, namely, to avoid pain and fear. And when this is once secured for us, all the tempest of the soul is dispersed, since the living creature has not to wander as though in search of something that is missing, and to look for some other thing by which he can fulfil the good of the soul and the good of the body. For it is then that we have need of pleasure, when we feel pain owing to the absence of pleasure; but when we do not feel pain, we no longer need pleasure. And for this cause we call pleasure the beginning and end of the blessed life. For we recognize pleasure as the first good innate in us, and from pleasure we begin every act of choice and avoidance, and to pleasure we return again, using the feeling as the standard by which we judge every good. . . .

> And again independence of desire we think a great good not that we
> may at all times enjoy but a few things, but that, if we do not possess
> many, we may enjoy the few in the genuine persuasion that those have
> the sweetest pleasure in luxury who least need it, and that all that is natural
> is easy to be obtained, but that which is superfluous is hard. And so plain
> savours bring us a pleasure equal to a luxurious diet, when all the pain
> due to want is removed; and bread and water produce the highest pleasure,
> when one who needs them puts them to his lips. To grow accustomed
> therefore to simple and not luxurious diet gives us health to the full, and
> makes a man alert for the needful employments of life, and when after
> long intervals we approach luxuries, disposes us better towards them, and
> fits us to be fearless of fortune.

For Epicurus, the experience of pleasure is the essence of the happy life, the blessed
life. Pleasure is fundamentally the absence of pain and fear. The person who is
happy is the person whose life is tranquil, peaceful, undisturbed by the anxious
yearning for pleasure unattained or unattainable. To achieve such tranquility we
must assess carefully our desires or wants. Some of our desires are natural—that
is to say, they are rooted in the innate needs of the self, as are the desire for
food and the desire for friendship. Other desires are vain, being the needs artificially
generated by society, such as the need to keep abreast of the ever-changing fashion
in clothes. The person who seeks happiness sloughs off all concern for these vain
desires and concentrates on the natural desires. Of these natural desires some
are necessary and some are not necessary. What seems to distinguish the one
from the other is the *object* of the natural desire. Consider, for example, the natural
desire for food. We could fix our desire upon plain, simple food like bread and
cheese, or we could yearn for something more exotic like lobster Newburg. The
bread and cheese would be adequate to satisfy our hunger, whereas the lobster
would also do that but with a touch of *unnecessary* extravagance. Accordingly,
the desire for food such as lobster would be deemed as an unnecessary natural
desire, whereas the desire for food such as bread and cheese would be judged a
necessary natural desire. The practical wisdom in this distinction is that persons
who wish to be happy will concentrate on necessary natural desires that are more
easily attained, but will not refuse a nonessential extravagance if it is offered to
them.

Considering Consequences

Fourth, we must learn to think correctly about the consequences of choosing specific
pleasures and specific pains.

> And since pleasure is the first good and natural to us, for this very reason
> we do not choose every pleasure, but sometimes we pass over many
> pleasures, when greater discomfort accrues to us as the result of them;
> and similarly we think many pains better than pleasures, since a greater
> pleasure comes to us when we have endured pains for a long time. Every
> pleasure then because of its natural kinship to us is good, yet not every

pleasure is to be chosen; even as every pain also is an evil, yet not all are always of a nature to be avoided. Yet by a scale of comparison and by the consideration of advantages and disadvantages we must form our judgment on all these matters. For the good on certain occasions we treat as bad, and conversely the bad as good.

If all pleasure is good in itself and all pain is evil in itself, should I welcome every pleasure and avoid every pain? Epicurus says, "No!" Some pleasures may generate future pains that far outweigh the value of those original pleasures. For example, the repeated ingesting of a certain drug may produce pleasant feelings now, but it may in due course lead to a drug dependency that involves unbelievable pain. Then too, some pains such as chemotherapy may lead to pleasures that justify the current pain. The pursuit of happiness thus requires careful attention to the consequences of the pleasure and pains one chooses.

Distinguishing Noble from Base Pleasures

Fifth, we must learn to discriminate correctly the noble from the base pleasures.

> When, therefore, we maintain that pleasure is the end, we do not mean the pleasures of profligates and those that consist in sensuality, as is supposed by some who are either ignorant or disagree with us or do not understand, but freedom from pain in the body and from trouble in the mind. For it is not continuous drinkings and revellings, nor the satisfaction of lusts, nor the enjoyment of fish and other luxuries of the wealthy table, which produce a pleasant life, but sober reasoning, searching out the motives for all choice and avoidance, and banishing mere opinions, to which are due the greatest disturbance of the spirit.

Although Epicurus does not speak of noble and base pleasures, nevertheless he clearly implies such a distinction. The "noble" pleasures are those derived from philosophical reasoning, in contradistinction to the "base" pleasure of profligates. The "noble" pleasures are preferable because they have the capacity to dissolve more of the pains and fears that afflict humans—pains and fears that steal from us the tranquility that is at the heart of happiness.

Becoming Prudent

Epicurus summarizes his advice to us in the directive that we should cherish and develop prudence.

> Of all this the beginning and the greatest good is prudence. Wherefore prudence is a more precious thing even than philosophy: for from prudence are sprung all the other virtues, and it teaches us that it is not possible to live pleasantly without living prudently and honourably and justly, nor, again, to live a life of prudence, honour, and justice without living pleasantly. For the virtues are by nature bound up with the pleasant life, and the pleasant life is inseparable from them. For indeed who, think you, is a better man

than he who holds reverent opinions concerning the gods, and is at all times free from fear of death, and has reasoned out the end ordained by nature? He understands that the limit of good things is easy to fulfil and easy to attain, whereas the course of ills is either short in time or slight in pain: he laughs at destiny, whom some have introduced as the mistress of all things. He thinks that with us lies the chief power in determining events, some of which happen by necessity and some by chance, and some are within our control; for while necessity cannot be called to account, he sees that chance is inconstant, but that which is in our control is subject to no master, and to it are naturally attached praise and blame. For, indeed, it were better to follow the myths about the gods than to become a slave to the destiny of the natural philosophers: for the former suggests a hope of placating the gods by worship, whereas the latter involves a necessity which knows no placation. As to chance, he does not regard it as a god as most men do (for in god's acts there is no disorder), nor as an uncertain cause of all things: for he does not believe that good and evil are given by chance to man for the framing of a blessed life, but that opportunities for great good and great evil are afforded by it. He therefore thinks it better to be unfortunate in reasonable action than to prosper in unreason. For it is better in a man's actions that what is well chosen should fail, rather than that what is ill chosen should be successful owing to chance.

Meditate therefore on these things and things akin to them night and day by yourself, and with a companion like to yourself, and never shall you be disturbed waking or asleep, but you shall live like a god among men. For a man who lives among immortal blessings is not like to a mortal being.

Prudent persons are those who know how to conduct themselves properly in the pursuit of happiness. Prudence involves correct thinking about the gods, about death, about our desires and the nature of pleasure, about the consequences of our choices, and about "noble" as distinct from "base" pleasures. The prudent person knows that happiness is of the self's own making, and self-made happiness cannot be stolen by external forces—neither by tyrants nor by death. Tyrants may take our goods and torture our bodies, but they cannot wrest from us the tranquility of soul that correct philosophizing has nourished. Indeed, prudent persons, wise persons whose happiness rests in their own hands, stand above the changing fortunes of the world and are truly dealing with immortal blessings.

It is not difficult to see why this lofty ideal of the tranquil sage appealed to Epicurus's contemporaries. It seemed to make the happy life accessible to all troubled souls who had the desire and courage to follow the mandates of Epicurus.

Assessment

Although Aristotle and Epicurus share the belief that human beings achieve their highest self-actualization in the use of reason and that the contemplative life is the most truly happy and most closely divine, the images of the happy, self-actualized person that they project seem to differ in at least one important respect. Aristotle's view blends social responsibility with individual fulfillment, whereas Epicurus's ideal seems to emphasize the individual facet at the expense of the social. You will recall that Aristotle firmly maintains that the chief good for the human being is a corporate good embracing all the persons of the state, that the role of politics is to identify and legislate the chief good for humankind, and that his ethical inquiry is appropriately called "political science." The individual, for Aristotle, is an inherently social being whose self-actualization and happiness are inextricably bound up with that of others.

Epirucus conveys quite a different impression. Perhaps because much of the suffering and anxiety he was seeking to combat came from other people such as Perdiccas of Thrace, he constructed a view of the happy self-actualized person whose tranquility was self-generated and self-sustained, secure from the changing fortunes and vicissitudes of life. Aristotle's model person is socially engaged, practicing the moral virtues as a good person would and developing the intellectual virtues as a wise person would. Epicurus's model person is socially disengaged, safeguarding the tranquility that is constantly assaulted by external events and internal fears.

This contrast between social engagement and disengagement in the pursuit of self-actualization has been repeated throughout the centuries, most notably perhaps with the rising and falling appeal of monasticism and asceticism. It is worth noting, however, that the different emphases of Aristotle and Epicurus can be blended effectively. After all, is it not the case that disengagement is the prerequisite for successful engagement? That is to say, must we not first learn to control the effect that changing external events have on our happiness and inner peace before we can strike out to shape society in a way that human self-actualization will be enhanced?

Clearly, both Aristotle and Epicurus had a great deal of confidence in reason as the agent of happiness. The twentieth century, however, does not share their degree of confidence. If everyone were to act rationally in Aristotle's and Epicurus's sense, human beings could live in peace and harmony. But the reality is far different. Intellect has become an instrument of excess: its power has extended human control over nature to such an extent that we face the possibility of destroying ourselves. The Greek vision of noble human beings, pursuing their fullest development and seeking the contemplative life, is an attractive prospect. But not only is the Greek vision based on a set of assumptions about human nature we no longer accept so confidently as they did, we also view their proposal as a somewhat aristocratic ideal better suited to an agrarian lifestyle than to a modern technological milieu. But the prospect of basing human conduct on developing that which is most distinctively human is an alternative that continues to be an attractive answer to the moral question.

Review Questions

1. How does Aristotle's explanation of change relate to his ethics?
2. What, according to Aristotle, is humankind's chief good, and of what does it consist?

3. How does Aristotle distinguish moral virtue from intellectual virtue? How are these virtues obtained? Does every human activity have a mean between extremes? Are all virtues equally productive of human happiness?
4. What are the five basic suggestions for achieving happiness presented by Epicurus?
5. Both Aristotle and Epicurus would have us actualize our human nature. How do their positions differ?

CHAPTER 6

Obeying the Will of God

Introduction

For the person who believes that God exists and that he has revealed his will to human beings, the response to the ethical question often is, I ought to do what God wills. Although many persons across the centuries and from different religious perspectives would agree that there are important relations between religion and ethics, they would not agree on how to characterize that relationship.

At the one end of the spectrum of views is the person who claims that God has issued timelessly true, specific laws for human conduct applicable to all persons irrespective of time and place. At the other end of the spectrum is the person who maintains that God's will varies according to time and place and that it must be discovered in the concrete human situation. The former may be called a *legalist* position, and the latter a *situationalist* position. Some people who give a theistic response to the fundamental ethical question blend features of legalism and situationalism in various ways. The two representatives of the will-of-God ethical view we have included in this chapter—William Paley and Emil Brunner—provide strikingly different mixtures of legalist and situationalist elements.

Concerning the content of God's will, even a cursory glance at the history of religions reveals the great variety of things people have identified with the will of God—from celibacy to polygamy, from the right of kingly rule to the right of social revolt, from the pursuit of peace to the prosecution of war, and from support of religious art to radical iconoclasm. Such diversity raises a number of perplexing problems. For example, if there is a Supreme Being, either he is pathologically addicted to changing his mind, or humans are perpetually misunderstanding or misrepresenting the revelation of his will. Or does such diversity call into question monotheism either by implying that there is a wide variety of deities corresponding to the variety of divine messages or by suggesting that there are no gods after all and that "God's will" is a convenient label used by people to legitimize their own desires? Both Paley and Brunner are stalwart monotheists in the biblical tradition. They would argue that the diversity of claims about God's will reflects a human problem rather than a divine defect.

Because both Paley and Brunner claim to be in the biblical tradition, one would expect certain important similarities in both the form and content of their will-of-God positions. Let us watch for any such similarities as we examine their thought, and let us also be alert to the significant differences in their thinking. Those similarities and differences will provide us with insights for criticizing will-of-God ethics in general.

William Paley: God's Will in Scripture and Nature

Natural Theology and Revealed Theology

William Paley (1743–1805) was a Christian philosopher of the eighteenth century who recognized fully that one of the problems faced by those who identify the right action with the will of God has been to sort out and identify what may be regarded as authentic knowledge of the nature and will of God. Most Christians would agree that God revealed his nature through his son Jesus the Christ, and through his encounters with the Hebrew people prior to the appearance of Jesus. Furthermore, they would agree that a record of this revelation is preserved in the scriptures of the Old and New Testaments. There would, however, be considerable disagreement about whether those scriptures are to be interpreted in a literalistic, legalistic fashion or in a situationalist manner. Also subject to a wide difference of opinion is the issue of the possibility of achieving genuine knowledge of God apart from the biblical revelation. This is the question of natural theology (what we can know about God through the use of human reason alone) versus revealed theology (what we can know about God through scripture). Defenders of natural theology have claimed that human reason, unaided by any special self-disclosure on the part of God, is able to achieve genuine knowledge of God. Is it not the case, for example, that the ethical reflections of Aristotle and the Bhagavad Gita of Hinduism contain insights into God's nature that are consistent with the view of God portrayed in the Bible? Opponents of natural theology have argued, on the other side of the issue, that human reason is sufficiently distorted by the beguiling power of sin and self-indulgence that unaided human reason cannot ascend to a true knowledge of God. Reason, it is claimed, needs the renewing power of divine grace associated with the biblical revelation to liberate it to achieve authentic knowledge of God. This issue was hotly debated in Paley's time and requires further comment in order to place Paley's thought in the proper context.

Early Christianity and Greek Philosophy

When Christianity existed in the womb of Judaism within which it was born, it encountered a Hellenistic world that had a rich philosophical heritage. That heritage could provide the early Christians with the intellectual concepts and logical skills to interpret their religious experience, to commend their gospel to a Hellenistic world, and to defend their beliefs against intellectual assaults from various quarters. Gradually, the early church borrowed the concepts and methods of Greek philosophy to achieve those tasks.

In relying so heavily upon the tools of Greek philosophy, Christian theologians sooner or later had to face up to the question, Does the content of Greek philosophy provide us with supplementary knowledge of God's nature and will? At least three different major responses appeared during the first millennium of Christianity. First, there were those who claimed that the biblical revelation was a substitute for all other so-called knowledge, including science, ethics, and metaphysics. The champion of this position was Tertullian (*circa* 160–220), who claimed that there was an unbridgeable chasm between Jerusalem and Athens, between divine revelation and Greek thought. Second, there were those who maintained that if one first believed in the God of the biblical tradition, then one could penetrate secular thought to discover the authentic gems of wisdom harbored within it. The great advocate of this position—a point of view often characterized as "faith seeking understanding"—was Augustine (354–430). Third, there were those who claimed that human reason unaided by the insights derived from the biblical revelation could achieve legitimate, albeit limited, knowledge of God. The classic proponent of this position was St. Thomas Aquinas (1225–1274). According to Aquinas, unaided philosophical reason could prove the existence of God, discover God's essential attributes, and demonstrate the existence and immortality of the human soul. Reason, aided by philosophy but independent of revelation, could serve as a guide to lead the person of good will and clear thought to the threshold of faith where the revealed truths of the scriptures supplemented but did not contradict the truths of philosophy. In ethics, the classic Greek virtues so ably articulated by Aristotle were accepted by Aquinas and crowned with the theological virtues of faith, hope, and love. God's will for humankind could be known by reason unaided by revelation. Revelation, it was thought, provided a confirmation of such knowledge.

The synthesis of Aristotelian philosophy and Christian theology achieved by Aquinas in the thirteenth century was truly impressive, so impressive that it continued to inform the work of such recent Thomists as Jacques Maritain and Etienne Gilson. Yet this synthesis soon disintegrated under pressures exerted by Duns Scotus (*circa* 1266–1308), who reduced the number of truths about the biblical God that unaided reason could establish, and William of Ockham (died 1349), who argued that nothing at all could be proved about God by natural reason—not even God's existence. As a result, the truths of philosophy and the truths of revelation were divorced from each other.

Modern Christianity and Philosophical Reason

As Christendom experienced the birth of Renaissance humanism, the rise of the Reformation, and the emergence of modern science, new relationships between philosophical reason and religious faith began to be forged. Protestant theologians—beginning with Philip Melanchthon (1497–1560) and Andreas Osiander (1498–1552)—in order to define, defend and commend theological positions against Roman Catholics and other Protestants, did what the early church had done. They borrowed the concepts and methods of Greek philosophy, which they applied to the divinely authored, and therefore inerrant, propositions contained in the scriptures. In so doing, they blended the biblical revelation with an Aristotelian-Ptolemaic view of the world, just at a time when that view was being discarded by scientists in favor of a Copernican cosmology. Needless to say, these Protestants became vigorous opponents of modern science. At the same time, they generated a biblical scholasticism that yielded a legalistic ethics comprising the laws laid down by God in scripture for the benefit of all humankind.

In contrast, there were those who cherished both the new science and religious seriousness. Their faith, however, was not tied so uncompromisingly to the biblical revelation as was that of the scholastics. Indeed, they, in Pythagorean fashion, marvelled at the power of mathematics to describe the relationships prevailing in the universe. They came to the conclusion that mathematics was the language of God. Johannes Kepler (1571–1630), for example, considered knowledge of mathematical harmony to be participation in the life of God, an act of worship in which knowledge of God surpassed even that which was obtained in the biblical revelation. Similarly, Galileo (1564–1641) adored mathematical order in the world and considered God to be the author of it. For him there were two important sources of knowledge: the Book of Scripture, which provided truths that transcended reason's unaided grasp, and the Book of Nature, which was clearer, more precise, and no less significant than scripture. While Galileo believed God to be the cause of the mathematical order pervading the Book of Nature, he claimed that God could not be directly perceived in and through that order. With that posture, Galileo set the stage for Deism, which discarded the Book of Scripture entirely in favor of the Book of Nature.

According to deists, God created the mathematically ordered universe which he now allowed to function on its own without the kind of divine intervention described in the scriptures. The truth of Christianity—that is, the Book of Scripture—was severely challenged. That challenge limited the knowledge of God to that which could be learned from the Book of Nature. Eighteenth-century apologists arose to address the challenge, making the case for Christianity on several grounds, including the miracles reported in scripture, the fulfillment of biblical prophecies, and the presence of purposeful design in nature as grounds for belief in a divine designer. William Paley was one of these eighteenth-century apologists who tried to defend the faith by embracing both the Book of Nature and the Book of Scripture as the twofold source of the knowledge of God. For him, the will of God is made known both in scripture and in nature.

Paley: Defender of Church and State

William Paley was born in England in 1743, the son of the headmaster of the school of Giggleswick in Yorkshire. His father considered him to be one of the clearest thinkers he had encountered, and, accordingly, sent him at the age of fifteen to study at Cambridge. After he was graduated in 1762, Paley rose slowly but steadily in the ecclesiastical and legal establishments, achieving eventually the ranks of archdeacon and justice of the peace. Upon the urging of a friend, he expanded some of his lectures into a book entitled *Principles of Morals and Political Philosophy,* which was published in 1785 and which immediately was adopted as a textbook at Cambridge. It is from this book, which went through fifteen editions during Paley's lifetime, that the following selections have been taken. His *Reasons for Contentment,* published in 1792 and which warned against revolutionary principles, and his enormously successful *Evidences of Christianity,* published in 1794 and which argued for the truth of the Christian religion, established Paley securely as an eminent defender of church and state. His last book, *Natural Theology,* published in 1802, attempted to derive the existence and attributes of God from natural phenomena. While he was writing this work (which received wide acclaim, passing through twenty editions in less than eighteen years), Paley was afflicted with ill health that occasioned great suffering for him and that eventually claimed his life in 1805.

The Task of Ethics

In the following selection from *Principles of Moral and Political Philosophy,* Paley begins with several important definitions.* First, he characterizes *ethics* as

> that science which teaches men their duty and the reasons of it. The use of such a study depends upon this, that without it, the rules of life by which men are ordinarily governed, oftentimes mislead them, through a defect either in the rule or in the application.

For Paley, ethics educates people concerning *what* they ought to do, and *why.* In response to the question, What ought I to do? Paley might say, You ought to do what is right. That, of course, would elicit the additional question, What makes something right? Paley's answer to this question is clear and unmistakable.

> *Right* . . . signifies consistency with the will of God.
>   Right is a quality of persons or actions.
>   Of persons; as when we say, such a one has a "right" to this estate;
> parents have a "right" to reverence from their children. . . .

* FROM William Paley, *The Principles of Moral and Political Philosophy,* seventh edition (Philadelphia: Thomas Dobson, 1788). The book was first published in London in 1785.

Of actions; as in such expressions as the following: it is "right" to punish murder with death; his behaviour on that occasion was "right." . . .

In this latter set of expressions, you may substitute the definition of right above given for the term itself, v.g., it is "consistent with the will of God" to punish murder with death—his behaviour on that occasion was "consistent with the will of God." . . .

In the former act, you must vary the phrase a little, when you introduce the definition instead of the term. Such a one has a "right" to this estate, that is, it is "consistent with the will of God" that such a one should have it . . . it is "consistent with the will of God" that children should reverence their parents. . . .

The Reason for Obeying God

Paley now explores the issue of why one ought to act in accordance with the will of God. In providing us with the reason, he offers definitions of virtue, moral obligation, prudence, and duty.

Virtue is the doing good to mankind, in obedience to the will of God, and for the sake of everlasting happiness. . . .

The four cardinal virtues are prudence, fortitude, temperance, and justice.

But the division of virtue, to which we are now-a-days most accustomed, is into duties: towards God . . . towards other men . . . towards ourselves. . . .

More of these distinctions have been proposed, which it is not worth while to set down. . . .

Why am I obliged to keep my word? . . .

A man is said to be obliged, when he is urged by a violent motive resulting from the command of another.

First, the motive must be violent. If a person, who has done me some little service . . . ask me upon some occasion for my vote, I may possibly give it him, from a motive of gratitude or expectation; but I should hardly say that I was *obliged* to give it him, because the inducement does not rise high enough. Whereas, if a father or a master, or any great benefactor, or one on whom my fortune depends, require my vote, I give it him of course; and my answer to all who ask me why I voted so and so, is, that my father or my master *obliged* me. . . .

Secondly, it must result from the command of another. Offer a man a gratuity for doing anything . . . he is not obliged by your offer to do it; nor would he say he is; though he may be induced, persuaded, prevailed upon, tempted. If a magistrate or the man's immediate superior command it, he considers himself as *obliged* to comply. . . .

Let it be remembered that to be obliged is to be urged by a violent motive, resulting from the command of another.

And then let it be asked, "Why am I obliged to keep my word?" and the answer will be, "because I am urged to do so by a violent motive" (namely, the expectation of being after this life rewarded, if I do, or punished for it, if I do not) "resulting from the command of another" (namely, of God).

This solution goes to the bottom of the subject, as no farther question can reasonably be asked.

Therefore, private happiness is our motive, and the will of God our rule.

There is always understood to be a difference between an act of *prudence* and an act of *duty*. Thus, if I distrusted a man who owed me a sum of money, I should reckon it an act of prudence to get another person bound with him; but I should hardly call it an act of duty. On the other hand, it would be thought a very unusual and a loose kind of language to say that, as I had made such a promise it was prudent to perform it; or that as my friend, when he went abroad, placed a box of jewels in my hands, it would be prudent in me to preserve it for him till he returned.

Now, in what, you will ask, does the difference consist? . . . The difference, and the only difference, is this, that, in the one case, we consider what we shall gain or lose in the present world; in the other case, we consider also what we shall gain or lose in the world to come. [Prudence has regard to the former; duty, to the latter.] Those who would establish a system of morality, independent of a future state, must look out for some different idea of moral obligation.

To us there are two great questions: Will there be, after this life, any distribution of rewards and punishments at all? If there be, what actions will be rewarded and what actions will be punished?

The first question comprises the credibility of the Christian religion, together with the presumptive proofs of a future retribution from the light of nature. The second question composes the province of morality. Both questions are too much for one work. The affirmative therefore of the first, although we confess that it is the foundation upon which the whole fabric rests, must in this treatise be taken for granted.

The Will of God in Scripture and Nature

Paley argues that one ought to obey the will of God in order to receive from God rewards after death that will produce personal happiness. But how does one determine what is and is not the will of God? Paley directs our attention at this point to God's word declared in scripture and God's work manifested in nature.

As the will of God is our rule, to inquire what is our duty, or what we are obliged to do, in any instance, is, in effect, to inquire what is the will of God in that instance? which consequently becomes the whole business of morality.

Now, there are two methods of coming at the will of God on any point: I. By his express declarations, when they are to be had, and which must be sought for in Scripture. II. By what we can discover of his designs and dispositions from his works, or, as we usually call it, the light of nature.

And here we may observe the absurdity of separating natural and revealed religion from each other. The object of both is the same—to discover the will of God—and, provided we do but discover it, it matters nothing by what means.

An ambassador judging by what he knows of his sovereign's disposition, and arguing from what he has observed of his conduct, or is acquainted with his designs, may take his measures in many cases with safety; and would have him act on most occasions that arise; but if he have his commission and instructions in his pocket, it would be strange not to look into them. He will naturally conduct himself by both rules: when his instructions are clear and positive, there is an end of all farther deliberation (unless indeed he suspects their authenticity): where his instructions are silent or dubious, he will endeavour to supply or explain them, by what he has been able to collect from other quarters of his master's general inclination or intentions. . . .

Even as the ambassador can have his sovereign's commission and instructions in his pocket, even so humankind can avail itself of God's written instructions in scripture. Those instructions, Paley believes, appear as general rules concerning piety, justice, benevolence, and purity. Some of those rules are occasionally illustrated, either in fictitious examples, as in the parable of the good Samaritan, or in instances that actually presented themselves.

God's will, then, is expressly declared in scripture in terms of general rules that are occasionally illustrated. But what if there are issues not treated in scripture? Then one must have recourse to God's will manifested in nature. Even as we can learn something about the will of an architect through the building the architect has designed and erected, so can we learn something about God's will from the universe he has designed and created.

The method of coming at the will of God concerning any action, by the light of nature, is to inquire into the tendency of the action to promote or diminish the general happiness. This rule proceeds upon the presumption that God Almighty wills and wishes the happiness of his creatures, and consequently, that those actions which promote that will and wish, must be agreeable to him; and the contrary.

As this presumption is the foundation of our whole system, it becomes necessary to explain the reasons upon which it rests.

When God created the human species, either he wished their happiness or he wished their misery or he was indifferent and unconcerned about both.

If he wished our misery, he might have made sure of his purpose, by forming our senses to be as many sores and pains to us as they are now instruments of gratification and enjoyment. . . . He might have made, for example, everything we tasted, bitter; everything we saw loathsome; everything we touched a sting; every smell a stench; and every sound a discord.

If he had been indifferent about our happiness or misery, we must impute to our good fortune . . . both the capacity of our senses to receive pleasure, and the supply of external objects fitted to excite it.

But either of these, and still more both of them, being too much to be attributed to accident, nothing remains but the first supposition, that God, when he created the human species, wished their happiness; and made for them the provision which he has made, with that view, and for that purpose.

The same argument may be proposed in different terms, thus: . . . The world abounds with contrivances; and all the contrivances which we are acquainted with are directed to beneficial purposes. Evil no doubt exists; but is never, that we can perceive, the object of contrivance. Teeth are contrived to eat, not to ache; their aching now and then is incidental to the contrivance, perhaps inseparable from it; or even, if you will, let it be called a defect in the contrivance; but it is not the object of it. This is a distinction which well deserves to be attended to. In describing implements of husbandry, you would hardly say of a sickle, that it is made to cut the reaper's fingers, though from the construction of the instrument, and the manner of using it, this mischief often happens. But if you had occasion to describe instruments of torture or execution, this engine, you would say, is to extend the sinews; this to dislocate the joints; this to break the bones; this to scorch the soles of the feet. Here pain and misery are the very objects of the contrivance. Now nothing of this sort is to be found in the works of nature. We never discover a train of contrivance to bring about an evil purpose. No anatomist ever discovered a system of organization calculated to produce pain and disease; or, in explaining the parts of the human body, ever said, "this is to irritate; this is to inflame; this duct is to convey the gravel to the kidneys; this gland to secrete the humour which forms gout: if by the chance he come at a part of which he knows not the use, the most he can say is, that it is useless; no one ever suspects that it is put there to incommode, to annoy, or torment. Since then God hath called forth his consummate wisdom to contrive and provide for our happiness, and the world appears to have been constituted with this design at first, so long as this constitution is upholden by him, we must in reason suppose the same design to continue. . . .

We conclude, therefore, that God wills and wishes the happiness of his creatures. And this conclusion being once established, we are at liberty to go on with the rule built upon it, namely, that the method of coming at the will of God concerning any action, by the light of nature, is to inquire into the tendency of that action to promote or diminish the general happiness.

In Paley's ethics, then, we can see a blend of natural theology and revealed theology, the Book of Nature and the Book of Scripture. In addition, we can observe a mixture of legalist and situationalist emphases. Clearly Paley believed that the scriptures set forth rules or laws that humans must obey if they are to achieve eternal happiness. That is a legalist posture. At the same time, Paley affirmed the general principles—on the basis of natural theology—that God wills human happiness, and that rules for various specific situations not covered in scripture can be derived from this principle. Here is an element of situationalism.

Disturbing Questions

Paley's synthesis, while clear and impressive, raises several troubling questions. First, could it not be argued that the motivation for obeying the will of God suggested by Paley—namely, to achieve personal and eternal happiness—is basically selfish and lacking the heroic and benevolent ingredients we usually associate with mature religious and moral consciousness? Second, does nature really declare that God wills human happiness? Could not a case be made that there is more evidence to suggest that he intends human suffering and misery as well as, or instead of, human happiness? Third, what does one do if the will of God declared in scripture and the will of God reflected in nature seem to be in conflict? What if obedience to a commandment in scripture clearly violates, in a particular situation, the pursuit of human happiness? Fourth, has Paley projected an ethics that is so heavily legalistic that the joy derived from creative human freedom is vitiated by a roster of wooden dos and don'ts? Questions such as these have led other will-of-God ethicists to offer alternative interpretations of obedience to the will of God. Let us consider the alternative offered by the twentieth-century thinker Emil Brunner.

Emil Brunner: God's Will in the Situation

Emil Brunner (1889–1966) was one of the major figures in a twentieth-century theological movement often referred to as neo-orthodoxy. The movement constituted a radical reaction to the prevailing thought of the eighteenth and nineteenth centuries. The eighteenth century, the century of Paley and his deistic adversaries, is frequently characterized as the century of the Enlightenment to draw attention to the critical examination of previously accepted doctrines and institutions that engaged human attention—a critical examination that achieved radical and concrete expression in both the American and French revolutions. Karl Barth (1886–1968), the Swiss Protestant theologian who was at the fountainhead of the neo-orthodox movement, preferred to describe the eighteenth century as the era of the "absolute man." Barth wrote the following:

> * Man, who discovers his own power and ability, the potentiality dormant in his humanity, that is, his human being as such, and looks upon it as the final, the real and absolute, I mean as something 'detached', self-justifying, with its own authority and power, which he can therefore set in motion in all directions and without any restraint—this is absolute man.

And that, says Barth, is eighteenth-century man.

---

* FROM Karl Barth, *Protestant Thought: From Rousseau to Ritschl* (New York: Harper & Brothers, 1959), p. 14.

Modern Promethean Man

Instead of being driven to unprecedented humiliation by the knowledge that human beings were as specks of dust in the vast, silent universe unveiled by science, eighteenth-century man marvelled that *humans* could unveil this sight and could describe it with mathematical precision. Dazzled by such accomplishments, eighteenth-century man construed himself a Prometheus unbound. Daniel Defoe's novel *Robinson Crusoe,* published in 1719, captured the age's Promethean spirit in the person of a shipwrecked English sailor who singlehandedly established human culture on a small tropical island. The Promethean spirit was everywhere. Barth observes the following.

> * This absolute man, whether he is called Louis XIV or Frederick the Great or Voltaire, whether he lives the obscure life of a philistine with secret revolutionary thoughts or of a friend of letters with liberal religious or even sceptical tendencies, or of a lady in her castle devoted to the mysticism of Tersteegen, or whether he sails the seas with James Cook or is a watchmaker in Geneva making tiny but useful improvements in the products of his handiwork . . . this absolute man is eighteenth-century man, who appears to us more or less distinctly, more or less open or veiled in conventional drapings, in all the human faces of that century which are so different amongst themselves.

In theological circles, this Promethean spirit found expression in a twofold confidence in the power of reason to grasp divine truth and in the power of human effort to achieve perfection. Eighteenth-century deists argued that human reason could establish three truths of traditional Christian orthodoxy: the existence of God, freedom, and immortality. Immanuel Kant (1724–1804) showed that not even these three could be established by reason, although they could be postulated as principles needed by reason if reason wished to make sense out of the human quest for moral perfection.

Kant's influence can be traced in the strong ethical bent of liberal theology of the nineteenth century, which is summarily represented in Adolf Harnack's volume *What Is Christianity?* published in 1900. According to Harnack, the essence of Christianity comprises three timeless truths: the fatherhood of God, the brotherhood of man, and the infinite value of the human soul. This simple, profound essence of Christianity was, says Harnack, overlaid with layer after layer of doctrinal formulations generated by alien ingredients (especially Greek philosophy) working on the pristine simplicity of original Christianity. Christianity, Harnack concludes, is basically a religion of inwardness (the cultivation of God-consciousness) and ethics (the pursuit of the brotherhood of man).

Opposed to this liberal theology, but sharing confidence in human rationality

* FROM *Protestant Thought: From Rousseau to Ritschl,* pp. 14–15.

and perfectability, was orthodox or dogmatic theology concretely depicted in a number of creeds such as "The Westminster Confession of Faith" in 1647, the "Methodist Articles of Religion" in 1784, and the "Articles of Religion of the Reformed Episcopal Church in America" in 1875. Although there is great diversity in these creeds, as one would expect from different denominations, there is nevertheless a uniform affirmation of the scriptures as a repository of divinely delivered propositions necessary for human salvation—propositions that can be manipulated by logical procedures to generate theological truths not expressly set forth in scripture. Clearly, such an attitude reflects confidence in human reason. In addition, while recognizing the continued presence of sin in the believer, these creeds hold out a growth model for believers whose goal is the perfection God requires of his people.

Nineteenth-century confidence in Promethean man was challenged only briefly by Darwin's evolutionary theory that seemed to erode human uniqueness and dignity. Defenders of Promethean man soon countered Darwin's thesis of the descent of man, they presented a portrayal of the ascent of man that emphasized how far humankind had come from its ancient primate ancestors. Such strategies reinforced the emerging doctrine of evolution-progress that encouraged humans to think they were getting better every day in every way.

The Apocalyptic Year

This unbridled confidence in human capacities was called into radical question during what Barth refers to as "the apocalyptic year"—1917. That was the third year of World War I, the year in which the full horror of the war was brought home. When the fighting began in 1914, the prevailing mood was one of optimism: the fighting would be brief and the troops would be home before Christmas. That optimism proved to be false hope. The war dragged on and on, and after three years of punches and counterpunches, the Western Allies were goaded into mounting a major offensive. Prompted largely by the submarine blockade of Britain and the collapse of the Russian front that would allow the Germans to transfer divisions from the eastern to the western front, the Allies attempted to make a major breakthrough at Flanders on July 31, 1917. On the first day, 60,000 men fell from guns and mustard gas. The battle continued to rage, and when a halt was finally called after one hundred days, the bodies of 440,000 Allied troops and 225,000 German soldiers were strewn over the fields of Flanders. As the horror of this carnage penetrated human consciousness, the Promethean vision began to fade.

At approximately the same time, in October 1917, the Bolsheviks, led by Lenin, overthrew the Kerensky government and inaugurated the Soviet system. The czar and his family were imprisoned and executed. The former ruling class was exterminated, and the systematic eradication of religion became an avowed state policy. This regime of the workers and peasants, of the hammer and the sickle, represented a radical transformation of the kind of society with which the nineteenth-century human had become accustomed. Once again, the Promethean vision of the nineteenth century seemed out of focus for the contemporary scene.

The Birth of Neo-Orthodoxy

From his study in Switzerland, Barth could hear the guns booming on the western front. With that awesome thunder in the background, he learned of the Russian revolution in the east. It was Barth's "apocalyptic year." For him, 1917 marked the end of the nineteenth century's intellectual vision of Promethean man progressively evolving into a better being. Barth, who had adopted that vision, cast it aside as incapable of providing spiritual sustenance for his parishioners. After much soul-searching and study, he rediscovered the biblical doctrine of sin and grace, which he shaped into a profoundly simple but potent message. For Barth, sin was the rejection of the living God of the Judaeo-Christian tradition. That rejection, according to Barth, is a universal characteristic of humankind, which occasions a universal faultedness in all human accomplishments. But, says Barth, God has rejected the human rejection of him; he has issued a divine "no" to the human "no" to him. That is the essence of grace. The gospel, accordingly for Barth, is simply the good news that "God is unrelentingly for us, not against us." Barth's new vision of the human being as a flawed, alienated creature who needs the transforming power achieved through accepting God's acceptance of him, was a striking departure from his former vision of the human as a potent being on the path to perfection.

Brunner: A Disciple of Barth

When Barth put his encyclopedic knowledge at the disposal of this new vision of humankind, he so startled, shocked, and challenged the theological establishment of his day that a new movement called neo-orthodoxy arose. One of the early disciples of that movement was Emil Brunner. Brunner was born in Winterthur, Switzerland in 1889. He studied theology in Zurich, Berlin and New York, receiving his doctorate in 1913 from Zurich University, where he became a professor of theology and lectured for many years. At first Brunner embraced liberal theology, but eventually he came under the influence of Barth and rejected the liberal perspective. Brunner did not adopt the extreme position of some Barthians who maintained that human reason apart from biblical revelation could know very little, if any, truth about religious matters. Instead, Brunner, while taking seriously the Barthian emphasis on the radical nature of sin, refused to subscribe to the notion that sin had utterly destroyed the sinner's capacity to know God's truth and to pursue it. Through his numerous books and extensive lecturing, Brunner exerted a powerful influence upon the world's theological scene; he was recognized and was awarded honorary doctorates from many institutions. The following selections are taken from his extended treatise on ethics, *The Divine Imperative*.

Rejection of Legalism

Like Paley, Brunner would respond to the ethical question, What ought I to do? by saying, I ought to obey God's will. Note, however, that Brunner is very careful to distinguish his view of God's will from a legalistic position.

* The Christian conception of the Good differs from every other conception of the Good at this very point: it cannot be defined in terms of principle at all.

Whatever can be defined in accordance with a principle—whether it be the principle of pleasure or the principle of duty—is legalistic. This means that it is possible—by the use of this principle—to pre-determine "the right" down to the smallest detail of conduct. . . .

The Christian moralist and the extreme individualist are at one in their emphatic rejection of legalistic conduct; they join hands, as it were, in face of the whole host of legalistic moralists; they are convinced that conduct which is regulated by abstract principles can never be good. But equally sternly the Christian moralist rejects the individualistic doctrine of freedom, according to which there is no longer any difference between "right" and "wrong." Rather, in the Christian view, that alone is "good" which is free from all caprice, which takes place in unconditional obedience. There is no Good save obedient behaviour, save the obedient will. But this obedience is rendered not to a law or a principle which can be known beforehand, but only to the free, sovereign will of God. The good consists in always doing what God wills at any particular moment.

This statement makes it clear that for us the will of God cannot be summed up under any principle, that it is not at our disposal, but that so far as we are concerned the will of God is absolutely free. The Christian is therefore "a free lord over all things," because he stands directly under the personal orders of the free Sovereign God. This is why genuine "Christian conduct"— if we may use this idea as an illustration—is so unaccountable, so unwelcome to the moral rigorist and to the hedonist alike. The moral rigorist regards the Christian as a hedonist, and the hedonist regards him as a rigorist. In reality, the Christian is neither, yet he is also something of both, since he is indeed absolutely *bound* and obedient, but, since he is bound to the *free* loving will of God, he is himself free from all transparent bondage to principles or to legalism. Above all it is important to recognize that even love is not a principle of this kind, neither the love which God Himself *has,* nor the love which He *requires.* Only God Himself defines love in His action. We, for our part, do not know what God is, nor do we know what *love* is, unless we learn to know God in His action, in faith. To be in this His Love, is the Commandment. Every attempt to conceive love as a principle leads to this result: it becomes distorted, either in the rigoristic, legalistic sense, or in the hedonistic sense. Man only knows what the love of God is when he sees the way in which God acts, and he only knows how he himself ought to love by allowing himself to be drawn by faith into this activity of God. . . .

"To know God in His action" is only possible in faith. The action of God, in which He manifests Himself—and this means His love—is His revelation. God reveals Himself in His Word—which is at the same time

* FROM *The Divine Imperative,* by Emil Brunner; translated by Olive Wyon. Copyright © MCMXLVII by W. L. Jenkins. Used by permission of The Westminster Press, Philadelphia, PA.

a deed—in an actual event—in Jesus Christ; and He reveals Himself operatively in His living Word, which is now taking place—in the Holy Spirit. Because only conduct which takes place on the basis of this faith (and indeed in this faith in God's Word) can be "good conduct," in the sense of the Christian ethic, therefore, the science of Good conduct, of ethics, is only possible within that other science which speaks of the Divine act of revelation, that is, within dogmatics. Reflection on the good conduct of man is only one part of more comprehensive reflection on the action of God in general. For human conduct can only be considered "good" when, and in so far as, God Himself acts in it, through the Holy Spirit. . . .

The specific element in the Christian ethic—as will become abundantly clear in all that follows—is precisely this: that the Good in human conduct only arises out of the fact that it is set within the action of God. All other forms of conduct are legalistic. . . . These considerations may now be summed up in a sentence, in which the special subject of Christian ethics is defined: *Christian ethics is the science of human conduct as it is determined by Divine conduct.*

Brunner is opposed to legalistic ethics. Legalism is the position generated by proud reason in the nineteenth century based on assumptions we now know to be false. Reason either took the words of scripture or the data of human experience and generated a set of general rules or principles applicable to all humans. Those sets of rules constituted, in effect, various legalisms which, according to Brunner, obscured the specific, concrete needs of one's neighbor whom God commands us to love. That love, says Brunner, cannot be encompassed in a principle because it is defined by God's action—and that action is situationally specific and, hence, incapable of generalization as a principle. If, then, Christian ethics rejects such generalizations, how can it be considered to be "scientific"?

The Christian ethic . . . since it cannot be scientific in terms of a general principle, can be scientific solely and simply if it represents its own subject in a strictly objective orderly process of reflection, and in a method which is suitable to its subject and precisely not after the pattern of a causal or normative science. The "organ" of reason is placed at the disposal of faith for its clarification. It aids the process of reflection on that which is not reason, but is always related to reason, precisely because it is related to man as man.

Blending Legalism and Situationalism

But if Brunner is going to answer the question, What ought I to do? will he not be forced into providing some generalizations which would commit him to the legalism that he is trying to avoid? Is he not committed to a curious inconsistency if he tries to answer our ethical question?

But what is the function of a system of ethics in regard to the central ethical question: What ought we to do? Can ethics tell us what we are to do? If it could, it would mean that the Christian ethic also is an ethical system

> based on law and on abstract principles. For where ethics is regarded purely
> as a science, there general, and to some extent timeless, propositions are
> stated. If these were to define what we ought to do, then the Good would
> be defined in legalistic terms. Therefore no such claim can be made either
> by or for ethics. The service it renders cannot be that of relieving us of
> the necessity for making moral decisions, but that it prepares the way for
> such decisions. How this takes place can only be made clear in the
> explication of the part which is played by law within a morality which is
> not legalistic. The significance of the law is the same as the significance
> of ethics, namely: that it prepares the way for a voluntary decision, or for
> the hearing of the divine command.

Notice how Brunner has incorporated strands of legalism and situationalism
in response to the problem of possible inconsistency. Christian ethics, in answering
the ethical question, does not tell us what we ought to do in a specific situation;
rather, it provides us with preparation for hearing God's command in the specific
situation. Brunner seems to have avoided inconsistency, but he has raised another
puzzle: How does one go about hearing the divine command? To hear the divine
command is to know God's will. In contrast with Paley, Brunner claims that
unaided reason cannot know God's will through nature, but it can achieve some
knowledge of his nature.

> Of ourselves we cannot know the Good or the Will of God. It is, of course,
> true that God manifests Himself as the incomprehensible One, mighty and
> wise in the works of His creation, with an impressiveness which, even in
> the most unseeing, awakens awe in the presence of the mystery of the
> universe, and fills with wonder everyone who has not entirely lost the child-
> spirit. But being what we are, with our limited vision, this manifestation is
> not enough to reveal to us the will of the mysterious power which rules
> in Nature. Nature speaks with two voices—and the heathen know this better
> than we do, for they are more defenceless in the presence of nature than
> we are—kindly and terrible, maintaining and destroying life. But even human
> nature, the human spirit, and its innermost sanctuary, the *conscience*, does
> not know God's will. It is of course true that every one knows "something
> of the divine"; I suppose everyone makes the distinction between good
> and evil—with that amazing precision which shows itself especially in
> criticism of others. But this knowledge always includes an element of
> ignorance, of misunderstanding, which is the counterpart of man's original
> sinful misunderstanding of his own nature. . . .

The Divine Command Interprets Oughtness

Human reason, without the help of God's revelation, can be aware of the distinction
between good and evil, and may have a sense of oughtness to pursue the good.
But reason needs divine revelation to understand this oughtness correctly: it needs
revelation to interpret God's will which is a command to love. That command
to love is disclosed in God's self-giving action.

God reveals His will, the Good, His self-giving, love itself, not only where
He gives us "something"—as He does every day in the ordinary processes
of nature—but where He gives Himself. In this event the meaning of the
word "love" is defined afresh, and indeed in such a way that only those
who understand this event as the real self-giving of God understand the
meaning of love. That which *we* call "love" is always a conditional self-
giving, whether it be the love of a mother, or the love of country, or the
love of an idea. It is always a love which is limited by some secret demand
for compensation, or by some relic of exclusiveness. It is never unconditional.
The message of Jesus Christ is the message of an historical fact; "the Word
was made flesh"—this means that God loves us without any conditions at
all. The very fact that this has happened, that in this happening God is
the One who acts, makes the love there manifested unconditional. The
word "Love" acquires its new meaning through the fact that in Jesus, the
"Suffering Servant of the Lord," *God* comes to us. It is thus that God reveals
to us His Nature and His Will.

It is His will to *give*. Therefore He can only be revealed in the reality
of His giving. It is His will to give Himself, to give His life to man, and in
so doing to give salvation, satisfaction, and blessedness. . . .

But this Divine giving is not accomplished in any magical way; it simply
takes place in the fact that *God "apprehends" man;* God *claims* us for
His love, for His generous giving. But this means that He claims our whole
existence for Himself, for this love of His; He gives us His love. He gives
us His love in such a way that He captures us completely by the power
of His love. *To belong* to Him, to this love, and through His love, means
that we are the *bondslaves* of this will. To believe means to become a
captive, to become His property, or rather, to know that we are His property.
The revelation which makes it plain that the will of God is lavish in giving
to man, makes it equally clear that His will makes a demand *on* man.
His will *for* us also means that He wants something *from* us. He claims
us for His love. This is His Command. It is the *"new* commandment,"
because only now can man perceive that it is the command of One who
gives before He demands, and who only demands something from us in
the act of giving Himself to us.

The Divine Command and Legalism

In his revelation in Jesus Christ, God gives his love to humankind, but that gift
of divine love is a gift that simultaneously demands love from human beings.
Brunner is quick to reiterate that this demand does not involve legalism.

But just as it is absolutely individual so also it is absolutely devoid of all
caprice. "I will guide thee with Mine eye." No one can experience this
"moment" save I myself. The Divine Command is made known to us "in
the secret place." Therefore it is impossible for us to know it beforehand;
to wish to know it beforehand—legalism—is an infringement of the divine

honour. The fact that the holiness of God must be remembered when we dwell on His love means that we cannot have His love at our disposal, that it cannot ever be perceived as a universal principle, but only in the act in which He speaks to us Himself; even in His love He remains our *Master* and Lord. But He is our "Lord" in the sense that He tells us Himself what it means to "love," here and now. . . . . Not even an Apostle can tell you what you ought to do; God himself is the only One who can tell you this. There is to be no intermediary between ourselves and the Divine Will. God wishes to deal with us "personally," not through any medium.

Preparation for Hearing the Divine Command

According to Brunner, God wills that human beings should love. What it means to love in a concrete situation cannot be determined in advance; if one could do so, then God's will would be imprisoned in a wooden legalism. The meaning of love in a concrete situation is made known by God to the individual in the situation. Must the believer, then, abandon all effort to think about God's will in advance and simply wait for some sort of special communication from God in the concrete situation? Brunner says "No."

What does God command? Only those who have a legalistic conception of the Good can imagine that they possess the answer to this question. God's Command is His free and sovereign act of commanding, which cannot be condensed into a regulation. But dangerous as it is to be in bondage to the legalism of orthodoxy, it is just as dangerous to fall into the opposite error of a fanatical antinomianism, which holds that it is impossible to lay down any rules at all, that it is impossible to have any knowledge beforehand of the content of the Divine Command. The will of God, which alone is the Good, is made known to us in His action, in His *revelation.* This Divine process of revelation, however, is not only present, nor is it only past; in fact, it is present, based on the past. We know God through His present speech—in the Holy Scriptures. He is the same yesterday, to-day, and for ever, and this not only in what He gives but also in what He demands. But in His historical revelation He has made Himself known to us as the Creator and Redeemer. Thus in this unity of His revelation He is the God of the Bible, the God who is revealed to us in Jesus Christ. As Creator He is the beginning and the ground of all existence, the source of all life; as Redeemer He is the End, the Goal, towards which all existence tends.

Precisely on the borderline between the past and the future stands the *present moment,* the moment of decision. The will of God which approaches us from the past differs from the will of God which calls to us from the future goal; it is different in its content, but its aim is the same. The work of the Creator differs from that of the Redeemer. The will of God is indeed only one, but we can only understand it in this twofold character. We see likewise how God looks at us both from the beginning and from the end, how He looks at this central point—which we call the "present"—which stands midway between the past and the future; it is this "present" moment which is so "pregnant" in ethical significance. We cannot control either the past or the future; all that we *can* control is this point, which we call "now." Owing to the fact that, for us, time is divided into the past and the future on the boundary line of the present, we are obliged to conceive of God and His action in a twofold conception, although in God Himself this action is only *one*. But for the very same reason this conception can *only* be twofold. For by our own act of free decision we divide time—which is nothing in itself—into past and future.

We, then, in the present stand on the border separating past from future. On that borderline, God's will appears as the will of the Creator who in the past affirmed this world by creating it and who in the present continues to affirm it by sustaining it. On that borderline, God's will also appears as that of the Redeemer who has a goal for His creation. Through his self-giving activity, God reveals his will. What he demands of us cannot be inconsistent with his revealed will. Accordingly, what Brunner perceives to be God's command to each of us on the borderline of the present is the demand to affirm his activity as creator and redeemer. Brunner summarizes the force of his view of God and its relevance for ethics.

> As Creator God preserves the world with His longsuffering "Yes"; as Redeemer He grasps it, breaks it, and re-creates it. *How* does God do this? He does this in Jesus Christ, in that act of judgment which is at the same time forgiveness, in that act of acceptance and justification which is at the same time renewal, in the sacrifice of the Cross. The divine love is to be known as that which enters into the world, by sacrifice, in order to tear it out of its present accursed existence.
>
> Thus God's Command becomes known to us as the demand to give ourselves to the world for the sake of the gift of Christ, for God's sake, that we may give a glimpse of the aim which lies beyond this mortal life. He who sacrifices himself pours himself out on the world as the Divine creation; indeed, he pours himself out for the God to whom we belong. But he who sacrifices himself is also quite free from the world, from the curse of seeking the world. This sacrifice is the right way of adjustment and of protest. As the "salt of the earth" it is our function to preserve; through self-devotion we are to attack.
>
> But this self-giving or self-sacrifice must not be interpreted as a principle. For it is impossible to define in legalistic terms what it means to "sacrifice" in any concrete, given instance, or to define how this aggressive and conserving activity is to be carried on. In any case, here the meaning of "sacrifice" is quite different from the meaning which it contains where "sacrifice" is regarded as a principle, that is, in asceticism, which may be in accordance with mysticism and pantheism, but is not in harmony with belief in God the Creator. True sacrifice consists in serving the world within the various "orders" of Society, and, moreover, of wholly personal service to the individual. . . .
>
> By itself ethics can decide nothing beforehand; *nothing at all.* But, by the consideration of all the points of view which have to be considered

by one who knows God's grace and God's demand, the Divine revelation in the Scriptures and in the Spirit, who knows God as Creator and Redeemer, it can prepare the decision of the individual as carefully as a conscientious legal adviser prepares the decision of the judge by the most careful consideration of all possibilities. In this interweaving of a definite demand and of its restriction, of our direct connexion with God Himself and with our actual neighbour, and of our indirect connexion through the Law: in this process—ever renewed before every fresh problem—of steering a clear course between legalism and fanaticism—between the aim at the One Good which alone exists, and the variety of all that can be said about the matter, the task of an evangelical ethic consists.

For Brunner, then, an ethic that provides a specific answer in advance to the ethical question is legalistic and, therefore, objectionable. Equally unacceptable to Brunner is an ethic which provides no preparation for moral decision making. Accordingly, Brunner presents an ethic that offers thoughtful analysis of the general nature of the divine command but awaits the specific content of the divine imperative to appear in the concrete situation. This will-of-God ethic is significantly different from Paley's. To a consideration of that difference we must now turn.

Assessment

Clearly both Paley and Brunner believe that God exists, that he has disclosed himself to some extent in nature, that he has revealed himself in certain historical events, and that scripture records that historical revelation. A thorough assessment of the positions of Paley and Brunner would require a scrutiny of these four beliefs that are fundamental to the will-of-God ethical postures they develop. We would have to ask what evidence and reasons can be proffered in support of those beliefs, and whether such evidence and reasons are sufficient to sustain belief. Such an investigation has engaged the attention of philosophers and theologians for centuries, and the consequence is a split decision: some conclude that the evidence and reasons are sufficient to support belief, whereas others conclude that they are insufficient. This might just be one of those loggerhead issues where rational persons can legitimately differ with each other in the absence of a conclusive case on one side or the other.

To push our assessment beyond a loggerhead stalemate, let us step inside the circle of faith with Paley and Brunner and ask a number of questions that probe the adequacy of their positions as representative of the biblical perspective. We have seen that Paley developed a strongly legalistic position. For him, God's will is contained in the rules set forth in scripture and in the rules that can be derived from God's will for human happiness evidenced in nature. Brunner, in contrast, articulated a situationalist and emphatically anti-legalistic position. For Brunner, God's specific commandment for us is made known only in the concrete situation, not beforehand in rules or laws.

Within the circle of faith, what are the relevant questions to ask in assessing the views of Paley and Brunner? Presumably one would be concerned about how consistent the ethic is with the biblical view of God, how consistent the ethic is with the biblical view of humankind, and how useful the ethic is in helping the believer to make sound moral judgments. Let us look briefly at the views of Paley and Brunner in the light of these three issues.

First, how consistent is each position with the biblical view of God? Needless to say, through the centuries there have been many different interpretations of the view of God portrayed in the Bible. Yet there has been a growing consensus during the twentieth century that the God of the biblical tradition should be described in terms of dynamic personhood rather than in terms of static perfection. Jesus is regarded as a window into God's nature, and through that window God appears as faithful, forgiving, self-giving, holy love. That love is seen to be endlessly resourceful in encounters with humankind. Legalistic ethics, however well-intentioned, through the rigidity of its fixed rules seems to be at odds with the resourceful freedom of divine love. Accordingly, Brunner's position appears to be more consonant with this view of God than does Paley's.

Second, how consistent are the views of Paley and Brunner with the biblical view of humankind? Here too, a variety of interpretations have appeared through the centuries. One of the most compelling of these interpretations suggests that the human, in being created in the image of God, is called upon to reflect God's creative freedom and love as a steward of creation. Humans are given sovereignty over the world and are summoned to rule with responsible freedom. Because the human situation is a dynamic process and not a static state, the human who is summoned to be a steward of creation must mirror the resourceful freedom of God's love. But such mirroring is possible only after the brokenness of the human relationship with God has been repaired by grace through faith. Even as legalistic ethics seems at odds with divine love, even so the static nature of legalistic rules seems to be at odds with the creative resourcefulness required of humans as they manage the ever-changing world of which they are the divinely appointed stewards. Here again, Brunner's position seems to be more consonant with this view of humanness than does Paley's.

Third, how useful are the views of Paley and Brunner in helping the believer to make sound moral judgments? What would it take to make a moral judgment "sound" within the circle of faith? Presumably such a judgment would be "sound" if it were consistent with one's other moral judgments and if it were consonant with the biblical view of God and humankind. Already we have suggested that Brunner's view of God and humankind is more consonant with biblical views than is Paley's. Yet the usefulness of Brunner's ethic is open to question. Brunner is so opposed to legalism that he disallows all rules and principles that attempt to express God's will; he claims that God's will can only be known in the immediacy of the concrete situation. If that be the case, can Brunner's ethic ever be useful in the development of legislation that seeks to set forth rules to guide the conduct of human affairs? If it cannot, how viable is an ethic that is incapable of helping to shape a society's laws? Furthermore, can Brunner's ethic prove to be useful in moments of crisis when moral decisions have to be made instantaneously without the benefit of moments to reflect?

Consider, for example, the situation confronted by the neonatal physician who must decide whether or not to withhold treatment from a newly born premature and radically deformed infant. To pause to deliberate would mean to decide in favor of withholding treatment, and the infant would die. If an ethic is to be effective, is it not essential that it be capable of generating rules *in advance* to guide human action in such crisis situations?

How does one perceive God's will in the immediacy of the concrete situation? Brunner suggests that the Holy Spirit will guide the believer to apprehend God's will. But cannot such an appeal to the influence of the Holy Spirit become the opportunity for emotions to exert their influence to the end that one's moral decisions lose the integrity and consistency of a reasoned approach? And is it not a discredit to the Creator to abandon the use of divinely given reason in the momentous matter of moral decision making?

Brunner seems to have sensed that his ethical posture was on the slippery slope that leads to emotionalism and subjectivism. He allows ethics a preparatory role for the moment of decision making. But how helpful is such preparation unless it develops principles to guide human conduct particularly in the face of moral dilemmas? Brunner has certainly held out for the believer an ethic that seems to be more consonant with divine and human freedom than does the ethic presented by Paley. Furthermore, Brunner suggests for obeying God's will a motivation that is rooted in love of God and love of neighbor; this strikes one as being far more heroic than Paley's, which is rooted in self-interest. Perhaps Brunner's ethic could be made more viable if it were to allow reason to develop provisional ethical principles that are based upon past divine-human encounters and that were subject to constant scrutiny and open to periodic revision.

Review Questions

1. Distinguish natural theology from revealed theology, and indicate the limits of natural theology.
2. Why, according to Paley, should one obey God? Is his reason adequate?
3. Compare and contrast the ways Paley and Brunner indicate that one comes to know the will of God.
4. "Neo-orthodoxy arose as a protest against the flawed portrayal of the human being as a Promethean man." Explain.
5. Why is Brunner so adamantly opposed to legalistic ethics?
6. "Brunner's ethics seems to be on the slippery slope that leads to emotionalism and subjectivism." Explain.

CHAPTER 7

Maximizing Human Happiness

Introduction

The ethical perspective that we will examine in this chapter, *utilitarianism,* originated in Great Britain in response to the Industrial Revolution, which changed the Western world from a basically rural, agrarian society to a fundamentally urban, industrialized society. The Revolution began in Great Britain during the mid-seventeenth century as a result of the confluence of a number of important factors. Britain had rich deposits of coal and iron, the essential ingredients of early industrialization. Among other things, Britain also had a vast colonial empire that provided not only raw materials but also markets for manufactured goods, and Britain possessed fine harbors and an extensive fleet to facilitate the movement of goods between it and the rest of the world. Given this legacy, when British businessmen introduced the factory system and power-driven machinery into the textile industry, the Industrial Revolution took hold and rapidly spread throughout the world, reshaping society in accordance with the needs of the new productive process.

As is the case with most technological advances, however, the moral consequences of the Industrial Revolution were mixed. There were benefits for humankind but not without attendant losses. On the one hand, the gross national product of Britain soared, as is evidenced by the more than tripling of iron production from 1788 to 1806. The wealth that accrued in Britain opened new opportunities for human fulfillment, especially for the middle and upper classes. On the other hand, that wealth accumulated at the expense of the working class, whose dire condition was documented by a wide variety of contemporary witnesses. Frederick Engels (1820–1895), the close collaborator of Karl Marx, documented these witnesses in his famous monograph "The Condition of the Working-Class in England," published in 1845.* Thomas Carlyle (1795–1881), an English essayist and historian, characterized the world of the textile worker as demonic. He wrote the following.

> ** English commerce, with its world-wide convulsive fluctuations, with its immeasurable Proteus Steam demon, makes all paths uncertain for them, all life a bewilderment; society, steadfastness, peaceable continuance, the first blessings of man are not theirs.—This world is for them no home, but a dingy prison-house, of reckless unthrift, rebellion, rancour, indignation against themselves and against all men. It is a green, flowery world, with azure everlasting sky stretched over it, the work and government of a God; or a murky, simmering Tophet, of copperas fumes, cotton fuzz, gin riot, wrath and toil, created by a Demon, governed by a Demon?

Children, being part of the work force, also were victimized by the inhumane working conditions in the factories. Sir David Barry (1780–1835), an English physician and a member of a parliamentary Factories' Inquiry Commission in 1833, made this next observation.

> *** The unfavourable influences of mill-work upon the hands are the following: (1) The inevitable necessity of forcing their mental and bodily effort to keep pace with a machine moved by a uniform and unceasing motive power. (2) Continuance in an upright position during unnaturally long and quickly recurring periods. (3) Loss of sleep in consequence of too long working-hours, pain in the legs, and general physical derangement. To these are often added low, crowded, dusty, or damp work-rooms, impure air, a high temperature, and constant perspiration. Hence the boys especially very soon and with but few exceptions, lose the rosy freshness of childhood, and become paler and thinner than other boys. Even the hand-weaver's bound boy, who sits before his loom with his bare feet resting upon the clay-floor, retains a fresher appearance, because he occasionally goes into the fresh air for a time. But the mill child has not a moment free except for meals, and never goes into the fresh air except on its way to them. All adult male spinners are pale and thin, suffer from capricious appetite and indigestion; and as they are all trained in the mills from their youth up, and there are very few tall, athletic men among them, the conclusion is justified that their occupation is very unfavourable for the development of the male constitution; females bear this work far better.

Concerning the living conditions of the factory workers, the comments of the Reverend B. Alston, pastor in Bethnal Green (one of the major working-class

---

* cf. Karl Marx and Frederick Engels, *On Britain,* second edition (Moscow: Foreign Languages Publishing House, 1962).

** FROM Thomas Carlyle, "Chartism" (London, 1840), pp. 34ff.

*** FROM *On Britain,* p. 190.

residential districts in London), are revealing. Of his parish, Alston observed as follows.

> * It contains 1,400 houses, inhabited by 2,795 families, or about 12,000 persons. The space upon which this large population dwells, is less than 400 yards (1,200 feet) square, and in this overcrowding it is nothing unusual to find a man, his wife, four or five children, and, sometimes, both grandparents, all in one single room of ten to twelve square feet, where they eat, sleep, and work. I believe that before the Bishop of London called attention to this most poverty-stricken parish, people at the West End knew as little of it as of the savages of Australia or the South Sea Isles. And if we make ourselves acquainted with these unfortunates, through personal observation, if we watch them at their scanty meal and see them bowed by illness and want of work, we shall find such a mass of helplessness and misery, that a nation like ours must blush that these things can be possible. I was rector near Huddersfield during the three years in which the mills were at their worst, but I have never seen such complete helplessness of the poor as since then in Bethnal Green. Not one father of a family in ten in the whole neighbourhood has other clothing than his working suit, and that is as bad and tattered as possible; many, indeed, have no other covering for the night than these rags, and no bed, save a sack of straw and shavings.

This kind of human deprivation inspired Marx and Engels to issue the *Communist Manifesto* in 1848. They called upon the exploited working class to unite, revolt, and cast off its socioeconomic chains. That same deprivation inspired Charles Dickens (1812–1870) to place his pen at the service of social reform by generating such works as *Oliver Twist,* published in 1837, which juxtaposed a weak child against the strong forces of crime, poverty, and unenlightened social legislation; he thereby beckoned the reader to liberate those countless children whose wretched condition did not have the happy outcome enjoyed by Oliver. And that same deprivation inspired Jeremy Bentham and his utilitarian disciples to fashion an ethical theory that would be acceptable to all rational persons and whose unqualified goal was the maximization of humankind's happiness.

Jeremy Bentham: Father of Utilitarianism

Jeremy Bentham (1748–1832) was born in London on February 15, 1748, the son of a lawyer. A precocious child, he studied Latin at the age of four, entered Queen's College, Oxford at the age of twelve, and was graduated at the age of fifteen. Although he went on to study law and was called to the bar at the youthful age of nineteen, Bentham's real interests were not in the practice of law but rather in the justification and reform of society's laws and institutions. The guiding thought of his effort was the principle of utility: the notion that an act should be judged

* FROM *On Britain,* p. 62.

right or wrong depending upon its tendency to generate the greatest happiness for the greatest number of persons. Bentham did not invent the principle of utility: earlier formulations of it are to be found in the writings of Joseph Priestley (1733–1804), Cesare Beccaria (1738–1794) and David Hume (1711–1776). What Bentham did was to make the principle of utility the foundation of his ethical theory and social reform. He is regarded, accordingly, as the founding father of utilitarianism.

Bentham was especially disturbed by the undue severity of the penal code and the inhumane conditions of the prisons in his day. He felt that not only did this situation violate humanitarian feelings, but that it also sinned against rationality. Clearly the penal system had been failing to serve the common good. What was needed was a system rationally generated on the foundations of the utility principle. In 1789, the year of the French Revolution, Bentham published his foundational work of utilitarian theory, *Introduction to the Principle of Morals and Legislation,* from which the following selection is taken. As an application of his theory, Bentham published in 1791 his plan for a model prison called *Panopticon,* and tried to induce the infant French republic to implement his scheme. Although the French National Assembly conferred citizenship upon him in 1792, it failed to adopt his Panopticon scheme. And although the British government encouraged Panopticon at first, the scheme came to naught, presumably through the subtle influence of the crown. At any rate, the British Parliament voted Bentham a handsome sum of money in 1813 to compensate him for his expenditures associated with the project.

Through his many writings, many of which were either abandoned unfinished or left to the agency of friends and disciples for publication, and through his personal advocacy, Bentham gradually became the leader of a group of radicals devoted to his principles. One of his disciples was James Mill (1773–1836) whose son, John Stuart Mill (1806–1873) became one of the most famous defenders of utilitarianism. Bentham's group founded a journal, the *Westminster Review,* in 1824, to provide a radical alternative to the prevailing conservative press. They also were instrumental in the founding of University College, London in 1828 to offer a third alternative to the two existing British universities, Oxford and Cambridge.

When Bentham died on June 6, 1832, his body—rather than being dissected for the benefit of science as he had instructed—was embalmed, dressed in his accustomed attire, and preserved in the college he had helped found.

Psychological Hedonism Affirmed

Bentham begins his discussion of utilitarian moral theory by affirming psychological hedonism as a fact. Hedonism as an ethical theory is the view that pleasure should be the goal of all action. Psychological hedonism is the view that all human beings are so constituted that they in fact always seek to attain pleasure and avoid pain. Upon this alleged fact about human nature, Bentham tries to establish the ethical basis for utilitarianism. In what sense, however, can it be meaningful to say that we *ought* to pursue pleasure and avoid pain if in fact we always do pursue pleasure and always do seek to avoid pain?

* Nature has placed mankind under the governance of two sovereign masters, *pain* and *pleasure*. It is for them alone to point out what we ought to do, as well as to determine what we shall do. On the one hand the standard of right and wrong, on the other the chain of causes and effects, are fastened to their throne. They govern us in all we do, in all we say, in all we think; every effort we can make to throw off our subjection, will serve but to demonstrate and confirm it. In words a man may pretend to abjure their empire: but in reality he will remain subject to it all the while. The *principle of utility* recognizes the subjection, and assumes it for the foundation of that system, the object of which is to rear the fabric of felicity by the hands of reason and of law. Systems which attempt to question it, deal in sounds instead of sense, in caprice instead of reason, in darkness instead of light.

Principle of Utility Articulated

Bentham proceeds to state the principle of utility and to clarify the key terms used in his statement.

But enough of metaphor and declamation: it is not by such means that moral science is to be improved.

The principle of utility is the foundation of the present work; it will be proper therefore at the outset to give an explicit and determinate account of what is meant by it. By the principle of utility is meant that principle which approves or disapproves of every action whatsoever, according to the tendency which it appears to have to augment or diminish the happiness of the party whose interest is in question; or, what is the same thing in other words, to promote or to oppose that happiness. I say of every action whatsoever; and therefore not only of every action of a private individual, but of every measure of government.

By utility is meant that property in any object, whereby it tends to produce benefit, advantage, pleasure, good, or happiness, (all this in the present case comes to the same thing) or (what comes again to the same thing) to prevent the happening of mischief, pain, evil, or unhappiness to the party whose interest is considered: if that party be the community in general, then the happiness of the community: if a particular individual, then the happiness of that individual.

The interest of the community is one of the most general expressions that can occur in the phraseology of morals: no wonder that the meaning of it is often lost. When it has a meaning, it is this. The community is a fictitious *body,* composed of the individual persons who are considered as constituting as it were its *members.* The interest of the community then is, what?—the sum of the interests of the several members who compose it.

It is vain to talk of the interest of the community, without understanding

* FROM Jeremy Bentham, *Principles of Morals and Legislation.*

what is the interest of the individual. A thing is said to promote the interest, or to be *for* the interest, of an individual, when it tends to add to the sum total of his pleasures; or, what comes to the same thing, to diminish the sum total of his pains.

An action then may be said to be conformable to the principle of utility, or, for shortness' sake, to utility, (meaning with respect to the community at large) when the tendency it has to augment the happiness of the community is greater than any it has to diminish it.

A measure of government (which is but a particular kind of action, performed by a particular person or persons) may be said to be conformable to or dictated by the principle of utility, when in like manner the tendency which it has to augment the happiness of the community is greater than any which it has to diminish it.

When an action, or in particular a measure of government, is supposed by a man to be conformable to the principle of utility, it may be convenient, for the purposes of discourse, to imagine a kind of law or dictate, called a law or dictate of utility; and to speak of the action in question, as being conformable to such law or dictate.

A man may be said to be a partizan of the principle of utility, when the approbation or disapprobation he annexes to any action, or to any measure, is determined by and proportioned to the tendency which he conceives it to have to augment or to diminish the happiness of the community: or in other words, to its conformity or unconformity to the laws or dictates of utility.

Of an action that is conformable to the principle of utility, one may always say either that it is one that ought to be done, or at least that it is not one that ought not to be done. One may say also, that it is right it should be done; at least that it is not wrong it should be done: that it is a right action; at least that it is not a wrong action. When thus interpreted, the words *ought* and *right* and *wrong,* and others of that stamp, have a meaning: when otherwise, they have none.

The Case for Utility Presented

Can the principle of utility be proved or disproved? If it cannot, why not? Bentham's reply contains detailed advice (a ten-point procedure of philosophical self-analysis) to those who find themselves opposed to the principle of utility.

When a man attempts to combat the principle of utility, it is with reason drawn, without his being aware of it, from that very principle itself. His arguments, if they prove anything, prove not that the principle is *wrong,* but that, according to the applications he supposes to be made of it, it is *misapplied.* Is it possible for a man to move the earth? Yes: but he must first find out another earth to stand upon.

To disapprove the propriety of it by argument is impossible; but, from the causes that have been mentioned, or from some confused or partial view of it, a man may happen to be disposed not to relish it. Where this is the case, if he thinks the settling of his opinions on such a subject worth the trouble, let him take the following steps, and at length, perhaps, he may come to reconcile himself to it.

1. Let him settle with himself, whether he would wish to discard this principle altogether; if so, let him consider what it is that all his reasonings (in matters of politics especially) can amount to?
2. If he would, let him settle with himself, whether he would judge and act without any principle, or whether there is any other he would judge and act by?
3. If there be, let him examine and satisfy himself whether the principle he thinks he has found is really any separate intelligible principle; or whether it be not a mere principle in words, a kind of phrase, which at bottom expresses neither more nor less than the mere averment of his own unfounded sentiments; that is, what in another person he might be apt to call caprice?
4. If he is inclined to think that his own approbation or disapprobation, annexed to the idea of an act, without any regard to its consequences, is a sufficient foundation for him to judge and act upon, let him ask himself whether his sentiment is to be a standard of right and wrong, with respect to every other man, or whether every man's sentiment has the same privilege of being a standard to itself?
5. In the first case, let him ask himself whether his principle is not despotical, and hostile to all the rest of the human race?
6. In the second case, whether it is not anarchical, and whether at this rate there are not as many different standards of right and wrong as there are men? and whether even to the same man, the same thing which is right today, may not (without the least change in its nature) be wrong tomorrow? and whether the same thing is not right and wrong in the same place at the same time? and in either case, whether all argument is not at an end? and whether, when two men have said, "I like this" and "I don't like it," they can (upon such principle) have anything more to say?
7. If he should have said to himself, No: for that the sentiment which he proposes as a standard must be grounded on reflection, let him say on what particulars the reflection is to turn? if on particulars having relation to the utility of the act, then let him say whether this is not deserting his own principle, and borrowing assistance from that very one in opposition to which he sets it up: or if not on those particulars, on what other particulars?
8. If he should be for compounding the matter and adopting his own principle in part, and the principle of utility in part, let him say how far he will adopt it?
9. When he has settled with himself where he will stop, then let him ask himself how he justifies to himself the adopting it so far? and why he will not adopt it any farther?
10. Admitting any other principle than the principle of utility to be a right principle, a principle that it is right for a man to pursue; admitting (what is not true) that the word *right* can have a meaning without reference to utility, let him say whether there is any such thing as a *motive* that a man can have to pursue the dictates of it: if there is, let him say what that

motive is, and how it is to be distinguished from those which enforce the
dictates of utility: if not, then lastly let him say what it is this other principle
can be good for?

Next, Bentham attacks all other ethical positions. His strategy is to reduce the
possible alternatives to the principle of utility to two in number: the principle of
asceticism, and the principle of *sympathy and antipathy.* Then he demonstrates
the irrationality of an ethics based on either of these two principles.

> If the principle of utility be a right principle to be governed by, and
> that in all cases, it follows from what has been just observed, that whatever
> principle differs from it in any case must necessarily be a wrong one. To
> prove any other principle, therefore, to be a wrong one, there needs no
> more than just to show it to be what it is, a principle of which the dictates
> are in some point or other different from those of the principle of utility:
> to state it is to confute it.
>
> A principle may be different from that of utility in two ways: 1. By being
> constantly opposed to it; this is the case with a principle which may be
> termed the principle of *asceticism.* 2. By being sometimes opposed to it,
> and sometimes not, as it may happen: this is the case with another, which
> may be termed the principle of *sympathy and antipathy.*
>
> By the principle of asceticism I mean that principle, which, like the
> principle of utility, approves or disapproves of any action, according to
> the tendency which it appears to have to augment or diminish the happiness
> of the party whose interest is in question; but in an inverse manner: approving
> of actions in as far as they tend to diminish his happiness; disapproving of
> them in as far as they tend to augment it.
>
> The principle of asceticism seems originally to have been the reverie of
> certain hasty speculators, who having perceived, or fancied, that certain
> pleasures, when reaped in certain circumstances, have, at the long run,
> been attended with pains more than equivalent to them, took occasion to
> quarrel with everything that offered itself under the name of pleasure. Having
> then got thus far, and having forgot the point which they start from, they
> pushed on, and went so much further as to think it meritorious to fall in
> love with pain. Even this, we see, is at bottom but the principle of utility
> misapplied.
>
> The principle of utility is capable of being consistently pursued; and it is
> but tautology to say, that the more consistently it is pursued, the better it
> must ever be for humankind. The principle of asceticism never was, or
> ever can be, consistently pursued by any living creature. Let but one tenth
> part of the inhabitants of this earth pursue it consistently, and in a day's
> time they will have turned it into a hell.
>
> Among the principles adverse to that of utility, that which at this day
> seems to have most influence in matters of government, is what may be
> called the principle of sympathy and antipathy. By the principle of sympathy
> and antipathy, I mean that principle which approves or disapproves of certain
> actions, not on account of their tending to augment the happiness, nor
> yet on account of their tending to diminish the happiness of the party whose

interest is in question, but merely because a man finds himself disposed to approve or disapprove of them: holding up that approbation or disapprobation as a sufficient reason for itself, and disclaiming the necessity of looking out for any extrinsic ground. Thus far in the general department of morals; and in the particular department of politics, measuring out the quantum (as well as determining the ground) of punishment, by the degree of the disapprobation.

It is manifest that this is rather a principle in name than in reality; it is not a positive principle of itself, so much as a term employed to signify the negation of all principle. What one expects to find in a principle is something that points out some external consideration, as a means of warranting and guiding the internal sentiments of approbation and disapprobation; this expectation is but ill fulfilled by a proposition, which does neither more nor less than hold up each of those sentiments as a ground and standard for itself.

In looking over the catalogue of human actions (says a partizan of this principle) in order to determine which of them are to be marked with the seal of disapprobation, you need but to take counsel of your own feelings: whatever you find in yourself a propensity to condemn, is wrong for that very reason. For the same reason it is also meet for punishment: what proportion it is adverse to utility, or whether it be adverse to utility at all, is a matter that makes no difference. In that same *proportion* also is it meet for punishment: if you hate much, punish much; if you hate little, punish little; punish as you hate. If you hate not at all, punish not at all; the fine feelings of the soul are not to be overborne and tyrannized by the harsh and rugged dictates of political utility. . . .

It may be wondered, perhaps, that in all this while no mention has been made of the *theological* principle; meaning that principle which professes to recur for the standard of right and wrong to the will of God. But the case is, this is not in fact a distinct principle. It is never anything more or less than one or other of the time before-mentioned principles presenting itself under another shape. The *will* of God here meant cannot be his revealed will, as contained in the sacred writings: for that is a system which nobody ever thinks of recurring to at this time of day, for the details of political administration: and even before it can be applied to the details of private conduct, it is universally allowed, by the most eminent divines of all persuasions, to stand in need of pretty ample interpretation; else to what use are the works of those divines? And for the guidance of these interpretations, it is also allowed, that some other standard must be assumed. The will then which is meant on this occasion, is that which may be called the *presumptive* will: that is to say, that which is presumed to be his will on account of the conformity of its dictates to those of some other principle. What then may be this other principle? It must be one or other of the three mentioned above; for there cannot, as we have seen, be any more. It is plain, therefore, that, setting revelation out of the question, no light can ever be thrown upon the standard of right and wrong by anything that can be said upon the question, What is God's will. We may be perfectly sure, indeed, that whatever is right is conformable to the will of God; but so far is that from answering the purpose of showing us what is right, that it is necessary to know first whether a thing is right, in order to know from thence whether it be conformable to the will of God.

The Hedonistic Calculus Explained

Bentham's goal is the rational reformation of society to maximize the happiness of humankind. The accumulation of many pleasures and the avoidance of pain generate a happy life. But how does one reform society to maximize happiness? Bentham's strategy is both profoundly simple and bewilderingly complex. According to psychological hedonism, human beings are always motivated by the pursuit of pleasure and the avoidance of pain. Therefore pleasure-producing actions and pain-producing actions can be used to condition people to act in ways that will maximize the happiness of humankind. That is the simple facet of Bentham's strategy, and it is very much akin to the behavior modification through environmental reinforcers advocated by B. F. Skinner in our own age. The complex part of Bentham's scheme involves the quantification of pleasures and pains so that a person can choose rationally to pursue those actions that will generate the most happiness for humankind. To perform this quantification, Bentham devised his famous *hedonistic calculus.* Step by step, this calculus seeks to reduce varying pleasures and pains to readily comparable quantities so that rational decision making will be facilitated. Suppose, for example, that one had the opportunity to allocate a large sum of money to one of several children's projects. Should one endow the Children's Television Workshop, or the Suzuki Violin Association of America, or the Junior Hockey League Program of America, or some other worthy project? Bentham's procedure would be to run each possibility through the categories of the hedonistic calculus, and then to choose the project that is likely to generate the greatest amount of net pleasure for human beings. The complexity of performing such a calculation will become apparent in Bentham's description of the calculus.

> Pleasures then, and the avoidance of pains, are the *ends* which the legislator has in view: it behooves him therefore to understand their *value.* Pleasures and pains are the *instruments* he has to work with: it behooves him therefore to understand their force, which is again, in other words, their value.
>
> To a person considered by *himself,* the value of a pleasure or pain considered *by itself,* will be greater or less, according to the four following circumstances.

1. Its *intensity.*
2. Its *duration.*
3. Its *certainty* or *uncertainty.*
4. Its *propinquity* or *remoteness.*

> These are the circumstances which are to be considered in estimating a pleasure or a pain considered each of them by itself. But when the value of any pleasure or pain is considered for the purpose of estimating the

tendency of any *act* by which it is produced, there are two other circumstances to be taken into the account; these are,

5. Its *fecundity,* or the chance it has of being followed by sensations of the same kind: that is, pleasures, if it be a pleasure; pains, if it be a pain.
6. Its *purity,* or the chance it has of *not* being followed by sensations of the *opposite* kind: that is, pains, if it be a pleasure: pleasures, if it be a pain.

These two last, however, are in strictness scarcely to be deemed properties of the pleasures or the pain itself; they are not, therefore, in strictness to be taken into the account of the value of that pleasure or that pain. They are in strictness to be deemed properties only of the act, or other event by which such pleasure or pain has been produced; and accordingly are only to be taken into the account of the tendency of such act or such event.

To a *number* of persons, with reference to each of whom the value of a pleasure or a pain is considered, it will be greater or less according to seven circumstances: to wit, the six preceding ones . . . and one other: to wit:

7. Its *extent;* that is, the number of persons to whom it *extends;* or (in other words) who are affected by it.

To take an exact account then of the general tendency of any act, by which the interests of a community are affected, proceed as follows. Begin with any one person of those whose interests seem most immediately to be affected by it: and take an account,

1. Of the value of each distinguishable *pleasure* which appears to be produced by it in the *first* instance.
2. Of the value of each *pain* which appears to be produced by it in the *first* instance.
3. Of the value of each pleasure which appears to be produced by it *after* the first. This constitutes the fecundity of the first *pleasure* and the *impurity* of the first *pain.*
4. Of the value of each *pain* which appears to be produced by it after the first. This constitutes the *fecundity* of the first *pain,* and the *impurity* of the first pleasure.
5. Sum up all the values of all the *pleasures* on the one side, and those of all the pains on the other. The balance, if it be on the side of pleasure, will give the *good* tendency of the act upon the whole, with respect to the interests of that *individual* person; if on the side of pain, the *bad* tendency of it upon the whole.
6. Take an account of the *number* of persons whose interests appear to be concerned; and repeat the above process with respect to each. *Sum up* the numbers expressive of the degrees of *good* tendency, which the act has, with respect to each individual, in regard to whom the tendency of it is *good* upon the whole: do this again with respect to each individual, in

regard to whom the tendency of it is *bad* upon the whole. Take the *balance;* which, if on the side of *pleasure,* will give the general *good tendency* of the act, with respect to the total number of community of individuals concerned; if on the side of pain the general *evil tendency,* with respect to the same community.

Modifications of Benthamism Required

Bentham believed he was rescuing ethics from the fickle sentiments and intuitions of human beings and grounding it upon careful, calculating reason. He viewed ethics built upon the principle of utility as unassailable. His disciples, however, found it necessary to make some modifications in Bentham's discussion as penetrating questions were raised. Can qualitative distinctions be introduced; are some pleasures "base" and others "noble"? If so, how does one decide between a noble and base pleasure if both of them generate the same quantity of pleasure? Is the hedonistic calculus at all practical? Is pleasure really quantifiable? Must one assess every act by the principle of utility, or can one utilize pre-established rules which themselves have been worked out on the basis of the utility principle? Consideration of these and many similar questions led to alterations and enrichments of utilitarianism, and utilitarians came to be labelled in a number of ways to indicate how they responded to the most important of these questions.

For example, *act utilitarianism* identified those who believed every act must be assessed directly by the principle of utility. *Rule utilitarianism* designated those who believed that actions are right or wrong depending on whether the rules that enjoin them have good or bad consequences. Such rules can assist a person in the moment of decision making when the time for extended philosophical assessment is seldom present. *Hedonistic utilitarians* were those who, like Bentham, believed that only the quantity of pleasure is relevant to the hedonistic calculus. *Ideal utilitarians* accepted a distinction between the quantity and the quality of pleasures and believed that human beings should strive for the higher ideals of life, not just the multiplication of the baser pleasures of human existence. Combining these terms gives rise to four possible varieties of utilitarianism: hedonistic act utilitarianism, ideal rule utilitarianism, hedonistic rule utilitarianism, or ideal act utilitarianism. Of these four possibilities—though the terms were not in use in Bentham's day—Bentham could probably be classified as a hedonistic act utilitarian. One of Bentham's younger contemporaries who did as much as any other single person to move utilitarianism beyond the simple calculations of the sheer quantity of pleasure and pain proposed by Bentham was John Stuart Mill, who became one of the nineteenth century's most eloquent defenders of utilitarian principles. It is to his interpretation of utilitarianism that we now turn.

John Stuart Mill: Interpreter of Utilitarianism

Although Bentham was the founder of utilitarianism as a philosophical movement, its popularization and defense was largely the work of John Stuart Mill (1806–1873). The son of James Mill, John Stuart was a brilliant child who began the study of Greek and mathematics at age three and turned to Latin at eight. Tutored under the careful eye of his father, who intended for his son to be a major interpreter of the utilitarian views of his friend Bentham, John Stuart Mill is the one to whom we owe a major reinterpretation of utilitarian theory. Given the classification mentioned previously, we would today classify John Stuart Mill as an *ideal rule utilitarian,* although this was not a distinction current in his own time.

Discriminating Higher from Lower Pleasures

Bentham's hedonistic calculus emphasized only the quantity of pleasure. "Pushpin is as good as poetry," Bentham said. But clearly this seems to imply that human beings cannot discriminate among the quality of pleasures. This seemed to John Stuart Mill to be simply false. That we are humans and not beasts implies the ability to enjoy the higher pleasures. But what are "higher" pleasures? Who decides? By what criteria? These are old questions, at least as old as the ancient hedonists, the Epicureans. We will let Mill speak for himself.

* The creed which accepts as the foundation of morals *utility,* or the *greatest happiness principle,* holds that actions are right in proportion as they tend to promote happiness, wrong as they tend to produce the reverse of happiness. By 'happiness' is intended pleasure, and the absence of pain; by 'unhappiness,' pain, and the privation of pleasure. To give a clear view of the moral standard set up by the theory, much more requires to be said; in particular, what things it includes in the ideas of pain and pleasure; and to what extent this is left an open question. But these supplementary explanations do not affect the theory of life on which this theory of morality is grounded—namely, that pleasure, and freedom from pain, are the only things desirable as ends; and that all desirable things (which are as numerous in the utilitarian as in any other scheme) are desirable either for the pleasure inherent in themselves, or as means to the promotion of pleasure and the prevention of pain.

Now such a theory of life excites in many minds, and among them in some of the most estimable in feeling and purpose, inveterate dislike. To suppose that life has (as they express it) no higher end than pleasure—no better and nobler object of desire and pursuit—they designate as utterly mean and groveling; as a doctrine worthy only of swine, to whom the followers of Epicurus were, at a very early period, contemptuously likened; and modern holders of the doctrine are occasionally made the subject of equally polite comparisons by its German, French, and English assailants.

When thus attacked, the Epicureans have always answered that it is not they but their accusers who represent human nature in a degrading light; since the accusation supposes human beings to be capable of no pleasures except those of which swine are capable. If this supposition were true, the charge could not be gainsaid, but would then no longer be imputation; for if the sources of pleasure were precisely the same to human beings and to swine, the rule of life which is good enough for the one would be

* FROM John Stuart Mill, *Utilitarianism.*

good enough for the other. The comparison of the Epicurean life to that of beasts is felt as degrading, precisely because a beast's pleasures do not satisfy a human being's conceptions of happiness. Human beings have faculties more elevated than the animal appetites, and when once made conscious of them, do not regard anything as happiness which does not include their gratification. I do not, indeed, consider the Epicureans to have been by any means faultless in drawing out their scheme of consequences from the utilitarian principle. To do this in any sufficient manner, many Stoic, as well as Christian elements require to be included. But there is no known Epicurean theory of life which does not assign to the pleasures of the intellect, of the feelings and imagination, and of the moral sentiments, a much higher value of pleasures than to those of mere sensation. It must be admitted, however, that utilitarian writers in general have placed the superiority of mental over bodily pleasures chiefly in the greater permanency, safety, uncostliness, etc., of the former—that is, in their circumstantial advantages rather than in their intrinsic nature. And on all these points utilitarians have fully proved their case; but they might have taken the other, and, as it may be called, higher ground, with entire consistency. It is quite compatible with the principle of utility to recognize the fact, that some *kinds* of pleasure are more desirable and more valuable than others. It would be absurd that while, in estimating all other things, quality is considered as well as quantity, the estimation of pleasures should be supposed to depend on quantity alone.

The Standard for Assessing Pleasures

So far, so good. But by what standard do we choose one pleasure, or set of pleasures, as *qualitatively* superior to others? One way, and the way suggested by Mill, is to ask the person who has experienced the widest variety of pleasures for advice.

If I am asked what I mean by difference of quality in pleasures, or what makes one pleasure more valuable than another merely as a pleasure, except its being greater in amount, there is but one possible answer. Of two pleasures, if there be one to which all or almost all who have experience of both give a decided preference, irrespective of any feeling of moral obligation to prefer it, that is the more desirable pleasure. If one of the two is, by those who are competently acquainted with both, placed so far above the other that they prefer it, even though knowing it to be attended with a greater amount of discontent, and would not resign it for any quantity of the other pleasure which their nature is capable of, we are justified in ascribing to the preferred enjoyment a superiority in quality, so far outweighing quantity as to render it, in comparison, of small account.

Now it is an unquestionable fact that those who are equally acquainted with, and equally capable of appreciating and enjoying, both, do give a most marked preference to the manner of existence which employs their higher faculties. Few human creatures would consent to be changed into any of the lower animals, for a promise of the fullest allowance of a beast's pleasures; no intelligent human being would consent to be a fool, no instructed person would be an ignoramus, no person of feeling and conscience would be selfish and base, even though they should be persuaded that the fool, the dunce, or the rascal is better satisfied with his lot than they are with theirs. They would not resign what they possess more than he for the most complete satisfaction of all the desires which they have in common with him. If they ever fancy they would, it is only in cases of unhappiness so extreme, that to escape from it they would exchange their lot for almost any other, however undesirable in their own eyes. A being of higher faculties requires more to make him happy, is capable probably of more acute suffering, and certainly accessible to it at more points, than one of an inferior type; but in spite of these liabilities, he can never really wish to sink into what he feels to be a lower grade of existence. We may give what explanation we please of this unwillingness: we may attribute it to pride, a name which is given indiscriminately to some of the most and to some of the least estimable feelings of which mankind are capable; we may refer it to the love of liberty and personal independence, an appeal to which was with the Stoics one of the most effective means for the inculcation of it; to the love of power, or to the love of excitement, both of which do really enter into and contribute to it: but its most appropriate appellation is a sense of dignity, which all human beings possess in one form or other, and in some, though by no means in exact, proportion to their higher faculties, and which is so essential a part of the happiness of those in whom it is strong, that nothing which conflicts with it could be, otherwise than momentarily, an object of desire to them. Whoever supposes that this preference takes place at a sacrifice of happiness—that the superior being, in anything like equal circumstances, is not happier than the inferior— confounds the two very different ideas, of *happiness* and *content*. It is indisputable that the being whose capacities of enjoyment are low, has the greatest chance of having them fully satisfied; and a highly endowed being will always feel that any happiness which he can look for, as the world is constituted, is imperfect. But he can learn to bear its imperfections, if they are at all bearable; and they will not make him envy the being who is indeed unconscious of the imperfections, but only because he feels not at all the good which those imperfections qualify. It is better to be a human being dissatisfied than a pig satisfied; better to be Socrates dissatisfied than a fool satisfied. And if the fool, or the pig, are of a different opinion, it is because they only know their own side of the question. The other party to the comparison knows both sides.

Utility, Ideals, and Rules

That Mill included the quality of pleasures as part of the hedonistic calculus meant that ideals could be considered a goal of an action. A person might choose to forego an immediate pleasure, gorging on food, for the sake of an ideal such as a trim and healthful figure. Or a person might forego the accumulation of money, which would be pleasurable, for the sake of a lower paying occupation in service of an ideal. This is where the term *ideal* enters into the label *ideal rule utilitarianism*. But Mill also went another step beyond Bentham. Whereas Bentham implied that each act should be evaluated in terms of the hedonistic calculus, Mill suggested that we use utilitarian principles to establish rules of conduct which then guide our lives. In practice, this means that a person accepts standards and rules for conduct that reflect utilitarian principles rather than having to calculate the pleasure accruing to each individual act.

> According to the 'greatest happiness principle,' as above explained, the ultimate end, with reference to and for the sake of which all other things are desirable (whether we are considering our own good or that of other people), is an existence exempt as far as possible from pain, and as rich as possible in enjoyments, both in point of quantity and quality, the test of quality, and the rule for measuring it against quantity, being the preference felt by those who in their opportunities of experience, to which must be added their habits of self-consciousness and self-observation, are best furnished with the means of comparison. This, being, according to the utilitarian opinion, the end of human action, is necessarily also the standard of morality; which may accordingly be defined, the rules and precepts for human conduct, by the observance of which an existence such as has been described might be, to the greatest extent possible, secured to all mankind; and not to them only, but so far as the nature of things admits, to the whole sentient creation.

By introducing considerations of quality rather than Bentham's exclusive emphasis on the quantity of pleasure, Mill faces an inconsistency. Suppose of two pleasures we are told that one is qualitatively superior to the other. On what grounds can we make such a judgment? Surely not on the grounds of pleasure: both are pleasures. So it must be a principle other than pleasure (such as an appeal to an ideal of human nature). But this would be inconsistent, because utilitarianism claimed that pleasure is the sole criterion. There is no evidence that Mill ever saw this difficulty or responded to it.

Assessment

What are we to make of utilitarianism as an answer to the question, What ought I to do? The first level of our assessment must be a historical one. As both an ethical and political force, utilitarianism was a significant factor in Britain in the nineteenth century. It inspired the rectification of some of the human deprivation occasioned by the Industrial Revolution. Through the reasoned argument of the followers of Bentham and Mill, many social reforms were adopted in England before they were accepted in the rest of the world—elimination of slavery, child labor laws, protection of the rights of workers, prison reform, just to name some. If a philosophical movement is to be evaluated by its results, utilitarianism has been more successful than many philosophical viewpoints.

But to point to the success of a movement does not gloss over its internal inconsistencies. One of the central ones that afflicts utilitarianism is its inability to take into account the rights of individuals as individuals. Remember that the principle of utility seeks *the greatest good for the greatest number.* But what are we to say, on utilitarian grounds, about an action that proposes to repress a minority group for the sake of the majority? Or an attempt to destroy one or more individuals in order to improve the pleasure of a larger number? To put the matter more bluntly, is it ever right to deprive a single individual of human dignity, no matter how much pleasure that deprivation might bring to society as a whole?

These kinds of questions loomed large in the critical debate about utilitarianism. Mill's response includes two works that have become classics in their own right: *Subjection of Women,* a powerful treatise for women's equality written in 1869; and his essay *On Liberty,* written in 1859. Both of these works would have been significant in their own right, apart from all utilitarian considerations. But that also points to a weakness of utilitarianism: it is hard to see how Mill, or any utilitarian for that matter, could argue for the equality of women, or the maximum amount of liberty for minorities, if it could be shown that these actions would not contribute to the happiness of the majority. The inequality of women, in fact, has usually been justified by an appeal to the beneficial results this situation has for society. And the repression of minorities has usually been justified in the name of some alleged benefit to society as a whole. What is needed, and what utilitarianism seems unable to provide, is an ethical theory that focuses on the rights of individual persons and treats them as deserving of dignity and respect simply because they are persons. For this additional dimension to our ethical thinking we turn to the work of another philosopher, Immanuel Kant.

Review Questions

1. Discuss the influence of the Industrial Revolution upon the development of utilitarianism.
2. What is psychological hedonism? Can it be combined meaningfully with utilitarianism as Bentham attempts to do?
3. What case does Bentham make in support of the principle of utility being accepted as the fundamental ethical principle?
4. What is the hedonistic calculus?
5. Discuss how John Stuart Mill modified Bentham's utilitarianism through the qualitative ranking of pleasures and the use of rules.

CHAPTER 8

Pursuing One's Duty

Introduction

Now that we have examined three ethical theories, the role of theory in ethics should be clearer to you. Rather than providing a set of rules that can be applied in a rather mechanistic fashion to an ethical problem, an ethical theory is an attempt to make explicit those considerations we use in responding to ethical problems. Not only does an ethical theory aim for explicitness, but it is also concerned with the consistency, coherence, and reasonableness of its point of view. How *exact* an ethical theory can be is a matter about which philosophers have disagreed. Aristotle, who was the first Western philosopher to develop a systematic ethical theory, admitted at the outset that ethics is not an exact science. In an often-quoted paragraph, Aristotle says that ethics can never be as precise as mathematics.

> * Our discussion will be adequate if it has as much clearness as the subject-matter admits of, for precision is not to be sought for alike in all discussions . . . for it is the mark of an educated man to look for precision in each class of things just so far as the nature of the subject admits; it is evidently equally foolish to accept probable reasoning from a mathematician and to demand from a rhetorician scientific proofs.

Other philosophers, notably Jeremy Bentham, thought ethics could be fairly exact; his hedonistic calculus was intended to be a model of exactness—a quantifiable

* FROM Aristotle, *Nicomachean Ethics* 1094, 12–14, 25–28.

approach to moral decision: add up the total amount of pleasure produced by various actions; add up the total amount of pain; do the calculations; and then choose the act that will create the greatest amount of net pleasure or happiness for the greatest number of people.

A different approach to ethical theory is found in the writings of Immanual Kant, who thought that a degree of exactness was possible in ethics. But it was a precision possible because ethics can achieve a *formal* exactness. To understand what Kant meant, consider the formal principles of the natural sciences or of mathematics. In physics one learns the principle $F = MA$, or in geometry the postulate that the shortest distance between two points is a straight line. But neither principle has any *content;* to give them content we have to observe, measure, and perform necessary calculations. The power of physics and mathematics lies in their ability to discover powerful formal principles (usually called formulas) that allow human reason to extend its scope far beyond what would be possible if we were limited to generalizations based on experience. Kant thought the same approach would be fruitful for ethics.

Immanuel Kant: Obeying the Inviolable Commands of Reason

Immanuel Kant (1724–1804) was born and lived all his life in the East Prussian town of Königsberg, now located in the Soviet Union and known as Kaliningrad. In his early work he focused his attention on problems of natural science and logic. But he soon turned his attention to a wider range of issues, including a critique of the power of reason to answer all the questions it can ask. His conclusion was that certain questions are not open to rational investigation; among these issues are ultimate reality, questions about the origins of the cosmos, and investigations into the nature of the human soul. In his lectures at the University of Königsberg, Kant developed what he referred to as his critical philosophy and also laid out his ethical theory.

The Break with Contemporary Approaches

Kant's ethical philosophy broke with contemporary approaches on two basic points. The *first* was Kant's denial of the claim that we have a special faculty for making ethical judgments—an ethical sense, or conscience. His claim was that we use the same faculty, *reason,* for making ethical decisions that we use in making judgments about the world we live in. The way reason functions in ethical thinking differs, but the difference is only in reason's employment. The *second* break with all previous ethical approaches was Kant's rejection of *consequences* as being the measure of the rightness or wrongness of an action. Hobbes, Butler, Bentham, and Aristotle all give variations on the theme that human actions should be judged in terms of their ability to achieve certain consequences. For Aristotle, as we have seen, actions are judged as they actualize our human potential and lead to a total sense of happiness or well-being. Hobbes, and in a more systematic way,

Bentham and Mill, argued that actions should be judged on the basis of their tendency to maximize pleasure and minimize pain. Even Paley could be viewed as arguing for judging actions by their tendency to bring about eternal rewards or punishments, again a consideration of consequences.

Shortcomings of Consequentialist Ethics

What is wrong with consequentialist ethics, that is, ethical views that base the rightness or wrongness of an action on an evaluation of consequences? From the writings of Kant we can see that there are three shortcomings to the consequentialist approach to ethics:

1. It lacks universality and necessity.
2. It can lead to rules that violate our ordinary moral sensitivities.
3. It reverses the proper relationship between ethics and happiness.

Consider the first point. Kant wants to make ethics into an objective but formal discipline (like logic). If ever ethics is to be respected as a rational endeavor, it must establish principles that apply to all rational beings at all times. And these principles must be recognized as being necessarily true, that is, subject to the same logical tests that we demand of formal principles in the sciences and mathematics. A principle of physics cannot be true for Americans but false for Chinese or Ugandans. We would never respect physics as a science if its principles were not universally recognized as true. And we should expect no less from ethics. When we apply the formal principles of physics, we can give reasons to demonstrate the necessity for the principles. And similarly, we should expect nothing less from ethics. In contrast, the consequentialist approach lacks this universality and necessity because it is based upon empirical generalizations (which can never be more than probabilities). That is to say, consequentialist ethics determines the rightness or wrongness of an action on the basis of projected consequences. And those consequences are projected on the basis of past experiences. But we cannot be absolutely certain that those projected consequences will in fact occur. This in turn means that our moral judgment of rightness or wrongness would be clouded with a measure of uncertainty. Such uncertainty is incompatible with the universality and necessity that Kant requires of the principles of science and of the principles of ethics.

The second point has already been touched upon in the chapter on utilitarianism. One might be able to justify on consequentialist grounds actions that we would judge to be immoral. Slavery, for example, was historically justified on the basis of its contribution to society, without regard for the wretchedness of those enslaved. Even if it could be proved that enslaving a minority contributed to the happiness of the majority (thereby producing a greater total amount of happiness), there is something outrageously unethical about enslaving another human being, regardless of how happy it makes others.

The inadequacy of the consequentialist approach is also reflected by the fact that our legal system appeals to factors other than consequences in determining guilt or innocence. If consequences were the only consideration, there would be no way legally to treat differently persons who caused the death of another, whether it be inadvertently or from "malice aforethought." Both legally and morally we want to distinguish between manslaughter (causing the death of another without intent to do so) and first degree murder (causing the death of another deliberately and with forethought). More than just the consequences of an act seem to matter in determining degrees of guilt: intentions, deliberations, and motives.

The third point is perhaps less obvious but nonetheless an important consideration in Kant's ethical viewpoint. The relation between happiness and morality in consequentialist theories is that happiness accrues to the ethical life. For Aristotle, the goal of life is happiness, and one cannot be said to be living a good life unless one is happy. Even more explicitly in utilitarian ethics, pleasure and the happiness it produces constitute the measure of an action's rightness or wrongness. But for Kant the basic question in ethics is not, Will my actions make me happy? but, Will my actions make me *worthy* of being happy? Again, Kant highlighted an important consideration in our prephilosophical ethical awareness. There seems to be something basically offensive to any rational person viewing an evil individual enjoying unbounded happiness. Reason tells us it should not be so. In a perfectly rational world, evil persons would be miserable and virtuous ones would be happy. But our world is not completely rational, and all too frequently we see persons who are terribly wicked enjoying life to its fullest and being happy in every respect. A rational being could not wish the world to be this way. In the world of fiction, the world we create, it is generally the case that crime does not pay. The villain is destroyed in the final reel. Good triumphs, evil is vanquished. But the world of fiction does not always mirror the real world. Alas, crime pays all too well. Good does not always triumph. At times, virtuous persons suffer simply because they are virtuous. Yet all this is an offense to reason. And worse, if we were building our ethical system on empirical observations, we would conclude that if the good life is the happy life, then the route toward happiness is not necessarily the way of virtue.

An Ethics of Duty

What Kant's ethical theory includes, which the consequentialist theories omit, is the recognition that some acts are right, and some acts are wrong, quite independent of their consequences. It is irrelevant in determining our moral obligation whether an action makes us happy, or whether it contributes to human pleasure. We do that which is right because it is the right thing to do. No other consideration is relevant to our moral deliberation. Theories of this type are called *deontological* (from the Greek word for obligation). A good definition of the *deontological approach* is that it is an ethical theory holding that acting from a sense of duty rather than concern for consequences is the basis for establishing our moral obligation. In short, a deontological theory is an ethics of duty. Human beings have often pursued an ethics of duty (note the legalistic moral codes of various religions), but Immanuel Kant was the first modern philosopher to formulate a deontological theory of ethics, and it is for that reason that we include selections from his writings here.

The Good Without Qualification

Where should we begin in our ethical thinking? Kant begins by making a transition from our ordinary, prephilosophical thinking about ethics to a philosophical level. When we begin thinking about ethics, we come to the issue of what is good. You will recall that understanding the nature of the good was central for Aristotle as well. But Kant gives an answer different from that of Aristotle. Aristotle distinguished between instrumental and intrinsic goods. Instrumental goods are those things that are desirable as a means to something else. The intrinsic good is that which is desirable in itself. For Kant the distinction is between that which is good without qualification and those goods that are qualified with reference to something else. Consider something you think is good—intelligence, for example. Kant points out that in an evil person, intelligence is not good but rather that it serves to magnify the evilness. It is better to deal with a stupid criminal than an intelligent one. We can think of something that is good without qualification as that which does not depend on anything else. The goodness of all the characteristics Kant lists depends upon the goodness of the will of the person who possesses these qualities. Therefore, none of these things is good without qualification—the qualification being that they are only good if accompanied by a good will. It all comes down to this: there is only one thing that is good without qualification, and that is a *good will.* No matter what else is lacking, a person of virtue is a person with goodness of intention, a person whose motives are good. Here is how Kant expresses this idea.

> * There is no possibility of thinking of anything at all in the world, or even out of it, which can be regarded as good without qualification, except a good will. Intelligence, wit, judgment, and whatever talents of the mind one might want to name are doubtless in many respects good and desirable, as are such qualities of temperament as courage, resolution, perseverance. But they can also become extremely bad and harmful if the will, which is to make use of these gifts of nature and which in its special constitution is called character, is not good. The same holds with gifts of fortune; power, riches, honor, even health, and that complete well-being and contentment with one's condition which is called happiness make for pride and often hereby even arrogance, unless there is a good will to correct their influence on the mind and herewith also to rectify the whole principle of action and make it universally conformable to its end. The sight of a being who is not graced by any touch of a pure and good will but who yet enjoys an uninterrupted prosperity can never delight a rational and impartial spectator. Thus a good will seems to constitute the indispensable condition of being even worthy of happiness.
>
> Some qualities are even conducive to this good will itself and can facilitate

* FROM Immanuel Kant, *Grounding for the Metaphysics of Morals,* translated by James W. Ellington, Copyright 1981 by Hackett Publishing Co., Indianapolis. Used by permission.

its work. Nevertheless, they have no intrinsic unconditional worth; but they always presuppose, rather, a good will, which restricts the high esteem in which they are otherwise rightly held, and does not permit them to be regarded as absolutely good. Moderation in emotions and passions, self-control, and calm deliberation are not only good in many respects but even seem to constitute part of the intrinsic worth of a person. But they are far from being rightly called good without qualification (however unconditionally they were commended by the ancients). For without the principles of a good will, they can become extremely bad; the coolness of a villain makes him not only much more dangerous but also immediately more abominable in our eyes than he would have been regarded by us without it.

A good will is good not because of what it effects or accomplishes, nor because of its fitness to attain some proposed end; it is good only through its willing, i.e., it is good in itself. When it is considered in itself, then it is to be esteemed very much higher than anything which it might ever bring about merely in order to favor some inclination, or even the sum total of all inclinations. Even if, by some especially unfortunate fate or by the niggardly provision of stepmotherly nature, this will should be wholly lacking in the power to accomplish its purpose; if with the greatest effort it should yet achieve nothing, and only the good will should remain (not, to be sure, as a mere wish but as the summoning of all the means in our power), yet would it, like a jewel, still shine by its own light as something which has its full value in itself. Its usefulness or fruitlessness can neither augment nor diminish this value. Its usefulness would be, as it were, only the setting to enable us to handle it in ordinary dealings or to attract to it the attention of those who are not yet experts, but not to recommend it to real experts or to determine its value.

But there is something so strange in this idea of the absolute value of a mere will, in which no account is taken of any useful results, that in spite of all the agreement received even from ordinary reason, yet there must arise the suspicion that such an idea may perhaps have as its hidden basis merely some high-flown fancy, and that we may have misunderstood the purpose of nature in assigning to reason the governing of our will. Therefore, this idea will be examined from this point of view.

In the natural constitution of an organized being, i.e., one suitably adapted to the purpose of life, let there be taken as a principle that in such a being no organ is to be found for any end unless it be the most fit and the best adapted for that end. Now if that being's preservation, welfare, or in a word its happiness, were the real end of nature in the case of a being having reason and will, then nature would have hit upon a very poor arrangement in having the reason of the creature carry out this purpose. For all the actions which such a creature has to perform with this purpose in view, and the whole rule of his conduct would have been prescribed much more exactly by instinct; and the purpose in question could have been attained much more certainly by instinct than it ever can be by reason. And if in addition reason had been imparted to this favored creature, then it would have had to serve him only to contemplate the happy constitution of his nature, to admire that nature, to rejoice in it, and to feel grateful to the cause that bestowed it; but reason would not have served him to subject his faculty of desire to its weak and delusive guidance nor would it have served him to meddle incompetently with the purpose of nature. In a word, nature would have taken care that reason did not strike out into a practical use nor presume, with its weak insight, to think out for itself a plan for happiness and the means for attaining it. Nature would have taken upon herself not only the choice of ends but also that of the means, and would with wise foresight have entrusted both to instinct alone. . . .

Reason, however, is not competent enough to guide the will safely as regards its objects and the satisfaction of all our needs (which it in part even multiplies); to this end would an implanted natural instinct have led much more certainly. But inasmuch as reason has been imparted to us as a practical faculty, i.e., as one which is to have influence on the will, its true function must be to produce a will which is not merely good as a means to some further end, but is good in itself. To produce a will good in itself reason was absolutely necessary, inasmuch as nature in distributing her capacities has everywhere gone to work in a purposive manner. While such a will may not indeed be the sole and complete good, it must, nevertheless, be the highest good and the condition of all the rest, even of the desire for happiness.

Actions Based on Impulses

Kant has argued that if happiness were the sole guide of life, then we would be better off not to have to *think* about our moral choices at all; instinct would be a better guide to the pleasant life. But since we are creatures of reason, and reason is to be our guide in making moral choices, it is necessary to examine in more detail the kinds of commands reason gives us. Kant uses the term "imperatives" in the extracts that follow to refer to the commands that we give to ourselves. It is not the case, however, that all our actions are in response to well thought out commands. Some of our actions (maybe even most of them) are the result of impulses: you decide to skip class and spend the afternoon at the lake. No rational command .here, merely the giving in to the impulse to enjoy the first spring day of the season. On an impulse you buy a new dress, even though that will leave you only $5.00 in your checking account. In spite of your better judgment, you spend the weekend visiting a friend at another college instead of studying for the mid-term examination on Monday.

Actions Based on Hypothetical Imperatives

Many of our actions are based on deliberation, though. Some of them are due to commands (imperatives) we give ourselves that are directed toward some end to be accomplished. We can characterize these commands as *if . . . then* sorts of commands. Kant calls these commands *hypothetical imperatives. If* I want to get good grades, *then* I should study. *If* I am to succeed in mastering the flute, *then* I must practice. *If* I want people to like me, *then* I should be friendly. Kant was steadfast in his insistence that we cannot build moral philosophy on hypothetical imperatives. Why? Basically for the same reasons already given against basing ethics on empirical generalizations: this approach would not yield universality and necessity in ethics or in any other discipline. Worse, there is nothing about a hypothetical command that tells us what our duty is. All that hypothetical imperatives tell us is that *if* we desire a certain consequence, *then* we ought to act in such and such a way. They do not tell us whether it is good to pursue that consequence or not. Even if we tried to build ethical philosophy upon the basis of hypothetical imperatives, we would still need some guide to help us determine which end and goals are good and which are not. All hypothetical imperatives tell us is how to act to achieve a certain goal, not whether we should be attempting to achieve it.

Actions Based on the Categorical Imperative

To do the job that moral reasoning requires of us (that is, to have commands that possess universality and necessity), we need a different kind of imperative, a command that commands absolutely, one that is not dependent upon varying conditions. This sort of imperative Kant calls a *categorical imperative*. A categorical imperative commands without any reference to an end to be achieved or a goal to be accomplished. Here is how Kant describes the two kinds of imperatives.

> Now all imperatives command either hypothetically or categorically. The former represent the practical necessity of a possible action as a means for attaining something else that one wants (or may possibly want). The categorical imperative would be one which represented an action as objectively necessary in itself, without reference to another end.
>
> Every practical law represents a possible action as good and hence as necessary for a subject who is practically determinable by reason; therefore all imperatives are formulas for determining an action which is necessary according to the principle of a will that is good in some way. Now if the action would be good merely as a means to something else, so is the imperative hypothetical. But if the action is represented as good in itself, and hence as necessary in a will which of itself conforms to reason as the principle of the will, then the imperative is categorical.
>
> An imperative thus says what action by me would be good, and it presents the practical rule in relation to a will which does not forthwith perform an action simply because it is good, partly because the subject does not always know that the action is good, and partly because (even if he does know it is good) his maxims might yet be opposed to the objective principles of practical reason.
>
> A hypothetical imperative thus says only that an action is good for some purpose, either possible or actual. In the first case it is a problematic practical principle; in the second case an assertoric one. A categorical imperative,

which declares an action to be of itself objectively necessary without reference to any purpose, i.e., without any other end, holds as an apodeictic practical principle.*

Whatever is possible only through the powers of some rational being can be thought of as a possible purpose of some will. Consequently, there are in fact infinitely many principles of action insofar as they are represented as necessary for attaining a possible purpose achievable by them. All sciences have a practical part consisting of problems saying that some end is possible for us and of imperatives telling us how it can be attained. These can, therefore, be called in general imperatives of skill. Here there is no question at all whether the end is reasonable and good, but there is only a question as to what must be done to attain it. The prescriptions needed by a doctor in order to make his patient thoroughly healthy and by a poisoner in order to make sure of killing his victim are of equal value so far as each serves to bring about its purpose perfectly. Since there cannot be known in early youth what ends may be presented to us in the course of life, parents especially seek to have their children learn many different kinds of things, and they provide for skill in the use of means to all sorts of arbitrary ends, among which they cannot determine whether any one of them could in the future become an actual purpose for their ward, though there is always the possibility that he might adopt it. Their concern is so great that they commonly neglect to form and correct their children's judgment regarding the worth of things which might be chosen as ends.

There is, however, one end that can be presupposed as actual for all rational beings (so far as they are dependent beings to whom imperatives apply); and thus there is one purpose which they not merely can have but which can certainly be assumed to be such that they all do have by a natural necessity, and this is happiness. A hypothetical imperative which represents the practical necessity of an action as means for the promotion of happiness is assertoric. It may be expounded not simply as necessary to an uncertain, merely possible purpose, but as necessary to a purpose which can be presupposed a priori and with certainty as being present in everyone because it belongs to his essence. Now skill in the choice of means to one's own greatest well-being can be called prudence in the narrowest sense. And thus the imperative that refers to the choice of means to one's own happiness, i.e., the precept of prudence, still remains hypothetical; the action is commanded not absolutely but only as a means to a further purpose.

Finally, there is one imperative which immediately commands a certain conduct without having as its condition any other purpose to be attained by it. This imperative is categorical. It is not concerned with the matter of the action and its intended result, but rather with the form of the action and the principle from which it follows; what is essentially good in the

---

* Apodeictic means *necessary,* and Kant refers to reason in its function of making moral judgments as its *practical* function. The phrase *apodeictic practical principle* therefore means a necessary moral principle. *The authors.*

action consists in the mental disposition, let the consequences be what they may. This imperative may be called that of morality.

Willing according to these three kinds of principles is also clearly distinguished by dissimilarity in the necessitation of the will. To make this dissimilarity clear I think that they are most suitably named in their order when they are said to be either *rules of skill, counsels of prudence,* or *commands (laws) of morality.* For law alone involves the concept of a necessity that is unconditioned and indeed objective and hence universally valid, and commands are laws which must be obeyed, i.e., must be followed even in opposition to inclination. Counsel does indeed involve necessity, but involves such necessity as is valid only under a subjectively contingent condition, viz., whether this or that man counts this or that as belonging to his happiness. On the other hand, the categorical imperative is limited by no condition, and can quite properly be called a command since it is absolutely, though practically, necessary.

There is a point stressed by Kant that is extremely important for understanding the categorical imperative. He says that the categorical imperative "is not concerned with the matter of the action and its intended result, but rather with the form of the action and the principle from which it follows. . . ." The distinction between *form* and *matter* is the distinction between the structure and the content of a moral decision. In mathematics there can be a purely formal statement of a mathematical principle, as in the following statement of the distributive law: $a(x + y + z) = ax + ay + az$. This law has no specific content in the sense that $a, x, y,$ and z can be any number, and, more importantly, this rule is universally true. We can also describe these principles as categorical, inasmuch as they are not hypothetical or dependent upon varying conditions. Any body of human knowledge becomes a *science* only when it bases itself on such formal principles that have universality and necessity. If ethics is to take its place alongside the other human activities that are accorded the respectability of rational thought, it too must discover the formal principles that will be true universally and necessarily. In short, we must be able to state the categorical imperative of ethics.

Maxims and the Categorical Imperative

One more point must be explored before we examine Kant's formulation of the categorical law of morality. Whenever we act deliberately (and this excludes those actions based on impulse already referred to), we first formulate a principle of our action. Kant calls this subjective principle our *maxim.* We might not explicitly formulate our maxim to ourselves, but we have one nonetheless and could formulate it were we to give it a moment's thought. When I decide to eat pizza even though I know that such food would be bad for my weight, my maxim would be something like this: Go for the pleasure of the moment, never mind the price to be paid tomorrow. Or if I choose to enter a field of study for which there are obvious vocational possibilities even though I would rather study something that lacks such explicit career paths, my maxim would be, Prepare for a lucrative job, don't seek education for its own sake. Part of the problem we face is that perhaps we do not examine our subjective principles or maxims frequently enough; were we to bring them to the level of rational examination, we might change our behavior in many ways.

Certainly the moral action must be one in which we examine carefully our subjective principle for acting, our *maxim,* to use Kant's phrase. So we bring our maxim to the level of rational examination. Then what? How are we to evaluate it? Remember that one of the goals of Kant's moral philosophy is to discover those ethical principles that will be accorded universal agreement. This obviously is a criterion for examining our maxim; *we must be able to make our maxim into a universal law.* Would you be willing to let everyone act on your maxim? Could everyone act on your maxim without self-contradiction? If the answer is "no," then your maxim is not a moral one. Here is how Kant describes the categorical imperative.

> If I think of a hypothetical imperative in general, I do not know beforehand what it will contain until its condition is given. But if I think of a categorical imperative, I know immediately what it contains. For since, besides the law, the imperative contains only the necessity that the maxim should accord with this law, while the law contains no condition to restrict it, there remains nothing but the universality of a law as such with which the maxim of the action should conform. This conformity alone is properly what is represented as necessary by the imperative.
>
> Hence there is only one categorical imperative and it is this: Act only according to that maxim whereby you can at the same time will that it should become a universal law.

Maxims Not Universalizable Consistently

Before we turn to Kant's examples of maxims that are not universalizable consistently, here is the procedure Kant suggests for applying the categorical imperative. First, determine the subjective principle, or maxim, on which you propose to act. Second, apply this maxim as a universal law. If you can do so without contradiction, then the maxim will result in a moral act. If you cannot do so, your action will not be moral. At no point in this procedure are you to consider the consequences of your action; to do so would be to transform the categorical imperative into a hypothetical imperative. Now let us turn to Kant's examples.

> 1. A man reduced to despair by a series of misfortunes feels sick of life but is still so far in possession of his reason that he can ask himself whether taking his own life would not be contrary to his duty to himself. Now he asks whether the maxim of his action could become a universal law of nature. But his maxim is this: from self-love I make as my principle to shorten my life when its continued duration threatens more evil than it promises satisfaction. There only remains the question as to whether this principle of self-love can become a universal law of nature. One sees at once a contradiction in a system of nature whose law would destroy life by means of the very same feeling that acts so as to stimulate the furtherance

of life, and hence there could be no existence as a system of nature. Therefore, such a maxim cannot possibly hold as a universal law of nature and is, consequently, wholly opposed to the supreme principle of all duty.

2. Another man in need finds himself forced to borrow money. He knows well that he won't be able to repay it, but he sees also that he will not get any loan unless he firmly promises to repay it within a fixed time. He wants to make such a promise, but he still has conscience enough to ask himself whether it is not permissible and is contrary to duty to get out of difficulty in this way. Suppose, however, that he decides to do so. The maxim of his action would then be expressed as follows: when I believe myself to be in need of money, I will borrow money and promise to pay it back, although I know that I can never do so. Now this principle of self-love or personal advantage may perhaps be quite compatible with one's entire future welfare, but the question is now whether it is right. I then transform the requirement of self-love into a universal law and put the question thus: how would things stand if my maxim were to become a universal law? He then sees at once that such a maxim could never hold as a universal law of nature and be consistent with itself, but must necessarily be self-contradictory. For the universality of a law which says that anyone believing himself to be in difficulty could promise whatever he pleases with the intention of not keeping it would make promising itself and the end to be attained thereby quite impossible, inasmuch as no one would believe what was promised him but would merely laugh at all such utterances as being vain pretenses.

3. A third finds in himself a talent whose cultivation could make him a man useful in many respects. But he finds himself in comfortable circumstances and prefers to indulge in pleasure rather than to bother himself about broadening and improving his fortunate natural aptitudes. But he asks himself further whether his maxim of neglecting his natural gift, besides agreeing of itself with his propensity to indulgence, might agree also with what is called duty. He then sees that a system of nature could indeed always subsist according to such a universal law, even though every man (like South Sea Islanders) should let his talents rust and resolve to devote his life entirely to idleness, indulgence, propagation, and, in a word, to enjoyment. But he cannot possibly will that this should become a universal law of nature or be implanted in us as such a law by a natural instinct. For as a rational being he necessarily wills that all his faculties should be developed, inasmuch as they are given him for all sorts of possible purposes.

4. A fourth man finds things going well for himself but sees others (whom he could help) struggling with great hardships; and he thinks: what does it matter to me? Let everybody be as happy as Heaven wills or as he can make himself; I shall take nothing from him nor even envy him; but I have no desire to contribute anything to his well-being or to his assistance when in need. If such a way of thinking were to become a universal law of nature, the human race admittedly could very well subsist and doubtless could subsist even better than when everyone prates about sympathy and benevolence and even on occasion exerts himself to practice them but,

on the other hand, also cheats when he can, betrays the rights of man, or otherwise violates them. But even though it is possible that a universal law of nature could subsist in accordance with that maxim, still it is impossible to will that such a principle should hold everywhere as a law of nature. For a will which resolved in this way would contradict itself, inasmuch as cases might often arise in which one would have need of the love and sympathy of others and in which he would deprive himself, by such a law of nature springing from his own will, of all hope of the aid he wants for himself.

These are some of the many actual duties, or at least what are taken to be such, whose derivation from the single principle cited above is clear. We must be able to will that a maxim of our action become a universal law; this is the canon for morally estimating any of our actions.

Treating Persons as Ends, Never as Means Only

Kant thought there was but one categorical imperative, although it could be stated in various ways to reveal various aspects of its force. One of the alternate ways was to speak of our duty to treat humanity, whether in the person of ourselves or of others, always as an end and never as a means only. Here is how Kant states this formulation and relates it to the examples just given.

If then there is to be a supreme practical principle and, as far as the human will is concerned, a categorical imperative, then it must be such that from the conception of what is necessarily an end for everyone because this end is an end in itself it constitutes an objective principle of the will and can hence serve as a practical law. The ground of such a principle is this: rational nature exists as an end in itself. In this way man necessarily thinks of his own existence; thus far is it a subjective principle of human actions. But in this way also does every other rational being think of his existence on the same rational ground that holds also for me; hence it is at the same time an objective principle, from which, as a supreme practical ground, all laws of the will must be able to be derived. The practical imperative will therefore be the following: Act in such a way that you treat humanity, whether in your own person or in the person of another, always at the same time as an end and never simply as a means. We now want to see whether this can be carried out in practice.

Let us keep to our previous examples.

First, as regards the concept of necessary duty to oneself, the man who contemplates suicide will ask himself whether his action can be consistent with the idea of humanity as an end in itself. If he destroys himself in order to escape from a difficult situation, then he is making use of his person merely as a means so as to maintain a tolerable condition till the end of his life. Man, however, is not a thing and hence is not something to be used merely as a means; he must in all his actions always be regarded as an end in himself. Therefore, I cannot dispose of man in my own person by mutilating, damaging, or killing him. (A more exact determination of this principle so as to avoid all misunderstanding, e.g., regarding the amputation of limbs in order to save oneself, or the exposure of one's life to danger in order to save it, and so on, must here be omitted; such questions belong to morals proper.)

Second, as concerns necessary or strict duty to others, the man who intends to make a false promise will immediately see that he intends to make use of another man merely as a means to an end which the latter does not likewise hold. For the man whom I want to use for my own purposes by such a promise cannot possibly concur with my way of acting toward him and hence cannot himself hold the end of this action. This conflict with the principle of duty to others becomes even clearer when instances of attacks on the freedom and property of others are considered. For then it becomes clear that a transgressor of the rights of men intends to make use of the persons of others merely as a means, without taking into consideration that, as rational beings, they should always be esteemed at the same time as ends, i.e., be esteemed only as beings who must themselves be able to hold the very same action as an end.

Third, with regard to contingent (meritorious) duty to oneself, it is not enough that the action does not conflict with humanity in our own person as an end in itself; the action must also harmonize with this end. Now there are in humanity capacities for greater perfection which belong to the end that nature has in view as regards humanity in our own person. To neglect these capacities might perhaps be consistent with the maintenance of humanity as an end in itself, but would not be consistent with the advancement of this end.

Fourth, concerning meritorious duty to others, the natural end that all men have is their own happiness. Now humanity might indeed subsist if nobody contributed anything to the happiness of others, provided he did not intentionally impair their happiness. But this, after all, would harmonize only negatively and not positively with humanity as an end in itself, if everyone does not also strive, as much as he can, to further the ends of others. For the end of any subject who is an end in himself must as far as possible be my ends also, if that conception of an end in itself is to have its full effect in me.

In examples one and two, there is a sense in which an attempt to universalize would be impossible if everyone acted on that maxim. That is, it would be impossible even to consider the action if everybody did it, because my being able to do it depends on the fact that most people do not do it. I can borrow money (from a bank, for example) by promising to repay because most people keep their promises. Examples three and four differ in that everyone could universalize the maxim without contradiction, but whether or not I would be willing to accept the maxim depends on my situation. If I were the one in poverty and needing help, I would urge a very different maxim than I would if I were wealthy and needing no help at all. Some interpreters of Kant point to the first two examples as failure of the *universalizable* aspect of the maxims; the second two are examples of the failure of the *reversible* aspect of the maxims.

We have said earlier that Kant locates the morality of the action in the intention, not in the consequences. You might think, however, that the examples just given show that Kant did indeed consider the consequences. But this is not the case. Just because a philosopher talks about consequences does not make that person a consequentialist. Kant is interested in rules that regulate our conduct; he is not interested in rules that achieve certain aims, such as promoting happiness or the good. The rule he defends is the categorical imperative, a rule that is guided by reason and that can be applied by every rational being. If we discover that when the principle we are acting on results in inconsistencies, then we can be sure that we are not being guided by the categorical imperative but by a principle of self-interest or a hypothetical imperative.

Morality and Freedom

Another formulation of the categorical imperative emphasizes the freedom and autonomy necessary for a moral action. Even our prephilosophic thinking about ethics holds that there is no moral praiseworthiness or blameworthiness to our actions if we do not do them freely. If someone holds a gun to your head and takes your money for the poor (as did Robin Hood), you can claim no moral praiseworthiness for contributing to the poor. Or if someone forces you on pain of death to assist in robbing a bank, your moral blame is diminished. Kant states the relation of freedom to morality in unequivocal terms: without freedom, there is no morality. But rather than attempting to prove that we are free in order to justify morality, Kant reverses the order and asserts that our moral sensibilities require that we consider ourselves as free. We cannot prove that we are free, we can only assert it as a necessary condition for morality.

> It is not enough to ascribe freedom to our will, on whatever ground, if we have not also sufficient reason for attributing it to all rational beings. For inasmuch as morality serves as a law for us only insofar as we are rational beings, it must also be valid for all rational beings. And since morality must be derived solely from the property of freedom, one must show that freedom is also the property of the will of all rational beings. It is not enough to prove freedom from certain alleged experiences of human nature (such a proof is indeed absolutely impossible, and so freedom can be proved only a priori). Rather, one must show that freedom belongs universally to the activity of rational beings endowed with a will. Now I say that every being which cannot act in any way other than under the idea of freedom is for this very reason free from a practical point of view. This is to say that for such a being all the laws that are inseparably bound up with freedom are valid just as much as if the will of such a being could be declared to be free in itself for reasons that are valid for theoretical philosophy. Now I claim that we must necessarily attribute to every rational being who has a will also the idea of freedom, under which only can such a being act.

For in such a being we think of a reason that is practical, i.e., that has causality in reference to its objects. Now we cannot possibly think of a reason that consciously lets itself be directed from outside as regards its judgments; for in that case the subject would ascribe the determination of his faculty of judgment not to his reason, but to an impulse. Reason must regard itself as the author of its principles independent of foreign influences. Therefore as practical reason or as the will of a rational being must reason regard itself as free. This is to say that the will of a rational being can be a will of its own only under the idea of freedom, and that a will must therefore, from a practical point of view, be attributed to all rational beings.

By now it should be clear that Kant's position on ethics is also a repudiation of the four challenges to ethics covered in Part One of this book. Morality, in Kant's analysis, can never be directed toward our own selfish good; the universalization of our maxim of action prevents that. Therefore, any principle of action based on egoism cannot be considered moral. Freedom being a necessary condition of morality, no view that sees human beings as determined by outside forces can be consistent with the recognition of our moral obligations. Likewise, relativism is to be rejected inasmuch as no view that fails to treat all rational beings as responsible to the same categorical imperative can be said to be a moral view. Furthermore, the categorical imperative aims at producing a statement of our maxim that has the force of a law of nature—the antithesis of the relativist view with its denial of cross-cultural moral principles. Finally, emotivism is an unacceptable viewpoint inasmuch as it would view all our actions as statements of emotion, equivalent to what Kant calls actions on impulse. For Kant, the key to the moral worth of an action is its rationality, not its emotional content.

Morality and Happiness

Finally, we raise again the issue of the relation between morality and happiness. Will the moral life make me happy? Aristotle, as you will recall, said yes. The utilitarians, given their view that human happiness is the aim of morality, would also say yes. Kant would say, Not necessarily. But let us rephrase the question. *Should* morality make me happy? To this Kant would say, Absolutely. But it is certainly not the case that morality is always conjoined with happiness in this life. Nor is it the case that those who aim for the development of a moral disposition will achieve it fully in this life. From considerations such as these, Kant concluded that to take seriously the moral life, reason demands that there be another life, a future life after death, in which we can continue to achieve moral perfection. Reason also demands that in this future life there be the conjunction of morality and happiness, so that ultimately the moral life is also the happy life, but only to those worthy of happiness. What can possibly bring about this future life? Only God could bring about a future life and insure that the rational demand is satisfied that morality and happiness should be conjoined.

This frequently overlooked aspect of Kant's moral philosophy is mentioned here to show how Kant thought moral philosophy provided a key to our highest human hopes. In his critical philosophy, Kant provided rigorous arguments against all the traditional approaches to proving that God exists or that human beings are free. Such questions, although expressing some of the most intensive concerns of human beings, are forever closed to rational proof and analysis. But in his moral philosophy Kant turns to these questions again, providing another way of thinking about them, a way that is legitimate for us as rational beings.

W. D. Ross: Assessing Conflicting *Prima Facie* Duties

One aspect of Kant's view is that when we recognize a moral duty, that obligation is universal and necessary. The term *universal* implies that all rational beings would recognize the same duty. But even more important is Kant's claim that one's moral duty is never affected by circumstances. No matter where or when, our duty remains the same. Given that it is our duty to tell the truth, we should never, under any circumstances, lie, no matter what harm might result from telling the truth. Even if your telling the truth resulted in great harm, even in the death of another, your duty is still to tell the truth.

Kantianism Criticized and Modified

It is against conclusions of deontological ethics such as this that utilitarians directed their greatest scorn. If a philosophical viewpoint says that I should tell the truth even if it causes the death of my best friend, then so much the worse for that moral viewpoint. The utilitarians pointed out that obviously the result of an action is important in considering its moral significance. How could anyone, in the final analysis, ignore the consequences of an action when considering its moral worth?

These are powerful objections to Kantian ethics. But utilitarians have problems of their own. True, we might want to consider the consequences of an action in considering the moral worth of that action, but are the consequences the *only* consideration, as utilitarians claim? And are there not actions that are wrong in themselves no matter how much happiness they might produce? Can we introduce some flexibility into a deontological approach without surrendering to utilitarianism?

Questions such as these are considered by William David Ross (1877–1971) in his important work *The Right and the Good.* Born in India of British parents and educated in England, Ross taught at Oxford University for nearly five decades, rising eventually to the position of Provost of Oriel (1919–1947) and Vice-Chancellor of Oxford University from 1941 to 1944. An Aristotelian scholar of great stature, Ross edited the Oxford translation of Aristotle published between 1908 and 1931. He himself translated, among other pieces, the *Nicomachean Ethics,* selections from which are included in chapter five of this book. His book on Aristotle, published in 1923, was considered by many scholars to be the most accurate and lucid survey of Aristotle's writings. In the realm of ethics, Ross made significant contributions, especially with the publication of *The Right and The Good* in 1930, from which the selections following have been taken. When it was first published, *The Right and the Good* stirred up considerable controversy, and for a time was the most widely read work on moral philosophy in England. Ross offered a modified form of deontological ethics that preserved the essential insights of Kant without surrendering to utilitarianism.

Teleological Ethics Examined

Ross's analysis begins with a statement of the issue upon which utilitarians and their opponents are divided: whether acts have a certain general characteristic that makes them right. Teleologists have argued that the rightness of an action depends upon the consequences of the action. Ross refers to three forms of teleological ethics, two of which we have already covered in this book: hedonistic egoism (such as that of Hobbes), hedonistic utilitarianism (Bentham), and an ideal utilitarian theory offered by a fellow English philosopher, G. E. Moore, a theory Ross describes as "productive of the greatest possible good" theory. G. E. Moore had argued that the goal of ethics is to produce good, and that "good" is a nondefinable term like *red,* which we recognize when we see it. We cannot define it because it is a primitive concept we use to define other concepts.

Ross's tactic in the material that follows is to dismiss egoism as patently inadequate and then to consider hedonistic utilitarianism's notion of right ("productive of the greatest pleasure") as a variant of G. E. Moore's view ("productive of the greatest good"). Then by attacking Moore's view he will have attacked teleologists in general, who, of course, include utilitarians.

> * The real point at issue between hedonism and utilitarianism on the one hand and their opponents on the other is not whether 'right' means 'productive of so and so'; for it cannot with any plausibility be maintained that it does. The point at issue is that to which we now pass, viz. whether there is any general character which makes right acts right, and if so, what it is. Among the main historical attempts to state a single characteristic of all right actions which is the foundation of their rightness are those made by egoism and utilitarianism. But I do not propose to discuss these, not because the subject is unimportant, but because it has been dealt with so often and so well already, and because there has come to be so much agreement among moral philosophers that neither of these theories is satisfactory. A much more attractive theory has been put forward by Professor Moore: that what makes actions right is that they are productive of more *good* than could have been produced by any other action open to the agent.
>
> This theory is in fact the culmination of all the attempts to base rightness on productivity of some sort of result. The first form this attempt takes is the attempt to base rightness on conduciveness to the advantage or pleasure of the agent. This theory comes to grief over the fact, which stares us in the face, that a great part of duty consists in an observance of the rights and a furtherance of the interests of others, whatever the cost to ourselves

* FROM W. D. Ross, *The Right and the Good.* Copyright 1930. Used by permission of The Clarendon Press, Oxford.

may be. Plato and others may be right in holding that a regard for the rights of others never in the long run involves a loss of happiness for the agent, that 'the just life profits a man'. But this, even if true, is irrelevant to the rightness of the act. As soon as a man does an action *because* he thinks he will promote his own interests thereby, he is acting not from a sense of its rightness but from self-interest.

To the egoistic theory hedonistic utilitarianism supplies a much-needed amendment. It points out correctly that the fact that a certain pleasure will be enjoyed by the agent is no reason why he *ought* to bring it into being rather than an equal or greater pleasure to be enjoyed by another, though, human nature being what it is, it makes it not unlikely that he *will* try to bring it into being. But hedonistic utilitarianism in its turn needs a correction. On reflection it seems clear that pleasure is not the only thing in life that we think good in itself, that for instance we think the possession of a good character, or an intelligent understanding of the world, as good or better. A great advance is made by the substitution of 'productive of the greatest good' for 'productive of the greatest pleasure'.

Not only is this theory more attractive than hedonistic utilitarianism, but its logical relation to that theory is such that the latter could not be true unless *it* were true, while it might be true though hedonistic utilitarianism were not. It is in fact one of the logical bases of hedonistic utilitarianism. For the view that what produces the maximum pleasure is right has for its bases the views (1) that what produces the maximum good is right, and (2) that pleasure is the only thing good in itself. If they were not assuming that what produces the maximum *good* is right, the utilitarians' attempt to show that pleasure is the only thing good in itself, which is in fact the point they take most pains to establish, would have been quite irrelevant to their attempt to prove that only what produces the maximum *pleasure* is right. If, therefore, it can be shown that productivity of the maximum good is not what makes all right actions right, we shall *a fortiori* have refuted hedonistic utilitarianism.

The Problem of Conflicting Duties

Over against teleologists, deontologists often claim that one should perform certain actions irrespective of the consequences. This is certainly the case in Kant's moral philosophy. Keeping one's promise is such a duty. Kant held that we should never, under any circumstances, break a promise. Now there is an important distinction to be made here. When we make a promise, we do so not because we expect certain good things to result from the promise. We feel obligated by our promise *because* we have made the promise, and we recognize that we ought to keep our promises. If we break our promise, it may be the result of a decision to act immorally; but it also may be the result of a conflict in our moral duties. We have other duties besides keeping promises. We have a duty to protect the life of others, to relieve the distress of others, to keep from harming others, and so forth. The difficulty in making moral decisions comes from the conflict of these various duties. What if acting on one duty causes me to violate other duties? What if keeping my promise results in harm to another? Which of these duties takes precedence? It was this problem that Kant sidestepped but which Ross faces squarely. But even when we break a promise for reasons cited above, this does not mean that we have surrendered our ethical principles to the teleologists.

> When a plain man fulfils a promise because he thinks he ought to do so, it seems clear that he does so with no thought of its total consequences, still less with any opinion that these are likely to be the best possible. He thinks in fact much more of the past than of the future. What makes him think it right to act in a certain way is the fact that he has promised to do so—that and, usually, nothing more. That his act will produce the best possible consequences is not his reason for calling it right. What lends colour to the theory we are examining, then, is not the actions (which form probably a great majority of our actions) in which some such reflection as 'I have promised' is the only reason we give ourselves for thinking a certain action right, but the exceptional cases in which the consequence of fulfilling a promise (for instance) would be so disastrous to others that we judge it right not to do so. It must of course be admitted that such cases exist. If I have promised to meet a friend at a particular time for some trivial purpose, I should certainly think myself justified in breaking my engagement if by doing so I could prevent a serious accident or bring relief to the victims of one. And the supporters of the view we are examining hold that my thinking so is due to my thinking that I shall bring more good into existence by the one action than by the other. A different account may, however, be given of the matter, an account which will, I believe, show itself to be the true one. It may be said that besides the duty of fulfilling promises I have and recognize a duty of relieving distress, and that when I think it right to do the latter at the cost of not doing the former, it is not because I think I shall produce more good thereby but because I think it the duty which is in the circumstances more of a duty. This account surely corresponds much more closely with what we really think in such a situation. If, so far as I can see, I could bring equal amounts of good into being by fulfilling my promise and by helping some one to whom I had made no promise, I should not hesitate to regard the former as my duty. Yet on the view that what is right is right because it is productive of the most good I should not so regard it.

Prima Facie and Actual Duties

But here a teleologist would seem to be able to make a telling point in favor of an ethical view based on consequences. When one's duties conflict, is not the only way to resolve the conflict to obey the most fundamental duty of maximizing the good? Ross once again disagrees with the views of G. E. Moore and introduces his key concept of *prima facie* duties. *Prima facie* duties are ones that we immediately recognize at first glance. Closer scrutiny, however, may confirm or deny that these *prima facie* duties are in fact our actual duties.

There are two theories, each in its way simple, that offer a solution of such cases of conscience. One is the view of Kant, that there are certain duties of perfect obligation, such as those of fulfilling promises, of paying debts, of telling the truth, which admit of no exception whatever in favour of duties of imperfect obligation, such as that of relieving distress. The other is the view of, for instance, Professor Moore and Dr. Rashdall, that there is only the duty of producing good, and that all 'conflicts of duties' should be resolved by asking 'by which action will most good be produced?' But it is more important that our theory fit the facts than that it be simple, and the account we have given above corresponds (it seems to me) better than either of the simpler theories with what we really think, viz. that normally promise-keeping, for example, should come before benevolence, but that when and only when the good to be produced by the benevolent act is very great and the promise comparatively trivial, the act of benevolence becomes our duty.

In fact the theory of 'ideal utilitarianism', if I may for brevity refer so to the theory of Professor Moore, seems to simplify unduly our relations to our fellows. It says, in effect, that the only morally significant relation in which my neighbours stand to me is that of being possible beneficiaries by my action. They do stand in this relation to me, and this relation is morally significant. But they may also stand to me in the relation of promisee to promiser, of creditor to debtor, of wife to husband, of child to parent, of friend to friend, of fellow countryman to fellow countryman, and the like; and each of these relations is the foundation of a *prima facie* duty, which is more or less incumbent on me according to the circumstances of the case. When I am in a situation, as perhaps I always am, in which more than one of these *prima facie* duties is incumbent on me, what I have to do is to study the situation as fully as I can until I form the considered opinion (it is never more) that in the circumstances one of them is more incumbent than any other; then I am bound to think that to do this *prima facie* duty is my duty *sans phrase* in the situation.

I suggest '*prima facie* duty' or 'conditional duty' as a brief way of referring to the characteristic (quite distinct from that of being a duty proper) which an act has, in virtue of being of a certain kind (e.g. the keeping of a promise), of being an act which would be a duty proper if it were not at the same time of another kind which is morally significant. Whether an act is a duty proper or actual duty depends on *all* the morally significant kinds it is an instance of. . . .

Ross now offers a provisional list of *prima facie* duties. Notice that by categorizing the duties of beneficence (the production of good for humankind) as one among several sets of *prima facie* duties, Ross is conveying the important insight that G. E. Moore's one overarching duty (maximizing the good) is merely one *prima facie* duty among others, and on some occasions it may prevail and on other occasions it may be overruled by another duty.

There is nothing arbitrary about these *prima facie* duties. Each rests on a definite circumstance which cannot seriously be held to be without moral significance. Of *prima facie* duties I suggest, without claiming completeness or finality for it, the following division.*

(1) Some duties rest on previous acts of my own. These duties seem to include two kinds, (a) those resting on a promise or what may fairly be called an implicit promise, such as the implicit undertaking not to tell lies which seems to be implied in the act of entering into conversation (at any rate by civilized men), or of writing books that purport to be history and not fiction. These may be called the duties of fidelity. (b) Those resting on a previous wrongful act. These may be called the duties of reparation. (2) Some rest on previous acts of other men, i.e., services done by them to me. These may be loosely described as the duties of gratitude. (3) Some rest on the fact or possibility of a distribution of pleasure or happiness (or of the means thereto) which is not in accordance with the merit of the persons concerned; in such cases there arises a duty to upset or prevent such a distribution. These are the duties of justice. (4) Some rest on the mere fact that there are other beings in the world whose condition we can make better in respect of virtue, or of intelligence, or of pleasure. These are the duties of beneficence. (5) Some rest on the fact that we can improve our own condition in respect of virtue or of intelligence. These are the duties of self-improvement. (6) I think that we should distinguish from (4) the duties that may be summed up under the title of 'not injuring others'. No doubt to injure others is incidentally to fail to do them good; but it seems to me clear that non-maleficence is apprehended as a duty distinct from that of beneficence, and as a duty of a more stringent character. It will be noticed that this alone among the types of duty has been stated in a negative way. An attempt might no doubt be made to state this duty, like the others, in a positive way. It might be said that it is really the duty to prevent ourselves from acting either from an inclination to harm others or from an inclination to seek our own pleasure, in doing which we should incidentally harm them. But on reflection it seems clear that the primary duty here is the duty not to harm others, this being a duty whether or not we have an inclination that if followed would lead to our harming them; and that when we have such an inclination the primary duty not to harm others gives rise to a consequential duty to resist the inclination. The recognition of this duty of non-maleficence is the first step on the way to the recognition of the duty of beneficence; and that accounts for the prominence of the commands 'thou shalt not kill', 'thou shalt not commit

* I should make it plain at this stage that I am *assuming* the correctness of some of our main convictions as to *prima facie* duties, or, more strictly, am claiming that we *know* them to be true. To me it seems as self-evident as anything could be, that to make a promise, for instance, is to create a moral claim on us in someone else. Many readers will perhaps say that they do *not* know this to be true. If so, I certainly cannot prove it to them; I can only ask them to reflect again, in the hope that they will ultimately agree that they also know it to be true. The main moral convictions of the plain man seem to me to be, not opinions which it is for philosophy to prove or disprove, but knowledge from the start; and in my own case I seem to find little difficulty in distinguishing these essential convictions from other moral convictions which I also have, which are merely fallible opinions based on an imperfect study of the working for good or evil of certain institutions or types of action.

adultery', 'thou shalt not steal', 'thou shalt not bear false witness', in so early a code as the Decalogue. But even when we have come to recognize the duty of beneficence, it appears to me that the duty of non-maleficence is recognized as a distinct one, and as *prima facie* more binding. We should not in general consider it justifiable to kill one person in order to keep another alive, or to steal from one in order to give alms to another.

The essential defect of the 'ideal utilitarian' theory is that it ignores, or at least does not do full justice to, the highly personal character of good, the question who is to have the good—whether it is myself, or my benefactor, or a person to whom I have made a promise to confer that good on him, or a mere fellow man to whom I stand in no such special relation—should make no difference to my having a duty to produce that good. But we are all in fact sure that it makes a vast difference. . . .

Prima Facie Duties Self-Evident

Like Kant, Ross thinks that all rational persons have the ability to understand *prima facie* duties as self-evident truths (like the principles of mathematics). But unlike Kant, Ross does not suggest the formalized procedure for arriving at these duties as was evident in Kant's description of the categorical imperative. We can see clearly in the following citation that Ross holds the view that there is an objective moral order that we as rational beings can grasp and defend. He uses repeatedly the term *qua,* the Latin term for *as.* When he speaks of an act *qua* fulfilling a promise he means an act such as fulfilling a promise.

There is another important point implied in Ross's approach. A common attack on an objective ethical view is to question how people come to a knowledge of right and wrong if such values are not imparted by their culture. Ross's implicit answer is that, like mathematics, values must be taught. But once learned, the principles of ethics, again like the principles of mathematics, are self-evident and need no further proof. Unless one accepts the axioms of geometry as needing no proof, one cannot make any progress in learning the mathematics of planes and solids. Similarly, unless one accepts certain ethical insights as given and needing no proof, one can never achieve moral understanding.

Something should be said of the relation between our apprehension of the *prima facie* rightness of certain types of acts and our mental attitude towards particular acts. It is proper to use the word 'apprehension' in the former case and not in the latter. That an act, *qua* fulfilling a promise, or *qua* effecting a just distribution of good, or *qua* returning services rendered, or *qua* promoting the good of others, or *qua* promoting the virtue or insight of the agent, is *prima facie* right, is self-evident; not in the sense that it is evident from the beginning of our lives, or as soon as we attend to the proposition for the first time, but in the sense that when we have reached sufficient mental maturity and have given sufficient attention to the proposition it is evident without any need of proof, or of evidence beyond itself. It is self-evident just as a mathematical axiom, or the validity of a form of inference, is evident. The moral order expressed in these propositions is just as much part of the fundamental nature of the universe (and, we may add, of any possible universe in which there were moral agents at all) as is the spatial or numerical structure expressed in the axioms of geometry or arithmetic. In our confidence that these propositions are true there is involved the same trust in our reason that is involved in our confidence in mathematics; and we should have no justification for trusting it in the latter sphere and distrusting it in the former. In both cases we are dealing with propositions that cannot be proved, but that just as certainly need no proof. . . .

Again, a common attack on an objectivistic view of ethics is to ask why there are moral disagreements if moral principles—our *prima facie* duties, to use Ross's phrase—are self-evident. Ross's answer is that, although the general principles of duty possess axiom-like certainty, specific judgments about one's concrete actual duty do not.

Our judgements about our actual duty in concrete situations have none of the certainty that attaches to our recognition of the general principles of duty. A statement is certain, i.e., is an expression of knowledge, only in one or other of two cases: when it is either self-evident, or a valid conclusion from self-evident premisses. And our judgements about our particular duties have neither of these characters. (1) They are not self-evident. Where a possible act is seen to have two characteristics, in virtue of one of which it is *prima facie* right, and in virtue of the other *prima facie* wrong, we are (I think) well aware that we are not certain whether we ought or ought not to do it; that whether we do it or not, we are taking a moral risk. We come in the long run, after consideration, to think one duty more pressing than the other, but we do not feel certain that it is so. And though we do not always recognize that a possible act has two such characteristics, and though there *may* be cases in which it has not, we are never certain that any particular possible act has not, and therefore never certain that it is right, nor certain that it is wrong. For, to go no further in the analysis, it is enough to point out that any particular act will in all probability in the course of time contribute to the bringing about of good or of evil for many human beings, and thus have a *prima facie* rightness or wrongness of which we know nothing. (2) Again, our judgements about our particular duties are not logical conclusions from self-evident premisses. The only possible premisses would be the general principles stating their *prima facie* rightness or wrongness *qua* having the different characteristics they do have; and even if we could (as we cannot) apprehend the extent to which an act will tend on the one hand, for example, to bring about advantages for our benefactors, and on the other hand to bring about disadvantages for fellow men who are not our benefactors, there is no principle by which we can draw the conclusion that it is on the whole right or on the whole wrong. In this respect the judgement as to the rightness of a particular act is just like the judgement as to the beauty of a particular natural object or work of art. A poem is, for instance, in respect of certain qualities beautiful and in respect of certain others not beautiful; and our judgement as to the degree of beauty it possesses on the whole is never reached by logical reasoning from the apprehension of its particular beauties or particular defects. Both in this and in the moral case we have more or less probable opinions which are not logically justified as conclusions from the general principles that are recognized as self-evident. . . .

Teleological Ethics Criticized Again

Ross has explained what *prima facie* duties are and how we discover them. Next he turns his attention once again to teleological ethics to expose what he considers to be the inadequacies of that approach to ethics. Because teleologists put the emphasis on the consequences of an action in assessing its moral significance, they are forced to conclude that an action is right to the extent that it optimizes pleasure or happiness or good. All three terms have been used by teleologists of various stripes. Ross refers to the view that measures the worth of an act by its tendency to optimize certain consequences as a view that places the primary emphasis on the *optimific*. (*Optimific* means the tendency to optimize certain desirable consequences.)

The conclusion Ross forces on teleologists is that, in their view, the terms *right* and *optimific* are "coextensive" terms. That is, any act that is *right* is also *optimific*, and any act that is *optimific* is also *right*. But how do they know this to be the case? Is it self-evident? (G. E. Moore said it was.) Is it deductively demonstrated? Is it inductively established? Using examples based upon the *prima facie* duty to keep one's promises, Ross argues that the coextensiveness of right and optimific is neither self-evident nor demonstrable by deductive or inductive means.

> Supposing it to be agreed, as I think on reflection it must, that no one *means* by 'right' just 'productive of the best possible consequences', or 'optimific', the attributes 'right' and 'optimific' might stand in either of two kinds of relation to each other. (1) They might be so related that we could apprehend *a priori*, either immediately or deductively, that any act that is optimific is right and any act that is right is optimific, as we can apprehend that any triangle that is equilateral is equiangular and *vice versa*. Professor Moore's view is, I think, that the coextensiveness of 'right' and 'optimific' is apprehended immediately. He rejects the possibility of any proof of it. Or (2) the two attributes might be such that the question whether they are invariably connected had to be answered by means of an inductive inquiry. Now at first sight it might seem as if the constant connexion of the two attributes could be immediately apprehended. It might seem absurd to suggest that it could be right for any one to do an act which would produce consequences less good than those which would be produced by some other act in his power. Yet a little thought will convince us that this is not absurd. The type of case in which it is easiest to see that this is so is, perhaps, that in which one has made a promise. In such a case we all think that *prima facie* it is our duty to fulfil the promise irrespective of

the precise goodness of the total consequences. And though we do not think it is necessarily our actual or absolute duty to do so, we are far from thinking that any, even the slightest gain in the value of the total consequences will necessarily justify us in doing something else instead. Suppose, to simplify the case by abstraction, that the fulfilment of a promise to A would produce 1,000 units of good for him, but that by doing some other act I could produce 1,001 units of good for B, to whom I have made no promise, the other consequences of the two acts being of equal value; should we really think it self-evident that it was our duty to do the second act and not the first? I think not. We should, I fancy, hold that only a much greater disparity of value between the total consequences would justify us in failing to discharge our *prima facie* duty to A. After all, a promise is a promise, and is not to be treated so lightly as the theory we are examining would imply. What, exactly, a promise is, is not so easy to determine, but we are surely agreed that it constitutes a serious moral limitation to our freedom of action. To produce the 1,001 units of good for B rather than fulfil our promise to A would be to take, not perhaps our duty as philanthropists too seriously, but certainly our duty as makers of promises too lightly.

Or consider another phase of the same problem. If I have promised to confer on A a particular benefit containing 1,000 units of good, is it self-evident that if by doing some different act I could produce 1,001 units of good for A himself (the other consequences of the two acts being supposed equal in value), it would be right for me to do so? Again, I think not. Apart from my general *prima facie* duty to do A what good I can, I have another *prima facie* duty to do him, and this is not to be set aside in consequence of a disparity of good of the order of 1,001 to 1,000, though a much greater disparity might justify me in so doing.

Or again, suppose that A is a very good and B a very bad man, should I then, even when I have made no promise, think it self-evidently right to produce 1,001 units of good for B rather than 1,000 for A? Surely not. I should be sensible of a *prima facie* duty of justice, i.e., of producing a distribution of goods in proportion to merit, which is not outweighed by such a slight disparity in the total goods to be produced.

Such instances—and they might easily be added to—make it clear that there is no self-evident connexion between the attributes 'right' and 'optimific'. The theory we are examining has a certain attractiveness when applied to our decision that a particular act is our duty (though I have tried to show that it does not agree with our actual moral judgements even here). But it is not even plausible when applied to our recognition of *prima facie* duty. For if it were self-evident that the right coincides with the optimific, it should be self-evident that what is *prima facie* right is *prima facie* optimific. But whereas we are certain that keeping a promise is *prima facie* right, we are not certain that it is *prima facie* optimific (though we are perhaps certain that it is *prima facie* bonific). Our certainty that it is *prima facie* right depends not on its consequences but on its being the fulfilment of a promise. The theory we are examining involves too much difference between the evident ground of our conviction about *prima facie* duty and the alleged ground of our conviction about actual duty.

The coextensiveness of the right and the optimific is, then, not self-evident. And I can see no way of proving it deductively; nor, so far as I know, has any one tried to do so. There remains the question whether it can be established inductively. Such an inquiry, to be conclusive, would have to be very thorough and extensive. We should have to take a large variety of the acts which we, to the best of our ability, judge to be right. We should have to trace as far as possible their consequences, not only for the persons directly affected but also for those indirectly affected, and to these no limit can be set. To make our inquiry thoroughly conclusive, we should have to do what we cannot do, viz. trace these consequences into an unending future. And even to make it reasonably conclusive, we should have to trace them far into the future. It is clear that the most we could possibly say is that a large variety of typical acts that are judged right appear, so far as we can trace their consequences, to produce more good than any other acts possible to the agents in the circumstances. And such a result falls far short of proving the constant connexion of the two attributes. But it is surely clear that no inductive inquiry justifying even this result has ever been carried through. The advocates of utilitarian systems have been so much persuaded either of the identity or of the self-evident connexion of the attributes 'right' and 'optimific' (or 'felicific') that they have not attempted even such an inductive inquiry as is possible. And in view of the enormous complexity of the task and the inevitable inconclusiveness of the result, it is worth no one's while to make the attempt. What, after all, would be gained by it? If, as I have tried to show, for an act to be right and to be optimific are not the same thing, and an act's being optimific is not even the ground of its being right, then if we could ask ourselves (though the question is really unmeaning) which we ought to do, right acts because they are right or optimific, our answer must be 'the former'. If they are optimific as well as right, that is interesting but not morally important; if not, we still ought to do them (which is only another way of saying that they *are* the right acts), and the question whether they are optimific has no importance for moral theory.

There is one direction in which a fairly serious attempt has been made to show the connexion of the attributes 'right' and 'optimific'. One of the most evident facts of our moral consciousness is the sense which we have of the sanctity of promises, a sense which does not, on the face of it, involve the thought that one will be bringing more good into existence by fulfilling the promise than by breaking it. It is plain, I think, that in our normal thought we consider that the fact that we have made a promise is in itself sufficient to create a duty of keeping it, the sense of duty resting on remembrance of the past promise and not on thoughts of the future consequences of its fulfilment. Utilitarianism tries to show that this is not so, that the sanctity of promises rests on the good consequences of the fulfilment of them and the bad consequences of their non-fulfilment. It does so in this way: it points out that when you break a promise you not only fail to confer a certain advantage on your promisee but you diminish his confidence, and indirectly the confidence of others, in the fulfilment of promises. You thus strike a blow at one of the devices that have been found most useful in the relations between man and man—the device on which, for example, the whole system of commercial credit rests—and you tend to bring about a state of things wherein each man, being entirely unable to rely on the keeping of promises by others, will have to do everything for himself, to the enormous impoverishment of human well-being.

To put the matter otherwise, utilitarians say that when a promise ought to be kept it is because the total good to be produced by keeping it is greater than the total good to be produced by breaking it, the former including as its main elements the maintenance and strengthening of general mutual confidence, and the latter being greatly diminished by a weakening of this confidence. They say, in fact, that the case I put some pages back never arises—the case in which by fulfilling a promise I shall bring into being 1,000 units of good for my promise, and by breaking it 1,001 units of good for someone else, the other effects of the two acts being of equal value. The other effects, they say, never are of equal value. By keeping my promise I am helping to strengthen the system of mutual confidence; by breaking it I am helping to weaken this; so that really the first act produces $1,000 + x$ units of good, and the second $1,001 - y$ units, and the difference between $+ x$ and $- y$ is enough to outweigh the slight superiority in the *immediate* effects of the second act. In answer to this it may be pointed out that there must be *some* amount of good that exceeds the difference between $+ x$ and $- y$ (i.e. exceeds $x + y$); say, $x + y + z$. Let us suppose the *immediate* good effects of the second act to be assessed not at 1,001 but at $1,000 + x + y + z$. Then its *net* good effects are $1,000 + x + z$, i.e. greater than those of the fulfilment of the promise; and the utilitarian is bound to say forthwith that the promise should be broken. Now, we may ask whether that is really the way we think about promises? Do we really think that the production of the slightest balance of good, no matter who will enjoy it, by the breach of a promise frees us from the obligation to keep our promise? We need not doubt that a system by which promises are made and kept is one that has great advantages for the general well-being. But that is not the whole truth. To make a promise is not merely to adapt an ingenious device for promoting the general well-being; it is to put oneself in a new relation to one person in particular, a relation which creates a specifically new *prima facie* duty to him, not reducible to the duty of promoting the general well-being of society. By all means let us try to foresee the net good effects of keeping one's promise and the net good effects of breaking it, but even if we assess the first at $1,000 + x$ and the second at $1,000 + x + z$, the question still remains whether it is not our duty to fulfil the promise. It may be suspect, too, that the effect of a single keeping or breaking of a promise in strengthening or weakening the fabric of mutual confidence is greatly exaggerated by the theory we are examining. And if we suppose two men dying together alone, do we think that the duty of one to fulfil before he dies a promise he has made to the other would be extinguished by the fact that neither act would have any effect on the general confidence? Any one who holds this may be suspected of not having reflected on what a promise is.

I conclude that the attributes 'right' and 'optimific' are not identical, and that we do not know either by intuition, by deduction, or by induction that they coincide in their application, still less that the latter is the foundation of the former. It must be added, however, that if we are ever under no special obligation such as that of fidelity to a promisee or of gratitude to a benefactor, we ought to do what will produce most good; and that even when we are under a special obligation the tendency of acts to promote general good is one of the main factors in determining whether they are right.

The Moral Consciousness of Humankind

Ross pauses to comment on what he considers to be the foundation upon which morality rests: the existing body of moral convictions that is the cumulative product of the moral reflection of many generations.

In what has preceded, a good deal of use has been made of 'what we really think' about moral questions; a certain theory has been rejected because it does not agree with what we really think. It might be said that this is in principle wrong; that we should not be content to expound what our present moral consciousness tells us but should aim at a criticism of our existing moral consciousness in the light of theory. Now I do not doubt that the moral consciousness of men has in detail undergone a good deal of modification as regards the things we think right, at the hands of moral theory. But if we are told, for instance, that we should give up our view that there is a special obligatoriness attaching to the keeping of promises because it is self-evident that the only duty is to produce as much good as possible, we have to ask ourselves whether we really, when we reflect, *are* convinced that this is self-evident, and whether we really *can* get rid of our view that promise-keeping has a bindingness independent of productiveness of maximum good. In my own experience I find that I cannot, in spite of a very genuine attempt to do so; and I venture to think that most people will find the same, and that just because they cannot lose the sense of special obligation, they cannot accept as self-evident, or even as true, the theory which would require them to do so. In fact it seems, on reflection, self-evident that a promise, simply as such, is something that *prima facie* ought to be kept, and it does not, on reflection, seem self-evident that production of maximum good is the only thing that makes an act obligatory. And to ask us to give up at the bidding of a theory our actual apprehension of what is right and what is wrong seems like asking people to repudiate their actual experience of beauty, at the bidding of a theory which says 'only that which satisfies such and such conditions can be beautiful'. If what I have called our actual apprehension is (as I would maintain that it is) truly an apprehension, i.e. an instance of knowledge, the request is nothing less than absurd.

I would maintain, in fact, that what we are apt to describe as 'what we think' about moral questions contains a considerable amount that we do not think but know, and that this forms the standard by reference to which the truth of any moral theory has to be tested, instead of having itself to be tested by reference to any theory. I hope that I have in what precedes indicated what in my view these elements of knowledge are that are involved in our ordinary moral consciousness.

It would be a mistake to found a natural science on 'what we really think', i.e. on what reasonably thoughtful and well-educated people think about the subjects of the science before they have studied them scientifically. For such opinions are interpretations, and often misinterpretations, of sense-experience; and the man of science must appeal from these to sense-experience itself, which furnishes his real data. In ethics no such appeal is possible. We have no more direct way of access to the facts about rightness and goodness and about what things are right or good, than by thinking about them; the moral convictions of thoughtful and well-educated people are the data of ethics just as sense-perceptions are the data of a natural science. Just as some of the latter have to be rejected as illusory, so have some of the former; but as the latter are rejected only when they are in conflict with other more accurate sense-perceptions, the former are rejected only when they are in conflict with other convictions which stand better the test of reflections. The existing body of moral convictions of the best people is the cumulative product of the moral reflection of many generations, which has developed an extremely delicate power of appreciation of moral distinctions; and this the theorist cannot afford to treat with anything other than the greatest respect. The verdicts of the moral consciousness of the best people are the foundation on which he must build; though he must first compare them with one another and eliminate any contradictions they may contain.

Ross's concluding point is that the task of philosophical ethics is to examine and clarify "the verdicts of the moral consciousness" of our society. The goal of such an examination is the consistency, coherence, and systematic nature of our ethical thought. But there is also the matter of applicability. Once we are convinced that our ethical viewpoint is consistent, systematic, and coherent in regards to our other views, can we apply it to actual ethical problems? How are we to apply our ethical theory to real-world issues? This is a concern that is looming ever larger in contemporary ethical writings. And it is the concern to which we turn in the final part of this book.

Assessment

This chapter has exposed the strong disagreement that exists between the teleologists and the deontologists. On the one hand, deontologists like Kant claim that we have duties, such as the obligation to tell the truth, that are inviolate and that must be pursued irrespective of the consequences. On the other hand, teleologists like Bentham, Mill, and Moore claim that our one overriding obligation is to maximize the good. Accordingly, for teleologists, consequences are crucial for evaluating an act as right or wrong.

A fruitful strategy employed by both sides in this debate is to try to construct a situation in which the views of one's opponent would commit that opponent to claims that would violate the moral sensibilities of most human beings. For example, the teleologists generate illustrations such as that of a deontologist whose unwavering commitment to truth-telling leads him to betray the whereabouts of his friend to vicious people intent on killing her. And the deontologists create illustrations such as that of a teleologist whose absolute commitment to maximizing the good leads him to punish an innocent person in order to maximize the happiness of society. These illustrations used by philosophers are not silly fantasies. Rather, they are the serious experiments deployed by philosophers to test the adequacy of various theories. And in this instance those experiments suggest that there is something inadequate about both teleological and deontological theories.

W. D. Ross attempts to meet the criticism of Kantian-type ethical theory with his discussion of *prima facie* duties. Ross's strategy is to make all duties in a sense provisional. No duty is absolute in the sense that it is to be pursued without reservation or qualification. All Ross's duties are *prima facie*—duties "at first glance." They are duties that may be in conflict with each other in a given situation, and it is only after carefully weighing the situation that one's actual duty in that situation—one's duty "at second glance"—appears. To the teleologist's criticism that when *prima facie* duties conflict, one is thrown back upon consequentialist conditions (i.e., maximizing the good) for determining which duties to pursue, Ross responds that maximizing the good is just one of the *prima facie* duties and not the supreme one to which all other duties are subordinated. As such, maximizing the good can be surrendered in order to obey another more pressing duty.

But how does one determine which duty is more compelling or more pressing in a given situation? Here Ross is not altogether clear, but he seems to be saying that even as the *prima facie* duties themselves are self-evident, even so the relative strengths of those duties will be self-evident in the given situation. And the teleologist will be quick to point out that what is self-evident to one person is not necessarily self-evident to another. Does that mean that Ross's position ultimately rests on a subjectivistic base where people can claim anything to be their *prima facie* duty on the ground that it is self-evident to them?

What, then, can we say about this debate between the teleologists and deontologists? Certainly we have only scratched the surface of the debate. But perhaps enough has been said to suggest that the debate is one of those loggerhead issues where people of noble motivations and keen minds can legitimately differ, and will continue to differ. Each side of the debate is, no doubt, convinced that its position is consistent, coherent, and comprehensive and is prepared to defend it against all comers.

Yet it is not only important that an ethical theory can be so defended: it is also important that an ethical theory can shed light upon the moral puzzles we encounter day by day in the lived world. Increasingly, moral philosophers are directing their attention to applied ethics—that is, to the bringing of ethical theory to bear on specific real-world problems. And it is to the domain of applied ethics that the final part of this book is devoted.

Review Questions

1. What, according to Kant, are the shortcomings of consequentialist ethics?
2. What does Kant consider to be good without qualification, and why?
3. Distinguish actions based upon impulses from those based on hypothetical and categorical imperatives.
4. What is a maxim, and how do the universalizability and reversibility of maxims help us to determine our duty without qualification?
5. "Kant does not seek to prove the existence of freedom and immortality, but he does allow them to be postulates of reason as it seeks to understand morality." Explain.
6. What problem in Kant's ethics leads W. D. Ross to modify Kant's position? Discuss that modification in terms of *prima facie* and actual duties.
7. Summarize W. D. Ross's critique of teleological ethics.

Retrospective to Part II

In response to the ethical question, What ought I to do? human beings have offered a variety of answers. We have examined four of the major ones: actualizing human nature, obeying the will of God, creating the greatest amount of happiness, and obeying the commands of reason. The advocates of these positions—Aristotle and Epicurus, Paley and Brunner, Bentham and Mill, Kant and Ross—were all eminently rational humans who had noble motivations. And each of their positions has significant strengths as well as weaknesses. Does that mean that one view is just as acceptable as any other, and that a person is forced into the situation of flipping a coin to select at random one of these views to affirm and defend?

To leave the selection of one's moral theory to the random toss of a coin would involve a rejection of reason. No philosopher committed to the examined life can consistently recommend this method. Instead, let us pause to consider the function of moral theory. Moral theory tries to provide a coherent, consistent, and comprehensive account of our moral experience and, in so doing, to give us guidance in finding our way through the moral puzzles that we encounter day after day as we, like Captain Scott in our introductory example, pause to ask, What ought I to do?

Now each of our four moral theories focuses on something to be valued in the human condition. In the light of that valued thing, each theory enables us to judge acts to be right or wrong. Because the human condition has many facets, and because each of these four theories focuses on one of those facets, each theory has a claim to a certain legitimacy. But because those theories focus primarily on just one facet with a relative neglect of the other facets, each of them has a marked incompleteness.

Consider the recommendation to actualize human nature. Would we not all agree that there is something distinctive about human beings, and would we not all agree that Aristotle has taken a giant step forward in identifying that distinctive aspect? And would we not agree with Aristotle that the distinctively human aspect of our nature is valuable? Would we not agree that the process of self-actualization, the "freedom to be me" is a feature of our human condition to be prized? But would we want to say that actions that promote self-actualization are right and those that inhibit it are wrong? That is where things begin to rub us the wrong way. After all, Hitler and Stalin were busy actualizing their human nature, but we would say that there is something morally repugnant about their particular self-actualization. Although self-actualization can be valuable, it is an incomplete basis for assessing acts as right or wrong.

Consider the recommendation to obey the will of God. Although some of us may be theists, and others atheists, and still others agnostic, we would all probably agree that Paley and Brunner have touched on an important facet of human moral experience, namely the dimension of transcendence. When we face a moral dilemma and ask, What ought I to do? we are assuming that one of the futures open to us is more desirable than the others and that it is more desirable because it possesses objective moral characteristics that invest it with greater moral worth than the other futures. We are assuming that reality harbors objective moral values that transcend, that stand over against and above our subjective feelings and preferences. When we ask, What ought I to do? we are submitting, subjecting ourselves to the dominion of those values. We are acknowledging the rule of a moral order that transcends us. With their will-of-God theory, Paley and Brunner intensify the focus on transcendence by drawing attention not only to the moral order that transcends the individual person but also to the Author of the moral order who transcends both the order and the person. But Paley's legalism and Brunner's situationalism both seem to fall short of an adequate basis for assessing right and wrong. Paley's system seems to violate the self-determination, the "freedom to be me," that we all prize, and Brunner's viewpoint so emphasizes human and divine freedom in the concrete situation that it fails to provide adequate preparation for resolving moral problems when one lacks the luxury of time to contemplate at length the particular problem.

Consider, also, the recommendation to maximize humankind's happiness. Surely we would all agree with Bentham and Mill that happiness is an intrinsic good, something desirable for its own sake. We don't ask others why they want to be happy, as if happiness were a means for achieving some other goal and received its legitimacy from that other goal. Happiness is desirable for its own sake. It is valued for its own sake. But although we agree that happiness is an intrinsic good, we might not go all the way with Bentham and Mill in making the greatest happiness for the greatest number the basis for assessing acts as right and wrong. There is something morally repugnant about punishing an innocent person in order to enhance the happiness of society at large, as was done in the Stalinist show trials of the 1930s so vividly portrayed by Arthur Koestler in his classic novel *Darkness at Noon*.

Consider, finally, the recommendation to obey the commands of reason. Once again, would we not find ourselves affirming, along with Kant, the values of a categorical imperative—a command issued by reason that is both universalizable consistently and reversible? Yet, would we feel comfortable in following Kant to the extremity of maintaining that these commands of reason must be held inviolable to the extent that we should tell the truth even if such truth-telling were to sacrifice the life of our friend? Surely there is something morally amiss in a moral theory that would require such a sacrifice of us. Then again, we might feel more comfortable with Ross's modified deontological approach with its *prima facie* duties that allow for competing values to yield the sacrifice of one duty in order to obey what is deemed to be a more commanding duty. Yet, Ross's *prima facie* duties are duties that are self-evident, and what is self-evident to one person may not necessarily be self-evident to another. A common defense used by Nazi war criminals was that they were only doing their duty to obey orders, a *prima facie* duty in their view. But those who found them guilty of war crimes did so on the basis of the *prima facie* duty to disobey an unjust command.

In brief, each of these moral theories, while revealing important insights about the things that we humans value, nevertheless falls short of accounting for all the kinds of moral judgments we would consider to be legitimate within our moral experience. Perhaps this shortcoming is built into a moral theory by the very nature of a moral theory.

The moral theories we have examined abstract a certain feature from the human moral experience—self-realization, transcendence, happiness, duty to reason's commands—and invest that feature with fundamental value and then employ it as the standard for right and wrong. In so doing, each theory invests those valued features with power and is able to penetrate the bewildering complexity of the human situation with a clarity that could not be achieved otherwise.

Yet the concrete human situation where real decisions must be rendered is complex. It seldom yields to neat applications of a single ethical theory. Perhaps what is needed of each advocate of these theories is a creative openness to the insights provided by the other advocates. Such openness does not mean surrendering the theory that you believe provides the most coherent, consistent, and comprehensive account of humankind's moral experience. Such openness does mean that you recognize the provisional and incomplete nature of your theory. And such openness does mean that you will be better prepared to deal with the complexities of applied ethics to which we turn in the next section.

PART III

Normative Ethical Issues

CHAPTER 9

Normative Ethical Issues

Introduction

At the center of the human moral experience is the question, What ought I to do? When human beings ask that question, they generally assume that they are free to pursue alternative futures and that moral judgments about those alternatives is possible. Several philosophical theories call into question those assumptions, and in so doing erode the significance people generally ascribe to the ethical question. In Part One we examined four of those theories: psychological egoism, determinism, ethical relativism, and ethical emotivism. We discovered that those theories do not possess a clear and compelling case that would lead us to abandon the significance with which most people invest the ethical question.

Then in Part II we explored a number of general responses to the ethical question offered by several eminent thinkers in the Western tradition. We studied the recommendations that we should actualize human nature, obey the will of God, maximize the happiness of humankind, and obey the commands of reason. And we discovered that each of these theories has a mixture of strengths and weaknesses. That led us to propose that one should adopt the ethical theory that seems to provide the most coherent, consistent, and comprehensive account of human moral experience while maintaining a creative openness to insights from other theories. Such a twofold commitment to a theory and to creative openness provides the kind of orientation needed for addressing contemporary normative ethical issues.

Accordingly, Parts I and II can be seen as preparation for Part III, which moves the ethical question from generality to specificity, from, What ought I to do? to, What ought I to do *in this instance?* And when we move to situationally specific ethical issues, we encounter almost bewildering complexity. Like most things in the world, ethical problems are seldom easy to analyze—or if they are easy they are not problems for us. Clouding our ability to understand fully the issues involved is a host of considerations: factual information or misinformation, religious beliefs, uncertainty about the outcome of our intervention, the possibility that trying to correct one situation will worsen another one, conflict between recognized ethical obligations, and so forth. How much simpler would be our moral judgments if we only needed to choose between a good and an evil action, between helping or harming someone. But our situation often forces us to choose among a series of obligations, to select that which is our *primary* obligation. Is it to self, to others, to country, to our family, or to some combination of all of these?

Various Responses to Applied Theory

Can we use the moral theory we adopt to help us to penetrate the bewildering complexity of the human situation and to generate a rationally consistent response to the real-world ethical problems? For some people an ethical theory provides a "cook-book" approach: identify the problem, look up the appropriate rule, and apply it. Problem solved. Issue settled. Some utilitarians who have great confidence in the hedonistic calculus seem to adopt this approach. For them the calculus provides a decision procedure: simply determine all the net units of pleasure likely to be produced by each alternative action open to the agent, select the action that generates the most net pleasure, and pursue that action as the moral thing to do. This approach toward moral decision making is somewhat akin to the casuistry that became well entrenched in the Middle Ages. Using a moral theory usually mixed with large doses of Christian theology, moral philosophers developed with great care intricate rules for applying moral principles. Fine distinctions, rules for the use of rules, and sometimes a trivializing of the issues characterized this approach. The term *casuistry* now connotes something negative, and to call someone a casuist is not to offer a compliment.

In contrast to the casuistic approach, Kant thought that applying ethical insights to actual problems was not the job of moral philosophy at all. He distinguished between moral philosophy and morals proper, the latter being the application of moral distinctions to real-world situations. He thought that the latter task belonged to anthropology, not to philosophy. The job of moral philosophy was to analyze the fundamental principles of ethics and to relate moral philosophy to the other tasks of philosophy.

The attitude expressed by Kant was assumed by many philosophers in the twentieth century. According to this view, the job of philosophers was to clarify our fundamental ethical terms, understand the role of ethical language, and investigate the nature of ethical judgments. Instead of calling this *metaphysics of morals* as Kant did, it was called *metaethics.* Dealing with actual ethical problems, called normative issues, was not understood to be the task of philosophers. To whom this task belonged was not clear, but it was certainly not the job of philosophers.

A New Attitude Toward Normative Issues

This attitude is now changing rapidly, at least in the United States. If philosophers give up their historic role in attempting to deal with normative ethical issues— that is, with specific moral problems—someone else probably less well trained in moral thinking will do the job, and maybe do it badly. In colleges and universities all across this country, departments of philosophy are including in their curricula courses in medical ethics, environmental ethics, business and professional ethics, and courses dealing with the ethical dimensions of public policy issues, such as income distribution and economic justice, criminal justice, and ethics for scientific researchers. Why the change in attitude among philosophers toward normative ethical issues? For one thing, the latter half of the twentieth century has presented us with a whole new set of pressing problems arising from developing technology. These problems must be resolved, and they can be resolved by the kind of thinking philosophers have traditionally pursued. New techniques in medicine, for example, have raised a whole set of important and perplexing issues such as the definition of death—especially germane to organ transplantation. (You must be sure the organ donor is dead, but not *too* dead; no one wants an organ from an unusable corpse.) Research in recombinant DNA has forced us to rethink the fundamental issues of our obligations as a species to future generations. Similar issues are raised by nuclear energy, both peaceful and other. Additionally, public alarm about actions by large corporations, as well as by the government, that harm individuals and the environment has forced us to rethink the obligations of individuals who run the large companies and government agencies. To whom is a corporation responsible? Its stockholders? Its customers? The public at large? The list of normative concerns could go on. It is getting longer every day.

The selections in Part III are merely samples of the enormous literature that is developing in normative ethics. Some of the best philosophical thinking of our time is being devoted to grappling with such issues, and there are many fine collections of such literature, some of which are listed in the bibliography at the end of the book. Clearly, the inclusion of Part III in this book indicates the rejection of the "hands-off" approach to normative issues. To advocate "hands-off" would constitute not only an abnegation of the traditional goal of moral philosophy (namely, the good life) but also an unacceptable disengagement from pressing moral issues that require the kind of insight philosophical thinking is able to provide. And the "cook-book" approach is also rejected because its neat solutions ignore the complexities of lived moral experience.

Ethical Theory and Normative Issues

Before turning to some of these normative issues themselves, more must be said about the relation between ethical theory and normative problems. Let us admit at the outset that to understand, accept, and defend a moral theory is no guarantee of an ability to deal adequately with normative ethical issues. Moral theory, as we have already suggested, provides a focused point of view with which one can penetrate the complexities of normative issues. It does not remove those complexities. Rather, it offers a vantage point from which to begin asking the morally relevant questions that in due course uncover the complexities of a specific normative issue. An adequate treatment of normative issues requires the asking of those questions and the openness to adopt insights provided by the other ethical theories in order to achieve the best possible judgment on an issue at a particular time.

This relationship between ethical theory and normative issues is not unlike the relationship between theory and practice in other disciplines. For example, a thorough grounding in quantum mechanics does not guarantee the discovery of a new subatomic particle. Nor does a theory, like Newtonian mechanics, become wholly useless when we discover its limitations. The space shuttle is guided by calculations based on Newton's laws of motion, even though we now know that predictability has its limits. When we turn to the social sciences, we find the same value and limitations to theories that attempt to guide research. Theories may instruct us as to where we should look for answers, but they do not guarantee that we will always find them.

Teleologists and Deontologists on Truthfulness

To illustrate the strategy we are suggesting for addressing normative ethical issues, let us consider the issue of lying and truthfulness and examine it from the teleological and deontological perspectives. Remember that teleologists emphasize the consequences of an action in determining its moral worth, and deontologists emphasize something in the action itself (such as the motive) that invests the action with moral worth. In our example, notice how each of these moral theories enables its advocate to penetrate the issue of lying by taking a provisional position on the issue. Then as that position is tested by concrete human situations, a cluster of additional morally relevant considerations is generated, and a modified position seems to be needed involving a blend of insights from several theories.

Agreement and Disagreement

Is it right ever to lie? Are we obligated always to tell the truth? A utilitarian, from a teleological stance, could argue for truthfulness on the grounds that a stable society depends upon certain agreements, and fundamental among these is the expectation that people tell the truth. Without this assumption, most of the institutions of a modern culture would simply collapse. So, on utilitarian grounds, one can argue for truthfulness as an important ethical standard. A Kantian, from a deontological perspective, could argue that truthfulness is required by the categorical imperative; the liar can be a liar because most people tell the truth, and the advantage to the liar comes about because the majority of people do not lie. Therefore, one could not universalize a maxim to lie.

So far, both utilitarians and deontologists would agree that truthfulness is an ethical requirement. But matters are not always so simple. Are there any circumstances, ever, when lying is not only allowed but required by our ethical commitments? Is it acceptable to lie to save a life? Should one lie during wartime to protect the security of the nation? If it could be proved that the public good is improved by a lie and would be harmed by the truth, is that sufficient justification for lying? To all these questions utilitarians would say, Yes. But Kantians would say, No. In the extreme cases the differences between deontological ethics and utilitarian ethics can be seen most clearly. Why was Kant so unyielding on this matter? For one reason, Kant wanted ethics to be consistent (remember the emphasis on universality and necessity); and for another, Kant thought that what one sacrificed in lying is fundamental: one's dignity as a human being. The selection that follows shows Kant's unmistakable word on this topic.

> * The greatest violation of man's duty to himself considered only as a moral being (the humanity in his person) is the opposite of veracity: lying. That no intentional untruth in the expression of one's thoughts can avoid this harsh name in ethics, which derives no authorization from harmlessness, is clear of itself. . . . For dishonor (to be an object of moral contempt), which goes with lying, accompanies also the liar, like his shadow. Lying can be either external or internal. By the former, man makes himself an object of contempt in the eyes of others; but by the latter, which is still worse, he makes himself contemptible in his own eyes and violates the dignity of humanity in his own person. . . . Lying is the throwing away as it were, the obligation of one's dignity as a human being. A man who does not himself believe what he says to another (even if it be only a person existing in idea) has even less worth than if he were a mere thing; for because of the thing's property of being useful, the other person can make some use of it, since it is a thing real and given. But to communicate one's thoughts to someone by words which (intentionally) contain the opposite of what one thinks is an end directly contrary to the natural purposiveness of his capacity to communicate his thoughts. In so doing, he renounces his personality and, as a liar, manifests himself as a mere deceptive appearance of a man, not as a true man.

Problems with Both Kantianism and Utilitarianism

Clearly, Kant's rejection of lies is unflinching. Lies made in jest, lies designed to do more good than harm, even lies that do no harm whatsoever—all are forbidden. But such a rigid rejection of lying seems to be unsatisfactory when it can be shown that telling a lie would save someone's life and telling the truth would cause someone's death. Even in these circumstances, Kant's insistence on truthfulness is absolute.

In the face of such rigidity, the utilitarian alternative seems attractive. When choosing to lie under some conditions, the consequences do seem important. If by lying you could save your best friend's life, most of us would choose to lie. The utilitarian emphasis on consequences, on *weighing* the consequences, seems

* FROM Immanuel Kant, *The Metaphysical Principles of Virtue,* translated by James Ellington. (New York: The Library of Liberal Arts, 1964), pp. 90–91.

preferable to most of us to Kant's unbending emphasis on truthfulness at all cost. Yet the utilitarian alternative, which seems at first to be so attractive, has its own problems, including all the problems previously discussed as difficulties with utilitarian approaches. In her perceptive book, *Lying,* Sissela Bok points out two of the major ones.

> * But, as soon as more complex questions of truthfulness and deception are raised, the utilitarian view turns out to be unsatisfactory as well. First of all, the more complex the acts, the more difficult it becomes to produce convincing comparisons of their consequences. It is hard enough to make estimates of utility for one person, keeping in mind all the different alternatives and their consequences. But to make such estimates for several persons is often well-nigh impossible, except, once again, in the starkest cases. The result is that, even apart from lying, those conflicts which are most difficult to resolve, such as questions of suicide or capital punishment, cause as much disagreement among utilitarians as among everyone else.
>
> But a second reason to be wary of a simple-seeming utilitarian calculation is that it often appears to imply that lies, apart from their resultant harm and benefits, are in themselves neutral. It seems to say that a lie and a truthful statement which achieve the same utility are *equivalent.*

If Kantian inflexibility offends our everyday, prephilosophic ethical sensibilities, and if we find ourselves confronting serious difficulties when attempting to apply utilitarian principles to the issue of lying, what are we to do? Both of the theories capture valuable insights that we would like to retain. So we seem to be caught in the middle between two valuable ethical sensibilities, in what philosophers call a dialectic. On the one hand, we recognize that telling the truth is important not just because of consequences, and that truthfulness is a duty in a fundamental sense, although in a sense that we may find difficult to formulate exactly. But on the other hand, we recognize that we should take consequences into consideration in some circumstances, that other duties such as saving lives, might override our duty to tell the truth.

Appreciating Insights from Both Perspectives

Sissela Bok, recognizing the assets and liabilities of both the teleological and deontological assessments of lying, unpacks a whole cluster of morally relevant features that must be taken into account in a crisis situation in which we feel obligated to lie in order to save a life. Here is an excerpt from her insightful analysis.

> How might the test of publicity discriminate among the many crisis situations where lies are told? Let us look back first at the case discussed

* FROM *Lying: Moral Choices in Public and Private Life,* by Sissela Bok, Copyright © 1978 by Sissela Bok. Reprinted by permission of Pantheon Books, a Division of Random House, Inc.

by Kant* and so many others—the murderer who asks where his victim has gone. This is a crisis in the most common sense of the word, a turning point at which a decisive change for better or worse may take place. It is a crisis, also, in the moral sense of that word: the turning point presents an opportunity to choose whether to intervene, and by what means. Not all crises afford such choice. The familiar scene from the past, where parents sat helpless by the bedside of a sick child whose illness had reached a critical point, is one of agonizing powerlessness. But here, the choice is clear, the stakes are high, and the likely damage without the lie irreversible. There seems no way to prevent the misdeed without the lie, and time is running out.

For those confronted with such a crisis, there is little time to reflect. But could they do so beforehand, they would, I believe, be able to justify such lies. First of all, they could argue, the limited time in which to make the decision rules out the chance to work out alternatives, such as appeals for assistance or rescue. (If, on the other hand, one could know a day ahead of time, there would, of course, be many alternative ways of protecting the victim.)

Second, if the claim that an innocent life can be saved is justified, it will offset in most minds the negative value ordinarily placed on lies. Non-maleficence, or the avoidance of harm, would be the principle invoked, and most would hold that it overrides the principles of veracity in these cases. Just as force would be justifiable as a means to prevent the murder, so it would be right to achieve the same objective through a lie.

Third, the life threatened is itself an innocent one. If, on the other hand, the pursued were a kidnapper, the lie to cover up for him would be very differently judged. One can conceive of innumerable variations in the degree of innocence of the pursued; of violence or coercion should the pursuer find him; and of loyalty to the pursued on the part of the person asked to reveal his whereabouts. All these variations could affect our judgment of how excusable the protective lie would be.

Finally, a lie to protect a murderer's intended victim is a very isolated instance. It would neither be likely to encourage others to lie nor make it much more likely that the person who lied to save a life might come to lie more easily or more often. In many lives, such emergencies arise rarely, if ever; should one arise, it is not likely to be repeated. And the situation is so extraordinary as to provide no reason to generalize the need for lying. There would be very little risk, therefore, of such a lie contributing in any way to a spreading deceptive practice.

For these reasons, the test of public justification could be satisfied. There would be no difficulty in defending openly the policy that persecutors

---

* In an essay entitled "On a Supposed Right to Lie," Immanuel Kant argued that one should tell the truth even to a murderer who asks the whereabouts of the intended victim. This essay can be found in Immanuel Kant, *Critique of Practical Reason and Other Writings in Moral Philosophy,* ed. and trans. Lewis White Beck (Chicago: The University of Chicago Press, 1949), pp. 346–50. *The authors.*

searching for their innocent victims can be answered dishonestly. In fact, not only can it be defended; it could be advocated in advance as preferable to a policy of honesty at all times. Someone who advocated the opposite policy of total honesty to persecutors would be a dangerous individual in times where life-and-death crises arise more frequently; one who could be trusted with no confidential information at all.

Does such a justification apply only to those lying to save other people from extreme threats, or does it apply equally to those who might lie to save themselves? That is, is there some greater justification for altruistic lies here than for self-serving ones? I cannot see that one is more justifiable than the other in such a crisis. Both can be equally advocated in advance and excused in retrospect. (Though if one person gives himself up to save another, the situation changes; such an act cannot be expected in advance,[1] yet it must be admired in retrospect.)

It has been argued that although lying might be justifiable on such occasions, most of us will, in fact, never encounter a situation where a lie might be excusable. We should proceed in life, therefore, as if no lie should ever be told. This is a comforting thought and makes everyday choices simple, but it holds little consolation for those many whose lives are touched more often and more crushingly by crisis than one might think. More individuals than not lead their lives under a continuous threat to survival or to their political or religious freedom. And even in societies where there are no such threats, there are professional groups—doctors or military personnel, for example—whose members can expect frequent crises in their work. For them, there can be no such easy certainty that a crisis where a lie will be necessary will probably never come into their lives.

Prolonged Threats to Survival

A crisis may be acute, as in the life-saving cases; but a state of crisis can also become chronic. The same elements are present—great danger and no escape—but the time frame is entirely different, and there is no one critical turning point. The threat may be continuous, so that one lie after another barely staves off disaster, or it may recur over and over again, each time posing the issue of deception.

In extreme and prolonged threats to survival, as in plagues, invasions, and religious or political persecution, human choice is intolerably restricted. Survival alone counts; moral considerations are nearly obliterated. People may still give each other help and protection in extremes of physical and mental stress; they may still forego lies and still share alike; but such choice goes far beyond duty. And for many, the moral personality is itself crushed; the ability to choose is destroyed.

Hume, describing such conditions, wrote that justice itself can be expected only in an intermediate range of scarcity and benevolence—where there is neither such abundance that all have what they need nor such scarcity that not all can survive; and where people are neither so completely good that they act justly and lovingly spontaneously, nor so incurably evil that nothing can make them do so.

And George Steiner evokes the "survival value" of lying under extreme circumstances:

> Fiction was disguise; from those seeking out the same waterhole, the same sparse quarry, or meagre sexual chance. To misinform, to utter less than the truth was to gain a vital edge of space or subsistence. Natural selection would favor the contriver. Folk tales and mythology retain a blurred memory of the evolutionary advantage of mask and misdirection. Loki, Odysseus are very late, literary concentrates of the widely diffused motif of the liar, of the dissembler elusive as flame and water, who survives.[2]

Under such circumstance, the luxury of alternatives is out of the question. The overwhelming justification is, once again, survival. It appeals to the most powerful aspect of the principle of avoiding harm—the battle against personal extinction. At such times, the spread of deceptive practices cannot be a consideration insofar as it has already taken place. Society *is* in a state of collapse, and a lie won't add to the chaos of the degradation. For all these reasons, public debate of how justifiable such lies are would then be largely beside the point.

These long-term threats to survival strain morality most of all. In shorter and more limited crises, as in mining disasters or shipwrecks, where some may survive and return to society, the ordinary expectations have more force. Such emergencies create exceptional circumstances, not qualifications of moral rules. Survivors may be brought to trial and held to existing standards, as in Conrad's *Lord Jim* or the famous lawsuit of *U.S. v. Holmes.*[3] In this case, the crew in a lifeboat threw overboard fourteen men to keep the vessel from sinking in a turbulent sea. One of the surviving crew members was convicted for unlawful homicide.

But to say that the long-term threats to survival strain morality is not to say that hindsight cannot make out differences in adherence to principles of justice or veracity at such times. Nor, obviously, is it to say that those who *impose* or tolerate such burdens for their fellow human beings must not be judged. It is merely to say that there comes a point of human endurance and of long-term threat beyond which justice is inoperative for sufferers, and where their adherence to moral principles cannot be evaluated by outsiders.

Totalitarian terror achieved its most terrible triumph when it succeeded in cutting the moral person off from the individualist escape and in making the decisions of conscience absolutely questionable and equivocal. The alternative is no longer between good and evil, but between murder and murder. Who could solve the dilemma of the Greek mother who was asked by the Nazis to choose which of her children should be killed?

1. In the absence of an acknowledged obligation such as that of captains of ships in distress, or the more general precept of "women and children first."

2. George Steiner, *After Babel,* p. 224.

3. *United States v. Holmes,* 26 Fed Cas. 360 (C.C.E.D. PA 1842). See also James Childress, "Who Shall Live When Not all Can Live?" in Thomas A. Shannon, ed. *Bioethics* (New York: Paulist Press, 1976), pp. 397–411.

Preserving a Moral Perspective

In conclusion, it is important to note that the examples Bok uses underscore the important distinction between ordinary moral choices we face and extraordinary moral choices. In many of our day-to-day moral decisions, in fact for most of them, we do not experience the moral ambiguity present in the examples given. And it would be a mistake to discard our moral viewpoint, whether it be teleological or deontological, because we find it difficult—even impossible at times—to apply it in limited situations. Recognizing that there are borderline cases does not imply that the principles we use are illegitimate or should be abandoned. Borrowing an observation made by John Searle in discussing philosophy of language, we could say of ethical borderline examples that "we could not recognize borderline cases of a concept as borderline cases if we did not grasp the concept to begin with. It is as much a test of a man's mastery of the concept *green* that he has doubts about applying it to a glass of Chartreuse, as that he has no doubt at all about applying it to a healthy lawn or withholding it from fresh snow."*

Most of the cases we will examine in the remainder of Part Three are borderline cases involving business, medical, and public policy issues. These cases will remind us that our commitment to a particular moral theory with its principles and key concepts must be held in creative tension with an openness that it be both aware of the limitations of our theory and also receptive to insights from other perspectives.

Review Questions

1. Is it important and necessary for ethical theory to be applied to concrete issues?
2. What is Kant's position on truthfulness and lying?
3. What is the utilitarian position on truthfulness and lying?
4. What criticisms can be registered against the Kantian and utilitarian positions on truthfulness and lying?
5. Does Bok blend insights from both deontologists and teleologists in her discussion of lying? How?

---

* John R. Searle, *Speech Acts: An Essay in the Philosophy of Language* (Cambridge: At the University Press, 1969), p. 8.

CHAPTER 10

Ethical Issues in Medicine

Introduction

During the past three or four decades, the concerns of medical ethics have expanded dramatically. This has been due both to advances in medical technology and to the desire of a better informed public to participate in medical decision making. Technological advances have driven concern beyond the physician's dilemma of being both an indispensable healer-comforter, and thereby also a favored money-maker, to the profound dilemmas associated with womb rentals, artificial insemination, genetic engineering, behavior control, organ transplantation, human experimentation, withholding or withdrawing treatment, neonatal euthanasia, and so forth. The list goes on and on.

In addition, the public—better informed, more alert to patient rights, and willing to pursue malpractice litigation—has fractured the mystique of the physician as the all-wise, not-to-be-questioned, trusted custodian of life and death. Accordingly, moral problems associated with the doctor/patient relationship have arisen. These problems include informed consent, confidentiality, paternalism, truth-telling, and so forth. Increasingly, colleges of medicine have responded to this expanding domain of medical ethics by infusing the traditional medical curriculum with courses in medical humanities. And professional organizations have been formed, such as the Society for Health and Human Values, by physicians, nurses, philosophers, theologians, attorneys, and other professionals "to encourage consideration of issues in human values as they relate to health services, the education of health care professionals, and research. . . ."*

* *Society for Health and Human Values By-Laws,* adopted May 3, 1983.

We have selected two of the many pressing normative medical issues for consideration in this chapter: abortion and allocation of scarce medical resources. Both of these topics bristle with difficult issues and thereby provide an excellent introduction to the complex domain of medical ethics. The selected bibliography at the end of the book provides additional resources illustrating how vast the field of medical ethics has become.

Issue One:
Abortion

Defining Abortion

What is an abortion? Shall we describe it as "the termination of a pregnancy"? If we do, how does it differ from birth, which is also the termination of pregnancy? Suppose, then, that we enrich our definition as follows: "Abortion is the induced termination of a pregnancy prior to birth." Will that do the job, or is there still something missing? Does not abortion differ significantly from medical procedures that terminate other conditions in the human body? Should we perhaps add that "abortion is the induced termination of a pregnancy prior to birth that results in the destruction of ———?" How shall we fill in the blank? How about "living tissue"? Surely that will not do, because cancerous growths are "living tissue," and certainly we would want to distinguish an abortion from a mastectomy. Suppose, then, that we insert in the blank "an embryo or fetus." Will that do the job? Or must we enlarge it to read "a *human* embryo or fetus"? Or should we simply insert in the blank "a human being"? Or perhaps more tersely "a person"? Clearly, there is an enormous difference between the terms "embryo or fetus" and "human or person." And clearly our willingness to authorize an abortion may vary considerably depending upon which term we believe is appropriate for the blank.

Suppose we fill in the blank with "human being." Then let us ask the question, Are there any circumstances under which we would agree that an abortion—the destruction of a human being—would be morally justified?" Some deontologists would argue that each human being possesses the inalienable right to life and that such a right must not be violated in any case, including this one. Other deontologists would argue that an abortion might be justified when the mother's right to life is in conflict with the fetus's right to life. Some teleologists would argue that the projected consequences of abortion are so dangerous to society— from the sacrifice of the physician's protective attitude toward life to the brutalization of humankind's sensibilities to the end that the retarded and senile would soon be added to the unborn as candidates for termination—that abortion cannot be morally justified. Other teleologists would argue that, in some cases, the consequences of allowing a particular fetus—such as one that is radically malformed and unwanted by the parents—to come to full term and be born would be so overwhelmingly painful for all parties concerned that the abortion would be morally justified. Presumably, if these pro-abortion teleologists could demonstrate to the anti-abortion teleologists that the overall painful consequences of not performing an abortion exceeded the overall beneficial consequences, then the anti-abortion teleologists would change their position. They would, accordingly, be only provisionally anti-abortion. But the anti-abortion deontologists have a position that seems to be cast in stone. For them, no consideration is strong enough to override the right to life.

When the anti-abortion deontologist encounters those who believe that under certain circumstances abortion is justifiable (whether they be deontologists or teleologists), we seem to have a loggerhead issue where rational debate between the two groups is likely to be unproductive. Yet, there is at least one point on which fruitful debate might still be engaged: the question of whether or not the embryo or the fetus should legitimately be regarded as a human being invested with the right to life. And that debate does not yield simple, quick solutions. For those who believe that, under certain circumstances, abortion can be morally justified, there is the challenge to work out precisely what are the morally relevant considerations that can justify such an action. Here, too, the task is far from easy.

Both of these tasks—exploring the appropriateness of calling embryos or fetuses "human," and identifying the morally relevant considerations that could justify an abortion—are carefully pursued by Sissela Bok in the selection that follows. We have already encountered Bok's careful philosophical reasoning on the subject of lying and truth-telling in a previous chapter. Here again, Bok provides us with philosophical analysis that blends both deontological and teleological concerns.

Reasons for and against Abortion

Bok begins her discussion by reminding us that although the U.S. Supreme Court in 1973 declared certain kinds of abortions to be lawful, nevertheless the moral issues of abortion still require careful debate. She then presents several of the major reasons people offer both against and in support of abortion.

> * The recent Supreme Court decisions[1] have declared abortions to be lawful in the United States during the first trimester of pregnancy. After the first trimester, the state can restrict them by regulations protecting the pregnant woman's health; and after 'viability' the state may regulate or forbid abortions except where the medical judgment is made that an abortion is necessary to safeguard the life or the health of the pregnant woman. But it would be wrong to conclude from these decisions that no *moral* distinctions between abortions can now be made—that what is lawful is always justifiable. These decisions leave the moral issues of abortion open, and it is more important than ever to examine them.
>
> While abortion is frequently rejected for religious reasons, arguments against it are also made on other grounds. The most forceful one holds

* FROM Sissela Bok, "Ethical Problems of Abortion," *Hastings Center Studies,* Vol. 2, No. 1 (January, 1974): 33–52. Used by permission of the author and Hastings Center.

that if we grant that a fetus possesses humanity, we must accord it human rights, including the right to live. Another argument invokes the danger to *other* unborn humans, should abortion spread and perhaps even become obligatory in certain cases, and the danger to newborns, the retarded, and the senile should society begin to take the lives of those considered expendable. A third argument stresses the danger that physicians and nurses and those associated with the act of abortion might lose their traditional protective attitude toward life if they become inured to taking human lives at the request of mothers.

Among the arguments made in favor of permitting abortion, one upholds the right of the mother to determine her own fertility, and her right to the use of her own body. Another stresses, in cases of genetic defects of a severe variety, a sympathetic understanding of the suffering which might accompany living, should the fetus not be aborted. And a third reflects a number of social concerns, ranging from the problem of overpopulation *per se* to the desire to reduce unwantedness, child abuse, maternal deaths through illegal abortions, poverty and illness.

Killing or Withdrawal of Support

Bok proceeds to analyze the fundamental conflict between the pregnant woman and the unborn life within her. There are two key questions in this conflict. First, is the unborn life within the woman to be considered a human being invested with rights and interests that can conflict with those of the mother? Second, must abortion be thought of as "killing" or can it legitimately be regarded as "the withdrawal of bodily life support on the part of the mother"? Bok addresses the latter question first of all.

In discussing the ethical dilemmas of abortion, I shall begin with the basic conflict—that between a pregnant woman and the unborn life she harbors.

Mother and Fetus

Up to very recently, parents had only limited access to birth prevention. Contraception was outlawed or treated with silence. Sterilization was most often unavailable and abortion was left to those desperate enough to seek criminal abortions. Women may well be forgiven now, therefore, if they mistrust the barrage of arguments concerning abortion, and may well suspect that these are rear-guard actions in an effort to tie them still longer to the bearing of unwanted children.

Some advocates for abortion hold that women should have the right to do what they want with their own bodies, and that removing the fetus is comparable to cutting one's hair or removing a disfiguring growth. This view simply ignores the fact that abortion involves more than just one life. The same criticism holds for the vaguer notions which defend abortion on the grounds that a woman should have the right to control her fate, or the right to have an abortion as she has the right to marry. But no one has the clear-cut right to control her fate where others share it, and marriage requires consent by two persons, whereas the consent of the fetus is precisely what cannot be obtained. How, then, can we weigh the rights and the interests of mother and fetus, where they conflict?

The central question is whether the life of the fetus should receive the same protection as other lives—often discussed in terms of whether killing the fetus is to be thought of as killing a human being. But before asking that question, I would like to ask whether abortion can always be thought of as *killing* in the first place. For abortion can be looked upon, also, as the withdrawal of bodily life support on the part of the mother.

Cessation of Bodily Life Support

Would anyone, before or after birth, child or adult, have the right to continue to be dependent upon the bodily processes of another against that person's will? It can happen that a person will require a sacrifice on the part of another in order not to die; does he therefore have the *right* to this sacrifice?

Judith Thompson has argued most cogently that the mother who finds herself pregnant, as a result of rape or in spite of every precaution, does not have the obligation to continue the pregnancy:

I am arguing only that having a right to life does not guarantee having either a right to be given the use of or a right to be allowed the continued use of another person's body—even if one needs it for life itself.[2]

Abortion, according to such a view, can be thought of as the cessation of continued support. It is true that the embryo cannot survive alone, and that it dies. But this is not unjust killing, any more than when Siamese twins are separated surgically and one of them dies as a result. Judith Thompson argues that at least in those cases where the mother is involuntarily pregnant, she can cease her support of the life of the fetus without infringing its right to live. Here, viability—the capability of living independently from the body of the mother—becomes important. Before that point, the unborn life will end when the mother ceases her support. No one else can take over the protection of the unborn life. After the point where viability begins, much depends on what is done by others, and on how much assistance is provided.

It may be, however, that in considering the ethical implications of the right to cease bodily support of the fetus we must distinguish between causing death indirectly through ceasing such support and actively killing the fetus outright. The techniques used in abortion differ significantly in this respect. A method which prevents implantation of the fertilized egg or which brings about menstruation is much more clearly cessation of life support than one which sucks or scrapes out the embryo. Least like cessation of support is abortion by saline solution, which kills and begins to decompose the fetus, thus setting in motion its explusion by the mother's body. This method is the one most commonly used in the second trimester of pregnancy. The alternative method possible at that time is a hysterotomy, or "small Cesarean," where the fetus is removed intact, and where death very clearly does result from the interruption of bodily support.

If we learn how to provide life support for the fetus outside the natural mother's body, it may happen that parents who wish to adopt a baby may come into a new kind of conflict with those who wish to have an abortion. They may argue that *all* that the aborting mother has a right to is to cease supporting a fetus with her own body. They may insist, if the pregnancy is already in the second trimester, that she has no right to choose a technique which also kills the baby. It would be wrong for the natural parents to insist at that point that the severance must be performed in such a way that others cannot take over the care and support for the fetus. But a conflict could arise if the mother were asked to postpone the abortion in order to improve the chances of survival and well-being of the fetus to be adopted by others.

Are there times where, quite apart from the technique used to abort, a woman has a *special* responsibility to continue bodily support of a fetus? Surely the many pregnancies which are entered upon voluntarily are of such a nature. One might even say that, if anyone ever did have special obligations to continue life support of another, it would be the woman who had *voluntarily undertaken* to become pregnant. For she has then brought about the situation where the fetus has come to require her support, and there is no one else who can take over her responsibility until after the baby is viable.

To use the analogy of a drowning person, one can think of three scenarios influencing the responsibility of a bystander to leap to the rescue. First, someone may be drowning and the bystander arrives at the scene, hesitating between rescue and permitting the person to drown. Secondly, someone may be drowning as a result of the honestly mistaken assurance by the bystander that swimming would be safe. Thirdly, the bystander may have pushed the drowning person out of a boat. In each case the duties of the bystander are different, but surely they are at their most stringent when he has intentionally caused the drowning person to find himself in the water.

These three scenarios bear some resemblance, from the point of view of the mother's responsibility to the fetus, to: first, finding out that she is pregnant against her wishes; second, mistakenly trusting that she was protected against pregnancy; and third, intentionally becoming pregnant.

Every pregnancy which has been intentionally begun creates special responsibilities for the mother. But there is one situation in which these dilemmas are presented in a particularly difficult form. It is where two parents deliberately enter upon a pregnancy, only to find that the baby they are expecting has a genetic disease or has suffered from damage in fetal life, so that it will be permanently malformed or retarded. Here, the parents have consciously brought about the life which now requires support from the body of the mother. Can they now turn about and say that this particular fetus is such that they do not wish to continue their support? This is especially difficult when the fetus is already developed up to the 18th or 20th week. Can they acknowledge that they meant to begin a human life, but not *this* human life? Or, to take a more callous example, suppose, as sometimes happens, that the parents learn that the baby is of a sex they do not wish.

In such cases the justification which derives from wishing to cease life support for a life which had not been intended is absent, since this life *had* been intended. At the same time, an assumption of responsibility which comes with consciously beginning a pregnancy is much weaker than the corresponding assumption between two adults, or the social assumption of responsibility for a child upon birth for reasons which will be discussed in the next section.

To sum up at this point, ceasing bodily life support *of a fetus or of anyone else* cannot be looked at as a breach of duty except where such a duty has been assumed in the first place. Such a duty is closer to existing when the pregnancy has been voluntarily begun. And it does not exist at all in cases of rape. Certain *methods* of abortion, furthermore, are more difficult to think of as cessation of support than others. Finally, pregnancy is perhaps unique in that cessation of support means death for the fetus up to a certain point of its development, so that nearness *to* this point in pregnancy argues against abortion.

Notice how important the appropriate definition and description of an ethical problem can be. If Bok had allowed abortion to be construed always as "killing," then it would have been more difficult for her to argue that killing does not necessarily involve a breach of a duty. But by regarding abortion as "ceasing bodily life support," Bok is able to draw the distinction between causing death *indirectly* through ceasing such support and *actively* killing the fetus. (Bok admits that the distinction does become a bit strained with some methods of abortion.) The former does not involve a breach of duty unless the woman voluntarily committed her body to provide life support for the fetus. If, then, the woman became pregnant involuntarily, such as during rape, would abortion in this case be morally justified because the woman would simply be withdrawing bodily support she had never promised to give? Or does the fetus, as a human being, have certain rights that must be protected?

Humanness and the Unborn Life

That brings us to Bok's other crucial question in the mother-fetus conflict: should the unborn life be regarded as a human being? If the unborn life is a human one, then it is entitled to the protection we accord to any other human, and abortion would be ruled out. But we must ask, When does the unborn life *become* a human being? Surely the sperm on its own and the ovum on its own would not be regarded as human beings entitled to the protection accorded to humans. Would the sperm become a human being when ejaculated into the woman? Would it become a human being when united with the ovum to form a zygote? Do we want to say that a fertilized ovum is a human being? Or do we want to say that the embryo becomes a human being at a later stage? If so, when? If we can identify the time at which the unborn life becomes a human, then presumably abortions prior to that time would not involve the violation of the right to life and protection we accord to all humans.

I would like now to turn to the larger question of whether the life of the fetus *should* receive the same protection as other lives—whether killing the fetus, by whatever means, and for whatever reason, is to be thought of as killing a human being.

A long tradition of religious and philosophical and legal thought has attempted to answer this question by determining if there is human life before birth, and, if so, when it *becomes* human. If human life is present from conception on, according to this tradition, it must be protected as such from that moment. And if the embryo *becomes* human at some point during a pregnancy, then that is the point at which the protection should set in.

Humanity

The point in a pregnancy at which a human individual can be said to exist is differently assigned. John Noonan generalizes the predominant Catholic view as follows:

If one steps outside the specific categories used by the theologians, the answer they gave can be analyzed as a refusal to discriminate among human beings on the basis of their varying potentialities. Once conceived, the being was recognized as a man because he had man's potential. The criterion for humanity, thus, was simple and all-embracing: If you are conceived by human parents, you are human.[3]

Once conceived, he holds, human life has about an 80% chance to reach the moment of birth and develop further. *Conception,* therefore, represents a point of discontinuity, after which the probabilities for human development are immensely higher than for the sperm or the egg before conception.

Others have held that the moment when *implantation* occurs, 6–7 days after conception, is more significant from the point of view of humanity and individuality than conception itself. This permits them to allow the intrauterine device and the 'morning after pill' as not taking human life, merely interfering with implantation.

Another view is advanced by Jerome Lejeune, who suggests that unity and uniqueness, "the two headings defining an individual" are not definitely established until between two and four weeks after conception.[4] Up to that time it is possible that two eggs may have collaborated to build together one embryo, known as a "chimera," whereas after that time such a combination is no longer possible. Similarly, up to that time, a fertilized egg from which twins may result may not yet have split in two.

Still another approach to the establishing of humanity is to say that *looking* human is the important factor. A photo of the first cell having divided in half clearly does not depict what most people mean when they use the expression "human being." Even the four-week-old embryo does not look human, whereas the six-week-old one is beginning to. Recent techniques of depicting the embryo and the fetus have remarkably increased our awareness of the "human-ness" at this early stage; this new *seeing* of life before birth may come to increase the psychological recoil from aborting those who already look human—thus adding a powerful psychological factor to the medical and personal factors already influencing the trend to earlier and earlier abortions.

Others reason that the time at which electrical impulses are first detectable from the brain, around the eighth week, marks the line after which human life is present. If brain activity is advocated as the criterion for human life among the dying, they argue, then why not use it also at the very beginning? Such a use of the criterion for human life has been interpreted by some to indicate that abortion would not be killing before electrical impulses are detectable, only afterwards. Such an analogy would seem to possess a symmetry of sorts, but it is only superficially plausible. For the lack of brain response at the end of life has to be shown to be *irreversible* in order to support a conclusion that life is absent. The lack of response from the embryo's brain, on the other hand, is temporary and precisely not irreversible.

Another dividing line, once more having to do with our perception of the fetus, is that achieved when the mother can feel the fetus moving. *Quickening* has traditionally represented an important distinction, and in some legal traditions such as the common law, abortion has been permitted before quickening, but is a misdemeanor, "a great misprision," afterwards, rather than homicide. It is certain that the first felt movements represent an awe-inspiring change for the mother, and perhaps, in some primitive sense, a 'coming to life' of the being she carries.

Yet another distinction occurs when the fetus is considered *viable*. According to this view, once the fetus is capable of living independently of its mother, it must be regarded as a human being and protected as such. The United States Supreme Court decisions on abortion established viability as the "compelling" point for the state's "important and legitimate interest in potential life," while eschewing the question of when 'life' or 'human life' begins.

A set of later distinctions cluster around the process of birth itself. This is the moment when life begins, according to some religious traditions, and the point at which 'persons' are fully recognized in the law, according to the Supreme Court. The first breaths taken by newborn babies have been invested with immense symbolic meaning since the earliest gropings toward understanding what it means to be alive and human. And the rituals of acceptance of babies and children have often served to define humanity to the point where the baby could be killed if it were not named or declared acceptable by the elders of the community or by the head of the household, either at birth or in infancy. Others have mentioned as factors in our concept of humanity the ability to experience, to remember the past and envisage the future, to communicate, even to laugh at oneself.

In the positions here examined, and in the abortion debate generally, a number of concepts are at times used as if they were interchangeable. 'Humanity,' 'human life,' 'life,' are such concepts, as are 'man,' 'person,' 'human being,' or 'human individual.' In particular, those who hold that humanity begins at conception or at implantation often have the tendency to say that at that time a human being or a person or a man exists as well, whereas others find it impossible to equate them.

Each of these terms can, in addition, be used in different senses which overlap but are not interchangeable. For instance, humanity and human life, in one sense, are possessed by every cell in our bodies. Many cells have the full genetic makeup required for asexual reproduction—so called cloning—of a human being. Yet clearly this is not the sense of those words intended when the protection of humanity or of human life is advocated. Such protection would press the reverence for life to the mad extreme of ruling out haircuts and considering mosquito bites murder.

It may be argued, however, that for most cells which have the potential of cloning to form a human being, extraordinarily complex measures would be required which are not as yet sufficiently perfected beyond the animal stage. Is there, then, a difference, from the point of view of human potential, between these cells and egg cells or sperm cells? And is there still another difference in potential between the egg cell before and after conception? While there is a statistical difference in the *likelihood* of their developing into a human being, it does not seem possible to draw a clear line where humanity definitely begins.

The different views as to when humanity begins are not dependent upon factual information. Rather, these views are representative of different worldviews, often of a religious nature, involving deeply held commitments with moral consequences. There is no disagreement as to what we now know about life and its development before and after conception; differences arise only about the names and moral consequences we attach to the changes in this development and the distinctions we consider important. Just as there is no point at which Achilles can be pinpointed as catching up with the tortoise, though everyone knows he does, so too everyone is aware of the distance traveled, in terms of humanity, from before conception to birth, though there is no one point at which humanity can be agreed upon as setting in. Our efforts to pinpoint and to define reflect the urgency with which we reach for abstract labels and absolute certainty in facts and in nature; and the resulting confusion and puzzlement are close to what Wittgenstein described, in *Philosophical Investigations,* as the "bewitchment of our intelligence by means of language."

Even if some see the fertilized egg as possessing humanity and as being "a man" in the words used by Noonan, however, it would be quite unthinkable to act upon all the consequences of such a view. It would be necessary to undertake a monumental struggle against all spontaneous abortions—known as miscarriages—often of severely malformed embryos expelled by the mother's body. This struggle would appear increasingly misguided as we learn more about how to preserve early prenatal life. Those who could not be saved would have to be buried in the same way as dead infants. Those who engaged in abortion would have to be prosecuted for murder. Extraordinary practical complexities would arise with respect to the detection of early abortion, and to the question of whether the use of abortifacients in the first few days after conception should also count as murder. In view of these inconsistencies, it seems likely that this view of humanity, like so many others, has been adopted for limited purposes having to do with the prohibition of induced abortions, rather than from a real belief in the full human rights of the first few cells after conception.

When Unborn Life Becomes Human

A strategy that often provides clarification in dealing with normative issues is to construct a continuum of a morally relevant feature. That is what Bok has done with the question, When does the unborn life become human? The continuum could be diagrammed as follows:

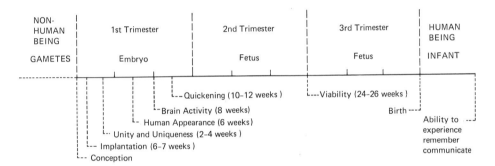

Presumably as we move from left to right along this continuum a human being comes. into existence. But where shall we draw the line to separate nonhuman from human? We would probably agree that the sperm and the ovum prior to conception are not human beings. We would call them gametes but hardly humans. Could we then fix a time after which we are certain that a human being is present? Could we say that birth guarantees the presence of a human being? If we did, then we would have to say that an infant born with a brain stem devoid of a brain (and, therefore incapable of brain functions) is a human. Would we really want to call that infant a human? If we would not, what level of brain activity is needed to qualify for being a human? Certainly we have very little difficulty identifying a fully developed human being when we confront one, but it is not at all easy to locate precisely the time (at or after conception) when a human being comes into existence.

In the light of such difficulty, why do people try to draw a line between the nonhuman and the human in our development? Some people, says Bok, do this in order to defend a preconceived position on abortion. For example, if you identify the emergence of a human with conception, then you can effectively rule out abortion as antihuman. Others try to draw the line as part of the effort to describe as fully and as accurately as possible the development of our species. Others may add to this descriptive purpose the desire to establish a model of what a good human being is in order to provide a goal for human aspirations. Then, too, others seek definitions of humanity in order to draw the line between life that is to be protected and life that can be used and dominated. Bok argues that definitions of humanity, as criteria for excluding life from protection, have been so abused throughout history and have such dangerous potentialities for continued abuse, that an appeal to a standard of humanity to determine what life merits protection and what life does not must be abandoned. She writes,

> And herein lies by far the most important reason for abandoning such efforts: the monumental misuse of the concept of 'humanity' in so many practices of discrimination and atrocity throughout history. Slavery, witchhunts and wars have all been justified by their perpetrators on the grounds that they held their victims to be less than fully human. The insane and the criminal have for long periods been deprived of the most basic necessities for similar reasons, and excluded from society. A theologian, Dr. Joseph Fletcher, has even suggested recently that someone who has an I.Q. below 40 is "questionably a person" and that those below the 20-mark are not persons at all.[5] He adds that:

> This has bearing, obviously, on decision making in gynecology, obstetrics, and pediatrics, as well as in general surgery and medicine.

> Here a criterion for 'personhood' is taken as a guideline for action which could have sinister and far-reaching effects. Even when entered upon with the best of intentions, and in the most guarded manner, the enterprise of basing the protection of human life upon such criteria and definitions is dangerous. To question someone's humanity or personhood is a first step to mistreatment and killing.

> We must abandon, therefore, this quest for a definition of humanity capable of showing us who has a right to live. To do so must not, however, mean any abandon of concerns with the human condition—with the quest for knowledge about human origins and characteristics and with aspirations for human goodness. It is only the use of the concept of 'humanity' as a criterion of *exclusion* which I deplore. . . . I submit that in the many borderline cases where humanity is questioned by some—the so-called 'vegetables,' the severely retarded, or the embryo—even the seemingly universal yardsticks of 'humanity' or rationality are dangerous.

Reasons for Protecting Human Life

If, however, we abandon the appeal to a standard of humanity to decide what life is to be protected, and thereby to gain some needed light on the issue of abortion, what alternative criteria do we have? Bok's answer is to identify the reasons why we protect life and then to see if those reasons apply to the embryo and the fetus. Notice how infused these reasons are with teleological considerations.

Reasons for Protecting Life
1. Killing is viewed as the greatest of all dangers *for the victim.*

- The knowledge that there is a threat to life causes intense anguish and apprehension.

- The actual taking of life can cause great suffering.
- The continued experience of life, once begun, is considered so valuable, so unique, so absorbing, that no one who has this experience should be unjustly deprived of it. And depriving someone of this experience means that all else of value to him will be lost.

2. Killing is brutalizing and criminalizing *for the killer.* It is a threat to others, and destructive to the person engaged therein.

3. Killing often causes *the family of the victim and others* to experience grief and loss. They may have been tied to the dead person by affection or economic dependence; they may have given of themselves in the relationship, so that its severance causes deep suffering.

4. *All of society,* as a result, has a stake in the protection of life. Permitting killing to take place sets patterns for victims, killers, and survivors, that are threatening and ultimately harmful to all.

These are neutral principles governing the protection of life. They are shared by most human beings reflecting upon the possibility of dying at the hands of others. It is clear that these principles, if applied in the absence of the confusing terminology of 'humanity,' would rule out the kinds of killing perpetrated by conquerors, witch-hunters, slave-holders, and Nazis. Their victims feared death and suffered; they grieved for their dead; and the societies permitting such killing were brutalized and degraded.

Turning now to abortions once more, how do these principles apply to the taking of the lives of embryos and fetuses?

Reasons to Protect Life in the Prenatal Period

Consider the very earliest cell formations soon after conception. Clearly, most of these reasons for protecting human life are absent here.

This group of cells cannot suffer in death, nor can it fear death. Its experiencing of life has not yet begun; it is not yet conscious of the loss of anything it has come to value in life and is not tied by bonds of affection to other human beings. If the abortion is desired by both parents, it will cause no grief such as that which accompanies the death of a child. Almost no human care and emotion and resources have been invested in it. Nor is a very early abortion brutalizing for the person voluntarily performing it, or a threat to other members of the human community. The only factor common to these few cells and, say, a soldier killed in war or a murdered robbery victim is that of the *potential* denied, the interruption of life, the deprivation of the possibility to grow and to experience, to have the joys and sorrows of existence.

For how much should this one factor count? It should count *at least* so much as to eliminate the occasionally voiced notion that pregnancy and its interruption involve only the mother in the privacy of her reproductive life, that to have an abortion is somehow analogous with cutting one's finger nails.

At the same time, I cannot agree that it should count enough so that one can simply equate killing an embryo with murder, even apart from legal considerations or the problems of enforcement. For it *is* important that most of the reasons why we protect lives are absent here. It does matter that the group of cells cannot feel the anguish or pain connected with death, that it is not conscious of the interruption of its life, and that other humans do not mourn it or feel insecure in their own lives if it dies.

But, it could be argued, one can conceive of other deaths with those factors absent, which nevertheless would be murder. Take the killing of a hermit in his sleep, by someone who instantly commits suicide. Here there is no anxiety or fear of the killing on the part of the victim, no pain in dying, no mourning by family or friends (to whom the hermit has, in leaving them for good, already in a sense 'died'), no awareness by others that wrong has been done; and the possible brutalization of the murderer has been made harmless to others through his suicide. Speculate further that the bodies are never found. Yet we would still call the act one of murder. The reason we would do so is inherent in the act itself, and depends on the fact that his life was taken, and that he was denied the chance to continue to experience it.

How does this privation of potential differ from abortion in the first few days of pregnancy? I find that I cannot use words like 'deprived,' 'deny,' 'take away,' and 'harm' when it comes to the group of cells, whereas I have no difficulty in using them for the hermit. Do these words require, if not a person conscious of his loss, at least someone who at a prior time has developed enough to be or have been conscious thereof? Because there is no semblance of human form, no conscious life or capability to live independently, no knowledge of death, no sense of pain, one cannot use such words meaningfully to describe early abortion.

In addition, whereas it is possible to frame a rule permitting abortion which causes no anxiety on the part of others covered by the rule—other embryos or fetuses—it is not possible to frame such a rule permitting the killing of hermits without threatening other *hermits.* All hermits would have to fear for their lives if there were a rule saying that hermits can be killed if they are alone and asleep and if the agent commits suicide.

The reasons, then, for the protection of lives are minimal in very early abortions. At the same time, some of them are clearly present with respect to *infanticide,* most important among them the brutalization of those participating in the act and the resultant danger for all who are felt to be undesirable by their families or by others. This is not to say that acts of infanticide have not taken place in our society; indeed, as late as the nineteenth century, newborns were frequently killed, either directly or by giving them into the care of institutions such as foundling hospitals, where the death rate could be as high as 90 percent in the first year of life. A few primitive societies, at the edge of extinction, without other means to limit families, still practice infanticide. But I believe that the *public acceptance* of infanticide in all other societies is unthinkable, given the advent of modern methods of contraception and early abortion, and of institutions to which parents can give their children, assured of their survival

and of the high likelihood that they will be adopted and cared for by a
family.

Dividing Lines

If, therefore, very early abortion does not violate these principles of
protection for life, but infanticide does, we are confronted with a new kind
of continuum in the place of that between less human and more human:
that of the growth in strength, during the prenatal period, of these principles,
these reasons for protecting life. In this second continuum, it would be as
difficult as in the first to draw a line based upon objective factors. Since
most abortions can be performed earlier or later during pregnancy, it would
be preferable to encourage early abortions rather than late ones, and to
draw a line before the second half of the pregnancy, permitting later abortions
only on a clear showing of need. For this purpose, the two concepts of
quickening and *viability*—so unsatisfactory in determining when humanity
begins—can provide such limits.

Before quickening, the reasons to protect life are, as has been shown,
negligible, perhaps absent altogether. During this period, therefore, abortion
could be permitted upon request. Alternatively, the end of the first trimester
could be employed as such a limit, as is the case in a number of countries.

Between quickening and viability, when the operation is a more difficult
one medically and more traumatic for parents and medical personnel, it
would not seem unreasonable to hold that special reasons justifying the
abortion should be required in order to counterbalance this resistance;
reasons not known earlier, such as the severe malformation of the fetus.
After viability, finally, all abortions save the rare ones required to save the
life of the mother, should be prohibited, because the reasons to *protect*
life may not be thought to be partially present; even though the viable
fetus cannot fear death or suffer consciously therefrom, the effects on those
participating in the event, and thus on society indirectly, could be serious.
This is especially so because of the need, mentioned above, for a protection
against infanticide. In the unlikely event, however, that the mother should
first come to wish to be separated from the fetus at such a late stage, the
procedure ought to be delayed until it can be one of premature birth, not
one of harming the fetus in an abortive process.

Medically, however, the definition of 'viability' is difficult. It varies from
one fetus to another. At one stage in pregnancy, a certain number of babies,
if born, will be viable. At a later stage, the percentage will be greater. Viability
also depends greatly on the state of our knowledge concerning the support
of life after birth, and on the nature of the support itself. Support can be
given much earlier in a modern hospital than in a rural village, or in a
clinic geared to doing abortions only. It may some day even be the case
that almost any human life will be considered viable before birth, once
artificial wombs are perfected.

As technological progress pushes back the time when the fetus can be
helped to survive independently of the mother, a question will arise as to

whether the cutoff point marked by viability ought also be pushed back. Should abortion then be prohibited much earlier than is now the case, because the medical meaning of 'viability' will have changed, or should we continue to rely on the conventional meaning of the word for the distinction between lawful and unlawful abortion?

In order to answer this question it is necessary to look once more at the reasons for which 'viability' was thought to be a good dividing-line in the first place. Is viability important because the baby can survive outside of the mother? Or because this chance of survival comes at a time in fetal development when the *reasons* to protect life have grown strong enough to prohibit abortion? At present, the two coincide, but in the future, they may come to diverge increasingly.

If the time comes when an embryo *could* be kept alive without its mother and thus be 'viable' in one sense of the word, the reasons for protecting life from the point of view of victims, agents, relatives and society would still be absent; it seems right, therefore, to tie the obligatory protection of life to the present conventional definition of 'viability' and to set a socially agreed upon time in pregnancy after which abortion should be prohibited.

To sum up, the justifications a mother has for not wishing to give birth can operate up to a certain point in pregnancy; after that point, the reasons society has for protecting life become sufficiently weighty so as to prohibit late abortions and infanticide.

When Reasons for Protecting Life are Present

Bok has suggested an alternative to the attempt to build a continuum from the nonhuman to the human. Instead, she suggests a continuum based on the absence or presence of reasons for protecting life. We can graphically present such a continuum as follows:

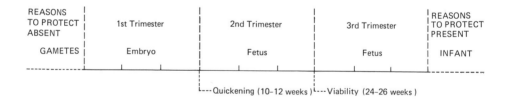

As we move from left to right along this continuum, we move from the absence of reasons to the presence of reasons for protecting life. Bok considers the presence of reasons to be negligible prior to quickening and suggests that during this period abortions could be permitted upon request. Between quickening and viability the presence of reasons for protecting life grows stronger and, therefore, Bok recommends that special reasons that weigh against the protection of the fetus should be required to justify an abortion. After viability the presence of reasons for protecting life are so strong that abortion should be prohibited, says Bok, except where the life of the mother is at stake.

Between the time of quickening to the viability of the fetus, abortion is much more difficult to defend and involves a number of factors that Bok explores with considerable precision. These involve such issues as how soon after quickening the decision to abort takes place, a consideration of the reasons why the abortion is desired, whether both parents are agreed upon the desirability of abortion, and a consideration of what alternatives there are to abortion. This section of Bok's article can provide additional insights for those wishing further analysis of the topic. For the present purposes, we will conclude with Bok's summary of her analysis.

Conclusion

There are many reasons which may lead a mother not to wish to give birth, but to have an abortion instead. They range from the most compelling to the most trivial. In early pregnancy, society's reasons for protecting life— the suffering and harm to the victim, to the agent, to the family and friends, and to society as a whole—do not apply, either to the zygote or to the embryo. Abortion, for whatever reasons, should then be available upon request. Preventing birth before conception or just after conception, however, presents fewer ethical conflicts than later abortions.

As pregnancy progresses, the social reasons for preventing killing are more and more applicable to the fetus. At the stage where a fetus is viable— capable of independent life outside the mother's body—these reasons begin to be as substantial as at birth and thereafter. In addition, viability represents the time when cessation of bodily support by the mother need not result in fetal death; as a result a viable fetus is capable of protection by others. For these reasons, I believe that after the established time of possible viability, methods separating fetus and mother so as to kill the fetus should be prohibited. But an earlier time—perhaps 17 rather than 24 weeks—is preferable for all but exceptional cases (such as those occurring after prenatal diagnosis of severe malformation).

Even though abortion may be *lawful* up to this time, however, it is not necessarily an act which an individual may consider right or justifiable. This discrepancy results, I believe, from the fact that the *social* reasons for protecting life may also be looked upon in each case as *individual* reasons. Society may not find that abortion harms either victim or agent, family or social practices. But the individual parent or physician may see risks to himself as a person from such acts and look at them as breaches of personal responsibility toward the unborn. They may then regard abortion as personally distasteful, even though it is lawful.

Some physicians, for example, do feel that they cannot participate in abortions without personal danger of brutalization and without sharing responsibility for killing. This may be especially true when they are called in, as in large hospitals, to perform one abortion after another without any chance to consult with the women involved and to hear their case histories. There should never be a requirement that a physician or nurse must participate in an abortion. Even if women have a right to abortion, they have not therefore the right to force others to perform such acts.

In the same way, a mother or a father may feel personal grief over the death of a fetus, and responsibility for killing it, quite apart from the legality of the act. This grief and this responsibility, which would be present as a matter of course where parents wish for the birth of their baby, may also accompany an unwanted pregnancy. The following factors should then be weighed by the mother before she can be confident that abortion is the right way out of her dilemma, and one she will not come to regret or view with guilt:

- whether or not the pregnancy was voluntarily undertaken.
- the importance and validity of the *reasons* for wanting the abortion.
- the technique to be used in the abortion; the extent to which it can be regarded as 'cessation of bodily life support,' rather than as outright killing.
- the time of pregnancy.
- whether or not the father agrees to the abortion.
- whether or not all other alternatives have been considered, such as adoption.
- her religious views.

And the father, if he weighs these factors differently, may feel the grief and responsibility differently too, and wish to take over the care of the baby after birth.

Abortion is a last resort, and must remain so. It is much more problematic than contraception, yet it is sometimes the only way out of a great dilemma. Neither individual parents nor society should look at abortion as a policy to be encouraged at the expense of contraception, sterilization, and adoption. At the same time, there are a number of circumstances in which it can justifiably be undertaken, for which public and private facilities must be provided in such a way as to make no distinction between rich and poor.

1. Roe v. Wade, *United States Law Week 41,* 1973, pp. 4213–33. Doe v. Bolton, *Ibid.,* pp. 4233–40.

2. Judith Thompson, "A Defense of Abortion," *Philosophy and Public Policy* 1 (1971), 47–66.

3. Noonan, *Morality of Abortion,* p. 51. For a thorough discussion of this and other views concerning the beginnings of human life, see Daniel Callahan, *Abortion: Law, Choice and Morality* (New York: Macmillan Company, 1970).

4. Jerome Lejeune, "On the Nature of Man" (Lecture at the American Society of Human Genetics at San Francisco, October 2–4, 1969).

5. Joseph Fletcher, "Indicators of Humanhood: A Tentative Profile of Man," *The Hastings Center Report* 2 (November, 1972), 1–4.

Assessment

In 1973, the U.S. Supreme Court's decision in *Roe v. Wade* made abortion legal under certain circumstances. In this case, a pregnant single woman adopted the pseudonym Jane Roe and filed a class action suit in federal court challenging the constitutionality of Texas criminal abortion laws that prohibited abortion except where the mother's life was in jeopardy. The Supreme Court refused to rule on the issue of when human life begins, but did declare the Texas statutes in violation of the right of privacy guaranteed in the Fourteenth Amendment to the Constitution. The Court, however, did not hold the right to privacy to be absolute. At some "compelling" point the state's interest in prenatal life and health care may supersede the mother's right to privacy and the state may decide to regulate abortion. The Court's decision was threefold.

1. During the first trimester, the abortion decision and method must be left to the judgment of the attending physician in consultation with the pregnant patient.
2. During the stage from the end of the first trimester to viability, the state can regulate the abortion procedure in ways related to maternal health.
3. During the prenatal stage following viability, the state can regulate and even outlaw abortion except where the life or health of the mother is at stake.

Thus, abortion was legalized without constraints during the first trimester but with the possibility of constraints during the second and third trimesters.

Bok's position parallels rather closely these stages of legality. For her, abortions in the first trimester are all morally justified, but abortions during the second trimester require special moral justification, and abortions in the third trimester require even more weighty moral justification. And her case is made with care and rigor.

Yet both Bok and the Supreme Court sidestep an issue that many people consider to be crucial: the question of whether the prenatal life is a human life and, therefore, invested with the rights accorded to other humans. Bok has certainly exposed the difficulty in drawing a line that separates nonhuman from human. But are her reasons for rejecting the relevance of that question for the abortion issue adequate and convincing? She uses what could be called the "slippery slope" argument: if you use criteria of humanness as relevant to abortion decisions, then you are on a slippery slope that will lead to the elimination of others in society who fall below these criteria. Bok's defense of abortion will not be acceptable to those who, for whatever reason, do find it necessary to draw a line between the human and nonhuman. If one draws that line at conception, because of a religious or philosophical belief that human life begins at conception, then no amount of rational argument and analysis is likely to change that person's mind. When does human life begin? Bok confesses that she does not know and that there is no empirical or scientific measure satisfactory to determine that crucial point. That being the case, she suggests that we not even try to answer that question but turn instead to issues with which we can deal.

The debate over abortion will continue. Why? Not because philosophy has failed to deal with the ethical issues involved in abortion, but because much of the opposition to abortion turns on a belief that can neither be proved nor disproved by philosophical analysis. If a person is not restrained by a commitment to the belief that it is wrong to terminate a pregnancy for any reason, or even to prevent a pregnancy by contraception (which is the official position of the Roman Catholic Church), then philosophical analysis can prove useful in determining when abortion is morally acceptable and when it is not.

Issue Two:
Allocation of Resources

As medical technology advances and health care costs soar, health care professionals are increasingly faced with demands for sophisticated health care resources that exceed the supply. At such times, health care professionals, together with the informed public, face the difficult question, Who shall live when
not all can live? The answer never comes easily; but to answer the question is
unavoidable.

Scarce Resources and Allocation Strategies

Consider, for example, the neonatal intensive care centers where profoundly sick
newborn infants are kept alive through sophisticated and expensive equipment
that is constantly monitored by professionals, and where costs can exceed a thousand
dollars per day. What should you do when all the units are occupied and another
neonate is brought to the center in need of treatment? You could pursue a teleological course of action, which might say, "Compare the new arrival's chances for
survival against the chances for survival of all the neonates already receiving treatment. If the new arrival's chances for survival are better than one of the neonates
already in the center, then replace that one with the new arrival. If the new arrival's
chances do not exceed those of any of the infants being treated, then exclude the
new arrival from the center." In so doing you would be attempting to maximize
life by going with the infants who had the best prognosis.

Then, too, you could pursue a deontological course of action that might say,
"Every human being has a right to life and protection. When the rights of a
group of infants are in conflict for scarce resources, the only fair and just thing
to do is treat all alike regardless of the prognoses and consequences. This can be
done by adopting a policy of 'first come, first served' or by instituting a lottery
in which all the names of the needy infants were placed in a hat and the name
of the infant first withdrawn from the hat is excluded from treatment." In so
doing you would be seeking not only to respect the universal right to life and
protection but also to serve the requirements of justice.

Whatever course of action you take, your action will contribute to the death
of an infant. That is why your decision and action will be fraught with pain.
And the pain and difficulty are intensified when you come to adult patients competing for limited resources, such as organ transplants. In the case of adults, you
have a record of their past contributions to society that raises the question of
the relative merit of those competing for the limited transplants. Also, you can
project the probable future beneficial contributions to society each of the competing
transplant recipients is likely to make, and that raises the question as to who is
most useful to society.

Childress's Approach

Issues such as these are explored by James F. Childress in the following article dealing with the allocation of scarce health care resources.

> * Who shall live when not all can live? Although this question has been urgently forced upon us by the dramatic use of artificial internal organs and organ transplantations, it is hardly new. . . . A significant example of the distribution of scarce medical resource is seen in the use of penicillin shortly after its discovery. Military officers had to determine which soldiers would be treated—those with venereal disease or those wounded in combat? In many respects such decisions have become routine in medical circles. Day after day physicians and others make judgments and decisions "about allocations of medical care to various segments of our population, to various types of hospitalized patients, and to specific individuals,"[1] for example, whether mental illness or cancer will receive the higher proportion of available funds. Nevertheless, the dramatic forms of "Scarce Life-Saving Medical Resources" (hereafter abbreviated as SLMR) such as hemodialysis and kidney and heart transplants have compelled us to examine the moral questions that have been concealed in many routine decisions. I do not attempt in this paper to show how a resolution of SMLR cases can help us in the more routine ones which do not involve a conflict of life with life. Rather I develop an argument for a particular method of determining who shall live when not all can live. No conclusions are implied about criteria and procedures for determining who shall receive medical resources that are not directly related to the preservation of life (e.g., corneal transplants) or about standards for allocating money and time for studying and treating certain diseases.
>
> Just as current SLMR decisions are not totally discontinuous with other medical decisions, so we must ask whether some other cases might, at least by analogy, help us develop the needed criteria and procedures. Some have looked at the principles at work in our responses to abortion, euthanasia, and artificial insemination. Usually they have concluded that these cases do not cast light on the selection of patients for artificial and transplanted organs. The reason is evident: in abortion, euthanasia, and artificial insemination, there is no conflict of life with life for limited but indispensable resources (with the possible exception of therapeutic abortion). In current SLMR decisions, such a conflict is inescapable, and it makes them so morally perplexing and fascinating. If analogous cases are to be found, I think that we shall locate them in moral conflict situations.

* FROM James F. Childress, "Who Shall Live When Not All Can Live?" in *Soundings*, Vol. 53, No. 4 (Winter, 1970). Used by permission of the author and publisher.

Insight From Analogous Cases

Childress, then, proposes to deal not with all resource allocation issues, but only with those where the survival of one life is in conflict with the survival of another life. And he proposes to garner some insight from analogous cases outside the domain of medical ethics—cases in which decisions have to be made to save some when not all can be saved.

Analogous Conflict Situations

An especially interesting and pertinent one is *U.S. v. Holmes*.[2] In 1841 an American ship, the *William Brown,* which was near Newfoundland on a trip from Liverpool to Philadelphia, struck an iceberg. The crew and half the passengers were able to escape in the two available vessels. One of these, a longboat, carrying too many passengers and leaking seriously, began to founder in the turbulent sea after about twenty-four hours. In a desperate attempt to keep it from sinking, the crew threw overboard fourteen men. Two sisters of one of the men either jumped overboard to join their brother in death or instructed the crew to throw them over. The criteria for determining who should live were "not to part man and wife, and not to throw over any women." Several hours later the others were rescued. Returning to Philadelphia, most of the crew disappeared, but one, Holmes, who had acted upon orders from the mate was indicted, tried, and convicted on the charge of "unlawful homicide."

We are interested in this case from a moral rather than a legal standpoint, and there are several possible responses to and judgments about it. Without attempting to be exhaustive I shall sketch a few of these. The judge contended that lots should have been cast, for in such conflict situations, there is no other procedure "so consonant both to humanity and to justice." Counsel for Holmes, on the other hand, maintained that the "sailors adopted the only principle of selection which was possible in an emergency like theirs,— a principle more humane than lots."

Another version of selection might extend and systematize the maxims of the sailors in the direction of "utility"; those are saved who will contribute to the greatest good for the greatest number. Yet another possible option is defended by Edmond Cahn in *The Moral Decision*. He argues that in this case we encounter the "morals of the last days." By this phrase he indicates that an apocalytic crisis renders totally irrelevant the normal differences between individuals. He continues,

In a strait of this extremity, all men are reduced—or raised, as one may choose to denominate it—to members of the genus, mere congeners and nothing else. Truly and literally, all were "in the same boat," and thus none could be saved separately from the others. I am driven to conclude that otherwise— that is, if none sacrifice themselves of free will to spare the others—they must all wait and die together. For where all have become congeners, pure and simple, no one can save himself by killing another.[3]

Cahn's answer to the question "who shall live when not all can live" is "none" unless the voluntary sacrifice by some persons permits it.

Few would deny the importance of Cahn's approach although many, including this writer, would suggest that it is relevant mainly as an affirmation of an elevated and, indeed, heroic or saintly morality which one hopes would find expression in the voluntary actions of many persons trapped in "borderline" situations involving a conflict of life with life. It is a maximal demand which some moral principles impose on the individual in the recognition that self-preservation is not a good which is to be defended at all costs. The absence of this saintly or heroic morality should not mean, however, that everyone perishes. Without making survival an absolute value and without justifying all means to achieve it, we can maintain that simply letting everyone die is irresponsible. This charge can be supported from several different standpoints, including society at large as well as the individuals involved. Among a group of self-interested individuals, none of whom volunteers to relinquish his life, there may be better and worse ways of determining who shall survive. One task of social ethics, whether religious or philosophical, is to propose relatively just institutional arrangements within which self-interested and biased men can live. The question then becomes: which set of arrangements—which criteria and procedures of selection— is most satisfactory in view of the human condition (man's limited altruism and inclination to seek his own good) and the conflicting values that are to be realized?

There are several significant differences between the *Holmes* and SLMR cases, a major one being that the former involves *direct* killing of another person, while the latter involves only *permitting* a person to die when it is not possible to save all. Furthermore, in extreme situations such as *Holmes,* the restraints of civilization have been stripped away, and something approximating a state of nature prevails, in which life is "solitary, poor, nasty, brutish and short." The state of nature does not mean that moral standards are irrelevant and that might should prevail, but it does suggest that much of the matrix which normally supports morality has been removed. Also, the necessary but unfortunate decisions about who shall live and die are made by men who are existentially and personally involved in the outcome. Their survival too is at stake. Even though the institutional role of sailors seems to require greater sacrificial actions, there is obviously no assurance that they will adequately assess the number of sailors required to man the vessel or that they will impartially and objectively weigh the common good at stake. As the judge insisted in his defense of casting lots in the *Holmes* case: "In no other than this [casting lots] or some like way are those having equal rights put upon an equal footing, and in no other way is it possible to guard against conflict." This difference should not be exaggerated since self-interest, professional pride, and the like obviously affect the outcome of many medical decisions. Nor do the remaining differences cancel *Holmes'* instructiveness.

Several strategies were suggested for dealing with the overloaded sinking lifeboat. The crew, on the basis of certain criteria that protected women and their spouses, selected the men who were to be killed in order that some could be saved. The judge declared that the occupants of the boat should have cast lots to determine who was to be sacrificed. Others have suggested that utilitarian criteria should have been used. And Edmond Cahn argued that all should have died together unless voluntary sacrifices would have made possible the survival of some. Childress rejects Cahn's recommendations as ultimately irresponsible. The judge's lottery is deontological. The crew's method and the utilitarian perspective are teleological. Let us watch carefully to see which of these perspectives Childress deploys in penetrating the problem of SLMR.

Stage One: Identifying the Medically Acceptable

Criteria of Selection for SLMR
Which set of arrangements should be adopted for SLMR? Two questions are involved: Which standards and criteria should be used? and, Who should make the decision? The first question is basic, since the debate about implementation, e.g., whether by a lay committee or physician, makes little progress until the criteria are determined.

We need two sets of criteria which will be applied at two different stages in the selection of recipients of SLMR. First, medical criteria should be used to exclude those who are not "medically acceptable." Second, from this group of "medically acceptable" applicants, the final selection can be made. Occasionally in current American medical practice, the first stage is omitted, but such an omission is unwarranted. Ethical and social responsibility would seem to require distributing these SLMR only to those who have some reasonable prospect of responding to the treatment. Furthermore, in transplants such medical tests as tissue and blood typing are necessary, although they are hardly fully developed. . . .

Childress recommends two stages in the selection process for determining who is to receive SLMR when not all can. First, from the pool of applicants, those who are "medically acceptable" must be identified. Being "medically acceptable" seems to mean that the patient has some reasonable prospect of responding to treatment. And although there is considerable debate about the relevant factors that determine "medical acceptability," it must remain an important factor in the decision process. Then from the pool of "medically acceptable" applicants, those to be given SLMR must be identified—not by using the medical criteria alone but by means of additional criteria. Childress proceeds to assess the utilitarian criteria for making this second stage selection.

Stage Two: Utilitarianism Rejected

The most significant moral questions emerge when we turn to the final selection. Once the pool of medically acceptable applicants has been defined and still the number is larger than the resources, what other criteria should be used? How should the final selection be made? First, I shall examine some of the difficulties that stem from efforts to make the final selection in terms of social value; these difficulties raise serious doubts about the feasibility and justifiability of the utilitarian approach. Then I shall consider the possible justification for random selection or chance.

Occasionally criteria of social worth focus on past contributions but most often they are primarily future-oriented. The patient's potential and probable contribution to the society is stressed, although this obviously cannot be abstracted from his present web of relationships (e.g., dependents) and occupational activities (e.g., nuclear physicist). Indeed, the magnitude of his contribution to society (as an abstraction) is measured in terms of these social roles, relations, and functions. Enough has already been said to suggest the tremendous range of factors that affect social value or worth. Here we encounter the first major difficulty of this approach: How do we determine the relevant criteria of social value?

The difficulties of quantifying various social needs are only too obvious. How does one quantify and compare the needs of the spirit (e.g., education, art, religion), political life, economic activity, technological development? Joseph Fletcher suggests that "some day we may learn how to 'quantify' or 'mathematicate' or 'computerize' the value problem in selection, in the same careful and thorough way that diagnosis has been."[4] I am not convinced that we can ever quantify values, or that we should attempt to do so. But even if the various social and human needs, in principle, could be quantified, how do we determine how much weight we will give to each one? Which will have priority in case of conflict? Or even more basically, in the light of which values and principles do we recognize social "needs"?

One possible way of determining the values which should be emphasized in selection has been proposed by Leo Shatin.[5] He insists that our medical decisions about allocating resources are already based on an unconscious scale of values (usually dominated by material worth). Since there is really no way of escaping this, we should be self-conscious and critical about it. How should we proceed? He recommends that we discover the values that most people in our society hold and then use them as criteria for distributing SLMR. These values can be discovered by attitude or opinion surveys. Presumably if fifty-one percent in this testing period put a greater premium on military needs than technological development, military men would have a greater claim on our SLMR than experimental researchers. But valuations of what is significant change, and the student revolutionary who was denied SLMR in 1970 might be celebrated in 1990 as the greatest American hero since George Washington.

Shatin presumably is seeking criteria that could be applied nationally, but at the present, regional and local as well as individual prejudices tincture the criteria of social value that are used in selection. Nowhere is this more evident than in the deliberations and decisions of the anonymous selection committee of the Seattle Artificial Kidney Center where such factors as church membership and Scout leadership have been deemed significant for determing who shall live. As two critics conclude after examining these criteria and procedures, they rule out "creature nonconformists, who rub the bourgeoisie the wrong way but who historically have contributed so much to the making of America. The Pacific Northwest is no place for a Henry David Thoreau with bad kidneys."[6]

Closely connected to this first problem of determining social values is a second one. Not only is it difficult if not impossible to reach agreement on social values, but it is also rarely easy to predict what our needs will be in a few years and what the consequences of present actions will be. Furthermore it is difficult to predict which persons will fulfill their potential function in society. Admissions committees in colleges and universities experience the frustrations of predicting realization of potential. For these reasons, as someone has indicated, God might be a utilitarian, but we cannot be. We simply lack the capacity to predict very accurately the consequences which we then must evaluate. Our incapacity is never more evident than when we think in societal terms.

Other difficulties make us even less confident that such an approach to SLMR is advisable. Many critics raise the spectre of abuse, but this should not be overemphasized. The fundamental difficulty appears on another level: the utilitarian approach would in effect reduce the person to his social role, relations, and functions. Ultimately it dulls and perhaps even eliminates the sense of the person's transcendence, his dignity as a person which cannot be reduced to his past or future contribution to society. It is not at all clear that we are willing to live with these implications of utilitarian selection. . . .

Clearly, Childress is opposed to utilitarian criteria for determining who among the pool of "medically acceptable" applicants should receive SLMR. He identifies three major problems with utilitarianism as it focuses on the relative social value of individuals. First, there is grave difficulty in determining the relevant criteria for social worth. Such criteria are usually tainted by regional prejudices, and agreement at a national or international level is not easy to achieve. Second, it is very difficult to predict not only future social needs but also what the future consequences of actions will be as well as which persons will fulfill their potential service to society. Yet such unreliable predictions are to be the basis for determining who gains access to SLMR. Third, the utilitarian approach tends to dehumanize humans by reducing a person's dignity to his or her contribution to society. Before moving on to consider the posture he advocates, Childress reminds us how important it is for us to preserve a sense of guilt when we are called upon to choose a person for SLMR and thereby to deny others access to these life-saving resources.

Stage Two: Randomness Advocated

The Values of Random Selection

My proposal is that we use some form of randomness or chance (either natural, such as "first come, first served," or artificial, such as a lottery) to determine who shall be saved. Many reject randomness as a surrender to nonrationality when responsible and rational judgments can and must be made. Edmond Cahn criticizes "Holmes' judge" who recommended the casting of lots because, as Cahn puts it, "the crisis involves stakes too high for gambling and responsibilities too deep for destiny."[7] Similarly, other critics see randomness as a surrender to 'non-human' forces which necessarily vitiates human values. Sometimes these values are identified with the process of decision-making (e.g., it is important to have persons rather than impersonal forces determining who shall live). Sometimes they are identified with the outcome of the process (e.g., the features such as creativity and fullness of being which make human life what it is are to be considered and respected in the decision). Regarding the former, it must be admitted that the use of chance seems cold and impersonal. But presumably the defenders of utilitarian criteria in SLMR want to make their application as objective and impersonal as possible so that subjective bias does not determine who shall live.

Childress, then, is an advocate of random selection, and he goes on to make a case for his position. First, randomness preserves human dignity by providing equality of opportunity.

Such criticisms, however, ignore the moral and nonmoral values which might be supported by selection by randomness or chance. A more important criticism is that the procedure that I develop draws the relevant moral context too narrowly. That context, so the argument might run, includes the society and its future and not merely the individual with his illness and claim upon SLMR. But my contention is that the values and principles at work in the narrower context may well take precedence over those operative in the broader context both because of their weight and significance and because of the weaknesses of selection in terms of social worth. As Paul Freund rightly insists, "The more nearly total is the estimate to be made of an individual, and the more nearly the consequence determines life and death, the more unfit the judgment becomes for human reckoning. . . . Randomness as a moral principle deserves serious study."[8] Serious study would, I think, point toward its implementation in certain conflict situations, primarily because it preserves a significant degree of *personal dignity* by providing *equality* of opportunity. Thus it cannot be dismissed as a "non-rational" and "non-human" procedure without an inquiry into the reasons, including human values, which might justify it. Paul Ramsey stresses this point about the *Holmes* case:

Instead of fixing our attention upon "gambling" as the solution—with all the frivolous and often corrupt associations the word raises in our minds—we should think rather of *equality* of opportunity as the ethical substance of the relations of those individuals to one another that might have been guarded and expressed by casting lots.[9]

The individual's personal and transcendent dignity, which on the utilitarian approach would be submerged in his social role and function, can be protected and witnessed to by a recognition of his equal right to be saved. Such a right is best preserved by procedures which establish equality of opportunity. Thus selection by chance more closely approximates the requirements established by human dignity than does utilitarian calculation. It is not infallibly just, but it is preferable to the alternatives of letting all die or saving only those who have the greatest social responsibilities and potential contribution.

Second, randomness safeguards the relationship of trust between the physician and patient. Such trust is incompatible with treating people on the basis of their value because trust is rooted in respect for another's dignity, and dignity is sacrificed by utilitarian considerations that reduce a person to a thing or means for achieving a certain quantity of social value.

This argument can be extended by examining values other than individual dignity and equality of opportunity. Another basic value in the medical sphere is the relationship of trust between physician and patient. Which selection criteria are most in accord with this relationship of trust? Which will maintain, extend, and deepen it? My contention is that selection by randomness or chance is preferable from this standpoint also.

Trust, which is inextricably bound to respect for human dignity, is an attitude of expectation about another. It is not simply the expectation that another will perform a particular act, but more specifically that another will act toward him in certain ways—which will respect him as a person. As Charles Fried writes:

Although trust has to do with reliance on a disposition of another person, it is reliance on a disposition of a special sort: the disposition to act morally, to deal fairly with others, to live up to one's undertakings, and so on. Thus to trust another is first of all to expect him to accept the principle of morality in his dealings with you, to respect your status as a person, your personality.[10]

This trust cannot be preserved in life-and-death situations when a person expects decisions about him to be made in terms of his social worth, for such decisions violate his status as a person. An applicant rejected on grounds of inadequacy in social value or virtue would have reason for feeling that his "trust" had been betrayed. Indeed, the sense that one is being viewed not as an end in himself but as a means in medical progress or the achievement of a greater social good is incompatible with attitudes and relationships of trust. We recognize this in the billboard which was erected after the first heart transplants: "Drive Carefully. Christiaan Barnard Is Watching You." The relationship of trust between the physician and patient is not only an instrumental value in the sense of being an important factor in the patient's treatment. It is also to be endorsed because of its intrinsic worth as a relationship.

Third, randomness would be the method selected as the most rational and fairest by persons who were self-interested, who were summoned to plan for themselves and their families, and who were ignorant of their own value to society. Here Childress is using a powerful argument developed in detail by John Rawls in his recent work *A Theory of Justice.*

> Thus the related values of individual dignity and trust are best maintained in selection by chance. But other factors also buttress the argument for this approach. Which criteria and procedures would men agree upon? We have to suppose a hypothetical situation in which several men are going to determine for themselves and their families the criteria and procedures by which they would want to be admitted to and excluded from SLMR if the need arose.[11] We need to assume two restrictions and then ask which set of criteria and procedures would be chosen as the most rational and, indeed, the fairest. The restrictions are these: (1) The men are *self-interested.* They are interested in their own welfare (and that of members of their families), and this, of course, includes survival. Basically, they are not motivated by altruism. (2) Furthermore, they are *ignorant* of their own talents, abilities, potential, and probable contributions to the social good. They do not know how they would fare in a competitive situation, e.g., the competition for SLMR in terms of social contribution. Under these conditions which institution would be chosen—letting all die, utilitarian selection, or the use of chance? Which would seem the most rational? the fairest? By which set of criteria would they want to be included in or excluded from the list of those who will be saved? The rational choice in this setting (assuming self-interest and ignorance of one's competitive success) would be random selection or chance since this alone provides equality of opportunity. A possible response is that one would prefer to take a "risk" and therefore choose the utilitarian approach. But I think not, especially since I added that the participants in this hypothetical situation are choosing for their children as well as for themselves; random selection or chance could be more easily justified to the children. It would make more sense for men who are self-interested but uncertain about their relative contribution to society to elect a set of criteria which would build in equality of opportunity. They would consider selection by chance as relatively just and fair.[12]

Fourth, Childress argues that rejection on the basis of randomness would generate less psychological stress for the rejected candidate than would rejection on the basis of inadequate social worth. Childress's fifth argument is that randomness is already practiced in the allocation of SLMR, and thereby its value is tacitly recognized.

His sixth argument is that randomness would remove the need for selection committees charged with the responsibility of weighing the relative social worth of applicants for SLMR. And seventh, randomness might cause the powerful and wealthy to commit their resources to the removal of the scarcity of life-saving medical resources in order to insure their own access to them when needed.

This proposal has yet another advantage since it would eliminate the need for a committee to examine applicants in terms of their social value. This onerous responsibility can be avoided.

Finally, there is a possible indirect consequence of widespread use of random selection which is interesting to ponder, although I do *not* adduce it as a good reason for adopting random selection. It can be argued, as Professor Mason Willrich of the University of Virginia Law School has suggested, that SLMR cases would practically disappear if these scarce resources were distributed randomly rather than on social worth grounds. Scarcity would no longer be a problem because the holders of economic and political power would make certain that they would not be excluded by a random selection procedure; hence they would help to redirect public priorities or establish private funding so that life-saving medical treatment would be widely and perhaps universally available.

Should exceptions to randomness be allowed? Childress says "No," but he does go on to suggest criteria for exceptions that are so stringent that exceptions would become almost impossible.

In the framework that I have delineated, are the decrees of chance to be taken without exception? If we recognize exceptions, would we not open Pandora's box again just after we had succeeded in getting it closed? The direction of my argument has been against any exceptions, and I would defend this as the proper way to go. But let me indicate one possible way of admitting exceptions while at the same time circumscribing them so narrowly that they would be very rare indeed.

An obvious advantage of the utilitarian approach is that occasionally circumstances arise which make it necessary to say that one man is practically indispensable for a society in view of a particular set of problems it faces (e.g., the President when the nation is waging a war for survival). Certainly the argument to this point has stressed that the burden of proof would fall on those who think that the social danger in this instance is so great that they simply cannot abide by the outcome of a lottery or a first come, first served policy. Also, the reason must be negative rather than positive; that is, we depart from chance in this instance not because we want to take advantage of this person's potential contribution to the improvement of our society, but because his immediate loss would possibly (even probably) be disastrous (again, the President in a grave national emergency). . . .

While I do not recommend this procedure of recognizing exceptions, I think that one can defend it while accepting my general thesis about selection by randomness or chance. If it is used, a lay committee (perhaps advisory, perhaps even stronger) would be called upon to deal with the alleged exceptions since the doctors or others would in effect be appealing the outcome of chance (either natural or artificial). This lay committee would determine whether this patient was so indispensable at this time and place that he had to be saved even by sacrificing the values preserved by random selection. It would make it quite clear that exception is warranted, if at all, only as the "lesser of two evils." Such a defense would be recognized only rarely, if ever, primarily because chance and randomness preserve so many important moral and nonmoral values in SLMR cases.

1. Leo Shatin, "Medical Care and the Social Worth of a Man," *American Journal of Orthopsychiatry,* 36 (1967), 97.

2. *United States v. Holmes* 26 Fed. Cas. 360 (C.C.E.D. Pa. 1842). All references are to the text of the trial as reprinted in Philip E. Davis, ed., *Moral Duty and Legal Responsibility: A Philosophical-Legal Casebook* (New York, 1966), pp. 102–118.

3. Edmond Cahn, *The Moral Decision* (Bloomington, Ind., 1955), p. 71.

4. Joseph Fletcher, "Donor Nephrectomies and Moral Responsibility," *Journal of the American Medical Women's Association,* 23 (Dec. 1968), p. 1090.

5. Leo Shatin, op. cit., pp. 96–101.

6. David Sanders and Jesse Dukeminier, Jr., "Medical Advance and Legal Lag: Hemodialysis and Kidney Transplantation," *UCLA Law Review,* 15:367 (1968) 378.

7. Cahn, op. cit., p. 71.

8. Paul Freund, "Introduction," *Daedalus* (Spring 1969), xiii.

9. Paul Ramsey, *Nine Modern Moralists* (Englewood Cliffs, N.J., 1962), p. 245.

10. Charles Fried, "Privacy," In *Law, Reason, and Justice,* ed. by Graham Hughes (New York, 1969), p. 52.

11. My argument is greatly dependent on John Rawls's version of justice as fairness, which is a reinterpretation of social contract theory. Rawls, however, would probably not apply his ideas to "borderline situations." See "Distributive Justice: Some Addenda," *Natural Law Forum* 13(1968), 53. For Rawls's general theory, see "Justice as Fairness," *Philosophy, Politics and Society* (Second Series), ed. by Peter Laslett and W. G. Runciman (Oxford, 1962), pp. 132–157 and his other essays on aspects of this topic.

12. Occasionally someone contends that random selection may reward vice. Leo Shatin (op. cit., p. 100) insists that random selection "would reward socially disvalued qualities by giving their bearers the same special medical care opportunities as those received by the bearers of socially valued qualities. Personally I do not favor such a method." Obviously society must engender certain qualities in its members, but not all of its institutions must be devoted to that purpose. Furthermore, there are strong reasons, I have contended, for exempting SLMR from that sort of function.

Assessment

Clearly, Childress has placed himself in the camp of the deontologists with his case for randomness as a way of preserving the key values of individual dignity, equality of opportunity, and trust between persons. His attack on utilitarianism is unrelenting. Utilitarianism, he says, is flawed by its threefold inability to generate criteria for determining the social worth of individuals, to predict the future (which is important for any teleological ethic), and to guarantee the dignity of human beings (which is so easily sacrificed when persons become means for achieving social utility).

But has Childress completely avoided consequentialist considerations? Consider the first stage of his selection process for allocating SLMR. At that stage, "medical acceptability" is to be determined by certain criteria which Childress does not specify but which he implies will identify "those who have some reasonable prospect of responding to the treatment." Does that not imply that in the first stage Childress is seeking to maximize life? And is that not a teleological consideration that is close to the utilitarianism he so stoutly rejected? But even if we accept his plea for random selection as preferable to utilitarian calculations of social worth, we still must face up to difficult borderline situations where randomness does not seem an appropriate moral guideline.

Suppose that among the "medically acceptable" applicants for the same SLMR there appeared a rapist murderer and one of his severely injured rape victims. Suppose, further, that random selection allocated the SLMR to the rapist and excluded the victim. Would not that outcome offend the moral sensibilities of most of us? One of Childress's major concerns is justice; justice is certainly concerned with equal opportunity as Childress suggests, but it is also concerned with *desert.* Justice asks if the treatment people receive is the treatment they deserve. By leaving out the possibility of making such decisions based on merit, Childress might be accused of leaving out an important aspect of justice.

Consider another borderline case in which Childress's random selection method allocated the SLMR to a severely mentally retarded person rather than to a research scientist who was nearing a breakthrough in cancer research. Would not most of us feel uneasy about a selection process that preferred the retarded person to the researcher? Should we not admit that the relative social worth of various individuals is not identical and is a morally relevant factor? Is the difficulty with determining and predicting accurately relative social worth adequate reason for discarding social worth as a morally relevant factor? Should perhaps an additional stage be inserted between Childress's first and second—a stage where certain people are excluded on the grounds of justice and others are given preferential treatment because of their extraordinary value to society? Would not such a blend of utility and justice (in the new second stage) and randomness (in the new third stage) be more consistent with our moral sensibilities? Would not Childress's deontological viewpoint benefit from more openness to the contributions of utilitarianism? Do not both perspectives contribute something toward answering the question of who shall live when not all can? These and similar questions will assure that the discussion of this important question is not finished but will continue as we attempt to probe more fully the ethical implications of this important issue.

Review Questions

1. Why is defining abortion such an important matter?
2. Bok argues that abortion should be construed as the cessation of bodily life support. What does that interpretation contribute to resolving the question of whether or not abortion can be justified?
3. Are attempts to delineate when an unborn life becomes human helpful in resolving the moral problem of abortion? Why?
4. What are the reasons for protecting human life, and can they be applied adequately to the unborn life to shed light on the justifiability of abortion?
5. What is the *U.S. v. Holmes* case, and what insight does it provide for the allocation of SLMR?
6. What are the two stages in the selection process advocated by Childress, and what are the reasons he gives for rejecting utilitarianism and for adopting randomness in the second stage? Do you find his reasons convincing? Why, or why not?

CHAPTER 11

Ethical Issues in Business

Introduction

Despite the clear changes in public attitudes toward business practices, there persists the widespread view that somehow the notion of ethics is incompatible with or irrelevant to business activities. This attitude is often appealed to by business leaders to justify their actions, as did Robert Guccione, publisher of *Penthouse,* in connection with his decision to publish some controversial photographs that precipitated the resignation of Vanessa Williams as Miss America. "It was not a moral decision, it was a business decision," said Guccione.

Can a collective such as a corporation be held accountable to moral criteria for its actions? Or is such accountability proper only for a human personality? *Should* businesses be held accountable to moral criteria for their actions? The first question raises the issue of who is responsible for the activities of a large corporation. We cannot put a corporation in jail, although we can fine a corporation for its activities. But if a company engages in criminal activity, what is the appropriate sanction? Should the chief executive officer be the one to pay for the company's errors? The executive most closely affiliated with the decision? The designers of a defective product? In one of the cases that follows, the issue of collective responsibility is explored in terms of issues relating to the moral and legal responsibilities of professional engineers in a corporate setting.

The second question is increasingly being answered in the affirmative by our society. We have recognized that corporations, which enjoy the benefits of society, must not be allowed to conduct their business affairs in an unrestrained fashion. Governmental legislation, as well as public opinion, now requires companies to

275

be good citizens and to be concerned for the general welfare of the community as a whole. The range of moral issues that affect a corporation's activities is vast, and is growing yearly in the public's view. These issues include the treatment of its employees, the company's role in assuring the safety and dependability of its products, its attitude toward the environment and restrictions placed upon it to prevent the pollution of the air and waterways, truth in advertising, personnel policies (including affirmative action and nondiscrimination in hiring and firing decisions), plant relocation and its effect on jobs, to mention the most prevalent topics.

There is a vast literature developing to survey the range of topics in business ethics. Business schools are now required by their accrediting agency to include business ethics courses in their curricula. Courses in business ethics are increasingly being included in the offerings of philosophy departments. From this literature, two topics have been chosen for presentation here: the first deals with the issue of individual and corporate responsibility involving the activity of professional engineers in a business context. The second clarifies some of the issues regarding truth-telling in advertising. Additional materials on business ethics are included in the bibliography at the conclusion of this book. Also included in the Appendix is a collection of ethical concepts useful for analysis of issues in business ethics. These were developed as a result of a project to develop courses in business ethics, a project funded by the National Endowment for the Humanities and involving business school deans, philosophy professors, and representatives from business and industry. Although the concepts were developed as part of a project involving the development of business ethics courses, they are useful for the analysis of normative issues in other contexts as well.

Issue One:
Corporate and Individual Responsibility

Diffusion of Authority in Corporations

One of the problems in holding business organizations accountable for their actions is the diffusion of authority in a modern corporation. Virtually gone from the scene is the one-person company where a single individual can set policy for an entire business. These days an individual employee who is aware of a design flaw or product fault may be so removed from the command structure as to have little effect on the decision to ignore or correct the flaw. What should an engineer, accountant, lawyer, or any other practicing professional do when becoming aware of misconduct by the employing company? "Whistle blowing" is a phrase that has come to describe the practice of publicly revealing corporate wrong doing. Suppose an engineer or other professional in a company becomes aware of a problem and does nothing about it? Is that person morally responsible for the problem? And if the engineer informs the next person in the chain of command of the problem, and the supervisor ignores the problem, is the engineer freed from moral responsibility? Or should the employee then engage in "whistle blowing"? Should a company be prevented from firing an employee who blows the whistle for the sake of public good? And how can we be sure that an employee is not just using the protection of whistle blowing to get back at the company for a personal grievance?

The selections that follow are from an article written by a philosopher, Charles Reagan, and an engineer, John Mingle. It points out the difficulties in assessing responsibility for a corporate decision involving several layers of authority, from design engineer through various supervisory levels to the chief executive authority. It also details two well-known cases involving corporate misconduct, one of which resulted in substantial loss of life, the other of which did not—mainly because of the actions taken by professionals in the corporate structure.

Difficulty in Affixing Responsibility in Corporations

* This discussion of moral and legal responsibility would be simplified if engineers were all independent practitioners, or in terms of the legal phrase, independent contractors. In particular cases, it would be much easier to say who was responsible, to what extent his or her acts or omissions caused harm, whether or not compensatory liability exists, and whether or not he or she had the capacity to be responsible; that is, to recognize his or her obligations and to direct applicable conduct toward their fulfillment. However, most engineers are employees. As engineers and as engineer-managers, they confront the questions of responsibility and legal liability in the context of a collective. In a large company, for instance, rarely is a single engineer solely responsible for a design, a product, a procedure, or a market.

The real difficulty in collective responsibility is in assessing the relative contributions that individuals have made to a collective action, which "involves assessment of various incommensurable dimensions of contribution—degrees of initiative, difficulty or causal crucialness of assigned subtasks, degrees of authority, percentage of derived profit, and so on."[1] The difficulty of knowing who is responsible and who is to pay compensation is usually legally resolved by application of strict liability. This means that the collectivity as a whole is punished or made to compensate for harm done, without answering the question of who is individually responsible. In many cases, the question of whether the collectivity itself is morally responsible is also avoided by strict liability.

Philosophers have produced a substantial literature of late on the question of group punishment. If individuals should be punished only for what they have done, how can society justify punishing them for acts of the group? One answer is a modification of the established principle of vicarious responsibility where masters are held liable for authorized actions of their

* FROM John O. Mingle and Charles E. Reagan, "Legal Responsibility Versus Moral Responsibility: The Engineer's Dilemma," *Jurimetrics Journal,* Vol. 23, No. 2 (Winter 1983). Used by permission of the authors and *Jurimetrics Journal.*

servants.[2] Another line of justification would be that responsibility and
authority are symmetrical in hierarchial organizations, and that therefore
groups should be punished by punishing those in authority in proportion
to their position in the hierarchy.

The authors have pointed out the difficulties in determining guilt in cases of
misconduct in a corporate organization. This difficulty also underscores how one
ethical issue easily, and frequently, leads to another. In this case, even if an employee
of a corporation is guilty of misconduct, and that employee is not the person
ultimately authorized to make a decision on behalf of the company, how much
blame, and punishment, should that person receive? There are two alternatives:
one is to say that a supervisor is responsible for actions of the persons supervised;
the other is to indicate that a person shares blame to the same extent that the
person shares authority for the decision. The difficulty for a business professional—
engineer, accountant, manager—is that the professional has duties to the profession
(whose goal is to serve humankind) and also to the corporation (whose goal is
to maximize profit). Not only is the business professional sometimes caught in
conflicting loyalties, but there is also the matter of legal liability for one's actions.
Both of these dimensions appear in the following two case studies.

Conflicting Loyalties and Legal Liability

Two cases from the engineering literature[3] which exemplify the problem
of allocating responsibility in organizations are known as the *DC-10* case
(now perhaps it should be called the first *DC-10* case), and the *BART* case.
In the former, some engineers at Convair, the subcontractor for the fuselage,
decided that the DC-10 fuselage and doors were improperly designed. The
test program showed that if a sudden decompression of the cargo hold
occurred, perhaps as a result of a cargo door failure, the floor of the passenger
compartment would collapse, in all likelihood jamming the controls to the
empennage.

On June 27, 1972, F. D. Applegate, Director of Product Engineering at
Convair, wrote his superior a letter in which he detailed his reasons for
worrying about the potential for Convair liability on the DC-10. He
enumerates the design flaws in the cargo door latching mechanism and
recites the history of the cargo hold, both on fuselages and on production
aircraft. At one point he says:

My only criticism of Douglas in this regard is that once this inherent weakness
was demonstrated by the July 1970 test failure, they did not take immediate
steps to correct it. It seems to me inevitable that, in the twenty years ahead
of us, DC-10 cargo doors will come open, and I would expect this to usually
result in the loss of the airplane.[4]

While his doubts are phrased in terms of legal liability, he thinks some
action should be taken to correct this apparent design flaw. His superior,
J. B. Hurt, Program Manager, DC-10 Support Program, answered Applegate's

letter on July 3, 1972. His objections to raising Applegate's doubts with Douglas were several. Among them were the fact that Convair did not object to Douglas's design of the fuselage and cargo doors when the aircraft was originally designed; the design satisfied FAA requirements; and, to raise doubts with Douglas at this point would be tacit admission that Convair was in error in originally accepting the Douglas design, so that Convair therefore would be liable for the costs for corrections.

He concludes by saying:

> We have an interesting legal and moral problem, and I feel that any direct conversation on this subject with Douglas should be based on the assumption that as a result Convair may subsequently find itself in a position where it must assume all or a significant portion of the costs that are involved.[5]

Convair's management accepted Hurt's reasoning and declined to approach Douglas with Applegate's criticisms of the fuselage design. No information is presented that would indicate Applegate pressed his criticisms in any other forum and certainly, from one point of view, he had fulfilled his responsibilities.

Engineering Constraints and Utilitarian Criteria

In proceeding to the next case study, the authors mention one of the reasons for the ambiguity felt by design engineers. They function within the framework of limitations—limitations of time, resources, even within the limits imposed by natural law. Within these limitations, which sometimes include political and economic restraints, they must fashion the best product possible, knowing that it will not be perfect. *Some* risk must be accepted. If the goal were to produce a perfect product, it would probably require so much time that it would never be manufactured and, if it were, it would be too costly for the market to bear. So, engineers do the best job they can within the limits imposed on them; in short, they adopt a more or less utilitarian standard of producing the best product for the greatest number at the lowest price. But this means accepting the possibility that some aspect of the product will fail, perhaps even resulting occasionally in injury or loss of life. How much risk of this type is acceptable? This is the question with which professionals in corporate settings constantly wrestle.

Legal Liability and Deontological Criteria

Conflict arises after an accident when, in a legal setting, considerations other than utilitarian ones come into play. When an aircraft crashes, resulting in loss of life, a jury holds the company to deontological criteria, or to what Reagan and Mingle refer to as egalitarian standards: no individual life should ever be traded off in design calculations, and one life is as valuable as any other. This conflict between utilitarian and deontological criteria for assessing moral and legal responsibility is at the heart of the problem of corporate responsibility.

Utilitarian Versus Deontological (Egalitarian) Concerns

The real engineering policy question in this *DC-10* case involved the design of the cargo door latching mechanism, and whether a forseeable occurrence is suggested by the probability of the door being improperly latched on the ground, yet satisfying all checks as far as the safety control system is concerned. A properly trained ground crew member, performing according to instructions, will naturally lock the cargo door successfully. Yet this design of the cargo door had been shown to be inferior in other airplanes already flying when the DC-10 was under development.[6] The nonusage of the latest state-of-the-art is not in itself a negligent act, yet under strict liability theory the product could be considered defective under these circumstances.[7] Regardless of whether Convair or Lockheed would be held legally responsible, are the Convair engineers morally responsible? The answer lies in the utilitarian concept of collective responsibility, which effectively allows the engineering profession to continually live with the imposition of potentially high risk situations upon society without chastising any one individual.

In contrast to the *DC-10* case is the famous *BART* (Bay Area Rapid Transit) case, where three engineers became alarmed about what they considered design flaws in the automatic control system and the computer system, as well as the general conduct of their management.[8] In this case, the three complaining engineers received no satisfaction from their superiors. So, they went outside the BART organization, first to their local engineering society, and finally to a local politician who was a member of the board of supervision of BART.

This forced a public meeting where the allegations of unsafe design were made and, to some extent, were answered by the manager of BART. The next day, the three engineers were fired. The technical merits of the dispute boil down to the degree of risk imposition to be subjected upon the public that the two sets of engineers can condone. The BART management, recognizing well that the development of a new type of control system will involve much feedback from actual operation, and recognizing the political situation and its necessity to have BART at least in partial operation quickly, opted to impose the risk upon the public of potential problems with the control system. But, knowing these problems will probably occur, additional safety precautions will naturally be enforced in the early operational phase. This concept of utilizing feedback from actual operation conditions is a standard utilitarian approach to product improvement. To BART management this increased risk to the public was not unreasonable, especially in the light of the public's demand that BART get rolling. Contrariwise, the fired BART engineers recognized that changes in the control system from the original design would lessen the safety factors and lead to increased public risk. Whether the new risk was unduly large was not of primary concern for these engineers, who had a more egalitarian outlook viewing any increase in public risk as unsatisfactory. The utilitarian management, well recognizing that the close-knit team effort required was impossible with these maverick employees, and recognizing that because of time and money constraints no effective change would be forthcoming in the partially completed system, promptly released the engineers.

Reagan and Mingle have pointed out an important aspect of weighing the moral implications of corporate conduct. Many managers assume something like a utilitarian standard to justify their conduct. As you will recall, utilitarian considerations are directed to the maximization of certain consequences that will provide the greatest happiness for the greatest number. On those criteria alone, business decisions can be defended that could not be justified on deontological criteria. A deontologist would argue that knowingly to put human lives at risk is immoral, no matter how much happiness might accrue to others if the risk is accepted. Reagan and Mingle point out that the conflict here between the engineering professional and the management of their employing company stems to a large extent from the clash between the deontological sensitivities of the engineers and the utilitarian calculations of their employer.

If the technical merits of their allegations are ignored, appreciation can be had for these engineers' willingness to fulfill their responsibilities, as they viewed them from a subjective sense, to the public even at the cost of their jobs. Some have countered that they had the duty of loyalty to their employer, which they did not fulfill. This is precisely the conflict of duties which employed engineers must face. Thus, what would have happened if Applegate had pursued his complaints outside of Convair and even Douglas? What would have happened if the BART engineers had remained silent after their worries were rejected by their supervisors?

This is the dilemma of the employee-engineer. As engineer he or she is committed, both by ethical code and by natural inclination, to benefiting mankind. Engineers see themselves as perfecting means rather than choosing ends and as engaged in improving the conditions of life. But as employees, they are subordinate members of an organization, with little actual control over the final decisionmaking process.

The bottom line of these *DC-10* and *BART* cases is that an engineer with an egalitarian outlook who cannot condone what he or she considers undue risk on the public, will get coverage from the press and sympathy from that sector of the public having like views. On the other hand, he or she will have to seek new employment because help in retaining the old position will not be forthcoming from the largely utilitarian engineering field. Further, the net result of the dispute likely will be no change in the product, but only an inefficient expenditure of resources because of lost technical time. Contrariwise, others feel that even if no effective change occurs in the subject situation, a better management environment more conducive to public safety may evolve from the situation. Yet from management's viewpoint the eventual promotion of an egalitarian engineer to a management position, where he or she would have to supervise utilitarian engineers, would be a gross mismatch and could not endure. Therefore, the minority of egalitarian engineers largely will migrate to positions of individual rather than collective responsibility, such as research laboratories, or universities or eventually leave engineering.

Alternatives When Ethical Concerns Conflict

Reagan and Mingle suggest that, in large part, the practice of engineering is driven by utilitarian considerations. In this respect the values of an engineer may not differ from the values of the company's management. When utilitarian considerations conflict with the egalitarian or deontological concerns of an individual engineer, there are two alternatives: either the engineer can leave the corporate setting and pursue the role of a consulting engineer in private practice, or the engineer can call public attention to the problem as did the engineers in the BART case. The term "whistle blowing" is used to refer to the practice whereby an individual employee brings public scrutiny to corporate practices deemed immoral or illegal. In the BART case, the engineers who engaged in whistle blowing lost their jobs. Should there be laws protecting engineers or other employees of a corporation who engage in whistle blowing? Is it reasonable to expect a person to have to choose between condoning immoral conduct or losing his or her job? The authors suggest that another alternative would be to find ways to encourage business organizations to change so as not to place their employees in such dilemmas.

Another view of this "whistle-blowing" situation is given by DeGeorge in discussing the ethical problems of engineers in a collective responsibility situation. He states:

Though engineers are members of a profession that holds public safety paramount, we cannot reasonably expect engineers to be willing to sacrifice their jobs each day for principle and to have a whistle ever by their sides ready to blow if their firm strays from what they perceive to be the morally right course of action.[9]

He concludes with the suggestions:

In addition to asking how an engineer should respond to moral quandaries and dilemmas, and rather than asking how to educate or train engineers to be moral heroes, those in engineering ethics should ask how large organizations can be changed so that they do not squeeze engineers in moral dilemmas, place them in the position of facing moral quandaries, and make them feel that they must blow the whistle.

Many of the issues of engineering ethics within a corporate setting concern the ethics of organizational structure, questions of public policy, and so questions that frequently are amenable to solution only on a scale larger than the individual—on the scale of organization and law. The ethical responsibilities of the engineer in a large organization have as much to do with the organization as with the engineer. They can be most fruitfully approached by considering from a moral point of view not only the individual engineer but the framework within which he or she works. We not only need moral people. Even more importantly we need moral structures and organizations. Only by paying more attention to these can we adequately resolve the questions of the ethical responsibility of engineers in large organizations.[10]

The next section on "Corporate Responsibility" elaborates on these questions.

One apparent result of the "whistle-blowing" engineer is to damage the confidence that the public has in the subject technology, because of the large negative press that is drawn to this type of controversy. However, rarely does the press transmit to the public sufficient information in a form that society can use to make a rational decision concerning the technical merits of the dispute. Many times a confused account of the issue is given. The public may not know whether the question is one of general social policy or one of technical efficacy. Sometimes the two problems are hopelessly intertwined, as the controversy surrounding nuclear power readily shows.

Unavoidable Risk and Morally Acceptable Risk

Even if we assume that some risk taking is unavoidable for anyone engaged in the manufacturing of a product, how much risk is acceptable? Where do we draw the line? A purely utilitarian calculation would accept much more risk than would a deontological orientation; the ideal for a deontologist would be minimal risk. Most business and engineering decisions are caught between these two extremes. And though it might be difficult to tell in a given situation what the right balance is between these twin demands, in some cases it is not difficult to tell when a corporate decision has been made at the utilitarian extreme.

The case referred to by Reagan and Mingle is the case of bad engineering design on the Ford Pinto. It was known beforehand that the placement of the gasoline tank created the possibility of fire when a Pinto was struck in a rear-end collision. But it would create an additional expense to protect the gasoline tank from this hazard, and multiplied by the number of Pintos being manufactured, the cumulative cost of modifying the design of the fuel tank would be a sizeable cost to the Ford Motor Company. After several rear-end collisions occurred and produced loss of life because of the ensuing fire, a lawsuit was filed against the Ford Motor Company. In the pretrial discovery process an internal memo revealed that management had calculated the cost of possible liabilities resulting from the faulty fuel tank design and had weighed this cost against the cost of improving the design of the car and removing the defect. Management had calculated that 180 burn deaths and 180 serious burn injuries would result in liabilities to the company of around $50 million. Improving the defective design was estimated to cost $11 per vehicle. On a total projected run of twelve and a half million vehicles, the cost of the improved design would be $137 million. On a strict cost-benefits analysis, corporate management decided not to improve the defective design. This corporate attitude so outraged the jury that they awarded punitive damages of $125 million.

But what about the liability of the company in this collective, moral responsibility situation? Naturally where imposition of some risk on the public is a daily occurrence, situations will occur when society rules, through the courts, that an unreasonable risk has been imposed, particularly since the courts have the benefit of hindsight, while the engineer must work from a forseeability viewpoint. This generally is negligence. Shifting to strict liability, one view is that constructive knowledge of a defective product creating undue risk of harm is imposed upon the manufacturer and the appropriate engineer staff. Thus, being in a risk imposition business, engineering can expect law suits as a common occurrence in the modern legal environment. The engineer naturally picks the utilitarian answer generated by a cost-benefit analysis, whereby the costs of law suits, insurance, lost time, increased design analysis, new material development, etc., are gauged against the benefits in terms of needed profits to stay in business, required product volume to keep a competent work force, including engineering, on the job, etc. In essence, this approach over the long range will result in some monetary value being placed upon a human life. To utilitarians, this is a perfectly reasonable concept, and their only question is: "What value should be employed?" This type of analysis[11] has produced a large variance in dollar amounts, expressed in terms of dollars invested in increased safety per potential life saved, from essentially zero dollars for some highway safety programs to 102 million dollars for the controversial one part per million OSHA benzene rule, which the Supreme Court later ruled was improperly generated.[12]

In contrast, to the egalitarian the very concept of placing a value on life is immoral. The awarding of punitive damages[13] by a largely egalitarian jury for intentional defective design is one result of this ethical dilemma. For instance, gasoline tank design for automobiles has been one such a controversial design subject.[14] The classic example was the *Ford Pinto* case,[15] where a $125 million punitive damage award was given by the jury; the Pinto gasoline tank ruptured in collision, seriously injuring the occupants because of the subsequent fire. Here an engineering memo, obtained during discovery from Ford, showed that a few dollars cost-per-car design addition would in some instances have protected the gasoline tank from rupturing. Management purposely deferred using this addition. The appeals court chastised Ford for "engaging in a cost-benefit analysis balancing human lives against corporate profits."[16] Again this was perfectly predictable utilitarian behavior by Ford, and likewise perfectly predictable egalitarian behavior by the court!

This value of human life situation requires the engineer to wear two hats, for under his or her employment placing a monetary value on an anonymous life in the population is perfectly reasonable and moral, while in his or her community no value can be placed upon a life of any known person. It is a common utilitarian trait of the engineer to be able to divorce himself or herself from the emotional regime associated with individuals and view the situation as a whole. Again to the egalitarian this approach is cold, cruel and immoral; yet to the utilitarian, it is a necessary part of the risk imposition business.

To engineers the level of risk society is willing to accept should be determined in the emotional environment of a well disciplined legislative debate. However, engineers recognize that the decisions can, and usually are, made by the courts before an emotional jury, especially if the legislative bodies refuse to act on a highly controversial issue, such as product liability.

Collective responsibility is a social invention that very well fits one of the previous definitions of utilitarianism which was "that normative ethical system which satisfies, in the most rational manner possible, the need for justifying a society's moral code to those who live under it."[17]

Reagan and Mingle have pointed out a principal reason for the moral dilemma faced by those working in a corporate context: the nature of corporate decision making, and especially the decisions made by engineers, is to balance risk against other values. It is impossible to eliminate risk entirely, so the question is how much risk is morally acceptable. A strict deontologist, or egalitarian (to use the author's term) tends to take the view that no risk is acceptable when it involves the possible death of a human being. Decisions by the courts, especially sympathetic juries, more and more tend toward the view that any injury caused by a company renders it liable for damages, whether the injury was intentional or not. This is the notion of *strict liability*. There will be an ongoing conflict between this notion of strict liability and the utilitarian considerations of business professionals until society resolves this conflict through legislation.

A Profession with Continuing Value Conflicts

The phrase "engineering profession" can encompass engineers, their employers or companies, and their technical and professional societies, when the concept of collective responsibility connects the groups together. From the discussions in this paper, no clear-cut line exists where the engineering profession's legal responsibility ends and its moral responsibility continues. The closest approximation to a concrete division lies in the field engineering area where contract terms try to limit legal liability, but the ethical duty to prevent foreseeable harm is still present. Naturally, if control is extended beyond the contract limits, liability will follow this morally based action.

Conversely, when legal liability is predicated upon strict liability concepts, the engineering profession suffers monetarily from the imposition by the courts of egalitarian ethical ideas upon their utilitarian views. Because the engineering profession generally possess a utilitarian ethical value system, with some strong meritocracy overtones, the courts usage of the "deep pocket doctrine," requiring the manufacturer to be in essence the insurer of his products, creates a bewildered engineering profession that wonders why society is picking on them. The engineering profession's answer has been to fight back with the help of its utilitarian friends in the insurance industry, by using the political process to have state legislatures pass "product liability acts." These acts essentially reintroduce the concepts of negligence into the product liability arena, and to the engineering profession shift the balance of justice more toward an utilitarian viewpoint.

On a separate front, the engineering profession's attempt to apply its utilitarian ethical principles to the establishment of behavior guidelines for its members and to the establishment of technically sound standards, both done in the interest of having the profession act in a manner most advantageous to the public, runs afoul of the libertarian antitrust principles and laws. Antitrust ideas can have utilitarian supporters when monopolistic situations work against the overall good of the public. But when antitrust laws are stretched to bring in peripheral parties clearly outside the action according to utilitarian conflict of interest principles, again the engineering profession wonders why society is picking on them.

How should the engineering profession respond? Should it change its ethical value system to egalitarian? Of course not! The business of risk imposition can only be handled with an utilitarian viewpoint. Thus, the engineering profession will have to learn to live with a certain amount of litigation fostered mainly by the egalitarian elements of society. In addition, society is making strong assertions that engineers need to do a better job of analysis and synthesis in creating their work-product, which further implies to the engineer that society is willing to pay the increased cost associated with more engineering services. However, society also seems to be making overtones that engineers should accept more of a continuing responsibility for their work-product, which responsibility should include a further search for methods to lower, not only the uncertainty associated with any risk imposition, but the actual risk itself.

Philosophers have been unable to show clearly and convincingly that either utilitarianism or egalitarianism is superior to the other.[18] Society must just live with this conflict of values. Indeed the Constitution states that Congress can pass laws designed to produce the maximum good for society as a whole, but these laws are limited by the rights enumerated and implied in the Bill of Rights. And many of the most famous Supreme Court cases have dealt, ultimately, with this conflict of values. In this paper the authors' hope was to explain to engineers the origin of some of these value conflicts, and to the non-engineer why engineers are naturally inclined to an utilitarian value system. One major source of the engineer's dilemma is that his or her utilitarian moral value system often conflicts with a legal system that is in large part based upon non-utilitarian moral principles.

1. Feinberg, Collective Responsibility, 45 *J. Philosophy* 684(L968).

2. Am. Jur.2d 407, *Agency,* 267(1962).

3. *See* R. Baum and A. Flores, Ed., 2 *Ethical Problems in Engineering.* 2nd Ed., Human Dimensions Center, RPI, Troy, NY(1980).

4. *Id.* at 183.

5. *Id.*

6. *Id.*

7. Robb, *A Practical Approach to Use of State-of-the-Art Evidence in Strict Products Liability Cases,* 77 Nw.U.L.J.1(1982).

8. Baum, *supra* note 126,80.

9. DeGeorge, *Ethical Responsibilitie of Engineers in Large Organizations: The Pinto Case,* 1 *Bus. & Prof. Ethics J.* (1982).

10. *Id.*

11. *See* Graham and Vaupel, *Value of Life: What Difference Does It Make?*, 1 *Risk Analysis* 89 (1981).

12. Industrial Union Dept. v. American Petroleum Institute, 448U.S.607, 100S.Ct.2844,65 L. Ed, 2d 1010(1980).

13. Annot. 13A.L.R. 4th 52(1982).

14. Annot., 96A.L.R. 3d 265(1979).

15. Grimshaw v. Ford, No. 197761, Orange County (California) Cup. Ct., 1978.

16. Grimshaw v. Ford, 174 Cal. Rptr. 348(Ct.App.1981)

17. P. Taylor, *Principles of Ethics,* 1(1975).

18. A. MacIntyre, *Why is the Search for the Foundations of Ethics so Frustrating?* Hastings Center Report, August 1979.

Assessment

What are we to conclude about the ethical evaluation of business practices that involve the calculation of risk? The conclusion suggested by Reagan and Mingle is that the conflict between the largely utilitarian calculations of the business manager or engineer in an industrial setting and the deontological demands placed on business by the courts and sympathetic juries is not going to be solved by further philosophical analysis. Why? Because it has not been possible to show conclusively that either utilitarianism or a deontological theory is adequate by itself to guide us through the thicket of moral decision making. As we found out in our examination of these two moral theories in Part Two of this book, each captures a valuable aspect of our moral insight; but neither by itself can guide our moral decisions totally. But this state of affairs is not a sufficient basis to give up on moral theory entirely.

As is true with other problems we face, we are caught between twin demands. This is not only true of ethics. Young professionals are caught between the demands of their career and their family life. Our political ideals are caught between the twin goals of freedom and order. A soldier is faced with dual demands for obedience and for individual initiative. And in ethics we are faced with cogent demands from both utilitarian and deontological considerations. What emerges from our study of the cases above is that we quickly fall into moral error when we surrender completely to one or the other of these moral demands. The utilitarian calculation by Ford Motor Company executives that placed a dollar value on human life offends our moral value of respect for individuals and strikes us as cold, calculating, and totally unacceptable. But many persons feel that it is unacceptable to set up strict deontological standards for conduct that would preclude such calculations and risk taking. After all, without such calculations and risk taking, the benefits of engineering would not be available to society.

Perhaps moral seriousness requires us to feel intensely the tension between these twin demands; to surrender totally to either of them would be to give up an important moral insight. We must keep the tension between these two demands alive; this is the moral posture. There is still much room for continued philosophical reflection and analysis on the proper balance between the two moral points of view: how much risk is morally acceptable? How should we accord blame when a corporation acts irresponsibly? How can we encourage business organizations to tolerate moral thinking on the part of their employees? And how should employees balance loyalty to their employer with their duty to blow the whistle when there is evidence of corporate misconduct? These are only some of the issues that will provide additional topics for the ongoing discussions in business ethics.

Issue Two:
Truth-Telling in Advertising

Another domain in business that exposes a number of ethical issues is marketing, and central among these is truth-telling in advertising. The last decade has seen the enactment of laws that, until a few years ago, would have seemed unthinkable— laws that require companies to prove the truth of their claims, that protect consumers against fraudulent advertising and levy penalties for disobedience to these regulations. These laws came about through the intervention of government into the free market; and although some conservatives argue that government ought to keep out of the free market entirely, there are others who counterargue that only by government intervention in the market can it remain free.

The Free Market, Utilitarianism, and Truth-Telling

The argument against governmental intervention is based on a view of the free market that goes back to the eighteenth century and the writings of Adam Smith (1723–1790), who defended the view that the free market is the most effective means of regulating the production and consumption of goods. In Smith's view, the forces of competition and the desire of entrepreneurs to sell their product will require that they make the best product and sell it at the lowest price. In a free market, the fact that each product has to compete with others will require its purveyors to keep the price low, the quality high, and the claims made for the product truthful. The history of industrial development paints a different picture. Various schemes were developed to restrain trade, to gain a monopolistic hold on a market, and to limit competition. To restore the free market, government had to intervene to break up large cartels, limit the share of any given market that could be dominated by a single firm, and in general to insure that the forces of the free market were left free to work inasmuch as is possible. When the market is truly free, its effect is like an "invisible hand," to use Adam Smith's phrase, insuring the widest possible distribution of the best possible products at the lowest possible price.

If this strikes you as a view compatible with utilitarianism, you would be correct, for one way of looking at Adam Smith's view is to see it as an economic counterpart of ethical utilitarianism. Through the forces of the free market, Adam Smith thought, the greatest good, in terms of the distribution of society's goods and services, could be had by the greatest number. But this noble vision of society can only occur if the market is truly free. If one accepts the free market view of how businesses ought to be allowed to function, then a corollary is that anything that detracts from the freedom of the marketplace is wrong. One could argue that failure of a company to tell the truth about its product is one kind of restraint on the free market; a company that lies about its products has an unfair advantage over its competitors, thereby distorting the effects of the free market.

If truthful advertising is seen as necessary to the functioning of a free market, it is seen as completely unnecessary by those who advocate a different method for distributing society's goods and services. In communist states, there is no advertising due to the view that it distorts how people view their real needs, results in unneeded production of unneeded goods, and unrealistically raises the expectations of the citizens in the society. Rather than allowing the effects of the free market to determine how the society's productive capacity will be used, Marxist countries view this task as one needing central control by the government. Therefore, the attack on advertising by Marxists is not directed at its untruthfulness; even truthful advertising would be seen as unnecessary and misdirected.

The following selection, from the contemporary philosopher Richard DeGeorge, carefully explores the ethical issues associated with advertising. The first task he sets for himself is to defend advertising against the charge that it is inherently immoral.

Advertising Not Inherently Immoral

* Once products are made, they must be sold. Marketing covers this process. Some products are produced only when ordered; others are first produced and then sold. The techniques by which a market is determined and goods sold is frequently complex, and the specific means chosen depends on the nature of the product, the potential buyer, the cost, and so on. Some goods are sold primarily by salespersons, others through store displays. But advertising is the major method by which consumer goods are sold.

Moral issues arise in other aspects of marketing besides advertising. Salespeople frequently use techniques of questionable character. We have already discussed in passing the question of bribery and the giving of gifts. Some salespeople use what are called high-pressure techniques of salesmanship, sometimes of dubious moral quality. Goods sold to one company by another are advertised as well as being marketed through sales representatives. Yet public and governmental concern has tended to focus on the advertising of consumer products to the general public. Corporations are thought capable of handling their own wants and of being qualified to determine on their own what they need. Although they are legally protected against fraud, they are less likely than the ordinary consumer to be taken in by misleading advertising or to be sold what they do not want.

Advertising is not in itself immoral. Once a producer makes a commodity, his object is to sell it. To do so he must inform potential buyers that the product is available, what it does, and how it might be a product they want or need. Advertising provides this information to large numbers of

* Reprinted with permission of Macmillan Publishing Company from *Business Ethics* by Richard T. DeGeorge. Copyright © 1982 by Macmillan Publishing Company.

people. A product might be advertised through a direct mail campaign or through use of the media—newspapers, magazines, TV. Advertising, therefore, is part of the process of selling one's products. Since any sale is a transaction between a buyer and a seller, the transaction is fair if both parties have adequate appropriate information about the product and if they enter into the transaction willingly and without coercion. From a moral point of view, since advertising helps achieve the goal of both seller and buyer, it is morally justifiable and permissible, providing it is not deceptive, misleading, or coercive. It can be abused, but it is not inherently immoral.

Attacks on Advertising Answered

Before going on to consider the proper limits of advertising, DeGeorge takes up a more basic criticism. There are those who object to advertising in principle, *any* advertising. There are three such attacks that have been made, and DeGeorge considers each of them. It is important to look at each of these, for if the enterprise of advertising is through and through immoral, then no amount of justification of specific advertising practices can rescue it. In an analogous way, if we agree that theft is wrong, then we could hardly discuss the moral versus immoral forms of theft.

The *first* attack on advertising comes from those who see it as an inevitable aspect of an immoral economic system. Supporters of this point of view argue that advertising is necessary to a capitalist, free-market economy, and that sort of economy is inherently immoral as opposed to a socialist form of economy. Without considering the basic attack on capitalism, which would take him into matters of political philosophy, DeGeorge points out that this criticism ignores the fact that in any economic system there will be some forms of advertising, even if it is something as simple as word-of-mouth advertising or display of products on a shelf. It is, therefore, not correct that advertising is an aspect of only capitalist economies. Advertising may be more widespread in capitalist economies, but this is due to the fact that capitalist economies are not usually economies of scarcity.

The *second* attack is that advertising is frequently in poor taste. DeGeorge's response is that poor taste is not immoral.

The *third* attack is that advertising takes advantage of people by forcing them to buy things they do not need. DeGeorge's response is that belief in the freedom of people to make their own choices is itself a value; furthermore, this criticism assumes that people are more easily misled than is probably the case.

> Before we examine in detail some of the abuses of advertising, we can put aside three morally irrelevant charges brought against advertising. The first charge that advertising is not necessary in a socialist economic system and that it is an immoral part of capitalism is vague and for the most part untrue. Any producer must make known that a product is available if people are to know that they can buy it. Displaying an item in a window so that people can see it is a form of advertising, as is displaying it on a shelf. In every economic system there must be some way of letting potential buyers know of the existence of goods. In a society of comparative scarcity, where

only essentials are available, people may constantly be on the lookout for products they want, spotting them when they arrive on a shelf. They may then transmit the information that the product is available through word of mouth. Before long there are lines of people waiting to purchase the item, and soon it is sold out. Those who did not get the item then wait for it to appear again. Or if an item is a staple, and generally available, people know where it can be purchased and simply go to that store when they need it. In such a society advertising plays a comparatively small role.

American society is not a society of comparative scarcity but one of comparative wealth. There are many items available to the consumer. Competition, moreover, encourages producers to enter a market in which there is consumer demand. If a company had a monopoly on an item, then it would have little need for advertising once people knew of its availability. Competition, therefore, accounts for the amount of advertising we have in the United States as opposed to that in the Soviet Union. The American automobile industry, for instance, produces a great many different kinds of cars—different styles and makes, with different accessories, price ranges, and so on. If there were only one kind of car made, clearly there would be less advertising by the automobile industry. Would it be better if there were only one car manufacturer—perhaps the government? The typical American answer is no. Once we allow competition—which has not been shown to be immoral—then advertising is a reasonable concomitant, and as such it is not inherently immoral.

A second charge against advertising which we can dismiss from a moral point of view is its frequent poor taste, offensive to one's finer sensibilities. The charge can hardly be denied. But poor taste is not immoral. As members of society we can make known our displeasure at such advertising either by vocal or written protest or by not purchasing the item advertised. We should keep distinct, however, what is in poor taste from what is immoral.

A third charge claims that advertising takes advantage of people either by forcing them to buy what they do not want or, more plausibly, by psychologically manipulating them to buy what they do not need. According to this view, people are not able to resist the lure of the vast resources available to producers for advertising campaigns. Manipulation and coercion through advertising are immoral, as we shall see in detail. But the charge is clearly an overstatement if it asserts that all members of the public are gullible, unsophisticated, and manipulable by media advertising. Advertising would be immoral if it always and necessarily manipulated and coerced people. But it does not. The difficulty is deciding what is manipulative and what is not, who should be protected from certain kinds of advertising, and who does not need such protection. The notion of protection from advertising is closely linked to governmental paternalism. To what extent are people to be allowed to make their own decisions and to what extent should government protect them against themselves because of its superior knowledge of their real needs and wants? The Federal Trade Commission (FTC) and the Food and Drug Administration (FDA) are the two American agencies with major responsibility for policing advertising. The standards they adopt are frequently more restrictive and paternalistic than morality requires. They have sometimes ruled advertising misleading if only 5 percent of the population would be misled by it. Whether morality demands this much protection is among the topics we shall investigate.

Functions of Advertising

Before considering the issue of truth-telling in advertising, DeGeorge enumerates the various functions of advertising: selling goods, supplying information, molding public opinion, and creating a favorable climate for a firm's products. Any view of advertising that limited itself to only one of these functions would miss much of advertising's force and would, accordingly, oversimplify the moral issues involved.

A major function of advertising is to sell goods. But this is not its only purpose, nor does it accomplish this only by supplying information. Advertising may educate the public or mold public opinion. Propaganda might be considered a form of advertising for a political party, a religious sect, or some special social group. Let us, however, limit this discussion to advertising in business and to the aim of selling a product. Informing the public of an item's availability is only part of the task of advertising. A manufacturer also wants to influence people to buy the product. Hence, ads are not only informative but also persuasive. Through advertisements some companies wish to achieve public notice and recognition. They feel that people will tend to buy products with a familiar name. The purpose of some advertising is the building of goodwill for the producer, who assumes that public goodwill will eventually help sales.

The approach to advertising which sees its function only in terms of supplying information takes too narrow a view of the objectives of advertising and tends to evaluate it from too narrow a moral perspective. If its proper function were exclusively the giving of information, and if information were always given in declarative sentences, then we could concern ourselves exclusively with the questions of truth in advertising. If what an advertisement says is true, it is morally permissible; if what it says is false, it is immoral. We shall initially approach advertising in this way. In doing so, we shall also see the shortcomings of this approach.

Advertising and Lying

If we considered advertising to be exclusively supplying information, then we would probably construe the issue of truth-telling in advertising to be merely the question of whether or not the information conveyed is true or false. That, in fact, seems to be the way the government construes truth-telling in its regulation of advertising when businesses are held accountable for every minute detail in their ads. DeGeorge's analysis points out that the morality of truth-telling in advertising is much more complex. This is so because language is used in many ways, not simply to convey information. Sentences that convey information are called propositions, and the claims they make can be assessed as true or false. But there are many other kinds of sentences, such as exclamations, interjections, questions, as well as a whole range of rhetorical devices such as hyperbole, metaphor, simile and so on. Advertising, exploring this rich variety of language, often does its job well without making any literally true statements, and also can mislead people without making any false statements. The ethical issue of truth-telling in advertising, accordingly, focuses not on falsehood but on *lying*. A careful analysis of lying is, therefore, needed.

Let us start with some distinctions that will be helpful in clarifying the complex question of truth in advertising. What is truth in advertising contrasted with? It can be contrasted either with falsehood or with lying. Lying is immoral; stating falsehoods is not necessarily immoral. Suppose, for instance, I were to tell a story. I could make a number of statements that were not factually true; yet I would not be lying.

The terms "true" and "false" are properly predicated of statements or propositions. Only a proposition can be true or false. An exclamation, a question, an interjection, cannot be true or false. A statement or a proposition contains a subject and a predicate. The subject has the property or is related to something else stated in the predicate. A statement or proposition is true, roughly speaking, if the relation stated to maintain between subject and predicate actually corresponds to the same relation in the world between what is designated or referred to by the subject and predicate. Hence the sentence, "This page of this book has words printed on it," is true if the page of this book does in fact have words printed on it. Obviously this page does have words printed on it. Therefore the sentence is true. The sentence, "This page is colored green," is false if in fact this page is not colored green. This rough characterization of truth and falsehood will suffice for our purposes.

Lying consists, however, not simply in making a false statement. From a moral point of view lying is an activity. Lying consists in making a statement which one believes is false to another person whom one has reason to think will believe the statement to be true. Lying consists both of my saying what I believe to be false and of my intending that another believe to be true what is actually false. I both say what I do not believe, and I intend to deceive or mislead the one to whom I make the statement.

Using this definition of lying, falsehood is not a necessary part of it. Suppose, for instance, that I believe there are four pints in a quart. A friend who is baking a cake asks me how many pints are in a quart. I reply, "There are four pints in a quart." Actually there are only two pints in a quart. What I have said is false. But I have not told a lie; I have made a mistake. Conversely, suppose I believe that there are four pints in a quart and the same person asks me the same question in the same situation. I want the cake to fail so that my friend will not spend any more of our time making cakes. So, intending to give false information, I say, "There are two pints in a quart." Morally speaking, I am guilty of telling a lie, even though, by accident, what I said was a true statement. It is a lie because

I thought that what I was saying was false and I said it with the intent to deceive and the expectation that what I said would be believed.

Whether a statement or proposition is true or false depends on the world; whether a statement is an instance of lying depends on the intent of the speaker.

Not all statements that are false and that I state believing they are false, however, are lies. Suppose, for instance, I say during a chilling wintry day, "I'm as cold as an iceberg." What I say is literally false. My body temperature is about 98.6 degrees, even if I feel cold. But my statement is not a lie. I have no intention of deceiving anyone when I make that statement; nor is it likely anyone will be deceived by it. I use language in many ways. Part of the normal person's use of language enables him to distinguish by context, phrasing, intonation, and other subtle techniques the difference between a sentence that is literally true and one that is figurative, exaggerated, or not to be taken literally. Metaphor, simile, hyperbole are all accepted figures of speech. We do not speak only in declarative sentences, and when we speak in declarative sentences we do not always speak literally. When I say, "I'm so hungry I could eat a bear," I do not expect people to point out that an average bear weighs much more than I do, that I could not possibly eat a whole bear, or that I probably would not even like bear meat. All that is true but beside the point. I am simply saying in an expressive way that I am very hungry. There is no moral reason why I should not use expressive language when I do not intend to deceive and when there is little or no likelihood that I will deceive, even if my statements are not literally true.

We can now turn to advertising. Some advertisements contain sentences and hence express propositions which are appropriately evaluated in terms of truth and falsity. If an ad makes a false claim, which the advertiser knows to be false, for the purpose of misleading, misinforming, or deceiving potential customers, then the ad is immoral. It is immoral because the advertiser in the ad is lying, and lying is immoral. An advertiser might also be morally guilty of lying if what he said in an ad was accidentally true, but he believed it to be false and intended to deceive. This problem, however, need not concern us, since it is of only peripheral interest.

The problem of truth in advertising, however, does not end here. For it is possible to deceive and mislead without making any statements that are false; and it is also possible, as we have seen, not to deceive or mislead while making statements that are not literally true.

Consider the following slogan used by Esso a number of years ago: "Esso puts a tiger in your tank!" The statement, of course, is not literally true. But did anyone think it was literally true? Do we really wonder if, after some customer had put Esso gasoline into his car, he worried about whether it had turned into a tiger? Exactly what Esso meant to convey by its slogan is to some extent a matter of speculation. It clearly did not want its slogan to be taken literally, but rather figuratively. The semantics of advertising properly allow the use of figurative language. To restrict ads to statements that are literally true is to fail to understand the semantics of advertising or of language in general. There is, however, no neat line between allowable figurative language and lying. An obvious exaggeration is not likely to be taken literally. But what is obvious to me and to you may not be an obvious exaggeration to everyone. Must we protect those who might be deceived by exaggeration by forcing advertising to be literally true in the statements it makes?

Advertising and Deception

The point DeGeorge makes is that advertising must be judged, from the moral point of view, on the basis of the advertiser's *intentions*. Truth-telling in advertising then becomes not simply an issue of whether or not the information conveyed is completely accurate (which is the major concern of the FTC and the FDA), but whether or not the advertiser's intention was to lie, to deceive. And deception can be achieved without the use of a false statement. Indeed, deception can occur even when an advertisement makes only true statements. DeGeorge continues to examine some of the many ways advertising can be deceptive and, hence, immoral.

From a moral point of view it seems sufficient that the vast majority of those at whom the ad is directed not be misled by it. In dealing with responsibility we used the rule that people are morally responsible for the foreseeable consequences of their actions. The test of what is foreseeable is what the ordinary person of goodwill in those circumstances would foresee. A similar approach can be taken to advertising. An advertiser will know whether he intends his ad to deceive. If he does, then the advertiser acts immorally in placing the ad. But if he does not intend to deceive, and we are to judge the ad on its merits and not on the advertiser's intent, then the ad is morally permissible if the ordinary person at whom the ad is directed is not deceived. Some ads directed at car owners might be misunderstood by children. This is not a matter of moral concern, however, since the ad is not directed at them but at the car owners.

The Better Business Bureaus, the FTC, and the FDA are all concerned with accuracy in advertisements. Advertisers are not allowed to make false statements. Moreover, advertisers must be able to document statements which make factual claims that are taken literally, if challenged. These agencies sometimes go beyond what is morally necessary according to our analysis. Even if a very small percentage of people might be misled, the ad is not allowed. The action of government agencies in these cases, if morally justifiable, depends not on the question of lying, but on the legitimate extent of paternalism which a government can practice. We shall consider this question later.

Without making any false statements, an ad might be misleading or deceptive. A misleading ad is one in which the ad does not misrepresent or make false claims but makes claims in such a way that the normal person, or at least many ordinary people reading it quickly and without any great attention and thought, will make a false inference or draw a false conclusion. Those who attempt to justify such ads claim that the mistake is made by the reader or viewer of the ad and that the responsibility for drawing the false conclusion rests with the reader or viewer and not with the advertiser. Strictly speaking, this is correct. But the intent in such ads is often clearly to mislead. They are written or presented that way, and their effect is predictable. Such ads are immoral because they intend to deceive even if they do not literally state what is false. The same is true of packaging. If a large box is only half filled, a consumer may erroneously think he will get more in a big box than in a smaller one. If no claim is made that the box is full, no false statement has been made. The mistake is the consumer's. But the maker of the product is morally at fault.

A deceptive ad is one which either makes a false statement and therefore lies, or which misrepresents the product without making any statement. Deception of the eye and mind may take place not only through sentences or propositions but also through pictures, through individual words, or through certain juxtapositions of objects. Such deception trades on a background of ordinary expectation. We are accustomed to having the contents of a box pictured on the box. We expect the pictures to be reasonably close to the product within. When this is not the case, the picture is deceptive. If an item is called "chicken soup" and it contains no chicken and was not made from chicken, the name is deceptive even if no statement is made that the soup contains chicken or is made from chicken. If an item is advertised as being at half price and the item was never sold at full price but is always sold at the price indicated, the ad is deceptive.

Advertising and Persuasion

One of advertising's functions is to persuade people to buy the product. Such persuasion can be achieved without intentional deception and is, accordingly, not immoral.

The semantics of advertising, however, allows a certain leeway in some products. The cosmetics field provides some examples. We expect cosmetics to be packaged in pretty bottles, boxes, or containers. Perfumes would smell just as sweet if they were packaged in mustard jars. But they would not sell as well. Face creams would cleanse and soften just as well without perfume; but they would not sell as well. Cosmetics are a luxury item. They are packaged as such. They are sold as much for their promise as for their chemicals. Shampoo, hair rinse, conditioners, and other hair products will not make the ordinary person's hair look like the hair of the models who claim in ads to use these products. Nor will the use of other beauty products make the average person look like the models pictured using them. Is this advertising misleading? Do people actually believe that a product will change their looks, their personalities, or their lives? Most people know that the semantics of cosmetic advertising is puffery and do not take the pictures or the implied claims literally. They hope the product will make them more attractive, and the products sometimes *do* make their users more self-confident. This is what the customer is paying for. Repeat sales for such products is an indication that the customer is not being deceived.

Advertisements not only make statements but also try to persuade people to purchase the product advertised. Persuasion may take the form of making statements. But it need not. Many ads simply create associations in the mind of the purchaser. An ad for an expensive scotch whiskey might simply show a couple in evening clothes sipping a drink in an elegant room, together with a picture of the bottle of scotch. The association of the scotch with elegance and class is all the ad wishes to convey.

Some ads simply show a picture of the product and aim only at recognition of the product when the consumer sees it on a supermarket shelf together with eight other brands of the same kind of item. Name recognition has an effect on purchasing. This is not inappropriate. A customer who knows little about the nine items on the shelf knows at least that one of the nine items is advertised. This is some information about it. An item which did not sell would not be advertised for very long. An item which depends on repeat purchases for success has a fairly large number of users if it is continuously advertised. That does not mean the product is the best of its kind. But it is information which makes the choice of products less than random.

Advertising and Half-Truths

DeGeorge concludes his discussion by looking at the immorality of half-truths in advertising, and then provides a brief summary of his position.

The final aspect of truth in advertising that we will consider is the question of half-truths. A statement made about a product may be true, may not mislead, may not deceive, and still may be morally objectionable. What the ad does *not* say is as important as what the ad does say. A dangerous product cannot morally be advertised and sold without indicating its dangers. If the background assumption of a certain product on the part of the ordinary person is that products of that kind are safe, and in fact the given advertised product is not safe, then the ad and/or box should include the caution that is appropriate. We expect lye to be caustic, and ads for lye which depend on its caustic property may not have to specify that it burns the skin, though that information should be prominent on the can. But we do not usually expect hair dye to contain lye or to be caustic. An ad for such a product that does not indicate its unusual potential danger would be immoral.

Our general rules concerning truth in advertising can be summarized in the following way. It is immoral to lie, mislead, and deceive in advertising. It is immoral to fail to indicate dangers that are not normally expected. It is not immoral to use metaphors or other figures of speech if these will be normally understood as the figurative use of language; nor is it immoral to persuade as well as to inform.

Assessment

Few of us would want to argue against truth-telling in advertising. It seems almost self-evident to us that advertising should be truthful. Deontologists and teleologists would blend their voices in defense of truth-telling. The deontologist might claim that lying is always immoral and would probably support that claim with Kant's argument (referred to in Chapter Nine) that the liar sacrifices dignity and humanness itself. The teleologist might argue (as was noted earlier in this chapter) that the free market is a device for maximizing human happiness by generating the best products at the lowest possible price and that lying and deception interfere with the functioning of the free market and are therefore unethical.

Given the widespread affirmation of truth-telling in advertising that exists today, it is understandable why the government has thrust itself into the free market to regulate advertising. Yet, governmental regulation has focused rather narrowly on the single issue of accuracy of information. DeGeorge has shown that even confining oneself to the accuracy of information is complex. But beyond this, DeGeorge, by focusing on intentionality, has shown how truth-telling in advertising involves more than simply conveying the truth or falsity of information. Deontologists, accordingly, provide an important corrective to the oversimplified hope that assuring the truth of statements in advertising is sufficient to correct unethical advertising practices.

An important dimension in advertising concerns the full disclosure of information, even information that might detract from the product's sale. Here the deontological emphasis on intentionality for determining the moral assessment of advertising needs to be enhanced by consequentialist considerations. Is it moral for a company to associate a product, such as cigarettes with their known health hazards, with health and vitality? Is it moral for companies to advertise infant formula in third-world countries to mothers unable to afford the product and who dilute it with unsanitary water? The companies respond that theirs is a good product, that the consumers have an obligation to use it correctly. But critics of this practice point out that by associating the product with the "modern" way of child rearing, the advertisers produce behavior that brings about malnutrition and death to the infants. Closer to home, such advertising practices as television advertising aimed at children (for sugared cereals, expensive toys, and so forth) is immoral, because children are not able to make discriminatory judgments.

In none of these cases is deception, or even the intent to deceive, the central issue. Debate about these advertising practices centers on the consequences they have for society—that is, on utilitarian considerations. So even after we have determined what is acceptable on the grounds of truth-telling in advertising, there are additional ethical issues to be explored. This discussion of truth-telling in advertising shows that the issue has not been put to rest by the governmental incursion into the free market to guarantee the accuracy of information conveyed in advertising. The morality of advertising has many facets, and insights from deontologists and teleologists alike will be valuable in the ongoing debate.

Review Questions

1. Describe the diffusion of authority in corporations, the resulting difficulty in affixing responsibility in corporations, and the doctrine of *strict liability*.
2. Indicate some of the constraints under which engineers operate and how this situation facilitates their adopting a utilitarian ethical posture.
3. Discuss how the utilitarian posture of engineers runs into conflict with deontological concerns held by the general public, the courts, and by engineers themselves.
4. "One of the major value conflicts in business in general and engineering in particular can be described in terms of unavoidable risk and morally acceptable risk." Explain.
5. Indicate the three attacks on advertising as inherently immoral and note DeGeorge's response. Do you find his response convincing? Why, or why not?
6. Why does truth-telling in advertising, from a moral point of view, involve a larger issue than simply the accuracy of information conveyed? Give examples.

CHAPTER 12

Ethical Issues in Public Policy

Introduction

The distinction between personal ethical issues and matters of concern to a society as a whole is not easy to draw. What starts as an issue for the individual quickly leads to matters of public policy. In sexual conduct, for example, the definition of a private relationship between consenting parties has implications for legislation and government action, or at least the debate quickly centers on what the appropriate role of government should be in intensely private matters such as this. Should government seek to regulate the private conduct of its citizens in matters of their sexual activity? Should prostitution be legalized, regulated, taxed? Should legislated restraints be placed on the distribution of pornography? Should homosexual activity be protected by law?

These questions reflect not only contemporary public issues but also show the intimate connection between private ethical conduct and larger issues of public concern. Lying and truthfulness, for example, can be considered as a personal ethical issue; but when the person lying is the head of a large corporation, and the lie concerns the company's activity as a polluter of neighboring lakes and waterways, the lie is also a public policy issue.

There are other issues, however, that are not so much matters of personal ethical choice with public policy ramifications as they are issues relating to broader concerns within society. Two of the most widely discussed such issues have to do with what philosophers call distributive justice and criminal justice. Distributive justice relates to that vast set of issues concerning how the goods and rewards of a society should be distributed. It also concerns the questions of what minimal standards

300

of living even the poorest person should be allowed, and what rights of access to society's institutions—educational, medical, governmental—should be guaranteed to all. Criminal justice, as the name implies, relates to how society should react to criminal behavior on the part of its citizens. It involves such issues as the moral right of the state to punish criminals, the rights of criminals, the purpose of punishment, and the limits of punishment, including whether capital punishment is to be tolerated. Such questions are not to be decided by the individual alone but by society in terms of the laws it passes and the institutions it creates.

Both of these issues—distributive justice and criminal justice—have been included in this chapter as an introduction to the domain of ethics and public policy.

Issue One:
Distributive Justice

John Rawls, a Harvard Professor, has written for many years on the theme of justice. This ancient topic, which received its first attention by Western philosophy in the dialogues of Plato, has proved to be a perennial topic for disagreement among thinkers and cultural traditions. Rawls's *A Theory of Justice* is one of the most important twentieth-century books to be written dealing with justice as it relates to the way society distributes its goods and service. The book itself, though long, is well worth reading. But instead of selections from the book, the following excerpt is an account of Rawls's principles by Allen Buchanan, a sympathetic but nonetheless critical interpreter. Number citations in parentheses in the citations refer to *A Theory of Justice*.

The Primary Problem of Justice

* The primary subject of justice is the basic structure of society because the influences of the basic structure on individuals are present at birth and continue throughout life. The primary problem of justice, then, is to formulate and justify a set of principles which a just basic structure must satisfy. These principles of social justice would specify how the basic structure is to distribute prospects of obtaining what Rawls calls *primary goods*. Primary goods include basic rights and liberties, powers, authority, and opportunities, as well as goods such as income and wealth. Rawls calls all of these benefits *primary* goods in order to emphasize that they are preeminently desirable. According to Rawls, primary goods are

. . . Things that every rational man is presumed to want. These goods normally have a use whatever a person's rational plan of life (62).

* Reprinted with permission of Ohio University Press from Allen Buchanan, "Fundamentals of the Rawlsian System of Justice," in *John Rawls' Theory of Social Justice,* edited by H. Gene Blocker and Elizabeth H. Smith. Copyright © 1980 by Ohio University Press.

Primary goods are perhaps best thought of as (a) maximally flexible means for the pursuit of one's goals, as (b) conditions of the effective pursuit of one's goals, or as (c) conditions of the critical and informed formulation of one's plans. Wealth, in the broadest sense, is a maximally flexible means in that it is generally useful for achieving one's goals, regardless of what one's goals are. Freedom from arbitrary arrest is a condition of the effective pursuit of one's goals. Freedom of speech and information are needed if one is to formulate one's goals and one's plans for attaining them in an informed and critical way. A just basic structure will be one which produces a proper distribution of prospects of obtaining primary goods, such as income and health care.

When applied to the fact about the basic structure of our society, principles of justice should do two things. First, they should yield concrete judgments about the justice or injustice of specific institutions and institutional practices. Second, they should guide us in developing policies and laws to correct injustices in the basic structure.

Rawls sets for himself, then, the task of discovering the primary principles of justice that will guide us in developing policies and laws concerning the distribution of society's primary goods. These are things that every rational person wants, and to get them involves certain additional guarantees about freedom of speech and freedom from arbitrary arrest. The primary principles of justice should relate to how society's basic institutions are structured and should guide us in attempting to correct inequities in those structures.

The Solution: Two Primary Principles of Justice

Rawls suggests and argues for two basic principles of justice. The first of these embodies principles that are well known to Americans and are embodied in the Bill of Rights. He calls this principle "The Principle of Greatest Equal Liberty." The second principle he calls "The Difference Principle," and it constitutes one of the most controversial aspects of Rawls's viewpoint. Unlike socialist political theorists who argue that justice prevails in a society only when differences among people are minimized, Rawls suggests that a just society can tolerate differences in wealth, privilege, and so forth. But he places two restrictions on such inequalities: (1) these inequalities in position and wealth must benefit the least advantaged in society; and (2) these inequalities must be attached to positions open to all.

Rawls proposes and defends the following two principles as a solution to the problem of specifying what would count as a just basic structure.
First Principle:

Each person is to have an equal right to the most extensive total system of equal basic liberties compatible with a similar system of liberty for all (250).

Second Principle:

Social and economic inequalities are to be arranged so that they are both:
(a) to the greatest benefit of the least advantaged, and (b) attached to offices

and positions open to all under conditions of fair equality of opportunity
(302–3).

Rawls calls the First Principle the Principle of Greatest Equal Liberty. The
Second Principle includes two parts. The first part of the Second Principle
is the Difference Principle. It states that social and economic inequalities
are to be arranged so that they are to the greatest benefit of those who
are least advantaged. The second part of the Second Principle is the Principle
of Fair Equality of Opportunity. It states that social and economic inequalities
are to be attached to offices and positions which are open to all under
conditions of fair equality of opportunity. Before we can hope to assess
Rawls' theory, each of these very general principles must be carefully
interpreted.

The Principle of Greatest Equal Liberty

The first principle includes two claims. First, each of us is to have an
equal right to the same total system of basic liberties. Second, this total
system of basic liberties is to be as extensive as possible. The key phrase
here is "basic liberties." By basic liberties Rawls means:

(a) freedom to participate in the political process (the right to vote, the right
    to run for office, etc.)
(b) freedom of speech (including freedom of the press)
(c) freedom of conscience (including religious freedom)
(d) freedom of the person (as defined by the concept of the rule of law)
(e) freedom from arbitrary arrest and seizure, and
(f) the right to hold personal property (61).

The idea of the First Principle, then, is that each person is to have an equal
right to the most extensive total system composed of the liberties listed in
(a) through (f), compatible with everyone else having an equal right to the
same total system.

The Difference Principle

The Difference Principle states that social and economic inequalities are
to be arranged so as to be to the greatest benefit of the least advantaged.
To understand this principle, two key phrases must be interpreted: "social
and economic inequalities" and "least advantaged."

For reasons which will become clearer later on, Rawls' First Principle
and the Difference Principle must be viewed as distributing two different
subsets of the total set of primary goods. The First Principle distributes one
subset of the total set of primary goods: the basic liberties listed above.
The Difference Principle distributes another subset: this subset includes the
primary goods of wealth, income, power, and authority. Thus the phrase
"social and economic inequalities" in the Difference Principle refers to the
inequalities in persons' prospects of obtaining the primary goods of wealth,
income, power, and authority.

The second key phrase in the Difference Principle is also to be interpreted as referring to this same subset of primary goods. The least advantaged are those who are least advantaged in their prospects of obtaining the primary goods of wealth, income, power, authority, etc. In other words, the phrase "least advantaged" refers to those persons who have the lowest prospects of gaining these goods.

We are now in a better position to understand the Difference Principle. The Difference Principle requires that the basic structure be arranged in such a way that any inequalities in prospects of obtaining the primary goods of wealth, income, power, and authority must work to the greatest benefit of those persons who are the least advantaged with respect to these primary goods.

An example will help illustrate how an institution of the basic structure might produce inequalities which work to the advantage of the least advantaged. Suppose that large-scale capital investment in a certain industry is required to raise employment and to produce new goods and services. Suppose that by raising employment and producing these new goods and services such capital investment will ultimately be of great benefit to the least advantaged members of the society. Suppose, in particular, that such capital investment, if it can be achieved, will greatly increase the income prospects of the least advantaged through employing many who are not now employed and by raising the wages of those who are already employed. Suppose, however, that individuals will not be willing to undertake the risks of this large-scale capital investment unless they have the opportunity to reap large profits from the enterprise, should it succeed. In such a case, tax advantages for capital investment and lowered taxes on profits might provide the needed incentives for investment. The Difference Principle would require such tax laws if they were required for maximizing the prospects of the least advantaged. In the case described, the successful investor would enjoy a larger share of the primary goods of wealth and power than other persons in his society. Yet this inequality in prospects of primary goods would be justified, according to the Difference Principle, granted that it is necessary in order to maximize the expectations of the least advantaged. If a different institutional arrangement would do a better job of raising the prospects of the least advantaged, then, according to the Difference Principle, that arrangement would be more just. As a more fundamental example of an inequality in the basic structure which might be viewed as maximizing the prospects of the worst-off, consider the United States constitution's provisions for special powers for the President. According to the Difference Principle, the inequalities in power which these provisions create are justified only if they maximize the prospects of the worst-off.

Though Rawls first introduces the Difference Principle in the form stated above, he quickly proceeds to restate it using the notion of the *representative worst-off man*. Rawls does not offer a detailed account of how the representative worst off man is to be defined. Instead he sketches two distinct definitions and suggests that "either of [them], or some combination of them, will serve well enough" (98). According to the first definition, we first select a particular social position, such as that of unskilled worker, and then define the worst off group as those persons with the average income for unskilled workers or less. The prospects of the representative worst off man are then defined as "the average taken over this whole class." The other definition Rawls suggests characterizes the worst off group as all persons with less than half the median income, and defines the prospects of the representative worst off man as the average prospects for this class.

This complication in the statement of the Difference Principle is not a minor point for Rawls. It is one instance of Rawls' emphasis on the notion of procedural justice. Rawls distinguishes several varieties of procedural justice, but for our purposes the main point is that procedural justice utilizes institutional arrangements and conceptions, such as that of the representative worst off man, which allow us to apply principles of justice without focusing on actual particular persons. According to Rawls, the great advantage of procedural justice "is that it is no longer necessary in meeting the demands of justice to keep track of the endless variety of circumstances and the changing relative positions of particular persons. One avoids the problem of defining principles to cope with the enormous complexities which would arise if such details were relevant" (87).

The Principle of Fair Equality of Opportunity
The Principle of Fair Equality of Opportunity requires that we go beyond formal equality of opportunity to insure that persons with similar skills, abilities, and motivation enjoy equal opportunities. Again an example may be helpful. Suppose that two individuals A and B both desire to attain a certain position which requires technical training. Suppose further that they are roughly equal in the relevant skills and motivation, but that A's family is extremely poor and cannot finance his training, while B's family is wealthy and willing to pay for B's training. Rawls' Principle of Fair Equality of Opportunity would presumably require institutional arrangements for financial aid to insure that the fact that A was born into a low income class does not deprive him of opportunities available to others with similar skills and motivation.

Buchanan suggests that Rawls has really proposed three principles, since the Difference Principle has two subprinciples. We could list them as follows:

1. The Principle of Greatest Equal Liberty.
2. The Difference Principle: Inequalities should benefit the least well off in society.
3. The Principle of Fair Equality of Opportunity: Positions to which inequality are attached should be open to all.

Our study of ethics has given us numerous examples of the difficulties we face in making ethical choices because of the conflict of principles. If we could always act on the basis of a single principle, we would face few ambiguities in ethics. The difficulties for us arise, however, when several principles—all of which embody important ethical values—are in conflict. That is, we find that we cannot simultaneously act on several principles, each of which we accept as important. In such cases it would help if we had *priority rules*, that is, rules that tell us which principles we should satisfy first.

The Priority of Justice

Rawls provides us with two such rules. These rules give us what Rawls calls *lexical* priority. Lexical priority means that we cannot go on to a second principle until we have satisfied the demands of the first principle; then we cannot go on to the third principle until we have satisfied the demands of the second principle, and so on. Rawls says that among the three principles stated above, Number 1 has lexical priority over the other two, and then principle Number 3 has lexical priority over principle Number two. In all, we have five things to guide us: three principles and two priority rules. The priority rules say that we cannot trade off basic liberties for economic well-being. It would not, for example, be just to take away freedom of speech and information as a trade-off for greater wealth or for equality of access to education or health care.

Since the Second Principle of Justice contains two distinct principles— the Difference Principle and the Principle of Fair Equality of Opportunity— there are three principles of justice in all. Having advanced these three principles, Rawls offers two priority rules for ordering these three principles. The need for priority rules arises because efforts to satisfy one principle of justice may conflict with efforts to satisfy another. The first priority rule states that the First Principle of justice, the principle of greatest equal liberty, is *lexically prior* to the second principle as a whole, which includes both the difference principle and the principle of fair equality of opportunity. One principle is *lexically prior* to another principle if and only if we are first to satisfy the requirements of the first principle before going on to satisfy those of the second. So Rawls' first priority rule states that the first priority of social justice is greatest equal liberty. Only after greatest equal liberty is secured are we free to direct our efforts to achieving the requirements laid down by the Difference Principle and the Principle of Fair Equality of Opportunity.

The second priority rule states a priority relation between the two parts of the Second Principle of Justice. According to this rule, the Principle of Fair Equality of Opportunity is lexically prior to the Difference Principle. We are to satisfy the demands of the Principle of Fair Equality of Opportunity before meeting those of the Difference Principle.

The priority on liberty expressed by the first lexical priority rule is one of the most striking features of Rawls' theory. This first lexical priority rule declares that basic liberty may not be restricted for the sake of greater material benefits for all or even for the least advantaged. Where conditions allow for the effective exercise of liberty, liberty may only be restricted for the sake of a greater liberty on balance for everyone. In other words, certain basic liberties may be restricted, but only for the sake of achieving a more extensive total system of liberty for each of us. Freedom of the press, for example, might be somewhat restricted, if this were necessary to secure the right to a fair trial in situations in which unrestricted freedom of the press would lead to biased trials. Trade-offs among basic liberties are allowed, but only if the resulting total system produces greater basic liberty on balance. Trade-offs of basic liberties for other primary goods such as wealth are not allowed. . . .

It should now be obvious that Rawls comes out on the side of the deontologists in his search for the principles of justice. He rejects utilitarian standards that would assess the justice of a society on the basis of consequences alone, insisting that unless a society provides basic liberties and fair equality of opportunities for all, no amount of material well-being can substitute for these fundamental liberties.

The Contractarian Perspective

As a social theorist, Rawls also is part of a tradition that includes Thomas Hobbes. Rawls, for example, suggests that the fairest principles of society are those that all would agree to were they in a position to make a social contract with each other. This position Rawls calls the *original position.* You will recall that Hobbes suggested the social contract as the way out of the unpleasant state of nature, in which life was "solitary, poor, nasty, brutish, and short." Of course, modern societies did not originate in a social contract, but the contractarian point of view asserts that we can use the social contract device to test the fairness of a society's institutions and social arrangements. Are they the sort of arrangements that would be agreed to by the members of that society if they were in a position to approve a social contract?

Using this social contract device, Rawls suggests that there are two additional insights we can gain concerning distributive justice. The first is that the fairest arrangements in a society are those that would be agreed to by participants who did not know where they would fit in society's social arrangements. Suppose you really did not know whether your parents would be rich or poor, whether you had a high or low IQ, whether your job in life would be one highly rewarded in monetary terms or a low-paying job, or whether you would need welfare payments and food stamps or not. Suppose you were really ignorant of how you would fare under the rules and arrangements you agree to as part of the social contract. If this were the case, Rawls suggests, you and the others agreeing to the social contract would choose the arrangements that would be the fairest possible.

Specifically, Rawls notes that the social contract theory works only when the participants are behind a *veil of ignorance;* that is, they really would not know how they would fare under the principles they agree to as part of the social contract. Under such conditions, the arrangements they agree to would probably be those under which the situation of the least worst off persons in society would be as good as possible. Rawls uses a term borrowed from economists to describe such a rule: the *maximin* rule. The maximin rule says that when forced to choose among undesirable alternatives, we choose the best of the worst situations.

The Advantages of Contractarian Views

The most distinctive feature of Rawls' conditions matching justification is his use of the traditional idea that acceptable principles of political organization can be viewed as the outcome of a mutually binding contract among the members of society. The conditions which together comprise the original position are then viewed as conditions under which suitably described parties make a contract with one another.

> . . . the principles of justice for the basic structure of society are the principles that free and rational persons concerned to further their own interests would accept in an initial position of equality as defining the fundamental terms of their association. These principles are to regulate all further agreements; they specify the kinds of social cooperation that can be entered into and the forms of government that can be established. This way of regarding the principles of justice I shall call justice as fairness (11).

The idea of a social contract has several advantages. First, it allows us to view the principles of justice as the outcome of a *rational collective choice*. Second, the idea of *contractual obligation* emphasizes that the persons participating in this collective choice are to make a *basic commitment* to the principles they choose, and that compliance with these principles may be rightly enforced. Third, the idea of a contract as a *voluntary agreement* for mutual advantage suggests that the principles of justice should be "such as to draw forth the willing cooperation of everyone" in a society, "including those less well situated" (15).

The Original Position

To utilize the idea of a hypothetical social contract, two things must be done. First, the hypothetical situation in which the agreement is to be made must be carefully described in such a way that it does yield agreement on a determinate set of principles. In other words, the hypothetical choice situation must be described in such a way that, granted the description, it is possible to derive the conclusion that rational persons who found themselves in this situation would choose one set of principles rather than another.

Second, the reasoning from this hypothetical situation must actually be gone through. We must determine exactly which principles of justice would be chosen by rational persons who found themselves in the hypothetical situation described in the first stage. Let us now examine in some detail Rawls' execution of the two stages of the argument, beginning with the first.

Rawls calls his description of the hypothetical choice situation the *original* position to signify that it is the situation of choice from which the principles of justice originate or derive. The original position includes four main elements: (a) the rational motivation of the parties, (b) the veil of ignorance, (c) the formal constraints of the concept of right, and (d) the list of competing principles of justice. To understand the nature of the hypothetical situation of choice as Rawls conceives it, and to see why he thinks it accords with our considered judgments about the conditions which are appropriate for the choice of principles of justice, we must now briefly explicate each of these four elements in turn.

(a) The parties to the contract are conceived of as being motivated to pursue their life plans in a rational way. By a life plan Rawls means a consistent set of basic goals to be pursued over a life time. Each party is conceived of as having a desire to gain as large a share of primary goods as possible, since primary goods are generally useful, whatever one's life plan happens to be. Rawls describes the parties as being mutually disinterested in the sense that each thinks of himself as an independent agent with a worthwhile life plan which he desires to pursue.

(b) The parties in the original position are subject to a set of informational constraints which Rawls refers to collectively as the "veil of ignorance." The idea is that the parties are deprived of certain information. No one knows whether he (or she) is rich or poor, black or white, male or female, skilled or unskilled, weak or strong. The main purpose of depriving the parties of this information is to avoid a biased choice of principles.

The principles of justice are chosen behind a veil of ignorance. This ensures that no one is advantaged or disadvantaged in the choice of principles by the outcome of natural chance or the contingency of social circumstances. Since all are similarly situated and no one is able to design principles to favor his particular condition, the principles of justice are the result of a fair agreement or bargain. For given the circumstances of the original position, the symmetry of everyone's relations to each other, this initial situation is fair between individuals as moral persons. . . . The original position is, one might say, the appropriate initial status quo, and thus the fundamental agreements reached in it are fair. This explains the propriety of the name "justice as fairness"; it conveys the idea that the principles of justice are agreed to in an initial situation that is fair (12).

The intuitive idea here is that the choice of principles of justice should not be influenced by factors that are arbitrary from a moral point of view. If, for example, a group of persons in the original position knew that they were rich while others were poor, they might choose principles of justice which produced even greater advantages for the rich while further disadvantaging the poor. Similarly, a person who knew that he was a member of the dominant racial majority might choose principles which would discriminate against certain minorities.

(c) The parties in the original position are also described as limiting their choice to principles which satisfy certain formal constraints. The rationale behind these constraints is that they must be satisfied if the principles of justice which the parties choose are to fulfill their proper role. The proper role of principles of justice, according to Rawls, is to provide a public charter which defines the terms of social cooperation by specifying how the basic structure is to distribute rights, wealth, income, authority, and other primary goods. Rawls suggests that if the principles of justice are to be capable of achieving this goal they must be (i) general, (ii) universal in application, (iii) universalizable, (iv) publicizable, (v) adjudicative, and (vi) final.

They must be *general* if they are to cover all or almost all questions of social justice which may arise. They must be *universal in application* in the sense that their demands must apply to all members of society. The principles of justice must also be *universalizable* in the sense that they must be principles whose universal acceptance we can endorse. If the principles of justice are to guide our actions and policies and to serve as justifying grounds in particular cases, they must be *publicizable* and understandable by everyone. Since questions of justice arise where different individuals come into conflict over the benefits produced by social cooperation, principles of justice must be *adjudicative* in the sense that they must provide a way of *ordering* conflicting claims and thereby settling disputes. Lastly, the principles of justice must be *final:* they must be ultimate principles which provide a *final* court of appeal for disputes about justice (131–35).

(d) Rawls' description of the original position also includes a list of competing principles of justice from which the parties are to choose. The main competitors, according to Rawls, are the two versions of utilitarianism (classical and average) and Rawls' principles of justice.

The Maximin Rule

Setting out the conditions listed in (a) through (d) completes the first stage of Rawls' contractarian argument, the description of the original position or hypothetical situation for the choice of principles of justice. We can now turn to a brief outline of the second stage of the contractarian argument—the attempt to show that granted this description of the original position, the parties would choose Rawls' principles of justice.

By construing the selection of principles of justice as a problem of rational choice, Rawls is able to enlist techniques developed by contemporary decision theorists. Granted the informational constraints imposed by the veil of ignorance, the problem of choosing principles of justice in the original position is what decision theorists call a problem of rational choice under uncertainty.

The idea is that the parties are to choose a set of principles which will then be applied to the basic structure of the society in which they live. Different sets of principles will produce different distributions of prospects for liberty, wealth, authority, and other primary goods. Since the parties do not know their present status in their society, they are not able to predict exactly how the choice of this or that set of principles will affect them personally. The parties are to choose principles which will profoundly influence their life-prospects, but they are to do so in a situation in which the outcome of the alternatives is uncertain.

Decision theorists have proposed various rules for making decisions under uncertainty. Rawls argues that the appropriate decision rule for the parties in the original position to employ is the *maximin rule.* The maximin rule states that one is to choose that alternative which has the best worst outcome. The maximin rule tells one, in effect, to choose the safest alternative.

Rawls' appeal to decision theory in defending the contractarian argument for his principles of justice has two stages. First, Rawls argues that the conditions which make up the original position are conditions which make it rational for the parties in the original position to employ the maximin decision rule. Second, he argues that if the parties employed the maximin decision rule they would choose his principles of justice over the competitors on the list. According to Rawls, the Principle of Greatest Equal Liberty, along with the Principle of Fair Equality of Opportunity and the Difference Principle, insure the best worst outcome of any of the sets of principles on the list.

Rawls Presents a Deontological Position

As was mentioned earlier, Rawls considers his views to have more in common with Kant than with Mill. The utilitarian point of view, he thinks, would allow trade-offs of liberty for greater wealth or security; he contends a group of persons in the original position would find these trade-offs unacceptable. It would be possible, in theory at least, for a utilitarian to argue for slavery for a group in society if the institution of slavery would contribute to the greatest happiness of the greatest number. No such trade-off is allowed by a deontologist, and Rawls shows us why. Persons behind the veil of ignorance would not know which of them would be the slaves in such a society. If it were genuinely possible that any of them would be slaves, then a society in which slavery were possible would be unacceptable. The same argument would be used against tolerating any other form of gross inequality.

It is important to understand exactly why Rawls thinks that the worst possible outcome under utilitarianism would be worse than the worst possible outcome under his principles. As we saw earlier, Rawls argues that utilitarianism might require or at least allow severe restrictions of liberty for some if this produced greater overall utility. Thus, the worst outcome under utilitarianism might be slavery or servitude or at least a lesser share of liberty than others have. A person in the original position is to consider the possibility that he might turn out to be a member of the worst off group in society. Rawls' claim is that since utilitarianism may sacrifice the interests of a minority to produce greater aggregate utility, the worst off under utilitarianism may be very badly off indeed. In contrast, the lexical priority of the Principle of Greatest Equal Liberty eliminates this possible outcome by insuring that no one's basic liberty will be sacrificed for the sake of maximizing overall utility. Further, the Difference Principle requires that inequalities in wealth, income, and authority must work to the greatest benefit of the worst off, subject to the lexical priority of the Principle of Greatest Equal Liberty and the Principle of Fair Equality of Opportunity.

Rawls concludes that parties in the original position would adopt a minimal risk strategy, choose his principles, and reject the alternative conceptions, including utilitarianism. . . .

Assessment

In the most populous nation on earth, there has been a concerted effort during the past thirty years to institute a society based on the notion of radical equality. Various policies have been followed that eliminated privilege whether attached to positions or special skills; plant managers, professors, and physicians have been sent to the countryside to learn the virtues of working the soil. Economic equality has been a national goal, and combined with disciplined work from all, there has been the virtual eradication of starvation and the guarantee of a minimal standard of living for all. This has been accomplished at the cost of great restriction of personal liberties—restrictions on freedom of speech and information, freedom of movement, and freedom to choose one's life work.

On the coast of the People's Republic of China is an enclave of both freedom and inequality. The structure of Hong Kong embodies the principle of maximizing both individual freedom and freedom for the marketplace. The result, due of course in part to its favored position as a tax-free port and its situation as an export platform—has been economic growth that is the envy of most industrialized nations. But coextensive with the creation of economic opportunity has been the toleration of vast inequalities. There are the poor struggling for a toehold on the economic ladder; but there are also the rich, many of whom can relate personal tales of rising from poverty to their present wealthy status. And although there are educational opportunities, they are not open to all.

Which of these societies embodies the greatest distributive justice? Each has become the model for partisans of a single ideal of distributive justice. On the one hand are the radical egalitarians who view the most just society as the one in which differences among people have disappeared. On the other hand are the supporters of free markets, who argue that the best guarantee of individual freedom is the freedom of the marketplace; they say that political and economic freedom go hand in hand. Supporters of the free market approach argue that there can be no justice in a radically egalitarian society when the only thing that is shared equally is poverty. Supporters of the egalitarian approach argue that a society cannot be just if it tolerates starvation in the midst of plenty and allows those of wealth and privilege to enjoy the educational, medical, and cultural resources of society while the disadvantaged go without.

John Rawls can be understood as offering an alternative to these two extremes. His model for distributive justice places primary emphasis on personal liberties; these cannot be traded off for other desirable goals. He also rejects the notion that the most just society is the radically egalitarian society in which all differences among people have been removed. He argues that we can allow differences in economic or social position as long as these differences help the worst off persons in society and are attached to positions open to all. In short, Rawls offers a model that emphasizes individual liberty and tries at the same time to eliminate radical inequality while perserving important differences in the way people function in society.

Although these goals are not difficult to articulate, they are much more difficult to apply. For example, one could argue that certain vocations—especially ones that require years of training and study—should be more adequately compensated than unskilled vocations. Why? Because it is to the advantage of the worst off in society to have available physicians, judges, engineers, and others whose value to society is a function of years of training and disciplined study. But how much inequality is just? And what mechanism can be developed to put a cap on the wealth, power, or privilege of those holding such positions? And what procedures should society adopt to guarantee equal access to such positions? Similarly, though both major political parties in the United States agree that minimal provisions should be guaranteed for the poor—the safety net approach—there is little agreement on how extensive such provisions should be. There are those who argue that too generous a safety net actually encourages the continuation of poverty by removing the incentive for persons to work their way out of it. So the debate on applying principles of justice will continue, even after there is agreement on what those principles are. Whether one takes a teleological approach or a deontological approach as Rawls seems to have taken, the challenge remains for both positions to find the proper blend between freedom and equality which, as we have seen, is not easy to achieve.

Issue Two:
Criminal Justice

Four Purposes of Punishment

A second area of intense public debate concerns issues of criminal justice. Such issues involve both questions of the purpose of punishment and the extent of punishment. The purpose of punishment is a topic on which there is no widespread agreement, and at least four views of punishment are widely suggested: (1) *deterrence* (that is, we punish criminals to deter others from committing criminal acts); (2) *rehabilitation* (punishment should reform a criminal, hence the title *reformatory* or *penitentiary,* i.e., a place of penance); (3) *protection* (of society by locking away criminals), and finally (4) *retribution* (that is, punishment inflicted as a deserved repayment for the wrong act). Not all these purposes for punishment are compatible. For example, it is difficult to understand how one rehabilitates a person by removing that person from the society to which one hopes the rehabilitated criminal will return.

These and other issues in criminal justice are considered in the following selection from Richard Brandt's book *Ethical Theory: The Problems of Normative and Critical Ethics.*

Criminal Justice and Justifying Unequal Treatment

* What is meant by an "examination of the ethical foundations of the institution and principles of criminal justice"? The job of such an examination is *not* to provide a moral blessing for the status quo, for the system of criminal justice as it actually is in the United States, or in the Commonwealth of Pennsylvania. (It would be impossible to do this for all states of the U.S.A. together, or for all the Western nations, for the legal systems of different political units differ in important particulars.) Rather, it is to identify the more important valid ethical principles that are relevant to the institution of criminal justice and to furnish a model in their use in criticism or justification of important features of this institution.

The broad questions to be kept in the forefront of discussion are the following: (1) What justifies anyone in inflicting pain or loss on an individual on account of his past acts? (2) Is there a valid general principle about the punishments proper for various acts? (Possibly there should be no close connection between offense and penalty; perhaps punishment should be suited to the individual needs of the criminal and not to his crime.) (3) What kinds of defense should excuse from punishment? An answer to these questions would comprise prescriptions for the broad outlines of an ideal system of criminal justice.

. . . There are two distinct ways in which there can be injustice in the treatment of criminals. First, criminals are *punished* whereas noncriminals are not. Punishment, however, is *unequal* treatment, in a matter that involves distribution of things good or bad. Therefore, if punishment is to be just, it must be shown that the unequal treatment is required by moral principles of weight. Thus, one thing that must be done in order to show that the practice of punishing criminals is not unjust, is to show that there are moral principles that require it. But second, the *procedures of applying* the principles directing unequal treatment for criminals may themselves operate unequally. One man gets a "fair" trial and another does not. There can be inequality in the chances given people to escape the application of legal sanctions in their case. Part of treating people "justly," then, is providing legal devices so that everyone has an equal hearing: scrupulous adherence to the rules of evidence, opportunity for appeal to higher courts for remedy of deviation from standard rules in the lower courts, and so on. We shall not here consider details about how legal institutions should be devised in order to secure equal application of the law; that is a specialized inquiry that departs too far from the main problems of ethical principle. It is a part of "justice," however. Indeed, we may view "criminal justice" as having two main aspects: just laws for the punishment of offenders and procedures

* Reprinted with permission of Richard B. Brandt from *Ethical Theory: The Problems of Normative and Critical Ethics.* Copyright © 1959 by Richard B. Brandt. Published by Prentice-Hall, Englewood Cliffs, N.J.

insuring just application of these laws by the courts and other judicial machinery.

The existence of just laws directing certain punishments for certain offenses, then, is not the whole of justice for the criminal, but we shall concentrate on identifying such laws.

We have seen that fundamental to the question of distributive justice is the issue of equality. Similarly, central to issues of criminal justice is the justification for treating people unequally. For to punish a criminal is to treat that person differently than other people in that society are treated. A just society would be one in which the reasons for this unequal treatment are themselves principles of justice. In addition, a just society would be one in which the procedures for administrating punishment are also just. Such procedures would have to ensure equality of treatment for the accused regardless of the persons's wealth, privilege or social standing.

Utilitarian and Deontological Purposes of Punishment

Although it does not capture all the differences between utilitarian and nonutilitarian principles of criminal justice, it would be accurate to say that the chief reasons for punishment on the utilitarian theory are *rehabilitation* and *protection*. That is, a utilitarian would argue that the justification of punishment resides in its social consequences, that punishment should have social utility. A deontological point of view, in contrast, would argue that the fundamental principle of criminal justice is *retribution*. That is, offenders are punished because they deserve punishment; and such punishment should not be any less or any more than they deserve. When discussing the deontological point of view, Brandt refers to it as the formalist position. Among the utilitarian points of view, he emphasizes the *rule utilitarian* position. The distinction between rule utilitarian and act utilitarian points of view is a contemporary distinction that emphasizes two applications of utilitarianism. The act utilitarian proposes that we judge each individual act by the test of social utility. The rule utilitarian proposes that we judge individual acts by general laws or rules for society that embody social utility considerations rather than judge each act directly by the principle of utility.

The Utilitarian Theory of Criminal Justice: Bentham

Historically there has been a cleavage of opinion about the kind of general ethical principles required for coherence with our concrete justified beliefs about criminal justice (those concrete beliefs that are compatible with our "qualified" attitudes)—a cleavage already found in the parallel problem of economic justice. Many writers have thought that a utilitarian principle is adequate. Others have thought that some nonutilitarian principle, or more than one, is necessary. Most of the latter writers (formalists) have espoused some form of *retributive* principle—that is, a principle roughly to the effect that a wrongdoer should be punished approximately in correspondence with either the moral reprehensibility of his offense or with the magnitude of his breach or of the public harm he commits. However, as we shall see, there are other types of formalist theory.

It is convenient to begin with the utilitarian theory. Since we have tentatively concluded that an "extended" rule-utilitarianism is the most tenable form of theory, we shall have this particular type of theory in mind. For present purposes, however, it would make no difference, except at two or three points where we shall make note of the fact, if we confined our attention to a straight rule-utilitarian principle. There is no harm in thinking of the matter in this way. We can ignore the distinction between hedonistic and pluralistic forms for the present topic.

The essence of the rule-utilitarian theory, we recall, is that our actions, whether legislative or otherwise, should be guided by a set of prescriptions, the conscientious following of which by all would have maximum net expectable utility. As a result, the utilitarian is not, just as such, committed to any particular view about how anti-social behavior should be treated by society—or even to the view that society should do anything at all about immoral conduct. It is only the utilitarian principle *combined* with statements about the kind of laws and practices which will maximize expectable utility that has such consequences. Therefore, utilitarians are free to differ from one another about the character of an ideal system of criminal justice; some utilitarians think that the system prevalent in Great Britain and the United States essentially corresponds to the ideal, but others think that the only system that can be justified is markedly different from the actual system in these Western countries. We shall concentrate our discussion, however, on the more traditional line of utilitarian thought which holds that roughly the actual system of criminal law, say in the United States, is morally justifiable, and we shall follow roughly the classic exposition of the reasoning given by Jeremy Bentham[1]—but modifying this freely when we feel amendment is called for. At the end of the chapter we shall look briefly at a different view.

Traditional utilitarian thinking about criminal justice has found the rationale of the practice, in the United States, for example, in three main facts. (Those who disagree think the first two of these "facts" happen not to be the case.) (1) People who are tempted to misbehave, to trample on the rights of others, to sacrifice public welfare for personal gain, can usually be deterred from misconduct by fear of punishment, such as death, imprisonment, or fine. (2) Imprisonment or fine will teach malefactors a lesson; their characters may be improved, and at any rate a personal experience of punishment will make them less likely to misbehave again. (3) Imprisonment will certainly have the result of physically preventing past malefactors from misbehaving, during the period of their incarceration.

In view of these suppositions, traditional utilitarian thinking has concluded that having laws forbidding certain kinds of behavior on pain of punishment, and having machinery for the fair enforcement of these laws, is justified by the fact that it maximizes expectable utility. Misconduct is not to be punished just for its own sake; malefactors must be punished for their past acts, according to law, as a way of maximizing expectable utility.

The utilitarian principle, of course, has implications for decisions about the severity of punishment to be administered. Punishment is itself an evil, and hence should be avoided where this is consistent with the public good. Punishment should have precisely such a degree of severity (not more or less) that the probable disutility of greater severity just balances the probable gain in utility (less crime because of the more serious threat). The cost, in other words, should be counted along with the value of what is bought; and we should buy protection up to the point where the cost is greater than the protection is worth. How severe will such punishment be? Jeremy Bentham had many sensible things to say about this. Punishment, he said, must be severe enough so that it is to no one's advantage to commit an offense even if he receives the punishment; a fine of $10 for bank robbery would give no security at all. Further, since many criminals will be undetected, we must make the penalty heavy enough in comparison with the prospective gain from crime, that a prospective criminal will consider the risk hardly worth it, even considering that it is not certain he will be punished at all. Again, the more serious offenses should carry the heavier penalties, not only because the greater disutility justifies the use of heavier penalties in order to prevent them, but also because criminals should be motivated to commit a less serious rather than a more serious offense. Bentham thought the prescribed penalties should allow for some variation at the discretion of the judge, so that the actual suffering caused should roughly be the same in all cases; thus, a heavier fine will be imposed on a rich man than on a poor man.

Bentham also argued that the goal of maximum utility requires that certain facts should *excuse* from culpability, for the reason that punishment in such cases "must be inefficacious." He listed as such (1) the fact that the relevant law was passed only after the act of the accused, (2) that the law had not been made public, (3) that the criminal was an infant, insane, or was intoxicated, (4) that the crime was done under physical compulsion, (5) that the agent was ignorant of the probable consequences of his act or was acting on the basis of an innocent misapprehension of the facts, such that the motivation to commit the offense was so strong that no threat of law could prevent the crime. Bentham also thought that punishment should be remitted if the crime was a collective one and the number of the guilty so large that great suffering would be caused by its imposition, or if the offender held an important post and his services were important for the public, or if the public or foreign powers would be offended by the punishment; but we shall ignore this part of his view.

Bentham's account of the logic of legal "defenses" needs amendment. What he should have argued is that *not* punishing in certain types of cases (cases where such defenses as those just indicated can be offered) reduces the amount of suffering imposed by law and the insecurity of everybody, and that failure to impose punishment in these types of case will cause only a negligible increase in the incidence of crime.

How satisfactory is this theory of criminal justice? Does it have any implications that are far from being acceptable when compared with concrete justified convictions about what practices are morally right?[2]

Many criminologists, as we shall see at the end of this chapter, would argue that Bentham was mistaken in his facts: The deterrence value of threat of punishment, they say, is much less than he imagined, and criminals are seldom reformed by spending time in prison. If these contentions are correct, then the ideal rules for society's treatment of malefactors are very different from what Bentham thought, and from what actual practice is today in the United States. To say all this, however, is not to show that the utilitarian *principle* is incorrect, for in view of these facts presumably the attitudes of a "qualified" person would not be favorable to criminal justice as practiced today. Utilitarian theory might still be correct, but its implications would be different from what Bentham thought—and they might coincide with justified ethical judgments. We shall return to this.

Criticisms of Utilitarianism Answered

After pointing out the main elements of the utilitarian theory of punishment, Brandt notes that the utilitarian arguments are based on factual assumptions that continue to be questioned. It is arguable whether the severity of punishment or the length of imprisonment are actual deterrents to criminal behavior. And there is much evidence to show that imprisonment does not reform criminals. Even though prisons are frequently called *reformatories,* their success in reforming criminals ought to call for a change in their name. A utilitarian could still argue on utilitarian grounds for punishment as deterrence, but the form such punishment takes would vary depending on whether there is solid, empirical evidence that punishment does in fact deter criminal behavior.

Another criticism of the utilitarian view is that it must assume a standard of *strict liability.* This means that a person who commits a certain offense must be punished; there are no exceptions allowed regardless of circumstances. Even the insane should be punished; there would be no such thing as innocence by reason of insanity.

Brandt thinks the utilitarian has a good response to such criticisms. The long-term good of society must be factored into our estimate of social utility. The utilitarian could argue that punishing the insane would have a hardening effect on society and would not really deter criminal behavior. And one could argue that it would not be socially useful to treat all behavior alike; there is a difference between someone accidentally hitting a child with an automobile and deliberately running a child down. To fail to make such a distinction would be to introduce into society a destabilizing factor that would not be socially useful.

The whole utilitarian approach, however, has been criticized on the ground that it ought not in consistency to approve of *any* excuses from criminal liability.[3] Or at least, it should do so only after careful empirical inquiries. It is not obvious, it is argued, that we increase net expectable utility by permitting such defenses. At the least, the utilitarian is committed to defend the concept of "strict liability." Why? Because we could get a more strongly

deterrent effect if everyone knew that *all behavior* of a certain sort would
be punished, irrespective of mistaken supposals of fact, compulsion, and
so on. The critics admit that knowledge that all behavior of a certain sort
will be punished will hardly deter from crime the insane, persons acting
under compulsion, persons acting under erroneous beliefs about facts, and
others, but, as Professor Hart points out, it does not follow from this that
general knowledge that certain acts will always be punished will not be
salutary.

The utilitarian, however, has a solid defense against charges of this sort.
We must bear in mind (as the critics do not) that the utilitarian principle,
taken by itself, implies nothing whatever about whether a system of law
should excuse persons on the basis of certain defenses. What the utilitarian
does say is that, when we *combine* the principle of utilitarianism with *true*
propositions about a certain thing or situation, then we shall come out with
true statements about obligations. The utilitarian is certainly not committed
to saying that one will derive true propositions about obligations if one
starts with *false* propositions about fact or about what will maximize welfare,
or with *no* such propositions at all. Therefore the criticism sometimes made
(for example, by Hart), that utilitarian theory does not render it "obviously"
or "necessarily" the case that the recognized excuses from criminal liability
should be accepted as excusing from punishment, is beside the point.
Moreover, in fact the utilitarian can properly claim that we do have excellent
reason for believing that the general public would be no better motivated
to avoid criminal offenses than it now is, if the insane and others were
also punished along with intentional wrongdoers. Indeed, he may reasonably
claim that the example of punishment of these individuals could only have
a hardening effect—like public executions. Furthermore, the utilitarian can
point out that abolition of the standard exculpating excuses would lead to
serious insecurity. Imagine the pleasure of driving an automobile if one
knew one could be executed for running down a child whom it was
absolutely impossible to avoid striking! One certainly does not maximize
expectable utility by eliminating the traditional excuses. In general, then,
the utilitarian theory is not threatened by its implications about exculpating
excuses.

It might also be objected against utilitarianism that it cannot recognize
the validity of *mitigating* excuses (which presumably have the support of
"qualified" attitudes). Would not consequences be better if the distinction
between premeditated and impulsive acts were abolished? The utilitarian
can reply that people who commit impulsive crimes, in the heat of anger,
do not give thought to legal penalties; they would not be deterred by a
stricter law. Moreover, such a person is unlikely to repeat his crime, so
that a mild sentence saves an essentially good man for society.[4] Something
can also be said in support of the practice of judges in giving a milder
sentence when a person's temptation is severe: at least the *extended* rule-
utilitarian can say, in defense of the practice of punishing less severely the
crime of a man who has had few opportunities in life, that a judge ought

to do what he can to repair inequalities in life, and that a mild sentence to a man who has had few opportunities is one way of doing this. There are, then, utilitarian supports for recognizing the mitigating excuses.

Next Brandt considers two additional criticisms of the utilitarian principle of punishment. The first is that, on utilitarian grounds, there is no fundamental difference between imprisoning a criminal and placing a quarantine on a leper. Both actions are designed to protect society. But, so the argument goes, this shows that utilitarianism must be mistaken; we feel it a duty to make the leper as comfortable as possible, but we feel no such obligation to the criminal. Brandt replies that the two cases are not parallel; the leper cannot help contracting leprosy, but the criminal can avoid committing crimes.

The second objection to the utilitarian theory is that a judge or prosecutor would be allowed to suppress evidence and send an innocent person to jail if such punishment would be in the public good. Again Brandt counterargues that the knowledge that innocent persons could be jailed for the sake of the public good would be a destabilizing influence on society that would undermine confidence in our judicial system.

> Sometimes it is objected to utilitarianism that it must view imprisonment for crime as morally no different from quarantine. This, it is said, shows that the utilitarian theory must be mistaken, since actually there is a vast moral difference between being quarantined and being imprisoned for crime. *Why* is it supposed that utilitarianism looks to the future; the treatment it prescribes for individuals is treatment with an eye to maximizing net expectable utility. The leper is quarantined because otherwise he will expose others to disease. The criminal is imprisoned because otherwise he, or others who are not deterred by the threat of punishment, will expose the public to crime. Both the convicted criminal and the leper are making contributions to the public good. So, quarantine and imprisonment are essentially personal sacrifices for the public welfare, if we think of punishment as the utilitarian does. But in fact, the argument goes on. We feel there is a vast difference. The public is obligated to do what is possible to make the leper comfortable, to make his necessary sacrifice as easy for him and his family as possible. But we feel no obligation to make imprisonment as comfortable as possible.
>
> Again the utilitarian has a reply. He can say that people cannot help contracting leprosy, but they can avoid committing crimes—and the very discomforts and harshness of prison life are deterring factors. If prison life were made attractive, there might be more criminals—not to mention the indolent who would commit a crime in order to enjoy the benefits of public support. Furthermore, the utilitarian can say, why should we feel that we "ought to make it up to" a quarantined leper? At least partly because it is useful to encourage willingness to make such sacrifices. But we do not at all wish to encourage the criminal to make his "sacrifice"; rather, we wish him not to commit his crimes. There is all the difference between the kind of treatment justified on utilitarian grounds for a person who may have to make a sacrifice for the public welfare through no fault of his own, and

for a person who is required to make a sacrifice because he has selfishly and deliberately trampled on the rights of others, in clear view of the fact that if he is apprehended society must make an example of him. There are all sorts of utilitarian reasons for being kindly to persons of the former type, and stern with people of the latter type.

Another popular objection to the utilitarian theory is that the utilitarian must approve of prosecutors or judges occasionally withholding evidence known to them, for the sake of convicting an innocent man, if the public welfare really is served by so doing. Critics of the theory would not deny that there *can* be circumstances where the dangers are so severe that such action is called for; they only say that utilitarianism calls for it all too frequently. Is this criticism justified? Clearly, the utilitarian is not committed to advocating that a provision should be written into the *law* so as to permit punishment of persons for crimes they did not commit if to do so would serve the public good. Any such provision would be a shattering blow to public confidence and security. The question is only whether there should be an informal moral rule to the same effect, for the guidance of judges and prosecutors. Will the rule-utilitarian necessarily be committed to far too sweeping a moral rule on this point? We must recall that he is not in the position of the act-utilitarian, who must say that an innocent man must be punished if in *his particular case* the public welfare would be served by his punishment. The rule-utilitarian rather asserts only that an innocent man should be punished if he falls within a class of cases such that net expectable utility is maximized if *all* members of the class are punished, taking into account the possible disastrous effects on public confidence if it is generally known that judges and prosecutors are guided by such a rule. Moreover, the "extended" rule-utilitarian has a further reason for not punishing an innocent man unless he has had more than his equal share of the good things of life already; namely, that there is an obligation to promote equality of welfare, whereas severe punishment is heaping "illfare" on one individual person. When we take these considerations into account, it is *not* obvious that the rule-utilitarian (or the "extended" rule-utilitarian) is committed to action that we are justifiably convinced is immoral. . . .[5]

The Deontological Theory of Criminal Justice: Kant

The major alternative to the utilitarian theory of criminal justice with its principal emphasis on deterrence and reformation of the criminal is the deontological—or formalist—approach which emphasizes the retributive nature of punishment. This is the view that the purpose of punishment is to give the criminal what the criminal deserves. Punishment should not be any less or any more than the criminal behavior deserves. Brandt fortifies his exposition of this theory of punishment by a lengthy quotation from Immanel Kant. Essential to Kant's point of view is that the only reason for punishing anyone is if that person has done something wrong. It is always immoral to punish an innocent person.

If utilitarian ethical principles are regarded as not enough, then the basic system of "axioms" may be enlarged or modified by further principles of a nonutilitarian sort. A formalist system of principles of course may, like Ross' system, contain utilitarian elements, for example, a principle asserting that there is a prima facie obligation to do what good we can.

Any system of basic principles that contains nonutilitarian principles relevant to the treatment of criminals may be called a "retributive" theory of criminal justice. However, it seems better to reserve the term "retributive theory" for a theory that asserts that it is a basic principle of ethics roughly that pain or loss should be caused to persons who have done wrong, with a severity corresponding with the moral gravity of their deed—and of course the "gravity" of the deed not being defined to accord exactly with the utilitarian theory about how severely wrongdoers should be made to suffer.[6] In saying that such a principle is a "basic" principle of ethics, proponents of the retributive theory deny the possibility of deriving this principle from any principle directing to do good, that is, from any kind of utilitarian principle.

Let us now examine some formalist theories, beginning with what may be viewed as the traditional retributive theory. In order to get a concrete account before us, let us look at a statement by Immanuel Kant. He writes:

Juridical punishment . . . can be inflicted on a criminal, never *just* as instrumental to the achievement of some other good for the criminal himself or for the civil society, but *only* because he has committed a crime; for a man may never be used just as a means to the end of another person or mixed up with the objects of Real Right—against which his innate personality protects him, even if he is condemned to lose his civil personality. He must first be found culpable, before there is any thought of turning his punishment to advantage either for himself or society. Penal law is a *categorical* imperative, and woe to him who crawls through the serpentine maze of utilitarian theory in order to find an excuse, in some advantage to someone, for releasing the criminal from punishment or any degree of it, in line with the pharasaical proverb "It is better that one man die than that a whole people perish"; for if justice perishes, there is no more value in man living on the earth. . . . What mode and degree of punishment, then, is the principle and standard of public justice? Nothing but the *principle of equality.* . . . Thus, whatever undeserved evil you inflict on another person, you inflict on yourself. If you insult another, you insult yourself; if you steal from another, you steal from yourself; if you strike another, you strike yourself; if you kill another, you kill yourself. Only the rule of retribution (*lex talionis*)—only, of course, before the bar of justice, not in your own private judgment—can determine the quality and quantity of punishment. . . . Now it appears that differences of rank and class do not permit the exact retribution of like with like; but even if retribution is not possible according to the exact letter, it is still always valid in respect of effect, taking into account the feelings of the superior party. . . . So, for example, a fine for slander has little proportion to the insult, since any one who is well off can then permit himself the luxury of such behavior at his own pleasure; yet the violation of the honor of one person can be the equivalent of damage to the pride of another party, if the court condemns the offender not only to retract and apologize, but to submit to some meaner ordeal such as kissing the hand of the injured person. . . .

[But] if a person has committed murder, he must die. There is no likeness
or proportion between life, however painful, and death; and therefore there
is no equality between the crime of murder and the retaliation of it but what
is judicially accomplished by the execution of the criminal. . . . Even if a
civil society decided, with the agreement of all, to dissolve (for instance, if
an island society decided to break up and scatter into all parts of the world),
the last murderer in the prison must first be brought to justice, in order that
everyone be meted out desert for his deeds, and in order that the guilt of
blood may not taint people who have failed to carry through the punishment—
because such a people would have to be regarded as parties to a public
violation of justice. . . . The equalization of punishment with offense is possible
only through the rule of retribution . . . as is manifest from the fact that
only then is sentence pronounced proportionate to internal wickedness. . .[7]

The essence of Kant's point is that the utilitarian theory of punishment
makes the false claim that man or society has the right to use another
man as a means to the welfare of others, as if he were a physical thing.
(The reverse of this is the equally false claim, he thinks, that a man need
not be punished if that suits the needs of society, irrespective of the quality
of his wrongdoing.) A man may be punished *only* if he has done something
wrong (and hence it is immoral to punish an innocent man); and if he has
done something wrong he *must* be punished. Kant does not hold merely
that there is a prima facie obligation on society to punish one who has
infringed the rights of others; it is an absolute over-all obligation—punishment
must absolutely be meted out or society itself is guilty of wrong. Moreover,
a person should be punished to the extent of his injury of his victim. Kant
suggests in the last sentences that this amount of punishment corresponds
with the moral turpitude of the criminal in that offense (presumably because,
at least in the ordinary case, a man may be supposed to have intended to
do what he does, so that what he does reflects the state of his character.)[8]

Brandt proceeds to offer a series of five criticisms of the retributive principle
advocated by deontologists like Kant.

Should we accept the retributive principle as a basic "axiom" about moral
obligation (or else the assertion that it is intrinsically better for offenders
to be punished than to go unpunished)? Various considerations suggest that
we should answer this question *negatively.*

(1) Our ethical theory is *simpler* without this principle, and therefore it
should be rejected unless it enables us to deduce, as theorems (when we
combine it with true factual premises), ethical principles which are valid,
and which cannot be deduced without it. But since our discussion of the
rule-utilitarian theory of punishment has not disclosed any major objection
to that theory—any concrete judgments coherent with our "qualified"
attitudes which are inconsistent with the rule-utilitarian theory, or which
do not follow from this theory (with the "extension" involving the intrinsic
worth of equality of welfare)—there is no reason to complicate our theory
by adding a retributive principle.

(2) We shall see that some people today question the whole practice of assigning "penalties to fit the crime." They think treatment of the criminal should be criminal-centered, not crime-centered. If their point is well-taken, the retributive principle is not true.

(3) The retributive principle, in whichever form we take it, asserts in effect that a principal aim of the law is to punish either moral guilt or intentional deviation from subjective obligation. But if so, then it ought to punish merely *attempted* crimes as severely as successful crimes. Moral reprehensibility, as we have seen, is equal in the two cases; and since an attempt is a case of setting oneself to commit a crime, it is as much a deliberate deviation from subjective obligation as the successful commission of a crime. Assuming that this implication is incorrect, clearly the retributive principle alone will not do as a principle guiding legislative practice.

(4) The "moral reprehensibility" form of the theory is open to serious objection. According to it, laws should be so framed that no one will be punished, no matter what he does, if he is morally blameless. This is objectionable. It is of great importance that the law be able to set up standards of conduct, and require all to conform, whether or not they are convinced of the desirability of the standards. The law must be in a position to demand certain conduct from individuals, say in the Defense Department, whose conscientious deliberations might lead them to betray secrets essential to the national defense. Again, the law must be in a position to ban some practice like polygamy, irrespective of the value judgments of any persons. Therefore we must again say that the retributive principle cannot be the only principle guiding the framing of law and judicial practice.

(5) The *lex talionis* version of the theory has its special difficulties. For instance, it is inconsistent with recognition of a difference between first degree murder, second degree murder, and manslaughter on account of provocation, since the degree of subjective obligation is equal in all these cases. Furthermore, the theory is inconsistent with holding that various circumstances are good reasons for imposing a relatively mild penalty, which in practice are regarded as good reasons and which we must agree morally are valid reasons. Thus we must conclude, again, that the retributive principle cannot be the only principle behind justified legal procedures, and one must question ever more forcibly what good reason there can be for saying that a retributive principle must be included in any satisfactory ethical theory.

A Modified Deontological Theory of Criminal Justice: W. D. Ross

In Part II of this book, you will recall that the chapter on deontological theories of ethics presented W. D. Ross as enlarging on the traditional Kantian viewpoint. Similarly, Brandt presents Ross's interpretation of a modified Kantian position as an expanded theory of retributive justice. Again, Ross makes use of his notion of *prima facie* duties.

Ross argues that when a person commits a criminal offense, this gives society a *prima facie* right, or permission, to punish the person but not an obligation to punish the offender. Whether or not society acts on this *prima facie* right depends on other considerations, among which is consideration of the public good. Finally, if the decision is made to punish the offender, it can remove his life, liberty, or property only to the same extent that the offender has injured the life, liberty, or property of others. This is another way of saying that the punishment should fit the crime.

An interesting nonutilitarian alternative to the traditional retributive theory has been proposed by W. D. Ross. The essential idea of his theory is stated thus:

> Rights of any human being are correlative to duties incumbent on the owner of rights, or, to put it otherwise, to rights owned by those against whom he has rights; and the main element in any one's right to life or liberty or property is extinguished by his failure to respect the corresponding rights in others. There is thus a distinction in kind which we all in fact recognize, but which utilitarianism cannot admit, between the punishment of a person who has invaded the rights of others and the infliction of pain or restraint on one who has not. The state ought, in its effort to maintain the rights of innocent persons, to take what steps are necessary to prevent violations of these rights; and the offender, by violating the life or liberty or property of another, has lost his own right to have his life, liberty, or property respected, so that the state has no *prima facie* duty to spare him, as it has a *prima facie* duty to spare the innocent. It is morally at liberty to injure him as he has injured others . . . exactly as consideration both of the good of the community and of his own good requires.[9]

Ross' view differs from the retributive principle, as stated, in several ways. (What he says is not quite consistent; that side of his view is here emphasized which permits his theory to be classified as an interesting and novel one.) First, the commission of a moral offense does not establish a prima facie obligation to punish to a degree corresponding with the gravity of the offense, but a *permission* to punish up to a limit corresponding with the gravity of the offense. Second, the extent to which society should avail itself of its right to punish is determined solely by considerations of promoting the public good, of protecting rights. Third, the state's right to punish the malefactor arises from the fact that the malefactor's rights *not* to be injured in respect of life, liberty, or property go only as far as he respects the rights of others. The culprit, Ross says, "has lost his *prima facie* rights of life, liberty, or property, only in so far as these rested on an explicit or implicit undertaking to respect the corresponding rights in others, and in so far as he has failed to respect those rights."[10]

Ross himself appears to think (like Kant) of the "moral gravity" of an offense as fixed by the actual injury done someone. His theory is made more plausible, however, if we think of it as construing "moral gravity" either in the moral reprehensibility, or in the *lex talionis* sense, as these have already been defined.

Ross' theory is closer to utilitarianism than is the retributive theory, on account of its second point: the proposal that considerations of public welfare are the sole determinant of how far society should avail itself (by passing laws to that effect) of its right to punish malefactors. But it is not a utilitarian theory because the right to punish is not established by appeal to utility.

Is this "permissive" type of retributive theory subject to the same objections as the standard retributive theory described above? First, if there are no objections to a straight form of extended rule-utilitarianism, we still do not *need* the theory; it is a cumbersome complication. Second, if we interpret it in the "moral reprehensibility" form, the fourth objection to the standard theory is a decisive objection to it. Where there is no moral blame, this theory implies (in this form) that there is no right to punish. Third, Ross' theory is at least *less* open to the second and third objections we raised to the traditional theory, since on his view the moral gravity of an offense only determines a right to punish. Everything considered, Ross' theory, especially in the *lex talionis* form, seems slightly superior to the traditional retributive theory as we have stated it (and much superior to Kant's formulation); but there is no reason for adopting it in preference to the simpler rule-utilitarian theory (with the "extension" already argued for).

Utilitarian Suggestions for Reform of the Criminal Justice System

Brandt concludes his discussion of criminal justice by considering several proposals for reform of the criminal justice system in Great Britain and the United States. Basic to these is that all considerations of retribution should be abandoned in favor of treatment programs that are designed to prevent criminal behavior in the future. These programs might be psychiatric or social in nature.

The difficulties of such proposals, Brandt suggests, is that removing the retributive aspect of punishment might make the police less protected in going about their tasks. Additionally, our techniques of treatment are simply not advanced enough to allow much confidence in our ability to reform criminal behavior.

Some thinkers today believe that criminal justice in Great Britain and the United States is in need of substantial revision. If we agree with their proposals, we have even less reason for favoring the retributive principle; but we must also question the traditional utilitarian emphasis on deterrence as the primary function of the institution of criminal justice.

Their proposal, roughly, is that we should extend, to all criminal justice, the practices of juvenile courts and institutions for the reform of juvenile offenders. Here, retributive concepts have been largely discarded at least in theory, and psychiatric treatment and programs for the prevention of crime by means of slum clearance, the organization of boys' clubs, and so forth, have replaced even deterrence as guiding ideas for social action.

The extension of these practices to criminal justice as a whole would work somewhat as follows: First, the present court procedure would be used to determine whether an offense has actually been committed. Such procedure would necessarily include ordinary rules about the admission of evidence, trial by jury, and the exculpating justifications and excuses for offenses (such as wrong suppositions about the facts). Second, if an accused were adjudged guilty, decisions about his treatment would then be in the hands of the experts, who would determine what treatment was called for and when the individual was ready for return to normal social living. The trial court might, of course, set some maximum period during which such experts would have a right to control the treatment of the criminal. What the experts would do would be decided by the criminal's condition; it would be criminal-centered treatment, not crime-centered treatment.

One might object to this proposal that it overlooks the necessity of disagreeable penalties for crime, in order to deter prospective criminals effectively. But it is doubtful whether threats of punishment have as much deterrent value as is often supposed. Threats of punishment will have little effect on morons, or on persons to whom normal living offers few prospects of an interesting existence.[11] Moreover, persons from better economic or social circumstances will be deterred sufficiently by the prospect of conviction in a public trial and being at the disposal of a board for a period of years.

Such proposals have their difficulties. For instance, would the police be as safe as they are, if criminals knew that killing a policeman would be no more serious in its consequences than the crime for which the policeman was trying to arrest them? However, there is much factual evidence for answering such questions, since systems of criminal justice along such lines are already in operation in some parts of the world, in particular among the Scandinavian countries. In fact, in some states the actual practice is closer to the projected system than one might expect from books on legal theory.

Another objection that many would raise is that psychiatry and criminology have not yet advanced far enough for such weighty decisions about the treatment of criminals to be placed in their hands. The treatment of criminals might vary drastically depending on the particular theoretical predilections of a given theorist, or on his personal likes and dislikes. One can probably say as much, or more, however, about the differences between judges, in their policies for picking a particular sentence within the range permitted by law.

An institution of criminal justice operating on such basic principles would come closer to our views about how parents should treat their children, or teachers their students, than the more traditional practices of criminal justice today.

We should repeat that this view about the ideal form for an institution of criminal justice is not in conflict with utilitarianism; in fact it is utilitarian in outlook. The motivation behind advocating it is the thought that such a system would do more good. It differs from the kind of institution traditionally advocated by utilitarians like Bentham only in making different factual assumptions, primarily about the deterrence value of threat of imprisonment, and the actual effect of imprisonment on the attitudes of the criminal.

1. In Principles of Morals and Legislation.

2. Act-utilitarians face some special problems. For instance, if I am an act-utilitarian and serve on a jury, I shall work to get a verdict that will do the most good, irrespective of the

charges of the judge, and of any oath I may have taken to give a reasonable answer to certain questions on the basis of the evidence presented—unless I think my doing so will have indirect effects on the institution of the jury, public confidence in it, and so on. This is certainly not what we think a juror should do. Of course, neither a juror nor a judge can escape his prima facie obligation to do what good he can; this obligation is present in some form in every theory. The act-utilitarian, however, makes this the whole of one's responsibility.

3. See H. L. A. Hart, "Legal Responsibility and Excuses," in Sidney Hook (ed.), *Determinism and Freedom* (New York: New York University Press, 1958), pp. 81–104; and David Braybrooke, "Professor Stevenson, Voltaire, and the Case of Admiral Byng," *Journal of Philosophy,* LIII(1956),787–96.

4. The utilitarian must admit that the same thing is true for many deliberate murders; and probably he should also admit that some people who commit a crime in the heat of anger would have found time to think had they known that a grave penalty awaited them.

5. In any case, a tenable theory of punishment must approve of punishing persons who are *morally* blameless. Suppose someone commits treason for moral reasons. We may have to say that his deed is not reprehensible at all, and might even (considering the risk he took for his principles) be morally admirable. Yet we think such persons must be punished no matter what their motives; people cannot be permitted to take the law into their own hands.

6. Notice that we do not need to use the word "punish" at all in stating the retributive theory. This is fatal to the contention of some recent writers that the "retributive" theory—which they interpret as asserting, "Only the guilty should be punished"—is true by definition . . . In fact, the traditional retributive theory has far more to it than merely the claim that only the guilty should be punished.

7. *Gesammelte Werke* (Cassirer edition, Berlin, 1922), VII, 138–40; see translation by W. Hastie of I. Kant, *The Philosophy of Law* (Edinburgh: T. and T. Clark, 1887), pp. 194ff.

8. A survey of historical opinions on the *lex talionis* is to be found in S. Pufendorf, *De Jure Naturae et Gentium* (Oxford: Clarendon Press, 1934), Bk. 8, chap. 3, pp. 1214ff.

9. *The Right and the Good* (Oxford: Clarendon Press, 1930), pp. 60–61.

10. *Ibid.,* p. 62.

11. It is said that picking pockets was once a capital offense in England, and hangings were public, in order to get the maximum deterrent effect. But hangings in public had to be abolished, because such crimes as picking pockets were so frequent during the spectacle! See N. F. Cantor, *Crime, Criminals, and Criminal Justice* (New York: Henry Holt & Company, Inc., 1932).

Assessment

Brandt's discussion is a good guide to the various proposals for criminal justice that are presently being considered in many societies. There is probably no public policy issue that is currently receiving more attention than criminal justice. The United States imprisons more of its citizens for criminal offenses than does any other western industrialized nation, yet criminal activity does not seem to be diminishing in direct proportion to the number of persons imprisoned.

There is no uniform agreement nationally about the ability of imprisonment to reform criminal behavior, yet the concern for greater severity in punishment seems to be gaining ground. It is seen in such demands as uniform sentencing laws and mandatory prison sentences for certain types of offenses. If anything, the national mood seems to be moving toward something like the rule-utilitarian considerations that Brandt addresses.

Alternatives that stress treatment programs in lieu of punishment evoke chilling visions of *A Clockwork Orange* and *1984*. There is strong resistance to the view that persons should be treated against their will for alleged psychotic behavior. The partisan of a retributive theory of justice would argue that the only reason for punishment is desert; unless a person deserves punishment as a result of criminal behavior, there is no justification for punishment. If a person is genuinely ill, then punishment should be no part of our reactions to that person's behavior.

Before meaningful reforms in the criminal justice system can be undertaken, there must first be agreement as to the purposes and justifications for punishment. There is currently no such agreement. Both deontologists in their concern for retribution and teleologists in their concern for deterrence and rehabilitation believe themselves acting consistently with the moral seriousness of humankind. Further discussion of the value questions underlying criminal justice proposals must be undertaken. Until such value questions are squarely faced, our criminal justice system will probably remain the ineffective and chaotic patchwork that it currently is.

Review Questions

1. What are Rawls's three primary principles of justice?
2. What is the lexical priority of justice?
3. Describe how Rawls's theory of the original position could promote distributive justice.
4. "Rawls's model for distributive justice can be seen as a mean between the extremes of equality with radically limited freedoms and freedom with radical inequalities." Explain.
5. What are the four purposes of punishment, and which ones do utilitarians and which do deontologists emphasize?
6. What responses does Brandt provide for the major criticisms of the utilitarian theory of criminal justice?
7. Recapitulate the case for the deontological or retributive theory of criminal justice.
8. "W. D. Ross's theory of criminal justice is a blend of utilitarian and deontological concerns." Explain.

Key Concepts in Normative Ethical Issues

The following key ethical concepts were developed for the Committee for Education in Business Ethics* and proved to be useful in the conceptual analysis of case studies. Professor Kurt Baier wrote the analysis of the following: honesty, fidelity and loyalty; obligation; autonomy-dependence-paternalism; freedom; justice; self-respect and dignity. Professor Norman Bowie wrote the analysis of rights. Although developed for use in courses in business ethics, these terms have a much wider application than this and will be useful in other normative contexts as well. It is for this reason that they are included as an appendix to this book.

Honesty, Fidelity, Loyalty

Honesty is the virtue of straightforwardness and trustworthiness in dealing with others. The honest man will not, for his own purposes, lie (veracity), deceive others (truthfulness), withhold relevant parts of the truth (candor, frankness, openness), misrepresent his own opinions, feelings, or attitudes (sincerity), or make false promises. Honesty refers to the element of straightforwardness in trustworthiness, fidelity to the element of reliability. As philosophers have recently used the term, 'fidelity' refers to the virtue of always keeping one's word or vows, of doing

---

* SOURCE: *Report of the Committee for Education in Business Ethics.* Newark, Delaware: American Philosophical Association, 1979, pp. 34–42. Used by permission.

what one has committed oneself to doing by one's promises, undertakings, or contracts. A person who gives a false promise is dishonest, but a person who breaks a promise honestly given, when the keeping of it is unexpectedly onerous or costly is not dishonest, but lacking in fidelity. Again, a person who fails to discharge an obligation he has *assumed* is not a man of his word and is falling short in respect of fidelity. But a person who fails to discharge an obligation he has *incurred,* fails in other ways. If he has been put under obligation by someone's kindness he is ungrateful. If he refuses to contribute his share in maintaining a just institution from whose functioning he has derived benefits, he is a "free rider," as when he regularly visits a museum or uses public tennis courts maintained by voluntary contributions.

Honesty, fidelity, doing one's fair share, are thought of as virtues. All three refer to manners of dealing with others. All three are aspects of trustworthiness, the virtue one looks for in others when one has dealings with them. Honesty refers to the willingness not to misrepresent things for one's purposes; fidelity refers to reliability in discharging assumed obligations even under difficult conditions, and doing one's fair share refers to the willingness to make a fair contribution to the maintenance of a cooperative enterprise from which one does and wants to profit. To think of these behavioral tendencies as virtues is to think of them as following underlying principles which are morally sound. Rawls speaks of the second as the principle of fidelity (that bona fide promises are to be kept) and of the third as the principle of fairness (no one is to gain from the cooperative efforts of others without doing his fair share). We could formulate a parallel principle of honesty: in cooperative enterprises, one is not to misrepresent, for purposes of his own, any matters relevant to the willingness of others to have dealings with him.

Loyalty is closely related to fidelity: Jones's loyalty to X is his readiness to promote the concerns and interests of X (whether a person or institution) ahead of those of other claimants, in the belief that Jones, through association with X, has become subject to legitimate claims on him by X going beyond the obligations he has assumed. It is much less clear whether loyalty is a virtue, that is whether there is a sound underlying moral principle of loyalty, and if so, how exactly it is to be formulated. The difficulty lies, of course, in determining under what conditions persons or institutions come to acquire such claims on one, and how strong such claims are in relation to other assumed or incurred obligations. The line between the virtue of loyalty and the vice of giving unjustified preference to one's friends and relatives (nepotism, simony) is hard to draw.

Obligation

For Smith to have an obligation or to be obligated to do A means that there is some act, A, by Smith which it would be wrong for him not to perform. Obligations can come into being in various ways. They may be incurred, as when a person causes another harm thus incurring the obligation to repair the harm done; or they may be assumed as when someone promises or undertakes to do something; or they may be imposed on others as when someone with authority to do so, orders someone under his authority to do something within the scope of his authority. If the obligation is *to* someone, Jones, then that person may release Smith from the obligation, thus making it not wrong for him not to perform A, or to set in motion some corrective machinery either punishing Smith or compensating Jones for Smith's failure.

Obligations should be contrasted with permissions. If you are permitted to do A, your not doing A is not wrong. If you are obligated to do A, your not doing A is wrong. Moreover, note that if you are obligated to do S, you are still physically free not to do it even though morality requires that you do it. In other words, obligation must not be confused with compulsion or force. Finally, the content of obligations may vary; obligations may be arbitrarily delimited in time and person as when I promise not to look until you count to ten: I am not obligated not to look, after you have reached ten, nor need anyone else be obligated not to look. Hence, obligations do not necessarily depend on the nature of the conduct in question or on its consequences. In this way obligations can be distinguished from intrinsic wrongs like killing or lying.

Autonomy—Dependence—Paternalism

Autonomy is either a psychological condition, reached by all normal adults, of being able to make rational decisions about what to do, or a right to make and act on such decisions. Dependence is the opposite of autonomy. It refers either to a psychological condition in which someone is in the habit of acting in accordance with the decisions made by someone else, usually one person such as his father or teacher on whom he is said to be dependent, or else to a legal or conventional position of dependence, in which a person (say, a minor) is conventionally precluded from making legally effective decisions on certain matters, as when he needs the approval, consent, or permission of a parent or guardian.

Paternalism is the view that in certain conditions people's autonomy should be disregarded, whether by the state (legal paternalism) or by other individuals, that they should not be asked or allowed to make decisions on certain matters, if it is clear to (specified) others that their decisions would gravely, perhaps irreversibly, affect their own good, as when a person decided to commit suicide, to take up heroin, or to embark on an extremely hazardous enterprise. Mill, the most widely respected anti-paternalist, opposed only the strong form of paternalism which insists that a person should not be permitted to harm himself even when he acts of his own free will and in full knowledge of the harm involved in his act. He did not object to interference where the person is not acting voluntarily (as when he is delirious, under hypnosis, or in a state of uncontrollable excitement) or is not adequately informed (as when he does not know the gun is loaded, the bridge is unsafe, or the drug lethal). However, Mill himself would seem to have embraced the strong principle of paternalism when he argued that no one should be allowed to sell himself into slavery, on the grounds that "the principle of freedom cannot require that he should be free not to be free." It is not clear to me why the principle of freedom, i.e., autonomy,—that every man has a right to determine the shape of his own life, whatever the effect on his own balance of goods—should not require this. In any case, it is worth noting that the strong form of paternalism is incompatible with Mill's first principle, the so-called "harm principle," which says that the only purpose for which people may be coerced by law is to protect *others* from harm they would, if not coerced, be inflicting on them.

Freedom

Freedom, in the important sense, with which we are concerned here, is a certain sort of ideal condition or state of affairs, considered by some to be so central to human lives that they are willing to fight in its defense or promotion. This condition concerns the structure of and relation between political societies. It is either the freedom *of* or *for* such societies, that is, their independence or autonomy or self-government. Or it is the freedom *in* such societies, consisting in the freedom *of* or *for* its citizens, that is, freedom for their major pursuits: freedom of religion, association, movement, economic enterprise, speech and communication, and so on, or the untrammelled functioning of the institutions promoting these activities: freedom of or for the press, the churches, the parties, the universities, the corporations. Societies can be less or more free in either or both of these two ways. A colony may be completely unfree, that is wholly governed by the mother country, but there may be complete freedom in that society. Conversely, after "liberation," the society may be wholly self-governing, but there may be little freedom in the newly sovereign society.

We think of freedom as tending towards a limit, complete freedom, beyond which it is impossible further to reform the society in respect of the extent of freedom. In such a completely free society, everyone is *free to do* what he ought to be free to do. And he ought to be free to do whatever he can do without thereby preventing others from doing what they ought to be free to do. Complete freedom thus prevails in a society if everyone has the greatest *possible extent* of freedom compatible with a like extent of freedom for everyone. That implies (i) that the law forbids no one to do anything he ought to be free to do, (ii) that it forbids people including government officials to interfere with other people's doing what they ought to be free to do, and (iii) that it has institutions designed to ensure that the substantive principles determining what people ought to be free to do are continually clarified and properly applied to individual cases as social conditions change.

Regarding the freedom of citizens in a society, some philosophers have distinguished between positive and negative freedom. Negative freedom is simply the absence of external constraints. For example, the freedom of speech is a negative freedom. We are free to speak our mind because there are no laws prohibiting it. The concept of positive liberty is a little harder to capture. The British philosopher Isaiah Berlin defines it as self-mastery. One lacks positive freedom if one cannot reach some end for reasons such as indecisiveness, compulsive desires or perhaps ignorance. Consider an alcoholic trying to stop drinking. No one forces him to take that drink, so he is, in the negative sense, free to drink or not. But his compulsion to drink is so strong, that he cannot help himself. Berlin would say he lacked freedom in the positive sense. Other philosophers suggest that rather than distinguish between types of freedom, we should define freedom simply as absence of constraints and distinguish between internal and external constraints.

Justice

Justice can be considered as a social ideal. While freedom is concerned essentially with mutual non-interference, with what people must (or need not) refrain from doing in order that others be able to do what they want to do, justice is concerned with determining *what is due from whom to whom.* It is often said that "a society is perfectly just if and only if everyone gets what is his due." I accept this for the present occasion, though I shall add the proviso: "and it has institutions designed to see to it that people get their due." These institutions serve two major tasks: determining *what* is due and distributing what is due either as benefits or sanctions.

Accordingly, we can distinguish various kinds of justice. We can distinguish, "horizontally," so to speak, between various domains of justice, such as distributive, economic, criminal, legal, parental, social, or cosmic justice. And we can distinguish "vertically," so to speak, between the first-order or declarative, and the second-order, or corrective levels of justice. An example may help make this distinction clearer. Thus horizontally, criminal justice covers a certain area, distinguishing it from economic justice. Vertically at first-order level, criminal justice determines what are crimes, that is, modes of behavior deserving the criminal sanctions (punishment). At the second-order or corrective level, criminal justice determines who, if anyone, has engaged in such criminal behavior and precisely what sanctions are to be imposed on him or her. Another example is obtained from the area lawyers call torts. The first-order level determines what sorts of behavior are torts, that is, behavior for which the agent deserves to be made to pay compensation. The second-order level determines who has become liable to pay compensation, to whom, and how much.

No one has so far worked out the proper relationship between these various domains of justice. Even the contemporary philosopher John Rawls speaks only of what he calls social or distributive justice, not the whole of justice. Moreover, Rawls does not make completely clear what exactly is to be included in his treatment. He refers to what he calls the basic structure of society, but he does not clearly identify precisely which institutions in our society are to be considered part of the basic structure. Does it, for instance, include the relation between the members of a family? If not, why is not this part of the basic structure? It surely is a very important factor in determining the character of the lives of those involved. And if it is part of the basic structure, then he does not make clear how his two principles of justice are to apply to it and how the roles of husband, wife, and child, are to be incorporated in the system of roles created by the economic and other institutions of our society.

Nevertheless, it is perhaps worth stating Rawls' two by now famous principles of social justice:

1st principle: each person is to have an equal right to the most extensive total system of equal basic liberties compatible with a similar system of liberty for all.

2nd principle: social and economic inequalities are to be arranged so that they are both (a) to the greatest benefit of the least advantaged and (b) attached to offices and positions open to all under conditions of fair equality of opportunity.

Priority Rule: The principles of justice are to be ranked in lexical order and therefore liberty can be restricted only for the sake of liberty.

Self-Respect and Dignity

Self-respect is normally respect for oneself as a person. A person has respect or is shown respect when his or her interests are taken into account and when his or her rights are honored. What these claims and rights are is contentious, but they include claims concerning life and health, claims to be dealt with honestly, and claims to be dealt with in a manner befitting the dignity of mankind.

To have self-respect, then, is to take seriously the claims and rights one has, simply on the grounds that one is a person. Hence one lacks self-respect if he or she is servile or craven, allows himself or herself to be humiliated or exploited without protest, fails to stand up for his or her rights, or submits to indignities as if he or she did not deserve any better, and so on. Such behavior suggests or implies that he or she does not think he or she has the basic rights of a person.

To lack self-respect in this sense is not a matter of degree: one either has it or one lacks it. However, people can differ from one another in respect of *how strong* their self-respect is, how easily they lose it under pressure, how firmly their readiness to stand up for their rights is entrenched, how sure they are of their basic rights as persons. Jones cannot (in this sense) have greater or a higher degree of self-respect than Smith, but his self-respect can be stronger, firmer, more deeply entrenched than Smith's.

Self-respect as a tendency to behave in certain ways on account of taking seriously the claims or rights one has as a person, should perhaps be distinguished from self-respect as a species of self-esteem, that is, respect for oneself by comparison with others. In this second sense, self-respect is a matter of degree. One may respect oneself more than one respects some other person, and more at one time than another. Self-respect in this sense is the opposite of self-contempt. It is not a tendency to behave in a right- or claim-respecting way, but simply represents a favorable opinion of oneself based on a comparison of one's worth with that of others. But while in cases of self-esteem the basis of the comparison may be any type of excellence, in cases of self-respect the basis is always a suitable character trait. One respects oneself as a consequence of a favorable comparative judgment based on the sorts of character traits, e.g., honesty, truthfulness, fidelity, trustworthiness, justice, rectitude, which one must have if one respects others as persons. Thus, self-respect in this second sense is simply self-esteem based on certain moral characteristics relevant to self-respect in the first sense.

Dignity is ordinarily a characteristic of persons: the self-assurance and poise acquired when one has no doubt about one's own worth and its recognition by others. Dignity is closely related to self-respect. To be subjected to indignities is to be treated in ways which tend to undermine one's self-respect and rob one of one's dignity. Such treatment is incompatible with the dignity of persons. Ordinarily, the rights and claims related to the dignity of persons are concerned primarily with the person's sense of his own worth. Insults, humiliations, degradations, ridicule, public mockery, are typical forms of such behavior. However, some philosophers have used 'self-respect' in a much wider sense, involving all those rights and claims which a person respects who respects another as a person, e.g., the right to honesty, fidelity, or fairness.

Rights

What are rights? They are moral entitlements—moral claims we can make against other persons and against institutions. They usually invoke corresponding duties on the part of others—be they persons or institutions. American democracy was born in a time when ethics was dominated by a philosophy of rights:

> "We hold these truths to be self-evident: that all men are endowed by their Creator with certain unalienable rights; that among these are life, liberty, and the pursuit of happiness."

Since Great Britain had allegedly denied these rights, the signers of the Declaration of Independence believed they had moral justification for rebelling. During the transition of the United States from a confederation to a federation, many individual states adopted the constitution only if a series of amendments (now called the Bill of Rights) were enacted to protect individuals from the state. The Bill of Rights is a statement of the moral entitlements that individuals have against the state. In political philosophy the vocabulary of rights has long been in use.

But what kinds of rights are there and more specifically what rights do we have? Basically rights have been divided into two classes, those which are created by societal agreement—e.g., rights created by a collective bargaining agreement, and rights persons have independently of any societal agreement. These latter are called natural rights. The rights referred to in the Declaration of Independence are natural rights. They are the rights that individual persons have against all social institutions. Rather than being created by society, natural rights are entitlements that morally constrain how social institutions ought to develop.

But how does one prove that one has natural rights? Those within the Roman Catholic tradition utilize the language of the Declaration of Independence. Just as God created laws of nature which transcend different cultures and which are available to human reason, so God created laws of morality which transcend different cultures and which are available to human reason. Applied ethics is the application of these universal laws to particular historical circumstances and business ethics is the application of these universal moral norms to business.

With the rise of secularism in intellectual life, Roman Catholic natural law philosophy declined in influence. Certain individualist philosophers, like John Locke, narrowed the natural law tradition to claims of individual natural rights which were taken to be self-evident. As a result of these claims of self-evidence in conjunction with so many competing theories of the natural rights, serious questions have been raised as to whether natural rights could be justified at all.

As a result, the natural rights philosophy did not fair well in competition with the ethical philosophy of utilitarianism. One of the chief intellectual spokesmen of utilitarianism, Jeremy Bentham, referred to natural rights as "nonsense on stilts."

Still additional problems were created when defenders of natural rights sought empirical support for the view that natural rights were possessed equally by all men and women. Whatever characteristic one picked out—intelligence, virtue, physical similarity—were all distributed unequally. If such characteristics were distributed unequally, how could they be the basis for an egalitarian theory of individual rights?

In the last few years there has been a tremendous resurgence in the philosophy of natural rights. Now there are a number of new proofs justifying their existence. All the arguments have as their starting point human experience. One then asks what must be presupposed to make sense of (explain) that experience. In every case the answer is *natural* (or as they are now sometimes called *human*) rights.

One of the chief characteristics of human beings is that they engage in moral discourse. Several philosophers (A. Phillips Griffiths, A. I. Melden, Robert Simon, and Richard Wasserstrom) argue that natural rights must be presupposed to account for our use of moral language and moral concepts. The following quotation is illustrative:

> Rights, we are suggesting, are fundamental moral commodities because they enable us to stand up on our own two feet, "to look others in the eye," and to feel in some fundamental way the equal of anyone. To think of oneself as the holder of rights is not to be unduly but properly proud, to have that minimal self-respect that is necessary to be worthy of the love and esteem of others." Conversely, to lack the concept of oneself as a rights bearer is to be bereft of a significant element of human dignity. Without such a concept, we could not view ourselves as beings entitled to be treated as not simply means but ends as well.

Alan Gerwirth starts with the fact that human beings are purposive agents. As purposive agents they must claim natural rights to freedom and well being since freedom and well being are the necessary conditions for purposive action. Each of the arguments is long and complicated and beyond the scope of this analysis. However, serious, able and sophisticated scholars are once again taking rights seriously.

If one successfully justifies the existence of natural rights, then the controversy focuses on the natural rights we have. All natural rights philosophers agree that we have a natural right to liberty although they disagree as to what liberty is. The natural right to liberty is especially central to libertarian political philosophy. The legal philosopher H. L. A. Hart has argued that all other rights have as a necessary condition the natural right to liberty.

Many other philosophers argue that persons also have a natural right to a minimum standard of well being. Libertarian philosophers reject the notion of such a natural right on the grounds that such a right cannot be universal (given the scarcity of material resources in some countries) and that such a right depends on the state. Proponents of the right concede that implementation of the right may depend on material circumstances and may need the support of the state. Such a concession would not show that a right is not universal. Moreover, the same arguments that establish a natural right to liberty establish a natural right to a minimum standard of well being.

Suggestions for Further Reading

CHAPTER ONE: Psychological Egoism

    Broad, C. D. *Five Types of Ethical Theory.* Paterson, N.J.: Littlefield, Adams, 1959. Chapter 3. An excellent, brief discussion of Butler's critique of psychological egoism.

    Gauthier, David P., editor. *Morality and Rational Self-Interest.* Englewood Cliffs, N.J.: Prentice-Hall, 1970. Offers ten selections assessing psychological and ethical egoism.

    Hospers, John. *Human Conduct.* New York: Harcourt, Brace and World, 1961. Chapter 4. Provides a clear and compelling criticism of psychological and ethical egoism.

    MacIntyre, Alasdair. "Egoism and Altruism." *The Encyclopedia of Philosophy,* vol. 2, pp. 426–66. Discusses the nature of egoism in ethics and offers a survey of the debate between Hobbes and Butler on this topic.

    Milo, Ronald D. *Egoism and Altruism.* Belmont, Calif.: Wadsworth, 1973. Contains selections from classical and contemporary authors discussing the pros and cons of egoism.

CHAPTER TWO: Determinism

    Berofsky, Bernard. *Determinism.* Princeton, N.J.: Princeton University Press, 1971. A sustained defense of determinism.

    ———., editor. *Free Will and Determinism.* New York: Harper & Row, 1966. A good collection of essays by various authors discussing the many dimensions of the problem.

    Farrer, A. *The Freedom of the Will.* New York: Scribner's, 1958. A sustained defense of free will.

    Gardner, Martin. *The Whys of a Philosophical Scrivener.* New York: Quill, 1983. Chapter 6 offers the author's reasons for rejecting determinism; included also is an analysis of James's position. Chapter 5 also gives the author's reasons for rejecting ethical relativism. The book is written in a popular style and can serve as an introduction to the issues for philosophical beginners.

Taylor, Richard. "Determinism." *The Encyclopedia of Philosophy,* vol. 2, pp. 359–73. The first part of this article deals with ethical determinism; it surveys both supportive and critical positions.

CHAPTER THREE: Ethical Relativism

Benedict, Ruth. *Patterns of Culture.* Boston: Houghton Mifflin, 1934. An affirmation of relativism by a prominent anthropologist. Note especially Chapters 2, 3, and 7.

Brandt, Richard B. "Ethical Relativism." *The Encyclopedia of Philosophy,* vol. 3, pp. 75–78. A good explanation of the theory showing its difficulties; an extensive bibliography appears at the end of the article.

Harrison, Jonathan. "Ethical Objectivism." *The Encyclopedia of Philosophy,* vol. 3, pp. 71–75. A survey of the arguments for and difficulties encountered by an objectivist theory of ethics.

Ladd, John, editor. *Ethical Relativism.* Belmont, Calif.: Wadsworth, 1973. A series of authors debate the merits of relativism.

Taylor, Paul W. *Principles of Ethics: An Introduction.* Encino, Calif.: Dickenson, 1975, pp. 13–29. A brief, careful criticism of four types of ethical relativism.

Westermarck, Edward. *Ethical Relativity.* New York: Harcourt, Brace, 1932. A classic defense of relativism.

CHAPTER FOUR: Ethical Emotivism

Brandt, Richard B. *Ethical Theory.* Englewood Cliffs, N.J.: Prentice-Hall, 1959. Chapter 9 includes some of the material from journal articles that both supports and attacks the emotive theory in ethics.

————. "Emotive Theory of Ethics." *The Encyclopedia of Philosophy,* vol. 2, pp. 493–96. Discusses the nature and difficulties of the emotive theory.

Stevenson, Charles L. *Ethics and Language.* New Haven: Yale University Press, 1944.

————. *Facts and Values: Studies in Ethical Analysis.* New Haven: Yale University Press, 1963. Both of Stevenson's works offer careful expositions and advocacy of emotivism.

Toulmin, Stephen E. *An Examination of the Place of Reason in Ethics.* Cambridge: Cambridge University Press, 1950. Chapter 3. Provides a careful critique of emotivism.

Warnock, G. J. *Contemporary Moral Philosophy.* London: Macmillan, 1967. Provides a valuable, brief critical discussion that locates ethical emotivism in the context of twentieth-century ethical theory.

Warnock, Mary. *Ethics Since 1900.* Third edition. Oxford: Oxford University Press, 1978. Interprets emotivism within twentieth-century philosophical developments.

CHAPTER FIVE: Actualizing Human Nature

Adler, Mortimer J. *Aristotle for Everybody: Difficult Thoughts Made Easy.* New York: Macmillan Publishing Co., 1979. Part III deals with the ethical and social views of Aristotle; the book is a good place for those unfamiliar with Aristotle to begin.

DeLacy, P. H. "Epicurus." *The Encyclopedia of Philosophy,* vol. 3, pp. 3–5. A brief discussion of all the philosophical views of Epicurus, including his ethical views.

Randall, John Herman, Jr. *Aristotle.* New York: Columbia University Press, 1960. Chapter 12. A highly readable introduction to Aristotle by a noted American philosopher.

Ross, David. *Aristotle.* New York: Barnes and Noble, 1964. First published 1923. Chapter 7. The classic exposition of Aristotle's life and thought.

Veatch, Henry B. *Aristotle: A Contemporary Appreciation.* Bloomington: Indiana University Press, 1974. Chapter IV offers a brief but good summary of Aristotle's views on ethics.

CHAPTER SIX: Obeying the Will of God

Beach, Waldo, and H. Richard Niebuhr. *Christian Ethics.* New York: The Ronald Press, 1955. A selection of readings from classic and modern theologians with helpful introductions by the editors.

Fletcher, Joseph. *Situation Ethics: The New Morality.* Philadelphia: Westminster Press, 1966. A classic statement of situationalism within a Christian context.

Niebuhr, Reinhold. *An Interpretation of Christian Ethics:* New York: Harper & Brothers, 1935. A classic statement of the role of religion in ethical theory.

Niebuhr, H. Richard. *Christ and Culture.* New York: Harper and Brothers, 1951. A lucid interpretation of five different ethical postures adopted by Christians through the ages.

Ramsey, Paul. *Basic Christian Ethics.* New York: Charles Scribner's Sons, 1954. A readable introduction to the subject.

CHAPTER SEVEN: Maximizing Human Happiness

Alston, William P. "Teleological Ethics." *The Encyclopedia of Philosophy,* vol. 8, pp. 84–88. A brief statement of the principal features of a teleological view in ethics.

Broad, C. D. *Five Types of Ethical Theory.* Paterson, N.J.: Littlefield, Adams, 1959. Chapter 6. Provides a careful, readable analysis of Henry Sidgwick's utilitarianism.

Ewing, A. C. *Ethics.* New York: The Free Press, 1953. Chapters 3 and 5. A brief criticism of utilitarianism.

Sidgwick, Henry. *The Methods of Ethics.* London: Macmillan, 1907. A classic statement of utilitarianism, but a bit difficult for beginners.

————. *Outlines of the History of Ethics.* Boston: Beacon Press, 1960. First published in 1886, this treatise sets utilitarianism within the context of the history of ethics, especially pp. 236ff.

Smart, J. J. C. "Utilitarianism." *The Encyclopedia of Philosophy,* vol. 8, pp. 206–12. Offers a comprehensive survey of utilitarianism and a full bibliography of additional sources.

CHAPTER EIGHT: Pursuing One's Duty

Broad, C. D. *Five Types of Ethical Theory.* Paterson, N.J.: Littlefield, Adams, 1959. Chapter 5. A clear, brief exposition of Kant's ethics.

Paton, H. J. *The Categorical Imperative: A Study in Kant's Moral Philosophy.* Philadelphia: University of Pennsylvania Press, 1947. A discussion of Kant's moral theory, detailed enough for the advanced student; Chapters 13–15 offer discussions of the aspects of Kant's views included in this textbook.

Ross, W. D. *Kant's Ethical Theory.* New York: Oxford University Press, 1954. An extensive treatment of Kant's ethical theory.

CHAPTER NINE: Normative Ethical Issues

Bok, Sissela. *Secrets: On the Ethics of Concealment and Revelation.* New York: Vintage Books, 1984. A companion volume to Bok's work on lying; deals with such issues as secrecy and power, whistle blowing, intrusive social science research, investigative journalism, and undercover police operations.

Narveson, Jan., editor. *Moral Issues.* New York: Oxford University Press, 1983. A collection of essays by contemporary writers on a variety of normative issues. Included are euthanasia and suicide, war, punishment, world hunger, abortion, sex, equality and inequality, and rights of future generations.

Nielsen, Kai. "Ethics, Problems of." *The Encyclopedia of Philosophy,* vol. 3, pp. 117–34. A comprehensive survey of major problems in ethics, this article includes a discussion of the relation of normative ethics to metaethics; also offers an extensive bibliography for the advanced student.

Wasserstrom, Richard A. *Today's Moral Problems.* Second edition. New York: Macmillan Publishing Co., 1975. Case studies and analysis of such normative issues as abortion, racism and sexism, preferential treatment, sexual morality, privacy, punishment, and such global issues as hunger, the ecology, and the rights of animals.

CHAPTER TEN: Medical Ethics

Callahan, Daniel. *Abortion: Law, Choice and Morality.* London: Macmillan, 1970. An exhaustive discussion of the abortion controversy.

Beauchamp, Tom L., and Laurence B. McCullough. *Medical Ethics: The Moral Responsibilities of Physicians.* Englewood Cliffs, N.J.: Prentice-Hall, 1984. Offers case studies of ethical issues in medicine with corresponding philosophical analysis and references to moral theories.

Clouser, K. Danner, and Arthur Zucker. *Abortion and Euthanasia.* Philadelphia: Society for Health and Human Values, 1974. Provides an annotated bibliography of over two hundred articles and books dealing with abortion.

Munson, Ronald. *Intervention and Reflection: Basic Issues in Medical Ethics.* Belmont, Calif.: Wadsworth, 1983. A first-rate survey of the topics in medical ethics, with readings, commentary, and bibliographies.

Pellegrino, Edmund, and David C. Thomasma. *A Philosophical Basis of Medical Practice: Toward a Philosophy and Ethic of the Healing Professions.* New York: Oxford University Press, 1981. An excellent guide written by a physician and a philosopher, dealing with a wide range of issues in which philosophy and medicine have something to contribute to each other.

Rescher, Nicholas. "The Allocation of Exotic Medical Lifesaving Therapy." *Ethics* 79 (April, 1969): 173–86.

CHAPTER ELEVEN: Ethical Issues in Business

DeGeorge, Richard T. *Business Ethics.* New York: Macmillan Publishing Co., 1982. A highly readable and good introduction to the basic issues in business ethics, written by one of the leaders in the movement to develop business ethics courses.

Donaldson, Thomas. *Case Studies in Business Ethics.* Englewood Cliffs, N.J.: Prentice-Hall, 1984. A good collection of actual business decisions showing the ethical issues arising from corporate actions.

Donaldson, Thomas, and Patricia H. Werhane. *Ethical Issues in Business: A Philosophical Approach.* Second edition. Englewood Cliffs, N.J.: Prentice-Hall, 1983. Offers case studies of a wide range of topics in business ethics.

Reagan, Charles E. *Ethics for Scientific Researchers.* Second edition. Springfield, Illinois: Charles C. Thomas, 1971. A good review of principles and cases dealing with ethical issues involving research both in an academic and business setting.

CHAPTER TWELVE: Ethical Issues in Public Policy

Arthur, John, and William H. Shaw. *Justice and Economic Distribution.* Englewood Cliffs, N.J.: Prentice-Hall, 1978. An anthology dealing with the economic dimensions of public policy issues.

Beauchamp, Tom L., and Terry P. Pinkard. *Ethics and Public Policy: An Introduction to Ethics.* Englewood Cliffs, N.J.: Prentice-Hall, 1983. A good collection of secondary literature on public policy issues, and a selection of materials on abortion and euthanasia.

Blocker, H. Gene, and Elizabeth H. Smith. *John Rawls' Theory of Social Justice: An Introduction.* Athens: Ohio University Press, 1980. An excellent collection of articles from a variety of perspectives dealing with the themes in Rawls's work.

Benn, Stanley I. "Punishment." *The Encyclopedia of Philosophy,* vol. 7, pp. 29–36. A thorough discussion of this important theme dealing with criminal justice; discusses the various theories of punishment and offers an extended bibliography.

Rawls, John. *A Theory of Justice.* Cambridge, Mass.: The Belknap Press of Harvard University Press, 1971. Rawls's massive statement of his political theory; beginners in philosophy should look to the shorter statements of his theory, such as the article cited in the next entry.

――――. "Justice as Fairness." *The Philosophical Review* 67 (1958), 164–94. A good introduction by Rawls to his social theory. This article is less difficult for the beginner than his massive work *A Theory of Justice.*

Glossary of Terms

Absolutism: In ethics the view that holds that there are moral standards applicable to all morally responsible persons regardless of time or place. *See* **objectivism.**

Act utilitarianism: A theory that holds that each act must be assessed directly by the principle of utility.

Aesthetics: The philosophical inquiry into the nature of art and beauty. Sometimes spelled *esthetics.*

Altruism: Unselfishly acting for the sake of others. Benevolence.

Analytic: A statement is analytic if its truth or falsity can be determined by analysis of the terms in the statement alone. Statements that are analytically true are said to be true by definition, or logically true.

Antinomianism: A term introduced by Martin Luther, which is used in general to describe freedom from law, from compulsion, and from the external regulation of human living.

A posteriori: Refers to knowledge that is derived from the senses.

A priori: Refers to knowledge that is derived solely from reason independently of the senses. The truth of a priori knowledge is claimed to be both necessary and universal.

Asceticism: The view that the body and its pleasures are detrimental to a moral and spiritual life. Hence, the ascetic practices self-denial even, at times, to the point of self-torture in order to stifle bodily desires.

Assertoric: Propositions can be classified as assertoric (i.e., asserting something as true), as problematic (i.e., asserting something as possible), and as apodeictic (i.e., asserting something as necessary).

344

Autonomy: The term literally means *self-legislated*. For Kant, autonomy was a key notion for morality, because an act can have moral significance only if it is willed freely and without compulsion by a rational being.

Benevolence: According to Butler, benevolence is a rational regulating principle that monitors the particular passions in order to direct the self to pursue those passions which would lead to the happiness of others, and to avoid those passions whose objects would generate misery for others. *See* **altruism.**

Casuistry: A method for resolving conflicting obligations by applying general moral principles, through intricate rules, to concrete cases of human conduct.

Categorical imperative: For Kant, the unconditional moral law; it can be expressed as the rule that we should act on that principle that we could make a universal law. If we cannot universalize our principle without contradiction, the action resulting from the principle is immoral.

Cognitive sentences: Sentences that are informational. When they bear information about the world, about states of affairs, they are synthetic and can be assessed as true or false. When they bear information about words or symbols, they are analytic and can be assessed as tautological or contradictory.

Conscience: According to Butler, a rational regulating principle in the self that passes moral judgment upon persons and actions, and that mediates disputes between cool self-love and benevolence.

Consequentialist ethics: Ethics that assess actions as right or wrong on the basis of the consequences generated by those actions. *See* **teleological ethics.**

Criminal justice: Relates to the pursuit of fairness in society's treatment of criminality.

Deduction: A method of reasoning in which a conclusion is claimed to follow necessarily from one or more premises.

Deism: The view that although God is the creator of the world, nevertheless he now has no immediate relation with it. God functions like an absentee landlord with whom humankind has no contact. Deism found considerable support from thinkers in England and France during the seventeenth and eighteenth centuries.

Deontological: Derived from the Greek word for *ought,* it refers to any ethical system that makes the morality of an action depend on one's acting out of a sense of duty. Kant's ethical system is deontological.

Determinism: The philosophical doctrine that claims that every event has a cause. Determinists are often divided into two groups: (1) extreme or *hard* determinists, who disallow free will entirely; and (2) moderate or *soft* determinists, who allow certain links in the causal chain to be called free will.

Difference principle: Rawls's second principle of justice (second in order of priority), which demands that any inequality in the distribution of social goods can be justified only if it contributes to the improvement of everyone in the society, especially the least well-off, and if the inequalities are attached to positions open to all.

Distributive justice: The pursuit of justice in the distribution of the goods and rewards of a society.

Egalitarian: Advocating equal political, economic and legal rights for all citizens.

Egoism: The ethical theory that holds that self-interest is the rule of conduct. **Psychological egoism** is the claim that people in fact only act out of self-interest. **Ethical egoism** is the view that people ought to act out of self-interest, not that they necessarily do so act.

Emotivism: The doctrine that claims that moral judgments do not convey information about the world but rather express the emotions of the speaker and perhaps attempt to evoke similar emotions in the hearers.

Empiricism: The theory that claims that all human knowledge is derived from the senses, which implies that humans neither possess inborn knowledge nor are able to generate knowledge by the use of reason alone.

Epicurean: Refers to followers of Epicurus (341–270 B.C.), who set forth a strategy for achieving truly human happiness by emphasizing the delights of the mind (over which a person has control) rather than the delights derived from material things (which are so often beyond one's personal control).

Ethical relativism: The view that there are no objective moral standards, and that the principles for conduct are relative to individuals or societies. Ethical relativists claim that there are no cross-cultural ethical norms by which to evaluate the conduct of persons in all societies.

Ethics: The philosophical investigation of the principles governing human actions in terms of their goodness, badness, rightness, and wrongness.

Ethnocentrism: The willingness to judge the actions and principles of other societies by the standards of one's own society because of the belief that one's own culture is superior to other cultures and that it is fitting, therefore, to judge other cultures on the basis of one's own cultural beliefs and practices.

Eudaemonism: From the Greek word for happiness or well-being; eudaemonism refers to the view that the aim of right action is the happiness or well-being of the human being.

Existentialism: A philosophical movement rooted in nineteenth-century philosophers such as Kierkegaard and Nietzsche, who emphasized the importance of exploring meaning for the concrete existing individual. Existentialists are opposed to grandiose philosophical systems, such as Hegel's, which provide extensive explanations of reality without raising the question of what it means to be an existing, struggling, choosing individual. The movement flourished especially after the Second World War through the writings of such thinkers as Jean-Paul Sartre, Gabriel Marcel, Jacques Maritain, Nikolai Berdyaev, and Martin Heidegger.

Freedom: Freedom is defined in various ways. Hobbes considered freedom to be the absence of external constraints. Blanshard, a soft determinist, argued that the human experience of freedom involves being determined by ideals. C. A. Campbell said that a free act, in the sense required for moral responsibility, requires that the agent be the sole cause of the act and that the agent could have exerted his or her causality in alternative ways. The authors of this book regard freedom to be the capacity to identify and pursue alternative futures.

Gnosticism: A variety of religious perspectives that were widespread in the Graeco-Roman world during the first centuries of the Christian era. Gnosticism had its roots in pre-Christian mystery religions and claimed that salvation consists in deliverance of the spirit from its imprisonment in the world of flesh. The deliverance was to be accomplished through secret knowledge or *gnosis.*

Good: According to Hobbes, any object that is desired by a person is good, and any object hated is evil. According to G. E. Moore, goodness is a unique, simple, indefinable, nonnaturalistic property that is discerned by intuition. For Aristotle, the chief good (that which is desirable for its own sake) is happiness. For Emil Brunner, the good consists in always doing what God wills at any particular moment.

Greatest equal liberty principle: Rawls's first principle of justice (first in order of priority); it requires that each person is to have an equal right to the most extensive total system of equal basic liberties compatible with everyone else having an equal right to the same total system.

Hedonism: Derived from the Greek word for pleasure, hedonism is the ethical philosophy that holds the view that pleasure and only pleasure is intrinsically good (that is, desirable for its own sake). Most philosophical hedonists have held, however, that intellectual pleasures are superior to sensual pleasures.

Hedonistic calculus: Bentham's strategy for quantifying the pleasure and/or pain that a given action is likely to generate, using the categories of intensity, duration, certainty, propinquity, fecundity, purity, and extent.

Hedonistic utilitarianism: Held by utilitarians who believe that only the quantity of pleasure is relevant to the calculations of the hedonistic calculus.

Hypothetical imperative: For Kant, commands that we give ourselves that are directed toward some end to be accomplished. They are *if . . . then* commands.

Ideal utilitarianism: Held by those utilitarians who accept a distinction between the quantity and quality of pleasures and advocate that humans should strive for the higher pleasures (that is, for higher ideals).

Indeterminancy principle: Also referred to as the Heisenberg uncertainty principle, this principle affirms the impossibility of knowing simultaneously the exact velocity and position of a subatomic particle.

Indeterminism: According to Brand Blanshard, the doctrine that there are some events whose antecedents do not make them necessary. In the words of William James, indeterminism claims that possibilities may be in excess of actualities and that of two alternative futures that we conceive, both may now be really possible. Indeterminists affirm the existence of human freedom.

Induction: A method of reasoning whereby one proceeds from a number of observed particular facts to a generalization about all such facts. Such generalizations can be supported by the particular facts, but the truth of those generalizations cannot be completely demonstrated by those facts.

Instrumental good: That which is desirable for the sake of an intrinsic good or for the sake of another instrumental good which will in turn lead to the intrinsic good.

Intrinsic good: That which is desirable for its own sake, as distinct from the instrumental good which is desirable because it leads to the intrinsic good.

Intuitionism: Refers to the direct and immediate apprehension by the self of knowledge about the self and the world without the need for deductive or inductive reasoning as the basis for affirming the truth of certain propositions. Intuitionism in ethics refers to those positions that hold that the basic propositions of ethics are known intuitively.

Laws of nature: According to Hobbes, the articles of peace suggested by reason whereby the state of nature is supplanted by a society ruled by law with sanctions. *See* **state of nature.**

Legalistic ethic: An ethic that spells out moral obligation in terms of specific laws for a wide range of human conduct. In religious circles, legalism is often evident in long lists of dos and don'ts that are represented as God's commands.

Lexical priority: The procedure advocated by Rawls that one should not pursue action on a second principle until one has satisfied the demands of the first principle, nor go on to the third principle until one has satisfied the demands of the second, and so on.

Libertarianism: The doctrine that affirms freedom of the will.

Logical positivism: A movement originating in Vienna in the early twentieth century; it tried to propagate the scientific outlook in all fields of human knowledge. A fundamental tenet of the movement was that statements are meaningful only if they can be verified or falsified either directly or indirectly through the data of experience. Applied to philosophy, this view eliminated as nonsense much of traditional philosophy that sought knowledge in the nonempirical realms of theology, metaphysics, and ethics. Some advocates of this view preferred to call it *logical empiricism.*

Materialism: The view that all reality is matter. Anything that is real is to be explained in terms of matter and the motion of matter. Materialism relegates mind (or spirit) either to a secondary, dependent status or to no status at all.

Mathematical reasoning: A method of scientific inquiry in which observed facts are quantified and synthesized into explanatory systems that are used to predict the behavior or phenomena. Those predictions are then subjected to empirical verification.

Maxim: According to Kant, the principle of action that is presupposed by a deliberate act.

Maximin rule: This rule states that when confronted by competing alternative futures, one should choose the alternative that has the best worst outcome.

Metaethics: A philosophical investigation of the terms and principles used in an ethical system, as opposed to an attempt to deal with an actual ethical problem. An example of metaethical analysis is the attempt to analyze how the term *right* functions in discourse or in an ethical theory. Metaethics is distinct from **normative ethics,** which seeks to answer the question, What ought I to do?; it prepares the way for normative ethics by examining the nature and presuppositions of moral discourse.

Metaphysics: The philosophical inquiry into the nature of ultimate reality. In contemporary usage, the term includes the analysis of fundamental philosophical principles.

Monism: A metaphysical theory that explains reality in terms of a single substance or principle. Materialism is an example of a monistic view.

Moral knowledge: Information about the world that involves assessing things as good or evil, right or wrong.

Mysticism: The belief that ultimate reality, such as God, is beyond usual empirical ways of knowing but can be apprehended through deep meditation or trance-like contemplation.

Naturalistic fallacy: According to G. E. Moore, this fallacy is present when someone attempts to interpret goodness as a natural, empirical property, when in fact it is a unique, simple, indefinable, nonnaturalistic property discerned by intuition. *See* **intuitionism.**

Neo-orthodoxy: A twentieth-century theological movement initiated by Karl Barth; it reacted against the optimism and confidence in human capacities evident in nineteenth-century theology by affirming the emphases of Luther and the Apostle Paul on the gravity of sin, the necessity of renewal through divine grace, and the purposeful action of God in history.

Noncognitive sentences: Sentences that are not used to convey information. Instead, they convey emotions, commands, questions, and so forth.

Normative: That function of philosophy concerned with establishing standards for distinguishing the correct from the incorrect, whether in ways of reasoning, believing, aesthetic judgments, or acting.

Objectivism: In ethics, the view that moral values and principles exist independently of a particular person's views and tastes. Such objective values and principles provide norms by which ethical statements can be judged as true or false. *See* **absolutism.**

Open question argument: G. E. Moore's argument that regardless of the property we select to define goodness, and even though we would all agree that a certain thing or event has this property, it is still an open question whether that thing or event is really good.

Optimific: Productive of the best possible consequences.

Optimism: The personal attitude of hopefulness about human destiny and a positive evaluation of the world.

Pantheism: The doctrine that identifies God with the forces of nature so that God is considered to be actually present in all things.

Particular passions: Butler's term to describe the drives of the self toward and away from specific objects.

Pessimism: The personal attitude of despondency, hopelessness, and gloom toward the self and the world. The most famous philosophical justification of this attitude is that presented by Schopenhauer.

Pragmatism: A philosophical position associated with such thinkers as C. S. Pierce and William James which interprets the meaning of a statement or idea generally in terms of its practical consequences.

Prima facie duty: W. D. Ross's term for a duty that a person recognizes at first glance to be a duty; closer scrutiny may confirm or deny it as one's actual duty.

Proposition: A sentence that has factual content and truth value; that is, it can be assessed as true or false.

Pseudo-proposition: According to logical positivists, sentences that look like propositions but on closer examination are seen to be in principle unverifiable and therefore have no truth value.

Psychological egoism: A theory of human motivation; it claims that humans are so constituted that they always act selfishly.

Psychological hedonism: The view that human beings are so constituted that they in fact always seek to attain pleasure and avoid pain.

Right of nature: According to Hobbes, the freedom all persons have to use their own power as they will to preserve their lives.

Rule utilitarianism: That form of utilitarianism which holds that rather than applying the utility principle to each act, our actions should be guided by general rules that are derived in advance using the utility principle.

Self-love: According to Hobbes, self-love is present when one possesses the objects one desires. According to Butler, self-love is a rational regulating principle that monitors the particular passions in order to direct the self to pursue those passions that lead to the self's happiness and to avoid those passions whose objects would lead to the self's misery.

Situationalist ethic: An ethic that claims that human moral obligations are discovered in concrete situations and cannot be determined in advance.

Skepticism: The view that certain kinds of knowledge are impossible to obtain.

Social contract: A theory articulated by Thomas Hobbes and others; it is used to explain the origin and nature of the state. The theory holds that the obligation men have to obey the laws and the reciprocal obligations and responsibilities of the state to its citizens is to be understood as though based on a mutually binding contract between citizens and government.

State of nature: The term used by the social contractarians to refer to the hypothetical condition of human beings before the institution of the state. According to Hobbes, the state of nature is the condition of humankind prior to the establishment of the state or commonwealth. Life in the state of nature is one of continuous conflict among selfish persons for possession of scarce resources. Right and wrong, justice and injustice, do not exist in the state of nature, and cultural development is inhibited.

Subjectivism: Any view that places primary emphasis on the knowing or acting subject. In ethics, subjectivism is the view that ethical statements are descriptions of the way people feel about certain things and involves the claim that moral values and principles represent the individual's subjective feelings and reactions which, in the absence of objective moral norms, cannot be assessed as true or false. According to subjectivism, there are no moral standards independent of human feelings. _See_ **ethical relativism.**

Syllogism: A form of deductive reasoning consisting of a major premise, a minor premise, and a conclusion. For example,

> All men are mortal. (major premise)
> Socrates is a man. (minor premise)
> Therefore, Socrates is mortal. (conclusion)

Synthetic propositions: Sentences that convey information about the world, about states of affairs. They can be assessed as true or false.

Teleological ethics: Ethical positions that determine the rightness or wrongness of acts on the basis of their consequences. The term is derived from the Greek word *telos,* which means "end" or "purpose."

Theist: One who believes in the existence of God.

Transcendence: That which stands above and beyond humankind. In ethics, objective moral values transcend the individual's subjective feelings and preferences. In theology, God (who is the author of the moral order) transcends humankind and the world as its creator and sustainer.

Utilitarianism: The ethical theory associated with the work of Jeremy Bentham, James Mill, and John Stuart Mill in the nineteenth century. Utilitarians hold that actions are moral if they aim at the general good, or the greatest good for the greatest number of people.

Utility: The property in any object by which it tends to produce benefit, advantage, pleasure, good, or happiness to the party whose interest is considered.

Utility principle: The principle of utilitarianism that says that we ought to do what will produce the greatest good for the greatest number of people. Sometimes it is referred to as "the greatest happiness principle."

Veil of ignorance: Rawls's term for the stipulation that the parties in the "original position," to insure their impartiality, must have no concrete knowledge as to who they are, from what economic background they come, what their specific talents are, and so on.

Virtue: According to Aristotle, virtue is related to function. When a thing is performing its proper function well, virtue is present. The proper and distinctive human function involves reason. Moral virtue is present when the appetites are regulated by a rational principle (the mean between the extremes of excess and deficiency directed toward a worthy goal). Intellectual virtue is present when the rational part of the soul possesses truth (which may be that of practical wisdom, art, intuitive knowledge, scientific knowledge, and philosophic wisdom). Moral virtue is acquired through habit, intellectual virtue through teaching. According to Joseph Butler, virtue is also related to function. When the parts of the human decision-making system are functioning properly, virtue is present; that is, when benevolence and cool self-love are monitoring the particular passions, and when conscience is overseeing that process. According to William Paley, virtue is doing good to humankind in obedience to the will of God and for the sake of everlasting happiness.

Index